Sophie Mayer is a writer, editor, ac   st for *Sight & Sound* and *The F-Word*, an affiliate lecturer in Screen Media and Cultures at the University of Cambridge, and was the first Poet in Residence at the Archive of the Now, Queen Mary University of London. Her previous books include *The Cinema of Sally Potter: A Politics of Love* (2009), *There She Goes: Feminist Filmmaking and Beyond* (co-edited with Corinn Columpar, 2010), *Lo personal es politico: Feminismo y documental* (co-edited with Elena Oroz, Punto de Vista, 2011) and *Catechism: Poems for Pussy Riot* (co-edited with Markie Burnhope and Sarah Crewe, 2012). She runs feminist cinema blog Political Animals (fuckyeahfeministcinema.tumblr.com), and is a member of feminist film collectives Club des Femmes and Raising Films.

'It is surely to become a canonical text when it comes to writing about film, writing about women, writing about society and culture, and is a must-read for anyone who loves film and loves women. I was incredibly impressed by several things, which have combined perfectly in this book: Sophie's depth of research and exhaustive knowledge of the art, craft, magic and business of cinema, and not just Western or studio film but international and independent work; her core grounding in feminism and muscular, gritty and unwavering gender-critical eye; and above all her passion for what film means and what it can achieve. She wants women to be the best we can be, film to be the best it can be, the society to finally change so that women's emancipation, in film, on film and in life, finally happens – and she'll be watching.

Of course, I recognise that while this isn't a dry academic exercise, Political Animals does presuppose a certain about of love of and knowledge of both film and feminism, it is rigorously referenced throughout. So I would expect that every single film studies, cultural studies, media studies and gender studies MA course, in every institution, should get one and make it essential reading on every syllabus.'

Bidisha, broadcaster and journalist

'Sophie Mayer is our foremost critic of contemporary feminist filmmaking and her exciting new book bristles with information, insight and discovery. *Political Animals* blasts through scarcity claims about women's participation in film by looking askance at the commercial industry. Her book is as bold and creative as the work she writes about.'

Patricia White, Professor of Film and Media Studies and English Literature, Swarthmore College, Pennsylvania

POLITICAL ANIMALS

THE NEW FEMINIST CINEMA

SOPHIE MAYER

I.B.TAURIS
LONDON · NEW YORK

Published in 2016 by
I.B.Tauris & Co. Ltd
London • New York
www.ibtauris.com

Copyright © 2016 Sophie Mayer

The right of Sophie Mayer to be identified as the author of this work has been asserted by her in accordance with the Copyright, Designs and Patents Act 1988.

All rights reserved. Except for brief quotations in a review, this book, or any part thereof, may not be reproduced, stored in or introduced into a retrieval system, or transmitted, in any form or by any means, electronic, mechanical, photocopying, recording or otherwise, without the prior written permission of the publisher.

Every attempt has been made to gain permission for the use of the images in this book. Any omissions will be rectified in future editions.

References to websites were correct at the time of writing.

International Library of the moving Image 33

ISBN: 978 1 78453 371 7 HB
         978 1 78453 372 4 PB
eISBN: 978 0 85772 994 1

A full CIP record for this book is available from the British Library
A full CIP record is available from the Library of Congress

Library of Congress Catalog Card Number: available

Typeset by Out of House

Printed and bound in Great Britain by T.J. International, Padstow, Cornwall

For all the feminist viewers, filmmakers, curators, critics and theorists who've kept me company, in person, online or through their words and images: thank you.

What I want to say is, there are all of us.

Joanna Russ, *On Strike against God.*

Having had nothing, I will not settle for crumbs.

Roxanne Dunbar-Ortiz, 'Female Liberation', quoted in
Mary Dore, *She's Beautiful When She's Angry* (2014).

Table of Contents

List of Figures ... ix
Acknowledgements ... xi

Introduction: Girls to the Front ... 1
1. Ain't about the (uh) Cha-Ching, Cha-Ching: Framing the New Feminist Cinema ... 12
2. Not in Kansas: Animal Selves and Becoming-Girls ... 29
3. Water Rites: Ecocinema's New Earth Mothers ... 45
4. Home Front: Women at War, Women against War ... 63
5. I Have No Country: British Cinema as a Runaway Girl ... 79
6. All Dressed Up: Costume Drama Loosens its Corset ... 97
7. Mirror, Mirror: Fairy Tales of the Feminist Fantastic ... 118
8. Girl 'Hood: A Body, a Room and a World of One's Own ... 133
9. Haunted Houses: Reclaiming 'Women's Cinema' ... 152
10. Come Together: Love, Justice and a New Sexual Politics ... 170

Conclusion: An Open Letter ... 188

Notes ... 204
Further Reading ... 230
Index ... 241

List of Figures

Fig. 1:	Elsa makes the *Frozen* ice rink (Disney, 2013)	2
Fig. 2:	Kathleen Hanna onstage, *The Punk Singer* (Dogwoof, 2014)	3
Fig. 3:	Shannen Koostachin dancing, *Hi Ho Mistahey!* (National Film Board of Canada, 2013)	7
Fig. 4:	Angela Y. Davis on stage, from *Free Angela and All Political Prisoners* (Codeblack Entertainment, 2013 [USA])	10
Fig. 5:	Ava DuVernay directing a crowd scene in *Selma* (Pathé, 2014) (Credit: Atsushi Nishijima/Paramount Pictures)	13
Fig. 6:	Aida El Kashef in Tahrir Square, *The Square* (Kaleidoscope Entertainment, 2014)	24
Fig. 7:	Adriana Barraza and Sally Potter shooting *Rage* (Adventure Pictures, 2009)	26
Fig. 8:	Feminist Godzilla Eats Male Gaze	27
Fig. 9:	Wendy and Lucy in the car, Lucy looking to camera, *Wendy and Lucy* (Soda Pictures, 2009)	30
Fig. 10:	Tanya Tagaq as Sedna, 'Tunjgijuq' (Isuma, 2009)	43
Fig. 11:	Asha in the desert, 'Pumzi' (Focus Features, 2009)	48
Fig. 12:	Girl floating in the sea, *Bloody Beans* (Allers-Retours Productions, 2013)	61
Fig. 13:	Baktay being kidnapped, *Buddha Collapsed out of Shame* (Slingshot Distribution, 2008)	64
Fig. 14:	Robyn trapped in her room, *The Time We Killed* (Argot Pictures, 2004 [USA])	77
Fig. 15:	Lucy reflected in the mall table, *The Unloved* (Channel 4 Television Corporation, 2009)	81
Fig. 16:	Joyce Vincent (left, turning towards the camera) at Nelson Mandela's talk, *Dreams of a Life* (Dogwoof, 2011)	88
Fig. 17:	*Belle* (20th Century Fox, 2014), cover star of BFI Film Fund Diversity Guidelines	99

List of Figures

Fig. 18:	Madeline Ivalu and Marie-Hélène Cousineau, directors of *Before Tomorrow* (Isuma Distributing International, 2007) at Toronto International Film Festival, 2014 (Credit: Arnait Video)	105
Fig. 19:	Frankenstein, *UNBOUND* (Abigail Child, 2013)	121
Fig. 20:	Stretch Goal Reached! Storm art for 'Rain', Maya Glick (Maya Glick, 2014)	130
Fig. 21:	Sabine watches her younger self, *Her Name is Sabine* (ICA Films, 2008)	136
Fig. 22:	Billie and James connect online and offline, *52 Tuesdays* (Peccadillo Pictures, 2015)	145
Fig. 23:	Isabel and Momi in Isabel's room, *The Swamp* (ICA Projects, 2001)	154
Fig. 24:	Sarah Polley and cinematographer Iris Ng making a home movie, *Stories We Tell* (Curzon/Artificial Eye, 2013)	168
Fig. 25:	Laila and Khanum meet cute, *Margarita, With a Straw* (Ishaan Talkies, 2014)	171
Fig. 26:	Lovers on the beach behind nets, *The Beaches of Agnès* (Artificial Eye, 2009)	186
Fig. 27:	Kate Bornstein with *My Gender Workbook*, *Kate Bornstein is a Queer and Pleasant Danger* (Sam Feder, 2014)	194
Fig. 28:	Crystal, with the star on her helmet, joins the Gnarlies youth team for her first jam, *In the Turn* (Erica Tremblay, 2014)	202

Acknowledgements

First and foremost, huge thanks to my editor Anna Coatman. *Political Animals* was her idea, and she has been an incredible ally, sounding board and reader through the process. Thanks also to Lisa Goodrum and the whole team at I.B.Tauris for producing a book rich in visual pleasure!

Asta Bradshaw and Rebekah Polding were crucial kickstarters, while Vicky Ainley, Sarah Crewe, Daniel Justice, Shelagh Rowan-Legg, S. F. Said and Preti Taneja were generous and attentive first readers; all of them offered incredible support throughout. Frances Morgan has been a tireless copy editor (no hyphen!), a reflective reader and brilliant company during the final stages.

The book has its roots in a decade of writing about feminist films and filmmakers for, in historical (and then alphabetical) order: at *Plan B*, S. F. Said, Nick Bradshaw and Frances Morgan; at *Vertigo* and *Artesian*, Gareth Evans; at *Sight & Sound*, James Bell, Nick Bradshaw, Kieron Corless, Nick James and Isabel Stevens; at Second Run DVD, Mehelli Modi; at *cléo*, Kiva Reardon, Julia Cooper and Mallory Andrews; and at *The F-Word*, Ania Ostrowska, who has been a passionate cheerleader with a critical ear.

Several of the ideas in this book were initially elicited, and subsequently developed, by academic editors Pam Hirsch (*Cinema of the Swimming Pool*), Alisa Lebow (*Cinema of Me*), and Anat Pick (*Screening Nature*). I'm particularly thankful that Anna Backman Rogers and Laura Mulvey invited me to tea to check we weren't writing the same book, and subsequently to contribute to the excellent *Feminisms*; it's been very special to have the two projects coming to fruition concurrently.

Rhidian Davis and David Edgar (BFI), Stuart Comer (Tate Modern), Gareth Evans (Whitechapel Gallery), Lucy Orr (Hackney Picturehouse), Adam Roberts (*À nos amours*), Chloë Roddick (Ambulante Michoacán), and Garth Twa (Trash Cannes) all extended invitations to developing these ideas through presentations and panels, as did academics Elinor Cleghorn (Ruskin School of Art), Kit Fryatt (Mater Dei), Holly Pester (Birkbeck), Anat Pick (Queen Mary University London), Sarah Turner (University of Kent), Emma Wilson (University of Cambridge), and the organisers of Screen 2014, who all improved my ideas through dialogue and cake.

Acknowledgements

Film Production at the London College of Communication and Film Studies at Queen Mary University London were warm homes while I was writing. Thanks especially at QM to my mentors Lucy Bolton and Guy Westwell for their collegial kindness, and to my co-convenors Jenny Chamarette, Janet Harbord and Alasdair King for their support and tolerance. Thanks also to my alternate, global feminist film & media studies 'staff room' on Facebook and Twitter: as well as many people already mentioned, gratitude goes out to Charlotte Richardson Andrews, Miriam Bale, Louis Bayman, Jane Bradley, Markie Burnhope, Ashley Clark, Corinn Columpar, Jemma Desai, Ariel Dougherty, Beti Ellerson, Marian Evans, Catherine Grant, Laura Hall, Simran Hans, Kate Hardie, Natalie Harrower, May Lui, Domino Renee Perez, Rebecca Porteous, Karin Ramsay, Elizabeth Treadwell, Tom de Ville, Thirza Wakefield and Patricia White.

The internet has also offered an unprecedented ability to connect with filmmakers, who have been incredibly generous with their time, thoughts and material. Especial thanks to Sandra Alland, Sini Anderson, Amma Asante, Maja Borg, Michelle Citron, Cheryl Dunye, Mia Engberg, Beth Freeman, Tina Gharavi, Barbara Hammer, Alexandra Hidalgo, Hope Dickson Leach, Alisa Lebow, Kim Longinotto, Leena Manimekalai, Carol Morley, Pratibha Parmar, Debs Paterson, Sally Potter, Elle-Máijá Tailfeathers, Erica Tremblay, Penny Woolcock, Jacqueline Wright, Campbell X and Andrea Luka Zimmerman.

Finally, this book is emerges from, and for, a collaborative community of feminist film curation. It has been thrilling to work with Bath Film Festival (Holly Tarquini), BFI Flare (Jay Bernard), Bluestocking Film Series (Kate Kaminski) Directed by Women (Barbara Ann O'Leary), London Feminist Film Festival (Anna Read), FRINGE! (Amelia Abraham), Punto de Vista (Elena Oroz), and above all with Club des Femmes. Selina Robertson, Alex Thiele, Sarah Wood and Campbell X are a unique queer feminist force. Curation has been key to the development of an intersectional feminist cinema and to this book. May it continue to equality – and beyond!

Introduction: Girls to the Front

Lovely and Vigorous and Brave

In 2014, a film written and co-directed by a woman, and featuring two female leads, was the highest grossing film worldwide, winning two Academy Awards. *Frozen* (Chris Buck and Jennifer Lee, 2013) is a world-beating cultural phenomenon.[1] It's been called 'Disney's first foray into feminism', and its theme song has been belted out by millions of small children everywhere. 'Let it Go' was simultaneously heralded as a coming-out anthem among lesbian, gay, bisexual, trans*, queer, intersex and asexual communities (LGBTQIA, although I prefer Nicola Griffith's and Kelley Eskridge's coinage QUILTBAG[2]).[3] Accompanied by dazzling animation, the song showcases Elsa (Idina Menzel) commanding the power of ice, a force 'stronger than a hundred men', according to opening number 'Frozen Heart'. Feminism's work appears to be done.

Elsa has been praised by feminist disability activists as the first Disney princess with a visible disability – one that is not 'cured' by the film.[4] Yet the film has also been criticized – rightly – for its overwhelming whiteness (including whitewashing Sámi characters while appropriating Sámi culture), its narrow range of female body types, and its class hierarchy.[5] At the end, Queen Elsa has changed social and personal perceptions about her icy powers, but she hasn't instituted democracy, recognized Sámi land rights, or formed a socialist feminist utopia. It makes me what Roxane Gay calls a 'bad feminist', but, from the privileged perspective of a white woman, I love *Frozen*. Its princess problem is offset by its riposte to what Antonia Senior judiciously calls 'the pernicious pinkification of little girls'.[6] As Stacy L. Smith reports, US children's media is still overwhelmingly produced by men, and sexualizes and renders passive the few female protagonists allowed onscreen.[7]

For my five year old goddaughter Asta, *Frozen* corrects that imbalance, placing active female characters centre-screen. 'I love all the girls, but I won't love the men', she told me during my second viewing and her umpteenth.[8] Her favourite moment

Political Animals

Fig. 1: Elsa makes the *Frozen* ice rink

is small but telling: when Elsa's sister Anna (Kristen Bell), despite being stricken by the ice in her heart, slides dramatically down a castle-high snow drift to initiate her own rescue. This moment, for Asta, is 'brave and fun'. She narrates the story as entirely focused on sisterly love, where Anna's and Elsa's 'true love's cuddle' (her words) is the climax of the story.

She loves that Anna chooses to save Elsa rather than herself, and that at the end, Elsa 'didn't make it snow – she made it like she did the first time, she made it lovely'. For her, the film ends with Elsa and Anna recuperating the traumatic 'first time', in which young Elsa made an ice rink for young Anna, and Anna got injured. The sisters get to re-vision their girlhoods, which had been rendered lost and lonely by the parental prohibition on Elsa's powers. Asta's observation chimes tellingly with a comment by musician and writer Lynnee Breedlove in documentary *The Punk Singer* (Sini Anderson, 2012). Looking back 20 years, s/he celebrates how the young 1990s North American feminists known as Riot Grrrls were 'reclaiming the girlhood that has been taken away from them, [saying] "I'm actually going to be a little girl but have power now so I can redirect my whole growing up experience from point A"'.

The feminist films I discuss in *Political Animals* all address, in one way or another, that deep longing to reclaim and redo childhoods that have been, at best, subliminally delimited by patriarchy, and, at worst, actively deformed by gendered violence, whether physical, sexual, emotional or psychological, particularly when intersecting with racist, colonialist, ableist, homophobic, transphobic and/or classist violence. Covering nearly 500 films by filmmakers who identify as female, trans*, intersex, non-binary and/or Two-Spirit (among other non-EuroWestern gender identities), from 60 countries, it celebrates key moments in feminist film

Introduction: Girls to the Front

Fig. 2: Kathleen Hanna onstage, *The Punk Singer*

in the twenty-first century, but looks beyond the mainstream. bell hooks offers a timely reminder:

> If we long to transform the culture so that the conventional mass media are not the only force teaching people what to like and how to see, then we have to embrace the avant-garde… Here is where we'll find radical possibility. We can deconstruct the images in mainstream white supremacist capitalist patriarchal cinema for days and it will not lead to cultural revolution.[9]

Frozen is important because of its broad reach and global impact, but it is a primer, rather than a closing statement, on the potential of feminist cinema.

That said, my first feminist film experience was probably *Labyrinth* (Jim Henson, 1986). Sarah (Jennifer Connelly) was a rare female and (proto)feminist protagonist in Anglophone 1980s children's cinema. Sarah – whose name means 'princess' – has lost her mother, as in so many fairy tales. The talismanic lines she reads at the start, and recites so memorably at the end, come from a play, according to A.C.H. Smith's novelization, in which her mother played the heroine Sarah comes to embody. 'Through dangers untold and hardships unnumbered', Sarah comes into her grrrlhood, finally telling Jareth the Goblin King (David Bowie), 'You have no power over me'. By offering variations of this declaration, feminist cinema has offered me a way of 'redirect[ing] my whole growing-up experience'. In

Chloé Hope Johnson's term, I am a 'becoming-grrrl', a subject for whom grrrlhood, transmitted through alternative audiovisual cultures, is the basis of my political formation.[10]

If we are to speak truth to power like Sarah, we need films that are 'lovely and vigorous and brave', as Asta sums up *Frozen*, films that are full of love, alive with energy, and courageous in their stands, in order to thaw the ice of internalized intersectional oppression. The films that I write about contain characters like Elsa and Anna, who, in recognizing and valuing each other, reclaim their identity together, in public. That's why, as seen in *The Punk Singer*, Riot Grrrl Kathleen Hanna used to call 'Girls to the front!' from the stage. Her strategy offered protection from gendered violence to audience members at gigs by her band Bikini Kill. As she notes in the film, it also created a safe zone for her as performer, a community in which grrrl-becoming could take place together, through each other.

Women Call the Shots

I'm indelibly shaped by coming of age in the early 1990s, an era in which it seemed that women definitively called the shots. *Point Break* (Kathryn Bigelow, 1991) was the first 18-rated film that I snuck into at the cinema; I discovered both Allison Anders (*Gas Food Lodging*, 1992; *Mi Vida Loca*, 1993) and Russian women's cinema via Channel 4's Women Call the Shots film seasons; I took my mum to see *Go Fish* (Rose Troche, 1994) in an awkward attempt at coming out; *Fire* (Deepa Mehta, 1996) went better as a date movie; and *Boys Don't Cry* (Kimberley Peirce, 1999) was the last film I saw as an undergraduate, literally my graduation film. It wasn't just the arthouse: mainstream US filmmakers Nora Ephron, Amy Heckerling, Mimi Leder, Kasi Lemmons, Penny Marshall, Mira Nair, Penelope Spheeris and Rachel Talalay appeared to have sliced the celluloid ceiling to shreds.

This diverse, playful and confident cinema was coeval with two interconnected, predominantly North American, counter-cultural movements. The first was Riot Grrrl, as documented in *The Punk Singer* and dramatized in *All Over Me* (Alex Sichel, 1997), which was also part of the second, named New Queer Cinema by B. Ruby Rich, and including *Go Fish*, *Fire* and *Boys Don't Cry*.[11] In the Riot Grrrl World in which my imagination still resides, it's normal that diverse filmmakers call the shots. As *Political Animals* proves, they do, across every mode of filmmaking, every budgetary scale, every medium and every genre. The new feminist cinema ranges confidently across the globe, from Albanian novelist Elvira Dones' *Sworn Virgin* (Laura Bispuri, 2015), adapted from her novel about a *burrneshë*, Hana Doda, who transitions to male to uphold his family honour, to Zimbabwean

Introduction: Girls to the Front

filmmaker Xoliswa Sithole's *Child of the Revolution* (2014), a personal essay on revolutionary politics.

But the connection between Riot Grrrl and the new wave of global feminist cinemas is not straightforward: in fact, it's marked by a hiatus at the turn of the millennium. As Laura Mulvey argues, 'the millennium concentrated into itself a widely perceived sense of change that had built up over the previous two decades, for instance the impact of the end of Communism, the advance of globalization, the shift in communication technologies, the decline of industry in the developed world'.[12] Both the availability of home broadband internet in the developed world and the launch of affordable MiniDV cameras in 2003 initiated a shift in film production and distribution, particularly for filmmakers who found it hard to secure funding, whether due to structural sexism or geographical location. When Shari Roman flagged up Agnès Varda's *Les glaneurs et la glaneuse* (*The Gleaners and I*, 2000) as visionary in 2001, it seemed that digital tools would offer a continuation, and indeed exponential expansion, of the extant indie feminist cinema.[13] It wasn't a cinematic version of the Y2K problem, or Millennium Bug, that struck – it was geopolitics.

'With the events of September 2001 in New York and Washington, DC', Mulvey continues, 'the indistinct sense of foreboding that belonged to the year 2000 found an emblematic embodiment'. As Guy Westwell argues in *Parallel Lines*, neo-conservative domestic politics altered US cultural production and distribution on a pervasive and profound scale, radically narrowing the range of subject positions available in US cinema.[14] There are similar temporal gaps in the oeuvres of Kathryn Bigelow (2002–2008), Jane Campion (2003–2009) and Kimberley Peirce (1999–2008). Although these are often explained through personal and economic rationales, it's notable that both Bigelow and Peirce returned to the big screen with war films, as explored in chapter four.

At the same time as conservatism engulfed Hollywood, US imperialism exported its own version of 'feminism' through illegal invasions. As Shahnaz Khan points out, 'the First Ladies of both the United States and Britain, Laura Bush and Cherie Blair, [suggested] that it was the misogynist Taliban (read terrorists) in Afghanistan who were responsible for the women's plight. The implication was that women in Afghanistan needed rescuing'.[15] Khan refers to this pervasive, missionizing gesture as 'colonial feminism'. In response, its more intersectional variants would actively provide a key motivation for the production and distribution of films from the other side of the conflict, including Women Make Movies' 'Response to Hate' free rental campaign for films about the Middle East.[16]

Patricia White points to both 'the worlding of women's cinema' and 'the gendering of world cinema' as twenty-first century effects in her new book *Women's*

5

Cinema, World Cinema.[16] She roots it in a diverse transnational women's cinema that was becoming visible on the festival circuit in the late 1990s, in the work of Claire Denis, Susanne Bier, Samira Makhmalbaf and Moufida Tlatli. What's 'new' about the twenty-first century 'new feminist cinema' observed here is its negotiation of a transgenerational feminist film history of four decades within a reflexive awareness of the interruption and re-vision of feminisms, and interconnectedly of film cultures, in the new millennium.

Any narrative of twenty-first-century cinema could be, and perhaps should be, written through feminist films. One such narrative would reflect the emergence of openly feminist cismale filmmakers (cis meaning identifying with the sex/gender one is assigned at birth). Their work is often informed by marginalized identities, notably (but not only) queer, indigenous and/or post-colonial. *Camera Obscura*'s special issue on Todd Haynes and Anna Dempsey's essay on women in public space in male-authored Iranian new wave cinema reflect on this intersectional filmmaking and its importance for feminism.[17]

Yet the work of filmmakers such as Jafar Panahi, Warwick Thornton and Apichatpong Weerasethakul is often emplaced as exemplary within national, auterial, aesthetic and political cinemas, and configured as universal, while non-cismale filmmakers' work is marked as niche. As Joss Whedon explained to Sheerly Avni:

> When I was in college, my then-girlfriend Gillian said something that I never forgot. I was mourning Orson Welles, who had just died… and I was getting all sad and sloppy about how this great genius had been trodden down, had shown such promise and not [been] allowed to speak, she said, 'Yeah, that's really interesting, I feel that way about the entire history of my gender'.[18]

I hope those cismale filmmakers whose work I don't discuss here will take Whedon's stance rather than James Cameron's. When Bigelow won the Academy Award for Best Director for *The Hurt Locker* (2008) in 2009, beating his nomination for *Avatar* (2008), Cameron was caught on camera making a throttling gesture – supposedly in jest.

Clearly, however, Bigelow's *The Hurt Locker* and *Zero Dark Thirty* (2012) exemplify far more precisely and knowingly than *Avatar* what historian Joanna Bourke calls US cinema's shift towards 'militainment'.[19] Feminist cinema is often in the political and aesthetic vanguard. The internationally garlanded *Firaaq* (2008), directorial debut of *Fire* star Nandita Das, represents Indian cinema 'beyond Bollywood' through its complex and confrontational account of the 2002 mass killings of Muslims in Gujarat. Laura Poitras' oeuvre, from *Flag*

Introduction: Girls to the Front

Fig. 3: Shannen Koostachin dancing, *Hi Ho Mistahey!*

Wars (2003) on gentrification in Middle America to her critiques of the National Security Agency in her *New York Times* 'op-doc' *The Program* (2012) and her internationally-recognized *CITIZENFOUR* (2014), is in the political avant-garde.

Andrea Arnold's *Red Road* (2006) essays a chilling critique of the surveillance state, and moreover was part of Advance Party, a constraint-based post-Dogme project that also includes Morag McKinnon's *Donkeys* (2010). Paz Encina's *Hamaca Paraguaya* (*Paraguayan Hammock*, 2006), a deeply political film about military service, may be the best representative of the most critically hyped auteurist movement on the festival scene, Slow Cinema (first categorized by Michel Ciment in 2003), as well as the first Paraguayan film by a woman.[20]

Lena Dunham's *Girls* (HBO, 2012–) is a keystone of auteurist television; generically, her brand of comedy is as zeitgeist-defining as that of *Girls* producer Judd Apatow, if not more so. Even the rise of the superhero blockbuster and the rise (and fall) of torture porn can be told as stories about gender. Feminist filmmakers have used both genres to analyse, rather than replicate, conventional gender dynamics and rape culture. *Boxing Helena* (Jennifer Chambers Lynch, 1993) at least attempts a critique of the heteropatriarchal erotic obsession with controlling women, while Iciar Bollaín's psychological thriller *Te doy mis ojos* (*Take My Eyes*, 2003) won awards internationally for its depiction of the reality of torture and/as domestic violence from a survivor's point of view.

7

First Nations feminist filmmakers have taken a similar approach to the superhero movie, re-purposing the idea of the action hero to query the heroism of violence. In Cree/Métis filmmaker Danis Goulet's 'Wakening' (2013), resistance fighter Weesakechak (Sarah Podemski) searches through a near-future dystopian city for the Cree cannibal spirit Weetigo (Gail Maurice) to aid in the fight against an army of occupation. 'Wakening' screened at Toronto the same year as the latest documentary by veteran Abenaki filmmaker Alanis Obomsawin. *Hi-Ho Mistahey!* (2013) is about teenage Cree education rights activist Shannen Koostachin, who also inspired superhero Equinox in the Justice League Canada comics.[21] Instead of holding out for Hollywood to grant us the next comic book heroine (and to recognize the filmmakers, such as Karen Kusama, Talalay and Lexi Alexander, capable of delivering her), why not celebrate the feminist superheroes we have and the filmmakers who engender them?

Remaking the World

As Asta puts it, 'The main thing that Anna does [in *Frozen*], she's always trying', and that is how I see feminist film and film criticism: alive in the attempt, often in the face of derision and erasure. The book's title arose from a conversation with my editor at I.B.Tauris, Anna Coatman, which turned 'political animal' from a backhanded compliment into a provocation to become *more* political, more full of love, vigour and courage. Getting to define what is and isn't political is a position of privilege; feminism, for me, is defined by refuting that privilege, and maintaining an inclusive engagement in transforming the world.

A stance of ongoing public activism, rooted in but not limited to gender equity, underlies my definition of a film, filmmaker, film theorist or film viewer as feminist. Film theorist David Bordwell has long argued for an 'active viewer' and active cinema.[23] Drawing on the modes of criticism laid out by Jill Dolan in *The Feminist Spectator in Action* – *argument* and *advocacy*, forming an *activist* criticism engaged with *artistry* – I suggest what lies beyond: activist viewers of an activist cinema.[24] Where the active viewer makes connections to and within the film, the activist viewer connects the film and the world.

Writing about Kim Longinotto's *Sisters in Law* (2005), Sharon Lin Tay points to a twenty-first-century 'empowered mode of feminist filmmaking: of being politically aware, infused, and grounded in the contingent so that it is always ready to posit an intervention'.[25] Winner of a Peabody award for campaigning journalism, as well as two awards at Cannes in 2005, Longinotto's thirteenth documentary is a model of her activist practice, which she has described as 'mak[ing] films that could reaffirm in a small way what the powerful are often trying to crush'.[26] In Cameroonian legal eagles Vera Ngassa and Beatrice Ntuba, leading the charge against domestic violence and sexual abuse with compassion, wit and jurisprudential insight, Longinotto and her co-director Florence Ayisi found the ideal icons for an activist feminist viewer.

Grace Lee Boggs, Hegelian philosopher and Black Panther associate, is another talismanic figure, still schooling young Detroit activists in her nineties, and delighting in getting schooled in hip-hop in turn. Grace Lee's documentary about Boggs, *American Revolutionary: The Evolution of Grace Lee Boggs* (2013) is, like Anderson's *The Punk Singer*, a sign of the return of what's been repressed by globalization. Neoliberal economics and increased surveillance have engendered protest cinemas globally that are looking forward for solutions by looking backwards to bold precursors, and feminist media makers are at the forefront.

The films I love thus share a commitment to and through the urgency of their resistant subjects, rather than a particular style or story. Flexing their forms inventively to fit their content, they tend to inhabit paradoxes: rich and raw; ambitious and chaotic; profound and funny; storytelling and poetic; cerebral and embodied; broad-ranging and local. Above all, they make me want to be part of their imaginative worlds, and to get involved in bringing them into being. As Angela Y. Davis, herself the subject of Shola Lynch's rousing documentary *Free Angela and All Political Prisoners* (2012), writes, 'The feminist critical impulse, if we take it seriously, involves a dual commitment: a commitment to use knowledge in a transformative way, and to use knowledge to remake the world so that it is better for its inhabitants – not only for human beings, for all its living inhabitants'.[27]

After setting the scene in chapter one by reviewing the twenty-first century's headlines on women in film from the stats to scandalous feminism, I turn in chapter two to a consideration of non-human political animals, and then, in chapter three, to water. Ecologically-engaged films offer us a model for feminist film beyond the mainstream, for a feminism that is (as it has to be) as large as the world and 'all its living inhabitants'. To 'remake the world', cinema needs to be remade: chapters four and five consider filmmakers tackling two prestigious (and destructive) frameworks, war films and the concept of a national cinema, disorienting them through a feminist point of view. Emma Wilson writes that, for Céline Sciamma, 'women's cinema is not an issue of aesthetics, but of politics. For her there is no female gaze or gesture in filmmaking; the question is rather one of point of view'.[28]

When feminist cinema works in a 'women's genre' such as costume drama, it politicizes it, as chapter six explores. This politicized point of view can be sensed

Fig. 4: Angela Y. Davis on stage, from *Free Angela and All Political Prisoners*

in an ethical approach to narrative choices, but also through film form, in what Carolee Schneemann called 'the persistence of feelings / hand-touch sensibilities'.[29] It's this that unites Elsa's power in *Frozen* with an experimental project such as Sarah Wood's short documentary 'For Cultural Purposes Only' (2009), in which we see the hands of artist Woodrow Phoenix as he illustrates lovingly-recalled descriptions of Palestinian films lost when an archive in Beirut was bombed.

Chapter seven considers how films touch our unconscious – perhaps awakening us politically – through the use of fairy tales and the fantastic, while chapter eight observes how young feminists make their mark on the world, creating a space that I call the 'girl 'hood'. In chapter nine, that space is both reinserted into and contrasted with the maternal home/body, reconfigured as a non-biological site of care and communion. These films often foreground the presence of two communities: the filmmaking collective, and the audience. Collaboration is connected to labours of love on a more intimate scale – particularly the contentious territory of romance – in chapter ten.

Films about the difficulties of love reflect the love needed to undertake the arduous process of making a film, something that Sally Potter refers to in her Barefoot Filmmaking manifesto as 'being an anorak': being committed and

Introduction: Girls to the Front

flexible, absorbed and curious, rigorous and open.[30] Potter is not the only feminist filmmaker to have committed her thoughts on filmmaking to paper; by considering these books as and alongside curation, the conclusion shows feminist cinema writing its own history.

Self-documentation is not unique to feminist cinema, but it is, in Melinda Barlow's phrase, 'gender-poignant'.[31] *Political Animals* is written in homage and gratitude to the feminist scholars, curators, critics and bloggers whose work opened, and opens, up a world of film to me, and preserves it for us all. Above all, B. Ruby Rich's feminist film history *Chick Flicks* brought news of films I couldn't yet see (and had never dreamed possible). Her search, delivered in effervescent style, for 'the kind of riveting, soul-replenishing work that can give girls and women the confidence and spirit to change the world', is the shoulder upon which my book stands.[32]

Although I hope it can be the book to throw at those who refute the existence and ability of feminist filmmakers, *Political Animals* isn't meant to inaugurate an alternative canon, or even prescribe a film festival programme. I acknowledge my economic, educational, cisgendered, white and able-bodied privilege; also my geographical privilege, as a London-based film critic with access to festivals, cinemas, DVDs and the internet. I also acknowledge practical limitations that contribute to the book's Anglophone focus. I look forward to future scholars throwing their own books at me, with intersectional film studies that far exceed my vision.

In celebration of the 'soul-replenishing' transformative worlds of feminist cinema I've been lucky enough to enter, *Political Animals*, finally, is a postcard saying WISH YOU WERE HERE. And if we wish, we also need to act together, to bring into being the liberatory qualities of the worlds we see on screen. Kathleen Hanna's words, which she would now rephrase as trans-inclusive (and I intend as such here), remain the best available invitation: ALL THE GIRLS TO THE FRONT. I'M SERIOUS.

1

Ain't about the (uh) Cha-Ching, Cha-Ching
Framing the New Feminist Cinema

Going Outside

From the set of *Selma* (2014), Ava DuVernay gave Manohla Dargis a powerful insight into the real struggle and practice of contemporary feminist cinema. 'It's not really all about money', she said, but 'about allowing our imaginations – and giving ourselves permission – to go outside'.[1] 'Go[ing] outside', whether speaking from the Selma courthouse or a blog post, may be the pre-eminent trend in feminist film this century, describing its ambition, reach and outspokenness. In the introduction, Elsa and Anna, Kathleen Hanna, Shannen Koostachin and Angela Y. Davis are all pictured 'go[ing] outside', representing both the new global feminist politics and feminist filmmakers' engagement therewith.

Permission may not arise from film funding, but the ways in which money is framed (as opposed to money itself) remain a key determinant of 'access to the means of inscribing one's vision and having it reckoned with as important in any way', as Sarah Brouillette phrases it.[2] It matters that *Selma* has passed the $50 million mark at the US box office, and that *Women and Hollywood* exists to report it, because of the incalculable potential social effects of that reportage.[3] Facts and figures on gender in film have been emerging with regularity and urgency since Kathryn Bigelow became the first woman to win Best Director at the Academy Awards and then the BAFTAs in 2010, galvanizing attention to the shameful statistics on unequal participation across the industry.

Martha Lauzen's work with the Center for the Study of Women in Television and Film, Stacy L. Smith's work with the MDSC Initiative at the Annenberg Center and See Jane (a programme started and promoted by Geena Davis), the European Women's Audiovisual Network and many more bodies and individuals are recording and reporting the numbers. This labour-intensive work is generally limited to the top 100 grossing films. While understandable, such a cap doesn't account for

Ain't about the (uh) Cha-Ching, Cha-Ching

Fig. 5: Ava DuVernay directing a crowd scene in *Selma*.

the full range of participation of women in the industry, and continues to allow monetary value and the mainstream to define success.

Frozen has made $1.3 billion worldwide, the eighth highest-grossing film of all time (as of August 2015), and the only film in the top 50 with a female (co) director, but those figures have had vanishingly little transformative effect.[4] As Bruce Handy concludes his analysis of the dramatic success of films with female protagonists at the US box office in 2013, 'according to math, the studios appear to be leaving money on the table, one sin they've rarely if ever been accused of'.[5] 'Ain't about the (uh) cha-ching, cha-ching', as the a cappella group sing in *Pitch Perfect* (Jason Moore, 2012, from a screenplay by Kay Cannon), covering Jessie J's 'Price Tag'. *Pitch Perfect* grossed nearly ten times its medium budget worldwide, its ensemble comedy cuing singalong events and a female-helmed sequel (Elizabeth Banks, 2015), the highest-grossing musical comedy ever, driven by fan culture. Both the box office and fandom are important – yet have done little to challenge the entrenched sexism and racism revealed through the leaked Sony emails in December 2014, as analysed by Lexi Alexander.[6]

Stacy L. Smith has demonstrated that women may be moving towards parity in US independent cinema, but not the studio system.[7] Melissa Silverstein quotes her succinct observation that, 'as U.S. studio money comes in, females are pushed out'.[8] In independent and alternative cinemas, representation is more equal, often due to an intersectional commitment from funders and programmers. Danis Goulet observes that, 'Within Indigenous cinema, women are a serious force to be reckoned with… approximately 37% of the [imagineNATIVE's] festival submissions had come from women in [2012], and 62% of official selections were made with Indigenous women in a key creative position'.[9] Systemic intersectional exclusion expresses itself through economies of scale, so that the higher budget accorded a film, the less likely it is to have a filmmaker or protagonist who is not, in Grayson Perry's resonant term, a 'Default Man'.[10]

The production narrative of *Selma* offers a keen reflection of systemic exclusion and its tenuous connection to balance sheets. Despite being a prestige biopic of a national hero, a favoured awards genre, the film's greenlight depended on star David Oyelowo, who brought not only director DuVernay on board (having worked on her Sundance-winning, self-distributed feature *Middle of Nowhere* [2012]), but also producer Oprah Winfrey, with whom he had been cast in *The Butler* (Lee Daniels, 2013). As he told Gary Younge:

> I had shared my dream with her of playing this role. She said, 'I'd do anything and everything I can to help you with that'. So, not wanting to look that gift horse in the mouth, I said, 'OK, I need you, mama'. And she came on board and that literally was the moment we were off to the races.[11]

Oyelowo's story bespeaks the complexity of a contemporary media landscape that cannot be summed up in statistics, in which Winfrey's anomalous position, as a hugely successful African American woman in US media, both does and does not counterbalance the persistence of systemic inequality. For a full picture of feminist cinema, we need to go outside the conventional narratives of film history and reportage.

Believing in Plenty

Like statistics, newsworthy 'firsts' such as DuVernay's Golden Globe and Academy Award nominations, are both a telling and delimiting way of reporting on feminist film in the twenty-first century. Firsts, such as Jennifer Lee being the first female co-director of a Disney animation feature, often tokenize, obscuring rather than illuminating the coherent and continuous history of innovation and activism by female-identified filmmakers. We need to link all the 'firsts' together into an alternate film history. Lee's current success might remind us that, in the 1920s, Lotte Reiniger pioneered silhouette animation, which, she noted, contained 'feminine and masculine elements that play into each other's hands'.[12]

Reiniger's impish account is included in Antonia Lant and Ingrid Periz's collection *Red Velvet Seat: Women's Writing on the First Fifty Years of Cinema*, which brings together innovating filmmakers such as Maya Deren, Germaine Dulac and Alice Guy-Blaché with early film theorists such as the poet H.D. (Hilda Doolittle). With her ex-husband and girlfriend, H.D. founded *Close-Up*, Britain's first serious film magazine, and made the experimental mixed-race bisexual romantic drama *Borderline* (Kenneth Macpherson, 1930). Lant and Periz's project is part of an ongoing initiative that begins with archival detective work and critical analysis in the 1970s, such as Claire Johnston's *The Work of Dorothy Arzner: Towards a Feminist Cinema*.[13] This essential recovery work informed and intertwined with the feminist counter-cinema called for by Laura Mulvey in her 1975 article 'Visual Pleasure and Narrative Cinema', and which she practised in her own films.[14]

Almost two decades later, Hollywood noticed, marking 1993 as 'Year of the Woman' at the Academy Awards, after the success of *Thelma and Louise* (Ridley Scott, 1991, from a screenplay by Callie Khouri), *The Piano* (Jane Campion, 1993) and *Orlando* (Sally Potter, 1992). The subsequent blossoming of global feminist cinemas, as described in the introduction, makes it possible to respond to statistics on the mainstream by 'rejecting models of scarcity, believing in plenty', as poet Jill McDonough responds to VIDA's depressing figures on women in literary publishing.[15] The committed coverage of blogs such as *Women and Hollywood*, African Women in Cinema and Wellywood Woman (and the online camaraderie of their authors Melissa Silverstein, Beti Ellerson and Marian Evans),[16] as well as journals such as the short-lived *Joan's Digest* and hopefully long-lived *cléo: a journal of film and feminism*,[17] further enables my refutation of scarcity.

At the same time, as the editors of *Celluloid Ceiling: Women Film Directors Breaking Through* observe, for many cisfemale and trans*, intersex and non-binary filmmakers worldwide, access is dependent on economic privilege (often linked to ethnic, class, caste, abled, cis, straight and/or educational privilege), a prior career as a performer (often connected to socially-constructed perceptions of physical beauty), and also to family networks.[18] Additionally, there remains a willed ignorance and determined erasure of history.

Clio Barnard's docudrama *The Arbor* (2010), like many contemporary feminist films, highlights the swiftness of this erasure, seeking out both personal and professional memories of the comet-like career of playwright Andrea Dunbar. Within our dual transitional phase of digital multi-platforming and global austerity, there are both ever more reasons for films and filmmakers to fall through the cracks, and ever-more inventive guerrilla distribution strategies to prevent further erasure. British feminist distributor Cinenova, formed following the merger of Circles and Cinema of Women, has set up a pay-what-you-can digital cinematheque at the Showroom Gallery in London, to ensure that some viewers can access rarities, from Tracey Moffatt's documentary on Aboriginal Australian feminists, *Moodejit Yorgas* (*Solid Women*, 1990) to Bev Zalcock and Sara Chambers' lo-fi sci-fi 'Space Dog Assassin' (1998).[19]

Feminist film scholarship has been critical in maintaining an awareness of inaccessible films, rather than seeking to institute a canon. Patricia White notes that she was wary of producing an 'updated, cosmopolitan edition of what Andrew Sarris notoriously called the "ladies auxiliary" to his pantheon of great directors [which] could be considered fundamentally at odds with feminist work on authorship'.[20] Authorship, like box office success, is at once crucial to coverage and circulation for feminist cinema, and deeply problematic, invoking Default Man models of the solitary genius. Corinn Columpar proposes the term 'auteure' for the ways in which female filmmakers both inscribe individual skill and question solitary prestige.[21] This auteure-ist lens is focal for the majority of monographs on female filmmakers, almost all of them written this century.[22] A very welcome development (although still running at 7 per cent or less of the series in which they appear), and a tribute to the persistence and critical acumen of feminist film scholars, they nevertheless primarily cover directors who are of white Western European or North American origin.

As Shohini Chaudhuri argues, 'feminist film theory increasingly needs to look beyond Hollywood and to engage with broader traditions of international filmmaking'.[23] There have been English-language studies of African, Chinese, Mediterranean and Latin American women's cinemas, but also Geetha Ramanathan's *Feminist Auteurs: Reading Women's Films* and Alison Butler's *Women's Cinema: The Contested Screen*, both of which, like White's *Women's Cinema, World Cinema*, inflect feminist film with the transnational, and vice versa.[24] White writes that, 'in the transnational feminist public sphere constituted around such [cinematic] work, the revolution will be subtitled' for Anglophone audiences.[25]

Firsts are still a major framework for global feminist cinemas, such as coverage of Haifa al-Mansour of Saudi Arabia and Siti Kamaluddin of Brunei making their countries' first ever commercial films.[26] At the same time, filmmakers such as Jane Campion, Sally Potter, Deepa Mehta and Agnès Varda, whose oeuvres began in the previous decades, continue luminously in the present. Such ongoing careers create a unique moment in feminist film history, where information, inspiration and expertise are flowing transgenerationally. That disarms Harold Bloom's oedipal model of the male writer's anxiety of influence, but also Sandra M. Gilbert and Susan Gubar's model of the female writer silenced by lack of female influence.[27] Lucy Bolton invites us to consider, instead, Luce Irigaray's model of feminist genealogies, offering an intergenerational 'horizon of accomplishment'.[28]

Campion's critically acclaimed mini-series *Top of the Lake* (with Gerard Lee, BBC/Sundance Channel/Screen Australia, 2013) features a young female detective who gets involved with an all-female commune comprised primarily of socially-excluded older women. The fifth episode (UK broadcast) ends with a funeral at Paradise, the commune. On a stage made from a shipping container, teenager Melissa (Georgi Kay) leads the commune in a cover version of Björk's 'Joga'. It's at once an image out of Greek tragedy, and an exciting reincorporation of Riot Grrrl's promise that alternative music offered a feminist route 'outside'. It soundtracks the first coming-together of all the different women in Laketop, as they take a communal stand against the corrupt patriarchal politics of the town.

Campion's change of medium is part of what makes her critique possible. Television – particularly *Sex and the City* (HBO, Candace Bushnell, 1998–2004) and *The L Word* (Showtime, Michele Abbott, Ilene Chaikin and Kathy Greenberg, 2004–2009) – has offered some preservation and continuity for 1980s and 1990s US indie feminist filmmakers. Allison Anders' direction of early *Sex and the City* episodes helped establish its smart address to a sophisticated audience. 'Thank fucking God I did', she told Alison Willmore, 'because it continues to take care of me in residuals – and I only directed four episodes'.[29] The breakaway successes of cable show *Girls*, network show *Scandal* (ABC, Shonda Rimes, 2012–) and online commissions *Orange is the New Black* (Netflix, Jenji Kohan, 2013–) and *Transparent* (Amazon Prime, Jill Soloway, 2014–) are directly attributable to the way in which US serial television was shaped by the earlier shows into a welcoming environment for women.

Independent webseries by women of colour build on this diversification of auteure-ist platforms. *The Slope* (Desiree Akhavan and Ingrid Jungermann, 2012) and *The Misadventures of an Awkward Black Girl* (Issa Rae, 2011–2013) are post-*Sex and the City* New York-set 'hot mess' comedies, while Cecile Emeke offers a London twist on the genre in *Ackee & Saltfish* (2015).[30] *Political Animals* celebrates what Miranda July calls 'the creative art of moving between the media', at which she excels.[31] 'Given the mutable cultural terrain of the twenty-first century, the work of female directors might be negotiating different, perhaps even disjunctive, [media] worlds', as Therese Davis and Belinda Smaill note, having to evince both flexibility and determination to work by any means possible.[32] Speaking from her experience as a woman of colour working in US media, documentarian Dawn Porter celebrates plenitude: 'We're all here. Despite the odds, despite people laughing at us, we're here'.[33]

Representational Justice

Feminist filmmakers face greater odds than just systemic exclusion from the Hollywood studio system. In *The Terror Dream*, her account of what happened to the USA after 11 September 2001, Susan Faludi argues that the progressive politics of the 1990s were stymied, and even reversed, by legislation and cultural shifts in the USA under the presidency of George W. Bush.[34] This led to a resurgence of overt structural sexism and violent misogyny in the over-developed world, which only since 2008 has seen the development of a 'fourth-wave' feminism focused on reversing the reverses.[35] From Tahrir Square to Rotherham to Steubenville to Delhi to Winnipeg, part of current feminist protest is about resisting the everyday violence that dominant culture enacts on bodies that are visibly female, queer, trans*, of colour, working class and/or disabled, which we could productively call – not least to assert ourselves as an allied majority – the bodies of the 99 per cent.

A public stand against the continuing crisis of gendered violence, and interrelatedly its reinforcement through on-screen depictions, is at the origin of feminist film and film theory. Yvonne Rainer, who moved from choreography to filmmaking in 1972, reminded us in 2006 that Mulvey's definitional article was 'a *cri de coeur* [against lived sexual violence] that was echoed in protests on both sides of the Atlantic'.[36] Mulvey was protesting 'rape culture', a now-widespread term that I first encountered in a 1999 essay by feminist media scholar Julia Lesage.[37]

In a 2014 editorial calling for more female film critics, *Sight & Sound* recognized 'how culpable movies have been in helping to create that nasty troll hinterland... [because] the male gaze is so deep-rooted in cinema as to be structural'.[38] Film's culpability in rape culture is the premise of the United Nations 2014 report on gender disparity in the global film industry. According to UN Women Executive Director Phumzile Mlambo-Ngcuka, who commissioned the study:

> Twenty years ago, 189 Governments adopted the Beijing Platform for Action, the international roadmap for gender equality, which called on media to avoid stereotypical and degrading depictions of

women. Two decades on, this study is a wake-up call that shows that the global film industry still has a long way to go.[39]

The report's headline figures showed that when films were made by women, whether as directors (7 per cent) or screenwriters (20 per cent), onscreen representation of women as protagonists improved by roughly 10 per cent.

Despite the much-vaunted success of *Gravity* (Alfonso Cuarón, 2013) and *The Hunger Games* tetralogy (Gary Ross, 2012; Francis Lawrence, 2013, 2014 and 2015), the solo strong female protagonist may be part of the problem, not of the solution. Sexy – and solitary – Strong Female Characters have long been fantasy figures for viewers of all genders. Isolated female-identified protagonists – however putatively strong – are often subjected to sexualized violence, and may be subtly blamed for taking the risk. Even Lisbeth Salander, 'the girl with the dragon tattoo', ends up trapped in a hospital bed and written out of her own narrative: what Tasha Robinson names 'Trinity Syndrome'.[40]

Aside from Paul Feig's highly successful, female-authored *Bridesmaids* (2011, from a screenplay by Kristen Wiig and Annie Mumolo) and *The Heat* (2013, from a screenplay by Katie Dippold), where big budgets and box office really baulk appears to be at female ensembles which truly pass the Bechdel Test.[41] This demands multiple rounded female-identified characters who interact with each other in solidarity – and not in ways that unthinkingly replicate other forms of oppression, as Roxane Gay identifies in her reading of *The Help* (Tate Taylor, 2011).[42] Simple 'representation' is not enough.

As Natalie Hill writes with respect to *Miss Representation* (2011), Jennifer Siebel Newsom's documentary about women on screen:

> The key slogan for *Miss Representation* is 'you can't be what you can't see'… Who don't we see in *Miss Representation*? Women with disabilities, for starters… We also see a whole lot of privileged white women doing most of the talking, which means we don't see a whole lot of anybody else.[43]

The MDSC Initiative's report 'Inequality in 700 popular films' is the first to offer the kind of intersectional breakdown Hill suggests would amplify claims to improve representation, and reveal new narratives about the complexity and specificity of global film production.[44] Anchalee Chaiworaporn notes that, since 1997, Tanwarin Sukkhapisit and Sarasawadee Wongsompetch, both kathoey (transgendered) directors who identify as female, have been the most productive female filmmakers in Thailand, each completing three features.[45]

Lana Wachowski is only the most visible figurehead of a non-cisgendered cinema. Foregrounded by trans-specific and LGBTQIA film festivals internationally, its best-known practitioners include Ester Martin Bergsmark, Sam Feder, StormMiguel Flores, Raphael Fox, Marcus Harwood-Jones, Gwen Haworth, Silas Howard, Wu Tsang and Kortney Ryan Ziegler. Sydney Freeland, a Navajo transgender woman, scored Sundance support – including Robert Redford as an executive producer – for her feature debut *Drunktown's Finest* (2014), which tells the intertwined stories of three characters, including Felixia, a transgender sex worker and aspiring model, played by Carmen Moore, a Diné transwoman in her first screen role.[46] Felixia's grandfather Harmon (Richard Ray Whitman), the local community's medicine man, recognises her as Nadleeh (third gender), telling her a traditional story in which Nadleeh mediate after a row between men and women.

Freeland introduced the film at BFI Flare 2015 by borrowing, approvingly, a fan's description of the film as 'a coming of age story for all three genders'.[47] The film takes its narrative shape from a four-day puberty ceremony for a tween girl, Max (Magdalena Begay), through whose unfolding the three late adolescent protagonists Felixia, Nizhoni (Morning Star Wilson) and SickBoy (Jeremiah Bitsui), undergo their own informal yet communitarian and connected rituals of coming of age. Freeland, Felixia and Moore represent how cinema is transforming, and – more importantly – transformative, because they also 'represent', in the hip-hop sense, both their nation and their gender.

Kara Keeling's *The Witch's Flight: The Cinematic, the Black Femme, and the Image of Common Sense*, the most original book of feminist film theory this century, begins from the premise that there is a crucial fissure in the word 'representation' as used in conversations about media equality. Drawing on Gayatri Chakravorty Spivak, Keeling identifies a dual meaning: in common usage, it means 'depiction,' a crafted visual and embodied re-presentation; but in legal (as in hip-hop) usage, it means to be empowered to speak for. In film, the former is the vehicle for the latter, so they are indubitably entangled. As Keeling explains, too much attention has been paid to increasing or changing the former, without attending to its tenor or meaning.[48] By taking time in *Selma* on both the crafting and delivery of public speeches by Martin Luther King, Jr., DuVernay shows the connection between speaking-for and depiction, leading up to his final speech with its multiple addressees including us, the future audience he dreamed.

DuVernay's use of film form offers what I call 'representational justice', in homage to the US-based movement for reproductive justice, fronted by women of colour. Reproductive justice foregrounds racial and economic inequalities that striate the health, education and political systems in the US, which frame and amplify the effects of the erosion of abortion rights.[49] Its necessity can be observed in the fact that Gillian Robespierre's charming and 'very reasonable', to quote Deragh Campbell, *Obvious Child* (2014), the first US comedy to address abortion, made headlines even as an online short film; the feature's trailer was initially banned by NBC.[50]

Documentaries such as *After Tiller* (Martha Shane and Lana Wilson, 2013) and *Vessel* (Diana Whitten, 2013), about pioneering doctors providing late-term abortions in the USA and on shipboard for territories where abortion is illegal, respectively, affirm both the centrality and scope of reproductive justice as a narrative framework for feminist cinema. Whitten has ensured that *Vessel* is widely available online, and for community screenings and fundraisers; an attack by three masked men on a screening by RFSU (the Swedish Association for Sexuality Education) in Stockholm confirmed the film's urgency.[51] Representational justice matters because, as the UN Women's report argues, it is a key determinant for claiming reproductive justice: a matter of life and death.

Reclaiming the Night

Inspiring the #ISupportDukhtar hashtag campaign against child marriage, Afia Nathaniel's *Dukhtar* (2014), was Pakistan's surprise entry for the 2014 Academy Awards. Loosely based on a real case, the film follows Allah Rakhi (Samiya Mumtaz) as she flees her husband's house with her lively, bright pre-teen daughter Zainab (Saleha Aref), in order to protect her from a tribal, dynastic marriage.[52] Having reached precarious safety, she leaves to meet with her mother, whom she hasn't seen since her own child marriage, risking capture by her husband's men in a Lahori night market. Patriarchal oppression can only be revealed and reversed by women 'go[ing] outside' *together*.

In the proto-feminist films of Dorothy Arzner, cads get what's coming to them, and wild girls get to live on. The feminist banner under which Rainer marched in the 1970s proclaimed that women would Take Back, or Reclaim, the Night. Reclaiming the night means taking up public space, but also dreamspace and desire. Jacqueline Rose's *Women in Dark Times* argues that feminism has neglected the play of the unconscious. Looking at the work of feminist artists including actor Marilyn Monroe and video artist Yael Bartana, she demands a 'scandalous feminism, one which embraces without inhibition the most painful, outrageous aspects of the human heart', wherein physical darkness, the darkness of the unconscious and of the cinema screen are all taken back.[53]

News that Nobel prize-winning novelist Elfriede Jelinek (author of *La pianiste* [*The Piano Teacher*, Michael Haneke, 2001]) is collaborating with Ulrike Ottinger, director of the lesbian BDSM cult classic *Madame X* (1978), on vampire film *La belle dormeuse* (*The Beautiful Woman Sleeping*, 2016), suggests just how productive the 'scandalous' territory of the feminist filmic unconscious could be.[54] In Ana Lily Amirpour's Iranian American vampire western *A Girl Walks Home Alone at Night* (2014) The Girl (Sheila Vand), a skateboarding vampire who tears apart the corrupt Bad City, is the post-*Buffy the Vampire Slayer* (WB/Fox, Joss Whedon, 1996–2003) fantastic heroine we have been waiting for.

Sophia Al-Maria's loving deconstruction of horror cinema in her installation *Virgin With a Memory* (Cornerhouse Manchester, 2014) riffs on her abandoned feature *Beretta*, which aimed to 'tell both the story of a woman who is pushed to extremes by her environment, and a country [Egypt] that was raped and degraded by its governments'.[55] The installation demonstrates the power that the genre retains, particularly for female viewers and artists seeking to represent violation and traumatic disruption. Feminist horror films such as *American Mary* (Jen and Sylvia Soska, 2012), *Jennifer's Body* (Karyn Kusama, 2009) and *Amer* (Hélène Cattet and Bruno Forzani, 2009) have developed the feminist potential of the genre as recognized by Carol Clover in *Men, Women and Chainsaws* (my all-time favourite feminist film book title).[56]

Films that flirt with sadistic voyeurism, however, even to turn the tables, perpetuate 'thrall', the romance of internalized sexism, which is legitimated by female-helmed arthouse fare such as *Contre toi* (*In Your Hands*, Lola Doillon, 2010), as well as blockbusters such as *Twilight* (Catherine Hardwicke, 2008) and *Fifty Shades of Grey* (Sam Taylor-Johnson, 2015). So the dual challenge is to reclaim the night against external violence and the more seductive internal violence of thrall. We need films that are like the dream described by Zapatista spokesman Subcomandante Marcos: 'one that takes away sleep. The only dream that is dreamed awake, sleepless. The history that is born and nurtured from below'.[57]

Cinema remains a useful site for such reclamations because it mediates between conscious and unconscious. Elisabeth Bronfen writes of the end of Campion's neo-*noir In the Cut* (2003) that, 'waking up and walking into the dawn of morning might just as well mean preserving the dialectic between night/day rather than insisting on a violent repression of the nocturnal side of the psyche'.[58] *In the Cut* ends with its protagonist having killed the serial killer who tried to enthral her (and the viewer). 'Lovely and vigorous and brave', it reclaims the night through its attention to gendered violence and its griefs.

The Revolution of My Country

Campion's protagonist moves through a New York scarred by the events of 9/11. She rescues herself not only from a serial killer, who is (pointedly) a police officer, but also from the rescue-and-confess narrative central to US domestic politics at that time. Reading the story of Private Jessica Lynch via *The Searchers* (John Ford, 1956), Susan Faludi identifies this as the controlling myth of US heteropatriarchal colonial violence.[59] Having a daughter who is inherently vulnerable under patriarchy, she argues, makes a manly man vulnerable, and thus non-masculine. Therefore the daughter's kidnap and rape first punishes her for emasculating our hero, then enables him to enact his hyper-masculinity against racialized Others, and finally to restore the status quo – but with the now 'damaged', i.e.: no longer virginal, daughter no longer able to make him vulnerable.

The resurgence of the western, and its post-apocalyptic variants, in the last decade and a half, has been mirrored by a vengeance trope that connects arthouse fare such as *Irréversible* (Gaspar Noé, 2002) to, as Hannah Hamad identifies, the endless iteration of testosterone-powered action thrillers in which a middle-aged dad has to rescue their/the President's daughter.[60] This cycle has left little or no room for the further development of Riot Grrrl/New Queer Cinema. Kelly Reichardt's thriller *Night Moves* (2013) aside, white feminist US indie has shied away from reclaiming the night.

Internationally, however, the same conflicts galvanized feminist filmmaking. Samira Makhmalbaf, already established on the international festival circuit with her debut *Sib* (*The Apple*, 1998), followed in her father Mohsen's footsteps by making a film in Kandahar among Afghan refugees, *Panj é asr* (*At Five in the Afternoon*, 2003) – indeed a second, after her short, 'God, Construction and Destruction', for the portmanteau film *11'09"01* (2002). She said that,

> The first day I went to Afghanistan, I didn't have any idea about Afghan women… I thought they were just victims. But then I started talking to then. They have big desires, they are full of hope… after one hour of talking, all of the class wanted to be president.[61]

Samira's 14-year-old sister Hana made a behind the scenes documentary, 'Lezate divanegi' ('The Joy of Madness', 2003) about *At Five*, and returned to Afghanistan to make her own first feature, *Buda as sharm foru rikht* (*Buddha Collapsed out of Shame*, 2007).

Hana's second feature film captures the political shift between the first and second decades of the twenty-first century: *Roozhaye sabz* (*Green Days*, 2009),

Fig. 6: Aida El Kashef in Tahrir Square, *The Square*

subtitled 'Dedicated to the People of Iran', weaves an intimate narrative around anonymous cellphone footage of the 2009 Green Wave protests. Hana had to leave the country to avoid arrest, and finished the film in Italy. Although it premiered at the Toronto International Film Festival, and screened on BBC Persia, it has been almost erased from history due to a ban in Lebanon. There are few clips online, although – according to the filmmaker – you can find copies on the black market in Iran.[62] Whereas *Buddha* is a delicate and devastating allegory of women 'go[ing] outside', *Green Days* documents the actuality. This book owes its existence in part to the ongoing uprising of which *Green Days* is a part, from Occupy to the Arab Spring and Idle No More – led, moreover, by women, such as Alicia Garza, Patrisse Cullors and Opal Tometi, founders of Black Lives Matter, and Camila Vallejo, a leader of the 2011 student protests in Chile.

Only a few films have yet documented this palpable, worldwide pulse. Jehane Noujaim's documentary *The Square* (2013), shot on the fly in and around the multiple occupations of Tahrir Square in Cairo, captures it best – because of the filmmakers' ongoing implication in the struggle. The film's editor Sanaa Seif was imprisoned in October 2014 for her continued participation in anti-government activism.[63] Like Hana Makhbalbaf's, Noujaim's oeuvre brackets the politics of the early twenty-first century; her second film, *Control Room* (2004), exposed the US military's spin in Iraq and the rise of al-Jazeera with wit and astonishing *chutzpah*. In *The Square*, Noujaim shows the same ability to speak truth to power by getting power to speak the truth to her.

Unlike *Control Room*, *The Square* also features significant feminist political animals in front of the camera, including human rights activist Radia Omran and filmmaker Aida El Kashef, co-founder of documentary collective Mosireen, whose footage is included in the film. Their experience tallies with that of Egyptian feminist activist Hend Badawi, who said, 'I had the opportunity to mix my inner revolution with the revolution of my country'.[64] In February 2014, Noujaim announced that *The Square* would be available for free to all Egyptian viewers. The Arabic message on the YouTube post reads: 'We were finally able to make it happen. So here it is. Hopefully we can watch it together in the square soon'. It was already being watched by protestors in Kiev, Istanbul and Caracas.[65]

Bodies On and Below the Line

Noujaim's and Hana Makhmalbaf's films speak of and from the digital revolution in political organizing, which also flashes up wittily onscreen in Alison Klayman's documentary *Ai Weiwei: Never Sorry* (2012), in the form of tweets that allow the titular artist to subvert his house arrest. Judith Butler draws a connection between the risks taken in physical public space by the protestors Noujaim and Makhmalbaf document, and the new risks of online space, noting that 'under conditions when those with cameras or internet capacities are imprisoned or tortured or deported, then the use of the technology effectively implicates the body'.[66]

Nowhere has this been more palpable than in the online video art of Pussy Riot.[67] Saluted by Kathleen Hanna for reviving the originary politics of Riot Grrrl with their queer, feminist eco-protests, Pussy Riot are a reminder of the vicious violence of the heteropatriarchal state; but also a reminder that, if we are political animals now, we are probably digital ones. Independent of the academy and of gatekeeper publications (and more problematically independent, generally, of payment), feminist bloggers and vloggers such as Anita Sarkeesian of Feminist Frequency are articulating the new feminist criticism as part of an engaged community, albeit one that is subject to the same patriarchal violence as its offline sisters.[68] The treatment meted out to Sarkeesian, for example, before and during the Gamergate controversy over sexism in videogaming, reiterates Lewis's law, coined on Twitter by journalist Helen Lewis, that 'the comments on any article about feminism justify feminism'.[69]

Just as it enabled the Green Wave, so the web carries the fourth wave: as well as online campaigns such as Everyday Sexism, the internet hosts responses such as Canadian journal *Feral Feminisms*, visceral feminism (via another Canadian journal, *GUTS*), hysterical feminism (via Swedish journal *HYSTERIA*) and Gay's

Fig. 7: Adriana Barraza and Sally Potter shooting *Rage*

bad feminism.[70] All of them name the movement's risk of ossifying and joining/becoming the system it's trying to change. Jessica Yee, a self-described 'Two Spirit multi-racial Indigenous hip hop feminist reproductive justice freedom fighter', captures this in her anthology *Feminism FOR REAL: Deconstructing the Academic Industrial Complex of Feminism*, which began in both offline and online organizing.[71]

Feminist cinema is reflecting back this online activity: filmmaker Astra Taylor has penned 'take back the internet' guide *The People's Platform*; Maja Borg distributed her utopian documentary *Future My Love* (2012) via an online 'pay it forward' scheme; and Sally Potter pioneered simultaneous theatrical, DVD and streaming release with *Rage* (2009).[72] Where Beeban Kidron's documentary *InRealLife* (2013) focuses on the negative impact of social media for young users, *Rage* uses the globalized medium of video-blogging to tell a story about globalization, as unseen documentarian Michelangelo, a young man of colour, captures workers from every level of the fashion industry backstage, under siege from both misogynist and politicized violence.

That violence is shown to be intersectional: Anita de los Angeles (Adriana Barraza) is an undocumented worker, and the first to suggest that the camera – and

Ain't about the (uh) Cha-Ching, Cha-Ching

Fig. 8: Feminist Godzilla Eats Male Gaze

online distribution – are themselves forms of violence, as visibility threatens her security. As *Rage* shows, activist stances emerge from embodied specificities. R-A-G-E: race and religion, ability and age, gender/sexuality, economic class. The word is an acronym of its own urgent, lived causes. On Black Girl Dangerous (BGD), Mia McKenzie writes of how persistent oppression can become a prompt to take action: 'My choices were to be silent and pushed around, or speak up for myself and be perceived as too aggressive, mean or violent. It's the story of a black girl's life. It is tiresome. And it is the reason I started BGD in the first place'.[73]

As in legendary feminist science fiction film *Born in Flames* (Lizzie Borden, 1983), intervention into broadcast media stands at the heart of feminist revolution. Her climactic image, of the Women's Liberation Army (including Bigelow as a journalist) blowing up the television transmitter atop the World Trade Center in order to take over the airwaves, remains among the most joyously radical in feminist cinema. Rage *for* is often practical and also witty in its reproach to phallocentrism – yet feminists are accused of not being able to take a joke because they don't like patriarchy's idea of pleasure. Hence feminist philosopher Sara Ahmed writes of 'killing joy as a world-making project'.[74] In her 'Feminist Killjoy' manifesto, she exhorts that: 'There can be joy in killing joy. Kill joy, we can and we do.

Be wilful [*sic*], we will and we are'.[75] It's not joy we're killing: it's the perversions of the patriarchy, thus creating a space in which intersectional feminist delights can take their place.

Feminist Godzilla's witty, anonymous, collective posts are a potent example of converting heteropatriarchal destructive pleasures into feminist constructive joys.[76] Using Tumblr, a microblogging site particularly popular with genre fans and teenagers, the authors wield an accessible, low-cost tool to address a toxic film culture, rather than bidding to become part of it. Godzilla reminds us that cinema is a massive power source, as dynamic – but also dangerous – as a nuclear reactor. It can illuminate our world, power our actions, energize our communities; but it can also be destructive. Feminist Godzilla isn't obliterated by the radiation coming off both blockbuster cinema and mainstream film criticism, she's irradiated and radiant with rage, spawning her own forms of media. Grrrlzillas, killjoys, riotous pussies, and other political animals power the new feminisms seen on our screens.

2

Not in Kansas

Animal Selves and Becoming-Girls

Girl Loves Dog

Girl loses dog. The narrative of Kelly Reichardt's third feature *Wendy and Lucy* (2008) is piercing in its simplicity, going to the deep core of all love stories. In the minimalist, almost wordless narration of the relationship between the human Wendy (Michelle Williams) and canine Lucy (Lucy, Reichardt's own dog), what it means to be a political animal unfolds. *Wendy and Lucy* is the perfect place to observe how we become political animals: representational justice is no more a solely human issue than it is solely for cisgendered straight white women. Putting human life in relation with animal life creates a site for political organization based in what we share, particularly shared needs and rights, and for transformation, as we learn to perceive with each others' senses. Through her relationship with Lucy, Wendy gets to reclaim, or redo, her girlhood as wild, out in the open, vulnerable, animal and for real.

In its dreamlike take on neo-realism, Reichardt's film is a subtle gloss on one of the founding myths of twentieth century US culture and its cinema: *The Wizard of Oz* (Victor Fleming, 1939). Famously one of the first films shot in Technicolor, it was made in an era when major Hollywood studio blockbusters weren't shy of female protagonists or antagonists, and their little dogs too. Wendy redoes her girlhood through Dorothy's, parsing feminist spectators' love of (and identification through) certain texts in classical cinema with our frustrations. The big screen is the place we yearn to be, despite it being the place we're so shoddily treated: it's 'no place like home'.

Toto is Dorothy's sounding board, the only character more vulnerable than she is: a reminder that women (particularly young women) are all too often rendered as pets in mainstream film, as in the world; Judy Garland's maltreatment by the film's producers is a sobering example. Animals on film are a feminist issue because

Fig. 9: Wendy and Lucy in the car, Lucy looking to camera, *Wendy and Lucy*

women and animals analogize each other in dominant culture. Whether cute or devouring, since Aristotle women have been imagined as nature to masculine culture. We are wild, outsiders, no longer in thrall to 'civilization': a total overthrow of the status quo. In *Wendy and Lucy*, as in the classic Garland musical, a young woman is blown away from home (here, by the winds of fortune) with her companion animal. But the bond between Dorothy and the mute, handbag-sized Toto pales compared to Wendy's with Lucy: Lucy is Toto (and *Return to Oz*'s [Walter Murch, 1985] opinionated hen Bellina), the Cowardly Lion, the Tinman and the Scarecrow, all in one. Unlike Toto, Lucy is a character in her own right, with her own needs and agency. And, brutally, it's this aspect of her – her subjecthood – that leads to the final separation.

Whereas Dorothy battles and befriends grand, mythic figures, for Wendy there is no Witch to crush or Wizard to confront behind the curtain: only the grinding reality of capitalism, which means that she has to acknowledge she cannot care for her dog. She is sleeping rough, reclaiming the night in a realist way, with all the attendant risks. For Wendy, there is literally no place like home. At the start of the film, she is driving to Ketchican, Alaska, to take a job, when her car breaks down in a small town in Oregon. Her sister in Indiana, also struggling economically, can't loan her the money to fix it, so Wendy shoplifts to feed herself and Lucy, her golden retriever, and is arrested. While she is in custody, Lucy is taken to the pound. In losing Lucy, Wendy *becomes* Lucy, a stray dog who, broke and alone, has to depend on the kindness of strangers. No longer a carer, she has to ask others to care for her.

Self-contained Wendy is the opposite of the archetypal vision of a politically engaged human, and perhaps even of a feminist. That's why she's so valuable to think with: she offers a representation of how a political animal becomes, of the difficulty of change and connection. Eventually Wendy just about engages in the community around her, and acknowledges her interdependence, but only when she loses her car (her protective, separatist shell) and her companion. She is anti-heroic: the film acknowledges her halting attempts at asking for assistance, and her final decision to alter her plans, as a very different kind of courage to superheroism, one grounded in and learned from her relationship with Lucy.

Talking to Sophie Brown, Reichardt pointed to the political dimensions of Wendy and Lucy's joint narrative.

> I'm drawn to outsiders. I mean, who wants to see a film about the winners? Fuck the winners, you know? I'm completely uninterested... The minutiae of things is very interesting to me, and people who don't have a big safety net and are trying to get a leg up. When we made *Wendy and Lucy* it was very much in the environment of the George [W.] Bush years, when there was this real disdain for poor people and a whole movement towards doing everything you can to further embrace people that are already the haves.[1]

44 per cent of US households told the Corporation for Enterprise Development in 2013 that they didn't have enough savings to cover their basic expenses for three months in the event of a financial emergency.[2] Wendy is a member – and a representative – of this precariat, whom poverty activist Linda Tirado calls 'Bootstrap America'.[3] She has budgeted carefully for her trip to Alaska, but not for the margin of emergency, which leads to a challenge from the jobsworth clerk who catches her shoplifting: 'If you can't afford dog food then you shouldn't have a dog'. In this harsh exchange, the film opens up its central premise: that affective relationships run counter to heteropatriarchal capitalism, and even act as a form of resistance to, or way out of, its narrow confines.

Feminist cinema also tells this story through same-species human relationships. But heteronormative partner and familial relationships remain the site of many over-familiar film tropes and of multiple, equally over-familiar, historical and enduring tensions. Our relation to what philosopher Donna Haraway calls 'companion species', by contrast, can disrupt audience expectations about love, friendship, labour, public space and vulnerability. Haraway offers a *Companion*

Species Manifesto that, like her better-known 'Cyborg Manifesto' of the mid-1980s, troubles boundaries and binaries, raising the possibility of new forms of political identity. She argues that humans and dogs (and horses) are 'constitutively, companion species [that] make each other up, in the flesh'.[4] For Haraway, we 'make each other up' in two senses: evolving together biologically; and culturally, inventing each other through story.

The films I discuss here engender this new story by foregoing the often-objectifying empathy of, say, *Marley and Me* (David Frankel, 2008) and moving towards a rigorous examination of the politics of what Haraway calls 'natureculture'. Here, the social construction of gender, race and class entwines with the impact of colonialism and capitalism on the land and water (discussed further in chapter three) and the attempted erasure of indigenous lifeways and folkways. Poet and environmental activist Stephen Collis coined the term 'biotariat' to refer to the shared stakes for 'the enclosed and exploited life of this planet'.[5]

As Andrea Luka Zimmerman explores in her Istanbul-shot documentary *Taskafa: Stories of the Street* (2013), even domesticated animals can step outside our comfort zone and become political, recognizing ourselves as members of the biotariat. Taskafa, we learn, was a former pet who became the pack leader of the dogs of Galata Square in Istanbul, with a liminal existence between domestic and wild. Zimmerman collects memories of Taskafa from human square dwellers, who describe a companionate environment in which humans and canines aided each other. The community stands together against the impersonal forces of gentrification (the installation of auto-locking doors to apartment building foyers, which has deprived the dogs of warm places to sleep), Ottoman imperialism and British colonialism (in the story of collusion between the British ambassador and Sultan to remove Taskafa's nineteenth-century precursors), and current state violence (Taskafa is said to have been disappeared by municipal workers). Zimmerman develops a low-angle, blurred 'dog's eye view' to make Taskafa a participant in, as well as object of, the discussion, and there are often at least as many dogs as humans on screen. Human behaviour is viewed in the ethical context of its companionship, or otherwise, to the square's dogs.

Like *Wendy and Lucy*, *Taskafa* and his tale-tellers lead us into the heart of a community where interconnection has replaced fear and alienation. Seen in the context of the Gezi Park protests of 2013, Taskafa and his canine community prefigure an engagement in public protest that made internationally visible Istanbul's counter-publics, including the LGBT Blok and the Sosyalist Feminist Kolektif.[6] *Taskafa*, like *Wendy and Lucy*, stands for a reclamation of public space as political space through diegetic space, which we could call Occupy Cinema. It's a politicized evolution of Slow Cinema, which itself often adopts an animal viewpoint or highlights companion species in rural landscapes, as Tiago de Luca describes.[7] Its slowness resonates with many Occupy camps' decision not to present a list of demands, but to take up space and time towards a new way of being, one that is learned from our companion species.

Without a Cat

It may seem counter-intuitive to start a chapter on feminist animal cinema with dogs rather than cats. Confused Cats Against Feminism (a blog parodying Women Against Feminism, which is sadly itself not a parody) not only demonstrates cats' dominance of online media, but also their longstanding association with negatively feminized qualities, and thus with women.[8] Film critic Anne Billson maintains the 'Cats on Film' blog, which notes the presence of 'catpanions' in two films that focus on female-dominated precariat families, *Bright Star* (Jane Campion, 2009) and *Little Women* (Gillian Armstrong, 1994).[9] As Kay Armatage describes, however, feminist animal cinema begins with Nell Shipman, a Canadian silent filmmaker who became an animal rights activist.[10] Her first film as filmmaker, *Back to God's Country* (1919), was an adaptation of James Oliver Curwood's short story 'Wapi the Walrus', in which Wapi – who is actually a Great Dane – is the narrator, and remains an important on-screen character.

Shipman's contribution thus predates by 25 years Maya Deren and Alexander Hammid's early diary film 'The Private Life of a Cat' (1944), shot in their Greenwich Village apartment. A cat also appears, notably, in Carolee Schneemann's legendary diary film 'Fuses' (1965): Kitch watches as Schneemann and her then-partner James Tenney make love, shifting the centre of attention. Agnès Varda pays homage, in 'Le Tombeau de Zgougou' (2006), to one of many highly significant feline companions for her, seen in charge of the computer monitor (and of the camera's gaze) in the opening shot of *The Gleaners and I*.

Both Deren and Schneemann play wittily with an association that lends the *frisson* to what Jenny Diski delights in calling 'Derrida's pussy': the gendering of cats as female via their association with feminized traits such as being high maintenance, selfish, appetitive and different. Deren's cat not only gives birth, but chases the father away with a feral hiss. As Diski points out in *What I Don't Know About Animals*, domestic cats are a reminder of the absolute Otherness of animal being. She notes that cats have a frightening undertone that is equally expressed in Jacques Derrida's concern about his cat observing him naked, and Lolcat's implied joke of feline world domination.[11]

Kitch is a mirror for the viewer, a way to look at Schneemann's radical erotic art that is at once cool and involved, accepting and amused, included and distanced; her presence de-pornifies the film. Feminist cat films favour 'the feral as a provocative call to untaming, queering, and radicalizing feminist thought and practice today', whereby the cat is a marker of the unpredictable, untame, erotic and disruptive because it is less domesticated than a dog, and more resistant to human hierarchies.[12] Cats often signify villainy in mainstream film, but for Deren and Schneemann they loosen the boundaries of domestic space, bringing the wild inside. The home, associated with the feminine, is disrupted by the presence of the pussy.

The domestic availability of the cat as subject is also indicative: Deren's and Schneemann's no-budget experimental home movies, made 'for what Hollywood spends on lipstick' in Deren's words, are the opposite of Shipman's ambitious epic.[13] *Wendy and Lucy*, shot for a micro-budget of $300,000 (oddly, roughly the same as the budget of Shipman's 1919 film), is a story about the exigencies of independent feminist cinema. As Reichardt commented wryly:

> Wendy's limited monetary situation was certainly relatable as far as the production went. It's just a very fragile situation making a film on such limited funds, there's not a lot of room for mistakes… And that's true for Wendy as well – the stakes are different for her but the whole fabric of her plan can easily fall away. It's either a really good idea to head off to Alaska, or to make a film, on a miniscule budget or a very stupid idea – in both cases it's a gamble.[14]

We could ask whether independent feminist cinema, with its commitment to a critical viewpoint and representational justice, might be analogized by Lucy's choices: like dog food, is it something that we can afford? What is at stake if we don't take the gamble and lose these alternate ways of seeing that rewild our cinema?

Most of the films I discuss in this chapter are micro-budget films: there is an alignment between the human/animal allegiance and the critique of mainstream forms. They show that a rewilding cinema might be both, environmentally and psychologically, what we need and all that we can afford. Through animal presences we can become political on a scale at once hyper-local and globally-connected. Annemarie Jacir's 'Sound of the Street' (2006) layers a soundtrack of found voices talking in Arabic about everyday issues over close-up footage of ants travelling over a small piece of ground. When a barrier is placed at one end, the ants begin to fight with each other, and the voiceover of repeated phrases is syncopated to the movement rather than synchronized. Jacir's short was part of the 'Summer 2006, Palestine' project of the Palestinian Filmmakers' Collective; Shuruq Harb notes that the film 'criticize[s] the internal division in the Palestinian street… safely… mirror[ing] the sentiment of the Palestinian public [without] necessarily challeng[ing] it'.[15]

Jacir's film uses a tight close-up to consider the bigger picture, in which internal division is less significant than external divide and rule. Jacir's choice, as well as being witty and economical, reminds humans that we are similar to ants when seen from an extraterrestrial vantage – and that ants are, as Harb says 'a symbol of rigor and teamwork'. An insect lifeform, often seen as an irritant in the EuroWestern optic, has to be re-viewed as Self rather than Other, but without personification. Animal beings turn out to be a way to stand aslant, outside, and/or against, capitalism, colonialism and patriarchy. Taking animals seriously means a different way of watching and attending to film, what Anat Pick calls a 'creaturely poetics': having the uncanny sense of being watched by our cats, or rather, watching with them. Drawing on Simone Weil's idea of *attention*, Pick argues that animal beings denote intervulnerability: watching them watching us watching them, we are asked to look closely and carefully.[16]

Mating Dances

Animals are usually regarded as outside the sphere of human politics. It is truer to say – insofar as animal beings are forced to take part in military, agricultural, environmental, medicinal and entertainment exchanges with humans – that animals, like women, are cast as having no political agency, as Pick explores. The films discussed here invoke animals at once as animal beings in themselves, and as animal selves of human characters. Inverting the association, animals and women represent each other's potential for agency. Like Jacir's ants, the animal beings act as an analogy for an activist being while retaining their species-specificity, drawing humans into their category. The animals not only speak *with* their human companions, but *for* them; representing them so they can become political, and be out in the world.

Observational documentaries are a primary route into companionable representation, often offering effective advocacy for change. Gabriela Cowperthwaite's *Blackfish* (2013) has led Southwestern Airlines to end their partnership with SeaWorld, home of captive killer whale Tillikum, the film's central subject. It also led to calls for the cancellation of dolphin tours; an attempt by legislators to introduce new rules for aquaria; and – the most salient measure for media coverage – to SeaWorld's stock dropping 30 per cent in the second quarter of 2014.[17] Cowperthwaite's documentary focuses on a localized story in order to expose human structures perpetuating animal cruelty, in parallel with campaigning human rights documentaries. A distance remains, in which the animal beings are still passive subjects, victims of circumstance. *Blackfish* has something narratively in common with Patty Jenkins' *Monster* (2003), her biopic *apologia* for Aileen Wuornos.

Feminist filmmakers have attempted to subvert this traditional, hierarchical manner of speaking, in order to return human and animal beings to kinship. Isabella Rossellini's short video series for the Sundance Channel, *Green Porno* (2008), *Seduce Me* (2010) and *Mammas* (2013), offer a subversive feminist biology that puts the filmmaker's body on screen to proclaim solidarity with living beings while questioning the specularization inherent in zoological documentaries. Rossellini's shorts, in which the filmmaker dresses up in elaborate animal costumes with a handmade aesthetic, celebrate a queer, desiring world while challenging popular pseudo-Darwinian notions about gender and sexuality. Alice Rohrwacher's bee-laden *Le meraviglie* (*The Wonders*, 2014) likewise draws parallels between colony collapse disorder and capitalist collapse, but also between bee-world and adolescent sexuality.

Athina Rachel Tsangari's *Attenberg* (2010), hailed as part of the 'weird wave of Greek cinema', negotiates the rich and problematic terrain of nature documentaries by imagining a character who lives her (human) life according to them.[18] Marina (Ariane Labed), a 23 year old driver, communicates with her dying father Spyros (Vangelis Mourikis) through their shared love of David Attenborough documentaries, excerpted within the film. This father-daughter family considers itself in relation to the prides, packs, mating rituals and primarily maternal parenting described in Attenborough's voiceovers. Marina performs animalian (particularly birdlike) gestures with Spyros, and with her friend Bella (Evangelia Randou), kissing her 'like two birds trying to feed each other'.[19] She has a sexual encounter with an engineer played by Giorgos Lanthimos, director of the more brutal allegories *Dogtooth* (2009, which Tsangari produced) and *Alps* (2011). Tsangari subjects him to the camera's naked gaze and Marina's almost-zoological exploration.

It is through the animal selves she has observed onscreen that Marina is able to interact with others. Like Wendy, she is a loner, isolated by a melancholy that Spyros, through a peroration about the postwar architecture of modern Greece, suggests is expressive of a correct maladjustment to rapid industrialization, a refusal to be other than angular and concrete in an angular, concrete world. The film fractures the happy consensus whereby TV nature documentaries supposedly reflect us while providing the frisson of the Other, yet it retains respect for Attenborough's work. It has a larger critique in mind, aimed at all the (mis)uses of animal selves and evolutionary biology that condition us to patriarchy, white domination and capitalism as 'natural' (red in tooth and claw, and so on). The schoolgirls taking their goats for a walk in Tsangari's subsequent short film 'The Capsule' (2012), led by a teacher played by Labed, take up the conjunction of femininity, animality and monstrosity to their own odd and thrilling ends.

Where 'The Capsule' is surreal and – as befitting a film sponsored by a fashion house – lush, *Attenberg* is brutally realist. Its sparsely populated scenes, coolly lit, tend towards cool grey and blue tones and bare industrial spaces, in contrast with the lush greens and reds in clips of Attenborough's television programmes, and with the super-saturated colours of *Dogtooth*. Marina's and Spyros' existence is what philosopher Giorgio Agamben calls 'bare life', underlined by Spyros' cancer treatment and death.[20] Bare life is what's left of Marx's argument for the workers of the world to unite: it's the scars that remain even if the chains can be thrown off. It is the place where political thought starts in the body, rather than separate from it, and there are stark images of bare life throughout feminist cinema.

What's compelling to me is that those images are also images of the source of the spark that leads us to rise up and represent. In this bare life, and its return to another kind of relationship with the animal and our ecology, innovative documentaries such as Agnès Varda's much-lauded *The Gleaners and I* and Mercedes Alvarez' less well-known study of the collapsing Spanish economy in *Futures Market* (2012) make productive kinship with those living barely on the margins, in and with waste. While Slavoj Žižek claims, as a provocative thought experiment, that we should learn to love our rubbish dumps in Astra Taylor's *Examined Life* (2008), Varda and Alvarez, like Tsangari, undertake the painstaking, affective work of discovering what this love might mean, beginning by recognizing our own animal selves.

Of Girls and Horses

Bare life is not confined to documentary or to neo-realism. Andrea Arnold's *Wuthering Heights* (2011) may register on the surface as a heritage drama, the tenth big screen adaptation of Emily Brontë's 1847 novel, but it strips off the generic associations to relocate Brontë's own concern with bare life. Conceived as both a riposte to, and piggybacking on, Stephenie Meyer's attribution, in the *Twilight* series, of Brontë's novel as Bella Swan's favourite book, Arnold's adaptation de-romanticizes the adult relationship between Catherine Earnshaw and her adoptive brother Heathcliff by re-romanticizing their relationship as children, with each other, with – and through – the moors.

Catherine (Shannon Beer) and Heathcliff (Solomon Glave) are, differently, marginal as a girl under patriarchy and a black child under colonialism. On Heathcliff's arrival, there is a brief shot of his back that suggests he has been branded or whipped, and so may be an escaped slave. Brontë's novel is a cry for freedom, and it is on the moors that the children find this, running away from domestic labour and an increasingly grim family situation. In these early scenes, Catherine teaches Heathcliff to ride, and they share sensory experiences through the body and movement of the horse. Close-ups of the horse's muscles even convey a cinesthetic sense of *being* the horse, and of the horse's being as movement, energy, scent and place, the horse-being that Rebecca Solnit cites as the beginning of motion pictures in her study of Eadweard Muybridge.[21]

Through Robbie Ryan's tight framing and handheld camera, the horse subsumes Cathy and Heathcliff so that the three become one flesh, and moreover, one being with the moor, rather than human/animal/landscape. The tragedy in Arnold's reading is that the older Catherine (Kaya Scodelario) separates herself from Heathcliff (James Howson), the horse and the moor in the hope that pretending to marriage and social mobility will rescue her from violence and poverty. Heathcliff, maltreated far more extensively, internalizes and acts out his adoptive brother Hindley's (Lee Shaw) racist equation of animal life, the moor, and Heathcliff himself with nullity and waste.

Just after puberty, each of them, misunderstanding the other, takes what seems a necessary path to survival – Catherine towards marriage and middle-class comforts; Heathcliff towards wealth – whereby they change utterly, emphasized by the change in casting. They lose their confident and joyful merging with each other and the world, their need for nothing beyond bare life. This is underscored by Arnold's choice to depict a scene usually omitted from adaptations, in which Heathcliff hangs a puppy to taunt Isabella (Nichola Burley), Catherine's ladylike sister-in-law. Hanged by its leash, the whimpering, squirming animal is emblematic of the ways in which both Heathcliff and Catherine are being strangled by their oppressions. The scene enquires fiercely and carefully into the similitude and difference between being a wife, being a pet and being a slave. Arnold's confrontational, elemental vision offers us a chance to opt for bare life by staying true to our animal selves.

As in *Attenberg*, there is a great howl of mourning at such a painful necessity. As a twenty-first-century, educated middle-class European woman, however, Marina – even in economically straitened contemporary Greece – has options that

Not in Kansas: Animal Selves and Becoming-Girls

Catherine and, even more so, Heathcliff utterly lack. Clio Barnard suggests in *The Selfish Giant* (2013) that this remains a middle-class advantage in the EuroWestern world: her young protagonists Arbor (Conner Chapman) and Swifty (Shaun Thomas) inhabit a northern English landscape even more ravaged by industrial collapse than Marina's. They get involved in horse-cart racing and scrap metal collection, in an almost all-male working-poor world overseen by the Dickensian trader Kitten (Sean Gilder), whose horse offers the sole permissible form of affection. As for young Cathy and Heathcliff in *Wuthering Heights*, it is the horse who is Arbor and Swifty's companion species and spirit animal; a chained horse acts similarly for Mia (Katie Jarvis) in Arnold's *Fish Tank* (2009). In all three cases, there is a riposte to the middle-class English girl's pony romance, a genre that has been satirized and queered in lesbian romantic dramas *She Monkeys* (Lisa Aschan, 2011) and *Of Girls and Horses* (Monika Treut, 2014), in which the stables set the stage for transgressive psychosexual encounters.

All the horses in these films are working horses, and it is through identifying with the horse as labouring body, signalling embodied agency and simultaneously oppression, that the characters find an equine affinity that also gives them a sense of self-worth. As Barnard puts it, 'One of the things I came to understand in the process of making this film was that the kids who live in this area called Homewood, they're very skilled horse people, and it's part of their culture… Embrace these boys because they're brilliant, skilled!'.[22] By seeing the mute suffering of the horse *Fish Tank*'s Mia comes to an understanding of herself as oppressed, but also able to resist – for the animal, if not for herself. In *The Selfish Giant*, it's similar for Arbor. Barnard's film shares an allegorical narrative of class and boyhood with Samira Makhmalbaf's *Asbe du pa* (*Two Legged Horse*, 2008), in which a poor boy is forced to bear a richer boy around on his back. Barnard's film, in maintaining the sentimental and moralistic conclusion of the Oscar Wilde story it updates, loses an opportunity to extend the realization that another world *could have been* possible through a full depiction of the hinted-at same-sex love story between Arbor and Swifty.

There is glimpse of freedom, by contrast, for Nasrine (Micsha Sadeghi), the protagonist of Tina Gharavi's *I am Nasrine* (2012). Leaving behind a middle-class life in Tehran after she is sexually assaulted in prison, Nasrine fetches up in a working-class area of Newcastle. There, she befriends a Traveller girl, Nicole (Nicole Halls), and becomes attracted to her brother, spending time with the siblings and their community's horses. Horse-riding is the medium through which Nasrine rediscovers joy in her body, and a sense of being in the world. She moves into an imaginative world without borders, beyond the difficult cultural moment for Middle Eastern immigrants in Britain, and simultaneously redefines the boundaries of her own body.

Like *Attenberg*, neither *Fish Tank* nor *I am Nasrine* is a conventional romance that ends with the girl getting the guy: in *Wuthering Heights*, Arnold explores why, taking apart a myth of destructive power, in which nineteenth-century novels are still seen to form the basis of a feminine erotic and affective imaginary. As an onscreen presence, horses – palpable and almost pungent – bring together both the girls' desires *and* the potential of reciprocity outside the girl-meets-boy norm. As Haraway asserts, companion species narratives are romances that reflect on human-human relationships and are separate from them. 'Significantly other to each other, in specific difference, we signify in the flesh a nasty developmental infection called love. This love is an historical aberration and a naturalcultural legacy'.[23]

Good Red Herring

At the end of *Wendy and Lucy*, Wendy leaves love behind, hitching a ride on an open cattle-car. From Dorothy, she has turned into the Littlest Hobo. Letting go of her car and her ownership of Lucy, she embraces bare life and her animal self. She is also a literal marker of the feminization of the precariat. In his review, Michael Sicinski casts doubt on the existence of contemporary hoboes, but Alison Murray's *Train on the Brain* (2000) and Sarah George's *Catching Out: Trainhopping and Living Free* (2003) document contemporary female hoboes.[24] Murray 'ambitiously attempts to ride from Canada to Iowa in order to experience the National Hobo Convention held annually on the second weekend in August in the hamlet of Britt', meeing hoboes of all genders.[25] Yet there are few notable female hoboes in US cinema. Driving alone, Wendy maybe follows in the tiretracks of *Wanda* (Barbara Loden, 1970) but on the train, she joins a short but potent lineage that includes Bertha (Barbara Hershey) in *Boxcar Bertha* (Martin Scorsese, 1972), a free adaptation of *Sister of the Road*, the autobiography of Bertha Thompson, the partner of union organizer Bill Shelly (David Carradine) – but both films have almost disappeared from circulation.

Reichardt's evocation acts as a reminder of a feminist counter-canon of 1970s independent US cinema, often omitted from studies and retrospectives, even within feminist film studies. As Bérénice Reynaud notes, '*Wanda* has been ignored by every major text of feminist film theory published in English over the last 20 years', although Marguerite Duras was a passionate fan, and attempted to distribute it in France.[26] A restored 35mm print of *Wanda* circulated to film festivals in 2011 after

Ross Lipman rescued the original 16mm AB reels, earmarked for landfill.[27] Interest in the film could be attributed to the emergence of contemporary women of the road, from *Thelma and Louise* to Wendy.

Unlike companions Thelma (Geena Davis) and Louise (Susan Sarandon), Nadine (Karen Bach) and Manu (Raffaëla Anderson) in *Baise-Moi* (Virginie Despentes and Coralie Trinh Thi, 2000), or the lesbian lovers on the run in *Benzina* (Monica Stambrini, 2001), Wendy is going it alone. The teens of the twenty-first century have seen the emergence of a sub-genre of conventionally-mark(et)ed 'women's cinema' in which Strong Female Characters (SFC) make solo journeys, often adapted from successful works of creative non-fiction or memoir. They stand as a significant contrast to the companionate films I've been discussing, which use their central relationships to move the viewer to a slower, quieter, more thoughtful and less consumerist way of viewing.

Eat Pray Love (Ryan Murphy, 2010), based on Elizabeth Gilbert's bestselling memoir, made $80 million at the US box office, compared to *Wendy and Lucy*'s $850,000. Two further transnational prestige adaptations have followed: *Tracks* (John Curran, 2013), adapted from Robyn Davidson's memoir by Marion Nelson, and *Wild* (Jean-Marc Vallée, 2014), adapted from Cheryl Strayed's memoir. Werner Herzog's *Queen of the Desert* (2015) focuses on a key origin figure for the solo SFC traveller: Gertrude Bell (Nicole Kidman). Instrumental in the post-World War I division of the Ottoman Empire into the current countries of the Middle East, the brilliant Bell is (to say the least) a divisive figure for intersectional feminism.

Davidson (played by Mia Wasikowska) walked across the deserts of West Australia with a camel train, and Strayed (played by Reese Witherspoon) walked 1,000 miles of the Pacific Crest Trail. These epic journeys, undertaken as invented rituals by young white women entering into indigenous landscapes they didn't understand, mirror tales of male heroism, as Bell's mirrors T. E. Lawrence's. *Wendy and Lucy* could similarly be criticized for focusing on a white woman, where women of colour are far more subject to structural impoverishment, surveillance, and incarceration for minor crimes against property. The repeated visual trope of Wendy or Lucy seen through bars or mesh fencing acts as a reference to what Angela Y. Davis has termed 'the prison-industrial complex' in the USA, not least because of the parallel between Wendy's arrest and Lucy's impounding.

In fact, Reichardt's film points to the racial divisions in the USA, as well as drawing attention to the white precariat. All her films have been set in the contemporary Pacific Northwest where she lives, bar her first, *River of Grass* (1994), set in Florida (where she grew up), and historical drama *Meek's Cutoff* (2010), set en route to the region, on the Oregon Trail. Oregon was recorded as 88 per cent white in the 2013 US census, and Reichardt's films reflect this, particularly given her focus on rural areas. Matt Novak notes that this statistic 'is not some accident of history. It's a product of oppressive laws and everyday actions', as, at statehood in 1859, Oregon had a constitution forbidding African Americans from living in the state; moreover, it 'was illegal for black people even to move to the state until 1926'. As visionary writer and social justice educator Walidah Imarisha tells Novak, 'Oregon was bold enough to write it down… [b]ut the same ideology, policies, and practices that shaped Oregon shaped every state in the Union, as well as this nation as a whole'.[28] Wendy is not an Oregonian; her presence and mistreatment there serve, implicitly, to highlight the state's exclusionary and punitive history.

Her destination, however, suggests her movement (and perhaps her nation's necessary movement) towards a more diverse community with a complex relation to the ecosphere: Ketchikan is the sixth-largest city in Alaska and is only 60 per cent white. Native Americans make up the second largest demographic, predominantly from the Tlingit-Haida and Tsimshian nations. The city stands on Tlingit land and has a Tlingit name. The association of fish canneries with sustaining indigenous communities in the circumpolar Arctic appears in both John Sayles' drama *Limbo* (1999) and Sarah Gavron's documentary *Village at the End of the World* (2012), in which a Greenland Inuit community successfully takes collective ownership of an abandoned cannery and re-opens it.

The short film 'Tungijuq' ('What We Eat', Félix Lajeunesse and Paul Raphaël, 2009) makes the strongest statement about indigenous spiritual pragmatics in relation to the animal kingdom. Inuit throat singer Tanya Tagaq (as Tanya Tagaq Gillis), who originated the idea for the film, appears as Sedna, the Inuit goddess of sea creatures, wearing furs, her mouth smeared with blood. Her movement and vocalizations are powerful, uniting the animal, human and spirit world in a shamanistic performance of the hunt. The film was made in response to Hollywood celebrities calling for an end to the Inuit seal hunt, which provides food and warm clothing for communities rendered increasingly precarious by settler colonialism, neo-liberal economics, pollution and global warming. Rather than adopt EuroWestern verbal discourse or dispassionate documentary, Inuit production company Isuma embraces and celebrates cultural specificity, with Tagaq embodying rather than explaining its worldview. Sensuously conceived, this heightened realism is an invocation of the creaturely rather than an analysis of it.

Tagaq's imagined confrontation with white liberal environmentalism exploded into reality at the 2014 Polaris (Canadian Music) Awards, when she accepted the award for Best Album for *Animism* with an impassioned speech ending 'Fuck

Not in Kansas: Animal Selves and Becoming-Girls

Fig. 10: Tanya Tagaq as Sedna, 'Tunjgijuq'

PETA!'. Connecting all the threads of representational justice, Tagaq noted in an interview,

> When there's a name [sic] of 1,200 missing and murdered indigenous women scrolling behind you [on a screen] at a big show like Polaris and everyone's losing their minds over seals? It's a little terrifying. Like c'mon, let's get with it. They're connected, it's important. If people are going to be worried about the welfare of animals – if you have a pet, their pet food had animal byproduct. More animals died for your pet food than 10 times the population of Inuit killing seals could do.[29]

The deaths of women and the deaths of seals are 'connected, it's important', but – as Tagaq argues – they have to be recognized as elements in a complex political network. Thus in *Wendy and Lucy*, salmon fishing is signalled as a subsistence strategy for indigenous communities, one that is environmentally problematic, but still connected to seasonal cycles and the natural world. When Wendy hops the train, she leaves behind the idea of ownership, setting Lucy free, and travelling to learn a new set of relations to the world in Ketchikan. On first viewing, *Wendy and Lucy*'s raw and emotive ending seems like a betrayal of companionate feminism, contrasting both with the expected ending of the romance (girl finds dog again) and with the culturally valued image of Dorothy and Toto.

When Wendy leaves Lucy (behind), it seems like a claim to self-sufficiency, a refusal of their interdependence and enmeshed lives; yet it signals her thinking like and with Lucy. She sees that Lucy is safe with her new carer, and the film neither forecloses on the idea of their reunion, nor confuses ownership with love. In Wendy's return to a mode of transport deemed anachronistic, associated with the Depression, there is a clear and powerful critique of late capital as it drives a wedge between companions, pricing them out of symbiosis and mutual respect. It turns out that a woman needs a fish more than she needs a man or a bicycle, to paraphrase Gloria Steinem's famous statement – but all four elements are in closer contact and relation than readings of Steinem's witty opposition often suggest. Women, fish and bicycles have all been shaped by capitalist patriarchy – and can thus reshape each other in resistance to it.

That subversive relation, between onwards travel and the underwater world, is present in Lucrecia Martel's short film 'Pescados' ('Fish', 2010).[30] As oblique (and as watery) as her features, 'Pescados' uses the separation of the audio and image tracks to create a haunting narrative. Martel intercuts shots of a motorway through a rainy windscreen at night with shots of fish crowding up to the surface of a tank. Opening their mouths to snatch food flakes, the fish appear to be speaking the distorted words sung on the soundtrack by musician Juana Molina, which relay a strange, fragmented tale that suggests the victims of a car accident have been reincarnated as these fish.

What might seem like a devolution by EuroWestern standards may actually be an evolution, allowing humans to move away from their dependence on ecologically and physically violent automobiles – and towards a co-dependent intervulnerability with animal beings that allow us to express and explore our animal selves. When Martel's fish, Lucy, Kitch or Catherine's horse communicate non-verbally via the camera, there is a direct challenge both to conventional spectatorship and to ideas of subjectivity. A profound, feminist question is asked about who (and how) we are in the world. Rather than being pets or property, political animals are our leaders, as Taskafa leads the camera through Istanbul and into a larger world unconstrained by the severe limitations of capitalism. '*All* life is bare in the sense of being susceptible to the interventions of power', and in becoming political animals, we immerse ourselves in the shared vulnerability of the biotariat.[31]

3

Water Rites

Ecocinema's New Earth Mothers

Seeds of Hope

'You wake up and want a glass of water'. It's a creative writing exercise I frequently use in workshops, to underline how narrative and its ethical conflicts can emerge from the simplest scenario – if that scenario has elemental significance for the biotariat. Set in a world without water, Wanuri Kahiu's short 'Pumzi' (2009) shapes the first-ever Kenyan science fiction film from this premise. Part-funded and mentored by Focus Features' 'Africa First' short film programme, 'Pumzi' premiered at Sundance in 2010 and screened at festivals around the world. Like the best science fiction, Pumzi resonates with big issues in the present day. Vandana Shiva, who co-authored the definitive guide to eco-feminism in 1993, has argued for over a decade that the twenty-first century marks, to quote her book title, an era of *Water Wars: Privatization, Pollution, and Profit*.[1] The world that 'Pumzi' imagines is coming.

For many, in fact, it is already a reality. Although it was shot in South Africa, 'Pumzi' takes a Swahili word as a title and a Kikuyu word, Maitu, to name its central, symbolic object. This connects the film to East Africa, and specifically to Kenya, where, according to UNICEF's the Joint Monitoring Programme's (JMP) 2012 report:

> access to safe water supplies… is 59% and access to improved sanitation is 32%. There is still an unmet need in rural and urban areas for both water and sanitation. Kenya faces challenges in water provision with erratic weather patterns in the past few years causing droughts and water shortages. Kenya also has a limited renewable water supply and is classified as a water scarce country.[2]

Climate change (and its denial), neo-colonial resource exploitation and a lack of infrastructure are the lived experience behind Kahiu's imaginings.

'Pumzi' is both local and global in its conception of water scarcity, acknowledging that water systems and climate change do not recognize national borders. It responds to a specific regional context, in which East Africa faces particularly stark water provision conditions, but situates the region as both indicative of, and central to, a coming global conflict. Set in our (not-too-distant) waterless future, 'Pumzi' shows its protagonist literally reclaiming a girlhood lost to waterlessness. In 2010, the World Health Organization and JMP estimated that more than 152 million hours of women and girls' time is consumed annually collecting water for domestic use. Lack of access to water for cooking, cleaning and personal sanitary use affects women and girls disproportionately.

Across feminist cinema, water marks a call for representational justice. Through its connective power, the intimate shared being of girls and animals seen in the previous chapter is expanded to a global scale. Through films concerned with the 'bare life' of closeness to nature I discussed there, I formulate a new feminist aesthetics in which beauty is a politics. It's beauty, not duty, that motivates the activists I discuss here, through the beauties of water that fill the screen and replenish our imagination. Their feminist aesthetics of water is not one of spectacle or scale; it emerges from and represents crisis, and it is taut, complex and – literally – a sight for sore eyes.

'Pumzi' tells the story of Asha (Kudzani Moswela), curator of a small museum in a futuristic dome city. Newspapers preserved in the museum reveal that 35 years have passed since World War III, the Water War that marked the end of life on planet Earth's surface. Realizing the lyrics of Joni Mitchell's 'Big Yellow Taxi', the museum also includes branches and a seed from the final living tree. Asha lives and works in one of the surviving underground communities, where water is severely restricted. Dome-dwellers collect and purify their sweat and urine, living close to their animal bodies despite their hi-tech surroundings.

Even in such a futuristic setting, the emphasis on embodiment signals the film's ecological focus, (re)generating a striking form of science fiction matched by a production process that eschewed CGI in favour of traditional Hollywood studio techniques. The film's mise-en-scène was created through matte painting and back projection, in which locations are constructed through a combination of handcrafted artwork and in-camera effects. Kahiu comments that the return to craft techniques was influenced by indigenous African artwork: 'We already have a tradition of tapestries and functional art and things like that, that loan a backdrop for films'.[3]

Funded and exhibited transnationally, 'Pumzi' retains a strong local claim. Kahiu told CNN's Screening Room that 'for both "Pumzi" and *From a Whisper*

[(2009), her first feature] she had to barter services with other local filmmakers in order to get the films done as economically as possible'.[4] Having created her own production company, Dada Productions, to ensure that she retained her rights to *From a Whisper*, Kahiu's experience has led her to formulate a vision of collaborative and co-operative filmmaking. 'I would like to work and build an industry, so that everyone walks away well-paid, with great hours… Just a humane society, of sorts'.[5]

Asha's community does not foster this humane equality. As a white-collar worker, she has privileges: she gets a daily water ration, and is not forced to work out (in a bitterly ironic scenario) on landlocked rowing machines to generate electricity, nor to clean toilets to obtain her water. She is faced with a difficult choice when a package that appears to come from Earth's surface prompts a repeated dream of being underwater, not prevented by prescribed dream-suppressants. The package, marked with co-ordinates, contains a soil sample that tests as radiation-free and contains high levels of water. She mixes the soil with some of her precious water ration, and moves the last surviving Maitu (Mother) tree seed from a display case to the jar, also 'borrowing' an old-fashioned brass compass.

Asha's overseers forbid her experiments on the soil, and have her arrested and consigned to the rowing machines. But like Wendy in *Wendy and Lucy*, Asha chooses to step outside safety once she sees the oppressive nature of her society. With the aid of a cleaner, to whom she had earlier donated water, Asha escapes through the women's toilets out to the roof of the dome, and follows the compass towards the co-ordinates, the seed wrapped in cloth in her belt-pouch.

'Pumzi' is such a miracle of compressed and comprehensive storytelling that it's astonishing to note it contains almost no dialogue – and none spoken aloud by the performers. An impersonal recorded announcement opens the film, while Asha types her impassioned statements to her overseers, to be read by a computer-generated voice, and their voices are similarly heard without the movement of their lips. No-one can afford to parch their throat by speaking. The film's title means 'breath' in Swahili, and it is Asha's breath that soundtracks her journey through the sand dunes outside the dome, replacing the indoor ambient muzak and announcements. Dream and reality blur – or come together – as Asha sees a Maitu tree that may be a mirage, or a vision of the future, and she decides to plant the seed under its imagined canopy. She gives the seed the last of her water, and her sweat, shielding it with her wrap. As the camera pulls up to the sky, Asha's body collapses, a forest covers the desert, and clouds return with the sound of thunder.

In contrast to mainstream science fiction films, there are no over-familiar shots of the destruction of New York or London. The focus remains on a local

Fig. 11: Asha in the desert, 'Pumzi'

community and a regeneration plan that is, literally, planted in a specific piece of ground. The co-ordinates on Asha's package are close to the hot springs at Kapedo heated by Mount Silali, a volcano created by the East African Rift (Great Rift Valley), proven by mitochondrial DNA to be the origin point and migration route of anatomically modern humans.[6] Asha's future is our past, and her local is our global: in planting the Maitu seed in the rift, close to an ancient lake bed, Asha returns us to our source and creates the possibility of starting again.

Still Waters

As the word Maitu suggests, there is also a complex, transcultural association of women, water and fertility, and this inspires/is inspired by an eco-feminist acknowledgement that reinfusing the sacred and mythopoeic dimensions of water and other ecologies is essential to our survival. Diana James, having worked in with the Pitjantjatjara and Yankunytatjara people around Uluru in southwestern Australia, acknowledges their stories 'as being the source of my desire to re-sacralize our connections to land and water... Symbolic consciousness is as important for sustainable use of water as technological knowledge and regulations'.[7] Here I consider how films, diverse across origin, mode and genre, use the resonance between film and water to engage us, like Asha, in a search for renewed springs and seeds of hope, both symbolic and real.

This is more visible in films that critique the EuroWestern optic, in which water is goods rather than a good. As Sharon Lin Tay writes of Liz Miller's documentary, set in a predominantly African American neighbourhood of Detroit, '*The Water Front* (2007) is an interdependent film that expresses an explicit feminist politics in its acknowledgement that the right to potable water is a feminist issue as it also concerns the community, environment, justice, and corporate attempts to commercialize public goods'.[8] Cisfemale, trans* and intersex characters often undergo a transformative aqueous experience, one that connects their bodily fluids with water in the natural world, re-embedding them as humans in the water cycle. This fosters interdependence, as seen in Vivienne Dick's experimental short 'The Irreducible Difference of the Other' (2013), in which Olwen Fouéré embodies, simultaneously, Antonin Artaud and Anna Akhmatova. Taking us back to 'a', the origin point of language, and to bodies of water in which Fouéré immerses herself, Dick's film is a wholesale renewal of water rites.

In Jane Campion's delicately speculative short film 'Water Diary' (2006), a group of teenagers take refuge in the power of dreams and metaphors, as Asha does, in order to bring rain after the longest drought in Australian history. Ziggy (Alice Englert) becomes a believer in the dream that Felicity Miles' (Isidore Tiller) viola playing can bring clouds. She is only open to this magical solution once she starts to grieve her father's murder of the family's horses, bringing together companion species and ecology. Together with the town's other young people, she cries into a jar then drinks an admixture of everyone's tears. Made for *8* (2006), a UNDP/UNESCO/World Wildlife Fund portmanteau project on global human rights issues that screened at Cannes, 'Water Diary' exemplifies telling a global story through hyper-local hydration centred on feminine transformation.

The leap of faith in these films is often small: a tear, a drop of sweat, a sip of water. These are not aestheticized or iconic like Man Ray's famous photograph 'Larmes' ('Tears', 1930–1932), which reifies and glamorizes a woman's grief. Instead, they are mobile, messy and most importantly shared. They mark, and are marked by, the transition between elements; Ada's (Holly Hunter) leap into the sea anchored by her piano in Campion's earlier film is an influential example. Jessica Hausner's *Lourdes* (2009) tentatively embraces the healing power of the town's waters, while (and by) maintaining an ambiguity about whether Christine's (Sylvie Testud) recovery is caused by faith, self-belief, performance, or the power of interpersonal connection. The sea off the southern Japanese island of Amami in Naomi Kawase's *Futatsume no mado* (*Still the Water*, 2014) also becomes a zone of connection, despite – or because of – its dangers. Kyoko (Jun Yoshinaga) braves the waters to cope with her mother's illness and death, swimming out to sea in her school uniform, in contrast to her shy neighbour Kaito (Nijiro Murakami). Once the mystery of his paternity is resolved, Kaito joins Kyoko naked in the sea in an honest and beautiful depiction of a first sexual encounter.

Swimming is a particularly potent expression of feminine, queer and non-binary subjectivity and emergent desire, most notably in the work of Lucrecia Martel and Céline Sciamma, two representatives of what B. Ruby Rich has identified as a new transnational New Queer Cinema, in which specificities of gender and sexuality interconnect with local/national politics, culture and myth.[9] All three of Martel's features explore the dual seduction and disgust of swimming in artificial pools as a metaphor for middle-class willed ignorance in Argentina. For Sciamma's young queer and trans* working-class, suburban Parisian characters in *Naissance des pieuvres* (*Water Lilies*, 2007) and *Tomboy* (2011), swimming is an escape, an alternative to their concrete domestic landscapes and the fixed gender expectations therein. Emma Wilson argues that:

> attention to the inception of sexual feeling, and its heightening and disorganization of the senses, has political purpose in Sciamma's filmmaking and its treatment of girlhood… What is particularly striking, in *Water Lilies*, is the way the public leisure space of the swimming pool is adopted as the stage, the locale, for this burgeoning feeling and for our sensing of its political purpose.[10]

For Wilson, Sciamma transforms the 'sterile, showy, wet public arena' of a suburban public pool into something analogous to the jar where Asha grows the Maitu seed. It is an immersive environment for 'burgeoning,' the emergence of new and hopeful political formations.[11]

Filling the Tank

Asha isn't the first feminist heroine to strike out for water: Tank Girl (Lori Petty), the first female comicbook superhero to headline her own film (*Tank Girl*, Rachel Talalay 1995), fought Water & Power (W&P), a mega-corporation that has a monopoly on the world's scarce water supplies after an 11-year drought caused by a comet striking the planet. After several cartoonish battles, Tank Girl defeats – and dehydrates – W&P executive Kesslee (Malcolm McDowell), freeing W&P's hoarded water, on which she goes water-skiing. *Tank Girl* shares its post-apocalyptic vision of desertification with the Mad Max films, but resourcefully creates a happy ending in which plenitude and pleasure return. This is particularly important because the film draws parallels between water privatization and the sexualized violence against women and children assayed by Kesslee.

Petty also played surfer Tyler in Kathryn Bigelow's *Point Break*, the only member of the central group assembled around Bodhi (Patrick Swayze) to call out the excess of testosterone in their thrill-based culture. Bigelow is often described as an expert and incisive narrator of hyper-masculinities, but, rewatching *Point Break* in light of figures on representations of women workers onscreen released by the

Geena Davis Institute in 2013, it's interesting to note how many of the subsidiary speaking roles are female.[12] There are female FBI officers, female bank tellers and female members of a drug gang, one of whom knocks out Johnny (Keanu Reeves). Tyler survives to the end of the film, despite Bodhi using her as an 'insurance policy', thus proving that she called correctly the issues with the male surfers' 'kamikaze look'. Through Tyler, Bigelow can both show the attraction of the characters' high-octane lifestyle (and the thriller genre's similarly high-octane storytelling) and its cost.

The potential for spectacular cinematography, whether over the water or under it, continues to inform Hollywood cinema. Bigelow's ex-husband James Cameron offered to lease his private fleet of submarines, developed for underwater photography on his films, to BP after the Deepwater Horizon oil spill.[13] In his quest for jaw-dropping spectacle, Cameron has actually superseded US government investment in scientific exploration; his cinema is literally science *fiction*, its technological capacity aggressively outstripping that of state science – while certainly not critiquing its politics. Reputedly marking a new wave of mainstream Hollywood environmental films, *Avatar*'s 3D spectacle may have got in the way of its message.

Kelly Reichardt's *Night Moves* deconstructs the conventional narrative of the eco-thriller, including the heroic male and passive female, while deploying its tropes. Like *The East* (Zal Batmanglij, 2013, co-written with its star, Brit Marling), released the same year, Reichardt's thriller wears its *Chinatown*-era (Roman Polanski, 1974) influences cleverly, adding a layer of social media anxiety to its water resource-related paranoia. In both *Night Moves* and *The East*, heterosexual desire is a faultline in groups of white eco/ego-activists, and violence against women the climactic moment. Reichardt takes it further, critiquing violent protest as a form of thrill-seeking similar to Bodhi's in *Point Break*, aligned with, and practised through, violent misogyny. Josh's (Jesse Eisenberg) paranoid actions towards Dena (Dakota Fanning) tally with Courtney Desiree Morris' argument that:

> radical social movements and organizations in the United States have refused to seriously address gender violence as a threat to the survival of our struggles… There are serious consequences for choosing ignorance. Misogyny and homophobia are central to the reproduction of violence in radical activist communities.[14]

Reichardt is searching for film language with which to reveal, critique and deflect the punitive gaze that is applied to the ecosphere as it is to female bodies, even in films such as *Avatar* that pretend to environmentalism.

While the Center for Media and Social Impact at the American University has created a code of best practices for sustainable filmmaking, it has yet to be adopted as an industry standard.[15] Individual filmmakers have worked from first principles to create a filmmaking practice that dovetails with their ecological subject matter. Franny Armstrong's *Age of Stupid* (2009) had its 'green-carpet' premiere in a solar-powered cinema tent in Leicester Square, London, linked by satellite to 62 cinemas around the UK, generating 1 per cent of the emissions of a normal blockbuster premiere while officially being the biggest simultaneous film screening up to that point.[16] Then-president of the Maldives, Mohammed Nasheed (subject of the documentary *The Island President* [Jon Shenk, 2011]), sent a video message to the London premiere announcing that the country would go carbon-neutral within ten years, a world-first. Armstrong then co-founded the 10:10 carbon emissions reduction campaign, in a dynamic example of activist cinema's real-world impact.[17]

Crossing the Watershed

Through their engagement with the facts of climate change and the struggles of activists, there is an incredible urgency about many of the films I discuss here, determinedly represented through low-budget, low-impact solutions that include a refusal to engage in conflictual narratives and spectacular effects as a way to hook an audience. Julia Bacha's *Budrus* (2010), mentored and produced by Jehane Noujaim, tells the story of Palestinian non-violent resistance via the village of Budrus's guardianship of its olive trees. It is led by Iltezam, the teenage daughter of previously imprisoned activist Ayed Morrar, and takes flight when the female elders join the protest. Bacha's choice is subtle and powerful: the olive branch is a treasured symbol of the Zionist right to the land of Israel, based on God's promise at the end of the story of Noah in Genesis. At the same time, the ancient trees are an undeniable empirical demonstration of the rootedness of Palestinians in the land. Without making it overt, the film indicates the necessity of irrigation and what Mark Zeitoun has called 'the hidden politics of the Palestinian-Israeli water conflict'.[18] They act as a contradiction to the myth of 'the land without a people' and to Zionist propaganda about Palestine's swamps and barrens. For both communities, the olive branch is supposedly a sign of peace. We see the trees inspiring the people of Budrus to develop tactics of non-violent resistance, which inspires anti-Occupation Israeli activists to join them.

Judith Butler, an outspoken Jewish anti-Zionist, defines non-violence as an active, and difficult, choice in her 2010 book *Frames of War*. She presents the choice as a response to a series of questions:

> How do I live the violence of my formation? How does it live on in me? How does it carry me, in spite of me, even as I carry it? And in the name of what new value can I reverse and contest it? In what sense can violence be redirected, if it can?[19]

In *Budrus*, violence is redirected into an energy of life, an uprising of tree branches and fruit that thrusts against the sky in protest of the concrete wall. It is from the rooted stillness of the trees that the protestors learn non-violence as a refusal to be moved.

Beth Stephens' 'ecosexual' documentary *Goodbye Gauley Mountain* (2013) combines familiar non-violent tactics of fixity and attachment, such as locking oneself to vehicles, with an unfamiliar one: marriage. Stephens and her wife, sex educator and feminist pornographer Annie Sprinkle, marry threatened landscapes and landmarks in mass weddings that are performance art-ritual-protests, acts of magical thinking that engage communities in practical awareness of, and responsibility towards, ecological issues. Gauley Mountain, which is threatened with mountain-top removal (MTR), a devastating form of coal mining using high-powered explosives, is close to Stephens' heart, as she grew up in the West Virginia coal-mining community around the mountain.

Unlike many eco-documentaries, *Goodbye Gauley Mountain* doesn't attempt to bring coal to West Virginia. Stephens returns to discover rich seams of environmental activism and creative protests by local coal people who feel excluded from the middle-class, mainstream environmental movement. She also finds a PFLAG group (formerly known as Parents, Families and Friends of Lesbians and Gays) that has emerged since she left home, further evidence of the community's openness, and of the intersection of eco- and sexual diversity. From the opening credits, in which HD close-ups of flowers, insects, grasses and birds are brutally interrupted by inserts of grainy video footage of MTR with its attendant explosive sounds, Stephens seeks to engage you as an activist by summoning your sensory memories of being in the natural world. The film, paced to the rhythm of West Virginian conversation and song, challenges the norms of the campaigning eco-documentary genre as *Budrus* challenges the norms of war documentaries, something I discuss further in the next chapter.

As Butler argues in *Frames of War*, that challenge has to start with the frame. Reichardt's *Meek's Cutoff* and Arnold's *Wuthering Heights* were, unusually for 2010, both shot in the squarer Academy ratio, 4:3; parts of Agnès Varda's autobiographical essay film *Les plages d'Agnès* (*The Beaches of Agnès*, 2008) which begins on an Atlantic beach, are also in squarer ratios. It's not too big a stretch to see the Hollywood classic widescreen establishing shot as, by analogy, the 'money' shot that displays mastery of the land, and these more contained frames as both a rejection of the insistence on spectacle and technological progress (contra filmmakers such as Cameron), and an inventive attempt to create what we could call a landscape-portrait. Rather than the clichéd sublime of the tiny figure dwarfed by nature (that he will come to command), the squarer ratio favours closer shots in which the human, animal and environment are enmeshed.

Experimental filmmakers Sharon Lockhart and Jennifer Reeves have taken this the furthest, both using the materiality of 16mm to formulate cinematic idiolects of twenty-first century eco-feminism. Reeves' *When it Was Blue* (2008) is a double 16mm projection with a live score by Skuli Sverisson that brings together diary film collected by Reeves as she lived and travelled, much of it hand-painted and edited back-and-forth in response to Sverisson's compositional process. Water predominates, as the title suggests; it is the connective tissue of a 'blue planet' that brings together disparate flora, fauna, textures and temperatures. For Reeves, who kept a blog called Not Dead Yet about her love of 16mm, the medium and the message are both engaged with the 'blues' of loss. Reeves told me: 'There are things in the film that don't exist anymore… I just wanted to bring the nature back. So the film goes backwards, away from civilization, towards a garden'.[20]

If *When It Was Blue* is made as if by an astronaut with a macro lens, Lockhart's *Double Tide* (2010) is a close-up at a distance. Composed of two 45-minute long shots of the same location, Seal Cove, Maine, on the same summer day, it plays on the Romantic sublime's *Rückenfigur*: instead of catching a gentleman of leisure admiring the (often lofty) view, Lockhart's camera focuses on the head-down, labouring figure of Jen Casad, a clam digger, as she follows the rare double low tides at dawn and dusk. In contrast to the constant, rhythmic movement of the tide, the earth and Casad, the frame remains fixed for each of the two 45-minute shots, but subject to tiny, irregular living movements of wind and weather. Lockhart's almost-breathing camera links the viewer to an ecology that is never allowed to be objectified as a 'landscape' or a 'view'. We work alongside Casad, feeling the pull of her muscles in ours, although the film cannot avoid the irony that we have the luxury of experiencing this from our cinema seats. The simplicity of Lockhart's concept – two fixed-frame shots of equal length – belies the time spent getting to know the wetland ecology in order to breathe with it. These films are contemplative, fragmented, quiet and 'haptic', in Laura U. Marks' term.[21] Rather than trying to tug your heartstrings or set your pulse racing with drama, they are exploring ways to give you the touch of the world, whether its beauties or – as with gas fires burning on a frozen lake in Siberia in *Perestroika* (Sarah Turner, 2011) – its manmade terrors.

Water Has a Memory

Turner's fiction-documentary hybrid *Perestroika* features multiple fixed shots looking out of (and with the camera just reflected in) the window of the Trans-Siberian Express, as the voiceover recalls the speaker's previous trip on the train. As well as stitching the landscape together with a rigorous continuity that contrasts with the fragmentation of the speaker's memories, it creates a pointed contrast with the canted angle shot of an anyplace of trees and sky from a car window that stands in for adolescent femininity, or the memory thereof, in too many indie dramas. It also recalls and dismantles the classic documentary establishing shot out of a car window, which situates the filmmaker as a technologically advanced tourist, capturing the location from their vantage point but separate from it. The difference, in *Perestroika*, is that the reflection, and the use of public transport, implicates the filmmaker/point of view character in a landscape, and a specific one at that.

Perestroika has significant reasons for trying to dislocate – and relocate – our relation to the world around us. The train is heading towards Lake Baikal, one of the most polluted bodies of water on earth, which functions as an analogy for memory because, as a totally enclosed freshwater lake, it retains pollution over aeons. Water flows through all these films for similar reasons: it is a metaphorical conduit for both trauma and healing, remembering and forgetting, purity and hybridity.

As for Turner, so for Natalia Almada: 'Water Has a Perfect Memory' (2001) is a short lyric documentary about grief and migration, drawing on Toni Morrison's essay 'The Site of Memory'.[22] While there are many campaigning documentaries about water rights, including Irena Salina's *Flow: For the Love of Water* (2008) and Jennifer Baichwal's *Watermarks* (2013), few of them capture the intimate and communal significance of water, its ability to define both individuals and larger groups such as nation-states, as Almada and Turner do. In the experimental films, water breaks the frame with its irregular movement, fracturing light, refusing to be contained; it washes up against the idea of 'landscape', a haptic reminder that our ecosphere is not only solid, stable dry land.

Penny Woolcock's *From the Sea to the Land Beyond* (2012) turns to a combination of archival footage and acoustic music to achieve both its mnemonic effects and its disruption of national boundaries. Here the sea, not the land, is what defines Britishness. With the run of the British Film Institute's archives, Woolcock produced a joyful, anarchic portrait of a nation at work and play, with a particularly sympathetic eye for working-class shoreline cultures and the appearance of women throughout the twentieth century, as cliff-climbers, fishwives, bathing beauties and blues singers. As crisply-preserved film gives way to degraded, lurid video, and communitarian uses of the littoral to capitalist ones, Woolcock's film balances aesthetic pleasures with sharp critique.

There is beauty even in a documentary that tackles a natural disaster and its devastating human cost: *Trouble the Water* (Tia Lessin and Carl Deal, 2009) sees the effects of Hurricane Katrina as exemplifying the intersections of systemic racism, rapacious environmental abuse and crony capitalism in the USA as a whole. Even beyond Spike Lee's testimonial in *When the Levees Broke: A Requiem in Four Acts* (Spike Lee, HBO, 2006), it is a work of representational justice. Its beauty derives from the filmmakers' use of citizen journalism: Lessin and Deal, who worked on anti-Bush documentary *Fahrenheit 9/11* (Michael Moore, 2004), travelled to New Orleans embedded with the National Guard returning from Iraq, but were refused access to the city centre. In a Red Cross shelter, they encountered Lower Ninth Ward residents Kimberly Rivers Roberts, an amateur hip-hop performer, and her husband Scott. Roberts told Lessin and Deal that she had home video of the hurricane's arrival and its effect on her home and beloved neighbourhood.

The beauty that emerges from Roberts' inclusion as a co-filmmaker is two-fold: her performance of her song 'Amazing', after she finds recordings of her performances as Black Kold Madina, which she had thought were lost in the storm; and her intimate knowledge of the Lower Ninth, a predominantly African American, working-poor area demonized in national news coverage of the hurricane as the scene of looting. Roberts' footage acts as a crucial corrective to the dominant media. She describes herself as, in essence, replacing them for her community, a form of filmmaking parallel to Chuck D's famous assertion that hip-hop is 'the CNN of the ghetto'. She told Lolis Eric Elie:

> The day before I shot the hurricane footage, I was going around talking to my neighbors and interviewing them, asking them what they were going to do for the storm, like I was a newscaster or something. People were really serious about not being able to leave and what they were doing. I was inspired to tell the story as people started opening up to me. I started feeling New Orleans was going to change somehow and I wanted to tell the whole story of before, during and afterward. It was as if I was on a mission. That's what inspired me to keep shooting.[23]

Rebecca Solnit, who also travelled to New Orleans as a volunteer after Katrina and stayed for a year, describes those who stayed, like Roberts, as forming 'disaster communities', in which 'ties… along with purposefulness, immediacy, and agency, also give us joy – the startling, sharp joy found in the accounts of disaster survivors'.[24] Roberts made a choice to document Katrina for the disaster community of which she was an elective and determined part. Even when stuck in her attic, with camera batteries failing, she kept recording. Unlike Turner, Almada and Woolcock, she was not reflecting on memories of water, but capturing them at source. And unlike the often-anonymous filmmakers whose work Woolcock uses, Roberts is an assertive presence on-camera as well as in control of it, a one-woman mission against water's tendency to erasure and forgetting.

Ama

As *Trouble the Water* shows, water rights are already a locus for political violence against the dispossessed. Martel's films, with their ambivalent swimming pools, offer oblique memorials both to those murdered by the *junta* and to those dispossessed by IMF-enforced water privatization in her home state of Salta after the economic collapse of 2001.[25] Spanish filmmaker Iciar Bollaín uses the Cochabamba Water Wars, sustained protests by indigenous communities against water privatization in Bolivia, as the backdrop to her meta-drama *También la lluvia* (*Even the Rain*, 2010). Costa (Luis Tosar), an autocratic European filmmaker, finds the Bolivian shoot for his biopic of Cristobal Colón drawn into close parallels with the continuing legacy of colonialism as the protests kick off. Bollaín settles, however, for a sentimental ending in which Costa realizes the error of his ways through a magical encounter with an indigenous family, while remaining at the centre of the story.

Bollaín's drama, from Paul Laverty's screenplay, does convey a number of stinging observations through its paralleling; particularly through Daniel (indigenous actor and filmmaker Juan Carlos Aduviri), an Aymara water rights activist who gets cast as Atuey, leader of the Taíno Cacique resistance to Colón. There is a similar charge in the casting of Blackfoot actor Misty Upham as Lila Littlewolf in *Frozen River* (Courtney Hunt, 2008). Lila drives migrants through the Mohawk Nation at Akwesasne to cross the Canada/US border of the St. Lawrence, the eponymous frozen river. For the Mohawk, the border is an imposition, evidence of lasting colonial power, and its policing erodes community. Through her actions Lila actively denies the force of the border, yet is ostracized from her community.

They believe that her smuggling operation led to her husband's death, so her mother-in-law has taken their son.

Ray Eddy (Melissa Leo) is the film's protagonist and point-of-view character. Like Wendy and Asha, she steps out onto risk. Through her association with Lila, she recognizes her white privilege, eventually taking the rap, in the knowledge she would get a shorter sentence, after the police stop her and Lila with two migrant sex workers in the car. Even in extremity – she is a working-poor single mother whose husband has abandoned her and gambled away their savings – Ray aligns herself with Lila. The viewer is also aligned, cheering as the film's point of view passes from Ray to Lila, who, living in Ray's double-wide, is able to reclaim her son. Tragically, Upham lost her life in October 2014 in what appear to be violent circumstances that resonate with the precarity of Lila's experience.[26]

Water on film often holds a mirror up to life. *The Cherokee Word for Water* (Tim Kelly and Charlie Soap, 2013) is a biopic of Wilma Mankiller (Kimberley Guerrero), and gains its authenticity and conviction from co-direction by its co-protagonist Charlie Soap (played in the film by Moses Brings Plenty). The film charts Mankiller's emergence as a political leader; she went on to become the first female chief of the modern Cherokee Nation. In tandem with Soap, she motivated her community to build a 16-mile pipeline to provide access to water, *ama* in Cherokee. While Mankiller's practical struggles to bring the community together in order to build the pipe provide the narrative structure of the film, its focus is on *gadugi*, a traditional Cherokee concept that translates as 'working together to solve a problem'. The pipeline is not the goal but the means towards a revival of gadugi as a small-p political strategy that combines self-help with a sense of reciprocity and interconnectedness.

Mankiller's struggle continues on a continental scale: Jeff Bear's *Samaqan: Water Stories* (APTN, 2012–), co-directed with Marianne Jones, has produced 39 episodes over three series considering indigenous water politics. Several focus on the Water Walks protests undertaken over the last decade by indigenous women in Canada and the US, due to the continuing prevalence of industrial pollution and resource abuse facing their communities across the Americas.[27]

Salt of Whose Sea

For Bollaín's countrywoman Chus Gutiérrez, there is a body of water closer to home than Spain's former colonies in the Americas with which to reflect on the legacy of colonialism. *Retorno a Hansala* (*Return to Hansala*, 2008) is the filmmaker's response to a newspaper article about Moroccan immigrants to Spain who drowned in the Mediterranean, and whose bodies washed up on a beach in Algeciras. Gutiérrez's protagonist Leila (Farah Hamed) is the sister of one of the dead men, and she persuades funeral director Martin (José Luis García-Pérez) to return to their village with his body.

Gutiérrez comments that Hansala is:

> inland, quite far from the sea. Most of the guys don't know how to swim, that's why they drown so easily… In one boat, there were 13 men from that village. So people in Spain living close to the tragedy were very touched by the event and they traveled to Morocco to offer their condolences.[28]

As for Lessin and Deal with *Trouble the Water*, a profound local connection was necessary for Gutiérrez in making *Return to Hansala*; in her case, on either side of the Mediterranean. The filmmaking galvanized the village women in Hansala, who were paid as extras and caterers on the film, and were inspired by the 50 per cent female crew. According to Gutiérrez, 'they do a lot of work, but they don't get paid normally. There was a women's revolution after we left. They told the men that they wanted to participate in the society. They created their own association'.[29]

The Mediterranean offers a measure of reciprocity and reflection for Gutiérrez, as a body of water conjoining southern Europe and North Africa, despite the former's desire for autonomy. The sea's Latin name means 'between the lands,' but it is often used only to refer to the southern European nations that border it. *Return to Hansala* challenges that claim on the model of Paul Gilroy's book *The Black Atlantic*, which rewrote the history of the African slave trade away from a focus on white imperialists to consider diasporic African histories.[30]

The poignant title of Annemarie Jacir's first feature (and the first full-length feature by a Palestinian woman) *Milh Hadha al-Bahr* (*Salt of This Sea*, 2008) refers to the Mediterranean at Jaffa, where Brooklyn-born Soraya (Suheir Hammad) arrives to retrieve her grandfather's pre-1948 savings. As Maymanah Farhat observes, the Jaffa littoral holds Soraya's family's memories:

> Her understanding of Palestine is based on notions of memory, heritage and community and she recounts the lives of her grandparents in Jaffa, giving the minutest details of their everyday being and environment. Emad [Saleh Bakri] remarks that it is as if she has already been to the seaside town she one day hopes to visit.[31]

The film stakes a claim, not least via the salt tears of the Nakba and exile, to the Mediterranean as a Palestinian sea.

Reclaiming the Mediterranean is an implicit feature of two first films from Algeria that, in addressing European colonial conflicts, start and end on the Mediterranean shore. At the end of Djamila Sahraoui's 1990s-set *Barakat! (Enough!*, 2006), Khadidja (Fettouma Bouamari) throws a gun into the sea, shouting 'Barakat!' She and Emel (Rachida Brakni) have failed to find Emel's missing journalist husband, but through their avoidance of conflict with male soldiers and militia on either side of the civil war, they reach the claim to non-violence that Butler identifies. Sahraoui's film is an inverse *Thelma and Louise*, a female-friendship road movie in which the women not only survive the threat of gendered violence, but reject, rather than wielding, the gun. Khadidja, the older, working-class woman, takes charge of Emel's search, and through her, Emel learns about the war of independence (1954–1962) and its implications for the political divisions of the civil war (1991–2002).[32] It is Khadidja, having lived through two wars, who takes to the sea to make her protest of 'Enough!'

The beach is the site of conflict, conversely, in Narimane Mari's *Loubia hamra* (*Bloody Beans*, 2013), but an unconventional one. Mari's hallucinatory feature, inspired by the rebellious students in *Zero de conduite* (*Zero for Conduct*, Jean Vigo, 1933), enacts the Algerian war of independence allegorically through an amorphous gang of children. For them, the beach is a space of pleasurable play that also represents resistance to both adult and French oppression. European dominance is envisioned as and through male violence against women, when the children chase off a pig-masked European man who has beaten his wife, Marcienne (played by Mari), whom the children comfort by singing Egyptian love songs. Later, Laila (Ghania Aïssani), a prominent member of the gang, reminds the boys when they try to perform a night raid without her, 'We aren't made for dishwashing… You don't own this war'.

After the raid, where violence is vividly analogized through a combination of coloured lighting, dance and puppeted silhouettes, the children kidnap a French (adult) soldier and bring him to the beach, where they debate how to punish him. The winning solution is to feed him the fart-inducing *loubia hamra*, red beans, a traditional dish that is all their families can afford while the French stockpile luxuries in their base. Bernard (Samy Bouhouche), a young conscript – the actor's name suggests he's of North African origin – seems happy to spend the night playing on the beach with the children, released from his duties.

Bernard is physically reminiscent of Gilles Sentain (Gregoire Colin), the young soldier in *Beau Travail*, Claire Denis' French Foreign Legion-set adaptation of Herman Melville's *Billy Budd*. Denis relocates the story to Djibouti, a French colony until 1977; in the saturated cinematography by Agnès Godard there is a

Water Rites: Ecocinema's New Earth Mothers

Fig. 12: Girl floating in the sea, *Bloody Beans*

productive tension between the blue Gulf of Aden, where the soldiers skin-dive, and the white salt flats where Sentain is abandoned by Galoup (Denis Lavant), his superior officer. Water, water everywhere, but – for the obsessed Galoup – not a drop to drink.

Similarly, in *Bloody Beans*, the liminal ecology evokes colonialism and resistance as the European tide goes out. After Bernard's night on the beach, dawn brings the roaring noise of jets and bombs, signalled by a white-out. The film, like the children's inventive, non-violent play by the sea, seems unable to withstand the reality of colonial power and military might. Yet Mari offers a coda that returns to her opening images of the children floating in the sea. As they float, the children now recite lines from 'Petit poème des poissons de la mer' (1927) by Antonin Artaud, in which a silver fish asks, 'Vaut-il mieux être que d'obéir?' – 'Is it better to be than to obey?' For Mari, the 'children never obey the reality of the war', and the ending may – like the end of 'Pumzi' – indicate the possibility of a new beginning rooted in the watery imagination.[33]

According to feminist water scholar Kuntala Lahiri-Dutt, the 'purificatory power of water, to wash away all pollution, all sin, all physical filth, is an essential feature in the religious symbolism in societies. This quality does not arise because of its intrinsic purity but because it absorbs pollution and carries it away'.[34] The Artaud poem speaks of 'the body of the sea', of which – the film implies – the children have become a part. Water is a site of life and death, pollution and purity, future and past, war and peace; its ambiguity is part of its potential for shaping representational justice. For feminist filmmakers, it is its necessity that makes it a place of politics; all of these films connect necessity to beauty, creating a politicized aesthetic that can be felt in the viewer's (thirsty) body. These films remind us how much we need the refreshment and reflection that they offer, and of the labour necessary to get it. Plunging into water politics, they destabilize hierarchies, refuse the thrall of solid ground, and ask us to draw a line, saying 'Enough!' Leaving the sterile scientific environment of Asha's museum for the salty tears of the Mediterranean, water films open up their protagonists and audiences to depths of emotion and a breadth of politics. Like the children in *Bloody Beans*, these films belong to the unstable, ever-changing, 'in-between' sea that connects many lands and communities, and holds our memories in a tentative vision of peace.

4

Home Front
Women at War, Women against War

Over There

Hana Makhmalbaf's third film *Buddha Collapsed Out of Shame* won the Crystal Bear at Berlin in 2008, voted for by the festival's young viewers. Set in Afghanistan, *Buddha* is the precise and perfect example of global feminist cinema's riposte to US international politics under George W. Bush, including his appropriation of white liberal feminism. Like *Bloody Beans*, it's seen from a child's eye view, and shows children enacting the war they have learned from their elders. This imitative play is a cautionary tale about the effect of a media dominated by narratives of spectacular violence.

Makhmalbaf places all of our girlhoods in a 'frame of war' through the Afghan girlhood she creates and depicts, contextualizing the familiar fears of rape culture as part of a continuum with the gendered violence of the war zone. Girls, she suggests, live war in our bodies; we are inherently political animals because of this. War films as a genre are used, appropriated and deconstructed by feminist filmmakers to make exactly this point: that war is not an exception (as it's staged in mainstream war porn), but the rule for the 99 per cent. Rather than celebrating an orgy of violence, these filmmakers use the political immediacy of the war zone to raise questions about, in Judith Butler's word, 'grievability', or whose lives and bodies count.[1]

Makhmalbaf was 18 when she made her first feature. She been banned from attending the premiere of her first release at the Venice Film Festival four years earlier, because minors are not admitted to unrated films, although she had made her first short film aged eight. Her focal character in *Buddha Collapsed*, Baktay (Nikbakht Noruz), is younger still: six years old, she wants to attend school and read funny books like her male next-door neighbour. She is shooed from his madrasa, kidnapped by boys playing at being the Taliban, and laughed out of the

Fig. 13: Baktay being kidnapped, *Buddha Collapsed out of Shame*

classroom at a UN girls' school that she eventually reaches, where the girls are more interested in lipstick than learning.

Makhmalbaf wrote the screenplay with her mother, Marzieh Meshkini, director of *Roozi ke zan shodam* (*The Day I Became a Woman*, 2000), the original girl-on-a-bike film echoed by Haifaa al-Mansour's global hit *Wadjda* (2012). Mother and daughter redeveloped the script based on a casting recce in Afghanistan, where Makhmalbaf found that: 'Unlike their counterparts in America who learn violence through Hollywood action films, the children of Afghanistan have learnt it by witnessing the atrocities suffered by their relatives. They have witnessed their fathers being beheaded in their own gardens'.[2] *Buddha Collapsed* aims its documentation and intervention both at those living through the war, and at those who wage it.

Butler notes, as Makhmalbaf does, that war is primarily an audio-visual experience for most of us, so 'if war is to be opposed, we have to understand how the popular assent to war is cultivated and maintained, in other words, how waging war acts upon the senses'.[3] In this chapter, I pay attention particularly to films that attempt to undo the war waged upon our senses, films that reframe war by querying stereotypes of heroism and victimhood, and challenging the viewer's expectations of a catharsis delivered via spectacular violence and embedded authenticity.

Buddha Collapsed starts with a brief excerpt of news footage of the event the sixth century CE sandstone Gandhara-style Buddhas being dynamited by the

Taliban in March 2001. The rest of the film takes place in their physical and symbolic absence, a powerful evocation of the geopolitical situation in Afghanistan, and a refusal to replicate the frame of war imposed by both the Taliban and the US. The film shares its use of allegory with other films of the Iranian New Wave, specifically those of Makhmalbaf's father Mohsen and her sister Samira. It also resonates with Fante Régina Nacro's singular *La nuit de la vérité* (*The Night of Truth*, 2004), a rare example of a feature by an African female filmmaker to receive international distribution.

Nacro's film is carefully set in an unnamed West African country; although it uses Dioula and Mooré, languages from Nacro's home country, Burkina Faso, its two nations are the (fictional) Bonandé and Nayak, torn apart by a decade of civil war. A reconciliation dinner between the nation's leaders becomes an inadvertent truth commission when Tomoto (Rasmane Ouedraogo) beats the Bonandé war drums. Tomoto is the village jester, a storyteller and inveterate stirrer. The film asks whether the truth Tomoto's actions indirectly uncovers is worth the violent consequences, as the families of the leaders are drawn into conflict. Nacro's film critiques both the neutrality of truth and reconciliation commissions and the over-used trope of the (almost always male) Fool whose actions appear carnivalesque. Tomoto certainly lends himself to cinematic spectacle, whether vividly narrating myths or drumming in the dark, but he risks social dissolution. His actions share a dangerous deniability – 'it's just a game' – with those of the leader (Abdolali Hoseinali) of the boys' gang in Makhmalbaf's film.

Buddha Collapsed played at many major international festivals, but I saw it via a slightly different venture: the 2008 Human Rights Watch (HRW) film festival in London. The London and New York HRW film festival began in 1997; from 2009, it became an international touring programme, predominantly screening documentaries, with a focus on international current events from a liberal perspective. The 2008 London programme featured several films that offer a rich context for *Buddha Collapsed*, particularly the opening night film, which was written and co-directed by an Iranian woman living in France, *Persepolis* (Marjane Satrapi and Vincent Paronnaud, 2007). Satrapi adapted her own autobiographical comics, telling the story of the post-revolutionary Iran into which Hana Makhmalbaf was born. While Satrapi's dark comedy did receive popular distribution in the West, it had a dual place at HRW, as a film concerned with human rights and as a film faced with censorship. As Patricia White reports, the Iranian Farabi Cinema Foundation objected to *Persepolis*' screening at Cannes. 'For Iranian officials, this exilic woman filmmaker is not a proper representative of the nation – though of course condemning her film made her just that'.[4] In a particular and painful sense, it was censorship that renewed the Iranian identity of both the film and the exiled Satrapi.

There were also two documentaries at HRW that related to *Buddha Collapsed*. Meg McLagan and Daria Sommers' *Lioness* (2008) focuses on the traumatic experiences of the first US women soldiers sent into direct ground combat, in contravention of official policy, due to a shortage of active combat troops caused by the US' dual illegal invasions of Iraq and Afghanistan. Lynn Hershman Leeson's *Strange Culture* (2007), meanwhile, offers a startling insight into the effects of US foreign policy on domestic human rights. It looks at the case of artist Steve Kurtz, who was arrested as a bio-terrorist in 2004, after his wife Hope's death from sudden heart failure while Kurtz was working on a project about food bio-engineering. Leeson had to employ dramatizations, featuring Thomas Jay Ryan (Steve) and Tilda Swinton (Hope), to subvert legal restrictions on representing aspects of the ongoing case. The scenes in which Swinton and Ryan discuss the project have an air of heightened reality, connecting play and profundity, reminiscent of Makhmalbaf's allegorical war games.

Chandra Talpade Mohanty, Minnie Bruce Pratt and Robin L. Riley note that: 'Feminists critiquing and organizing against war in most places in the world will thus need to contend with the effects of US imperial wars in their own backyards, whatever part of the globe they happen to be living in'.[5] By co-programming these documentaries, HRW does not prioritize the North American point of view and experience. Rather, it queries it by including critical voices from within alongside a range of global voices.

The HRW films' complex range of approach to representation challenges the viewer's expectations of what exactly we hope to gain from watching human rights films. They offer more than a sense of satisfaction in the rightness of our own politics or the mastery of issues occurring 'over there'. An animation, a fiction feature and two documentaries: the mix of modes also queries the idea of war film as a genre and war's relation to aesthetics. All three films press on the metaphor of the 'theatre of war', the risk and rewards of performance with reference to war as 'the real', and the ways in which mediatized representations of war inform lived experience – for people of all genders.

Armories

In 'We Have Always Fought', her Hugo Award-winning essay 'challenging the "women, cattle and slaves" narrative', Kameron Hurley is concerned with the erasure of women fighters from the historical record, citing in particular Shaka Zulu's female troops as well as pirates, sailors and soldiers who might be read as transvestite or transgender.[6] Comments on her article also call attention to the Soviet women soldiers and pilots, whose struggles for full equality after the World War II can be seen in Larisa Shepitko's film *Krylya* (*Wings*, 1966). Few other feminist filmmakers have explored these aspects of the historical record, either within the war genre or outside it. Participation in military and paramilitary fields is a part of women's history, but feminist cinema, at least in the West, tends to focus on women as the victims of war and violence; fighting, at best, on the home front.

Cate Shortland's *Lore* (2012) and Lucia Puenzo's *Wakolda* (2013) both, differently, exemplify the feminist potential of the grey area between warrior and victim, soldier and civilian, through their use of adolescent girls as figures of complicity and resilience. Lore (Saskia Rosendahl) and Puenzo's Lilith (Florencia Bado) are both daughters of Nazi-supporting families; after the war ends, they are shown continuing the Resistance fight within their own subjectivities, seeking to define themselves against their families' politics. Dragging her siblings across Germany in 1945, Lore makes a literal and psychological journey from faithful believer, through disbelief about her parents' complicity in the Final Solution, to a final act of sharp rebellion against both the regime and postwar forgetting.

Puenzo's Lilith has to extricate herself, her family and their German-Argentinean community from their thrall to a German doctor (Àlex Brendemühl) living in Patagonia, who offers to draw on his gruesome medical experimentation to normativize her embodiment. Lilith, small and underdeveloped compared to her classmates, contrasts with Puenzo's more typical female warrior, the Israeli spy Nora (Elena Roger), who has identified the doctor as Josef Mengele. Yet the film suggests that Lilith's resistance is more successful than Nora's, a challenge to both the typical war film and the current investment in female action heroism.

Kathryn Bigelow and Susanne Bier, the only two women to win recent Academy Awards as feature filmmakers, have both directed war films. As White puts it, 'Given the content of Bigelow's combat film, the moment seemed to represent the convergence of American exceptionalism with the director's own'.[7] Angelina Jolie likewise followed her Balkan war drama *In the Land of Blood and Honey* (2011) with *Unbroken* (2014), a biopic of athlete and prisoner-of-war Louis Zamperini (Jack O'Connell), which adheres to the Greatest Generation trope of World War II films. Hence the importance of *Lioness* and Beth Freeman's Canadian equivalent *Sisters in Arms* (2011), which interrogate the complex and often contradictory experiences of women in active combat. Freeman's film received international attention the year after its release when the USA lifted its combat role ban.[8]

While underlining Hurley's argument that women have always fought, Freeman's is an intimate documentary that includes her sister Tamar, an army medic, among its central subjects. Freeman has said that while her sister's move from reserves to regular forces was a prompt, making the film led to a broader 'decision... to present a female voice/perspective on frontline combat, whatever that was'.[9] Master Corporal Kimberley Ashton, a combat engineer and armaments specialist, whom we see interviewed in an armory, represents the full range of that perspective, from applying for active combat because of a line in the application that stated women were not physically strong enough, to her eventual decision, after the traumatic death of a close colleague and her husband's PTSD diagnosis, to transfer out of combat to raise her daughters.

'I'll always be a sapper, regardless', she says of losing her rank, a statement that blurs the traditional distinction between battlefield and home in a way that seems positive, in contrast to the bleak nightmare of unsurvivable PTSD for female combatant Suzy (Joanne Froggatt), who returns home from Iraq in British drama *In Our Name* (Brian Welsh, 2010). Freeman's film balances video diaries by combatants with at-home interviews that contextualize combat. It overlaps with a sub-genre that seems particularly compelling to female filmmakers: critical films that explore the liminal zone between front line experience and returning home. Kimberley Peirce returned to cinema after nearly a decade with *Stop-Loss* (2008), a feature film critical of the US military's policy of recalling soldiers who had completed their tours, due to the same shortages that also saw the subjects of *Lioness* called to the frontline. After the suicide of his comrade Tommy (Joseph Gordon-Levitt), Brandon King (Ryan Phillippe) – tellingly named to represent maximum masculinity – decides to flee from Texas to Mexico with the assistance of his mother Ida (Linda Emond) and his girlfriend Michelle (Abbie Cornish), but turns back from this feminized act of dishonour, returning to active duty as ordered. Liza Johnson's *Return* (2011) tells a similar, albeit quieter and grittier, story about National Guard reservist Kelli (Linda Cardellini) choosing to return to the front line.

Peirce's film joins Bigelow's and Bier's better-known contributions. While they may not depict women in active combat roles, they have been widely covered as 'courageous' war films by women filmmakers, as if filmmaking were itself an active combat role. It was 2007's *Things We Lost in the Fire*, the US remake of her film *Brødre* (*Brothers*, 2004), that brought Bier to international attention. Both films concern a woman who opens her house to her lost soldier husband's brother, only for her husband to return from the war. In this version of *Martin Guerre*, the home becomes a claustrophobic version of the battleground and the woman and her children an allegory for contested territory. Bier foregrounds this familiar trope and unnerves us with the ways in which domestic and military violence are as connected as domestic and foreign policy. Bigelow, likewise, uses claustrophobia – tight shots, a small ensemble, deadlined narratives – to engage her viewer in the realities of war. *The Hurt Locker* follows directly from her prior film, submarine drama *K-19: The Widowmaker* (2002), made for what was then the highest budget ever granted to a female filmmaker in Hollywood.

Like its predecessors in Bigelow's oeuvre, *The Hurt Locker* is concerned with toxic masculinity. It has *Point Break*'s pitch-perfect grasp of genre even as it deconstructs it. A similar strategy can be seen in Antonia Bird's powerful docudrama *The Hamburg Cell* (2004), one of the earliest films to address the 9/11 attacks, and a rare film to look empathetically at the bombers. The adrenalized elation of Bigelow's action films can be read as 'complicitous critique', in Linda Hutcheon's valuable term: an attempt to use the thrills of mainstream film against itself, engaging an audience only to confront them with the cost of their own investments.[10] But there is more at stake in using this approach with ongoing current events than with surfing. Alisa Lebow, in her study of war documentaries, suggests the term 'paramilitarist' for films that 'excel… in the "war is hell" approach, in which the politics and historical contexts for war are understood as less significant than some generic humanism that sees war as a form of the sublime, in which everyone is living more authentically in the face of death'.[11]

Whereas King in *Stop-Loss* returns to base out of moral concerns and Johnson's Kelli returns out of necessity, William James (Jeremy Renner) returns to Delta Company because he is not only inured but addicted. Bigelow makes this explicit from the opening intertitle, a quotation from war correspondent Chris Hedges: 'The rush of battle is a potent and often lethal addiction, for war is a drug'.[12] The quotation is addressed to the viewer as much as to James, but since we experience the 'rush of battle' through his point of view, a rush that has potent parallels with action movies and first-person shooter video games, complicity here may be stronger than critique.

Bigelow's film forms an instructive contrast with Claire Denis' *Beau Travail*, discussed in chapter three, which resonates with the analogy between toxic masculinity and colonial violence; Denis makes far more clear-cut the emergence of that violence from the repression of homoeroticism, particularly from the dehumanizing eroticization of the non-white Other. Sam Whitsitt identifies *The Hurt Locker* with the western, particularly with with *The Searchers* (a lone wolf classic) and with *The Last of the Mohicans*, with James as Natty and his African American subordinate Sanborn (Anthony Mackie) as Chingachgook.[13] In overlaying the solo and companionate stories of colonial conquest, Bigelow and her screenwriter Mark Boal insist on these twenty-first-century conflicts as a continuation of imperial wars, renewals of manifest destiny extended to other landmasses.

This Bloodpath

Bigelow's follow-up *Zero Dark Thirty*, whose climax was already international news, forms a fascinating comparison with a Canadian short film that resituates the war narrative, also focusing on a female avenging angel. Elle-Máijá Tailfeathers' 'A Red Girl's Reasoning' (2012) extends Butler's 'frames of war' further, asking who gets to define the parameters of conflict. As Delia (Jessica Matten), clad in bike leathers, tracks down two white men – one a cop and one a criminal, their interchangeability implied by intercutting – her voiceover insists:

> I've been on this bloodpath for six, long, lonely years. But white boys have been having their way with Indian girls since contact [onscreen, Delia's boot connects with the groin of the man she's fighting]. Forget what Disney tells you: Pocahontas was *12* when she met John Smith. It's pretty little lies like this that hide the ugly truth.

Delia's bloodpath, 'both a calling and a curse', drives her to avenge First Nations women subjected to gendered and raced violence throughout the long war of colonialism that is still ongoing. Her reference to Pocahontas is a reminder that, as Cowlitz/Watlala writer Elissa Washuta titles a recent blog post with dark irony, 'Violence against Indigenous women [is] fun, sexy, and no big deal on the big screen'.[14] Lived reality is the exact inverse of the wish-fear fantasies of the western: it is Indigenous women, not white women, who are most at risk. Indigenous communities in North America have been at war since 1492.

Tailfeathers is planning to develop 'A Red Girl's Reasoning' as a feature; the short leaves the viewer with a long take of Delia, in her leathers, riding her motorbike through a tunnel, reflections sliding over her helmet in an optical illusion that turns the future ahead of her into the past behind her. Her possible act of vengeance remains in the viewer's imagination: she has tied up and poured gasoline on a rapist, after he shuts down the opportunity she's offered for reconciliation, calling her 'a dirty fucking squaw'. In response, she places her lit cigarette between his lips. Thus, Tailfeathers navigates the ethics of non-violence: neither the rape nor the revenge are represented, but only inferred. Delia – who has told us that her bloodpath is a curse – appears, finally, like a cyborg riding into an unknown future. Her actions, and Tailfeathers' filmmaking, are exhilarating and, in Corinn

Columpar's useful term, 'unsettling', shifting the cinematic point of view from settler to Indigenous culture.[15]

Like Bigelow, Tailfeathers freely appropriates popular genre semantics to frame her story, including the action genre's return to the Strong Female Character (SFC). *Zero Dark Thirty*'s Maya (Jessica Chastain) is part of the lonely SFC trend. Boal and Bigelow based the character on a CIA analyst called Jen, who may be a cover name for a composite, or may not exist at all.

> According to [to Greg Barker's 2013 documentary] *Manhunt*, there was a team of female analysts known within the CIA as 'The Sisterhood', who issued report after report warning about the threat bin Laden posed to America – and whose warnings were repeatedly ignored… Maya is something of a composite of these women.[16]

Jen's (non-)existence has proven one of the many points of dissonance or compression for which critics have taken Bigelow to task, the most serious being her spec(tac)ularization of torture. Emily Bazelon, writing for *Slate* in defence of the film, nevertheless states that: 'At the end of the interrogation scenes, I felt shaken but not morally repulsed, because the movie had successfully led me to adopt, if only temporarily, Maya's point of view: This treatment is a legitimate way of securing information vital to US interests'.[17] As with James, so with Maya: Bigelow's powerful filmmaking creates a point of view character with whom white liberal viewers might align themselves, even against their politics and against all evidence that torture does not work.

As a proxy for the viewer, Maya initially seems troubled by the torture meted out by other CIA operatives to Ammar (Reda Kateb), but when left alone with him, adheres to the policy of torture legitimated by confession, telling him, 'You can help yourself by being truthful'. Maya – whose name, tellingly, means illusion in Sanskrit – is as much in thrall to the addiction of war as her *Hurt Locker* counterpart James; more so, perhaps, in that she is a singular female operative who has internalized the machismo of her surroundings in order to succeed. Her final moments are framed very differently to his: where James returns to the companionship of his battalion, to the neverending cycle of creating and diffusing violence, Maya is alone, crying. Bigelow offers this as a potential reaction to the viewer, asking us what it would mean to cry, instead of punch the air, on hearing of the successful completion of the mission in Abbottabad. In some ways, Maya's tears are as inscrutable, or at least ambiguous, as Delia's mirror-visored helmet in 'A Red Girl', a kind of mask of tragedy that refuses to be coded as either masculinist triumphalism or feminine emotional susceptibility.

Checkpoints

US cinema is exported globally, acting as ideological 'soft' warfare. Likewise, it was ideologically crucial for Soviet cinema to portray its women as liberated, equal and powerful, as seen in Sally Potter's television documentary *I am an Ox, I am a Horse, I am a Man, I am a Woman: Women in Russian Cinema* (1986). One country has continued the Soviet tradition of the female soldier sub-genre: Israel. Within a different political context, there is a similar rationale, wherein female soldiers represent the nation-state's view of itself as modern, progressive and powerful. Female soldiers are at once a marker of Israel's self-described status as a liberal democracy, in which women have equal rights (it is the only country that drafts women), and of its preparedness or toughness, such that *even* women are deployed in combat.

Melanie Kaye/Kantrowitz refers to the Israeli Defence Force (IDF) as 'gender-integrated but not women-liberated', contrasting the armed forces with the largely female-driven, and often invisibilized, peace movement since 1987.[18] Unlike the female peacenik, the female soldier is part of the Israeli cinematic self-image to such an extent that Talya Lavie's *Zero Motivation* (2014) can mock it, focusing on a group of female conscripts marking time behind the lines in a Human Resources office. Like Lavie's dark comedy, Vardit Bilu and Dalia Hager's *Karov La Bayit* (*Close to Home*, 2005) examines the normalization of army life for its female characters, but its protagonists Smadar (Smadar Sayar) and Mirit (Naama Schendar) do not have the security of a desk behind which they can hide their involvement in an occupation. We see the micro-aggressions of the checkpoint through Smadar and Mirit's point of view, but we also see that their high-handed and arbitrary behaviour towards Palestinians takes place in the context of their gradual attrition of all the army rules, including Smadar's off-hours shoplifting game. Both *Zero Motivation* and *Close to Home* chip away at the heroization of the IDF, while simultaneously normalizing female army service, and using that femininity, potentially, as a post-feminist strategy to disarm criticism of the films as mocking and/or glorifying the army.

Kirby Dick's Oscar-nominated *The Invisible War* (2013) unpicks the representation of female soldiers as the (anti-) heroic face of nation. A campaigning documentary exposé of rape in the US military, it focuses on survivor testimony. Its release has supported, and been supported through, the Invisible No More coalition working to end male-on-female sexual assault in the military.[19] Kori Cioca, one of the survivors who appears in the film, summed up the army's attitude in an interview with *Bitch* magazine, telling interviewer Natasha Guzman, 'I understand there's no honor or valor in being raped in the military'.[20] Cioca, tellingly, does not say that there's no honour or valour in being a rapist in the military: what she identifies is the insistence that soldiers must be invulnerable. This underlies the narrative *frisson* available in depicting the female soldier or spy as vulnerable – to the enemy.

Rape is both a weapon of war and a metaphor for it. Dick's film draws on and inverts the use of rape as a narrative trope by which female characters are commonly embedded in the war genre, undertaking the process observed by Yifat Susskind of international women's right organization MADRE. Stating that 'the most destructive power of rape as a weapon of war lies in the deep-rooted stigma attached to it', she quotes an impassioned argument by Iraqi women's rights activist Yanar Mohammed, that we should not see 'a ruined, raped girl, but… a prisoner of war who was strong enough to survive weeks of torture and brave enough to escape'.[21]

That transformational strategy, in which rape is recoded from shame to survival, is palpable not only in Jolie's *In the Land of Blood and Honey* and her international activism for the recognition of rape as a war crime, but also in fiction features by Bosnian filmmaker Jasmila Zbanić and Irish filmmaker Juanita Wilson. Internationally-co-produced and -distributed (albeit on a small scale than Jolie's), their films address the use of rape as a weapon of war in the Balkan conflict from the point of view of resourceful female survivors.

Zbanić's *Grbavica* (*Esma's Secret*, 2006) gives its secret away in the English title: the film's plot drives powerfully towards the main character, Sara (Luna Milović), questioning her mother Esma (Mirjana Karanović) about the identity of her father, whom she has been told was a war hero. Under pressure, Esma reveals that she was raped by a Chetnik, a Serbian paramilitary, in a prison camp. The mother-daughter bond is stronger than the act of the father, erasing it. When Sara joins her fellow students on a field trip for the children of war heroes, she claims allegiance to her mother and preserves her secret.

Esma's secret is only secret to Sara, not to viewers: the use of rape as a weapon of ethnic, as well as gendered, violence was widely reported in coverage of the Balkan conflict. Wilson's first feature *As If I Am Not There* (2010) draws on testimony to the International Criminal Tribunal in the Hague collected into a novel, *S. A Story about the Balkans*, by novelist Slavenka Drakulić.[22] It tells the story of Samira (Natasa Petrovic), a schoolteacher who leaves her modern family in Sarajevo to take a job in the country. After her first day in the village, Samira and the women are taken hostage by Serbian soldiers. Samira is singled out for her youth and beauty and gang-raped. The scene is uncompromising, utterly bleak and grey, using Petrovic's powerful gaze – focused on a fly – to convey the internal effects of the soldier's actions. The film enters trickier territory when Samira is romanced by The Captain (Fedja Stukan), a charismatic warlord who offers her a bath and food, separating her from the other women being kept in a hay-loft by the soldiers. Her decision concerning the Captain is denied to her by the soldiers' abandonment of the farm.

Samira ends up giving birth in wintry Stockholm, where we see her at the start of the film, in Wilson's feeling strategy to ensure that we know her protagonist survives. The frame narrative implies that Samira, looking detachedly at her daughter, has to recall the events in Bosnia in order to form a maternal bond. As in *Esma's Secret*, the bond between mother and daughter is a healing complement to, and sets the stage for, testimony. Yet there is a question of whose testimony is deemed presentable. There has yet to be a similar wave of prestige arthouse cinema testifying to the use of rape as a weapon of war in the Democratic Republic of Congo, or by UN peacekeepers, or by US soldiers in Vietnam, or child marriages occuring in Syrian refugee camps.

20,000 Bosniak Muslim women and girls were raped during the Balkan conflict, according to UN figures.[23] A genocide within a genocide, the figures bear witness to the central way in which war is different for women. Esma and Samira *are* combatants; they endure, resist and contemplate enacting violence. Their stories require us to reframe our understanding of the war film in the same way that 'A Red Girl's Reasoning' contests our frame of war. For women, rape culture is an everyday war. As acts of representational justice, these films alter the war genre away from masculine heroics, even when undertaken by bored female soldiers. But the frame is still narrow.

Lighthouses

Both war films and anti-war films focus on military action: invasions, explosions and exposition set the pace of the narrative. Denis' *Beau Travail* is a counter-example of a female filmmaker immersing herself in the masculine world of the armed forces, but producing a film of inaction and delay, where desire and violence blur out of boredom. In *White Material* (2009), she uses a female character as a focal point for a similarly tense examination of the (un)calm before the storm.

White Material has strong resonances with Marguerite Duras' novels about her family life in Indochina before the anti-colonial First Indochina War (1941–1949). Duras' *Un barrage contre le Pacifique* (*The Sea Wall*, 2008) which was adapted for the screen by Rithy Panh, tells the story of a French woman building a King Canute-like sea wall. The saline inundation prefigures the coming revolution, and also her willed ignorance of both natural and political forces. Isabelle Huppert, who played the mother in Panh's adaptation, took the role of Maria Vial in *White Material* a year later. Maria owns a coffee plantation in an unnamed African country in which civil war is imminent. She gives shelter to a rebel leader, Le Boxeur (Isaach De Bankolé), and finds herself in a tense conversation with a local warlord (Ali Barkai), navigating both sides of the conflict with wary respect. Meanwhile, her drunk husband (Christophe Lambert) and psychotically violent son (Nicholas Duvauchelle) enact the legacy of European colonialism, trying to dominate the locals and Maria, creating an unbearably tense situation as their irresponsible and arrogant actions undo the delicate balance of survival that Maria has negotiated.

As in Duras' work, there is an autobiographical note to Denis' return to Cameroon, the location of her first film, *Chocolat* (1988), which drew from the filmmaker's childhood memories of time spent in the country with her father, a colonial administrator before independence. *White Material* was co-written with French-Senegalese novelist Marie NDiaye, winner of the 2001 Prix Femina. Her novels, as described by Andrew Asibong, take place in 'a world of obscenely casual betrayal and humiliation, much of which is facilitated by social and familial structures of cruelty, complicity and abuse', a description that resonates with Denis' films and their continual analogy between the patriarchal colonial state and family home.[24]

White Material shares many qualities with the documentaries that Lebow describes as 'unwar films', which look:

> away from the main event, as it were, to that which is happening just outside the field of frenetic action… [to] do the destabilizing work of unthreading the very fabric of the militarist paradigm… engag[ing] various techniques and approaches to make the imperceptible perceptible.[25]

Lebow gives as an example of these techniques the use of offscreen sound to indicate the potentiality of violence without spectacular depiction. In Denis' film, this latter mainly comes through the radio, through which the rebel leader announces his plan to clear the country of 'white material', likely a reference to the coded 'hate radio' broadcasts of Radio-Television Libre des Mille Collines in Rwanda.

In Maria Saakyan's film *Mayak* (*The Lighthouse*, 2006), it is the sound of the train that similarly promises and threatens. Saakyan was forced to leave Yerevan, Armenia at the age of 12 because of war in the South Caucasus; she subsequently studied film at the Gerasimov Institute of Cinematography (VGIK) in Moscow. We meet Lena (Anna Kapaleva), the protagonist of *The Lighthouse*, returning from Moscow to her home village, intending to bring her grandparents back to the capital with her. Only the elderly, the damaged and those with small children remain in the village, whose exact location remains indeterminate.

Like Maria in *White Material*, Lena is an active character whose plans are thwarted by the chaos in which she finds herself, created by the illogic of the encroaching war, to which the villagers respond with humour and gentleness. There are startling episodes of violence: one night soldiers with guns come to the village; and Lena's games on the hillside with her friend's toddler son are brutally interrupted by the appearance of a helicopter. The village represents an unwar, rather than a peace, a reminder of the continuing cycle of conflict and its effects. Even so it stands determinedly apart, insisting on the right to frame its own narrative in its own temporality.

It Came Into My Room

War comes close even in contemporary films that appear to be exempt from it; some are in denial, but some engage obliquely. As a thriller in which the cops are useless; a romance in which the male protagonist might be a serial killer; a New York film in which the only diegetic landmark is practically in New Jersey, Campion's *In the Cut* is not an obvious war film, whether pro-, anti-, para-, or un-. But it was the first film given a permit to shoot in Manhattan after 9/11, the shoot having been delayed from winter 2001 to summer 2002. Campion pairs the protagonist's loss and endangerment with the city's, framed by the coming of Homeland Security.

Franny (Meg Ryan) lives near Washington Square; despite Marcel Duchamp's 1917 declaration of the 'Free and Independent Republic of Washington Square', it is one of the most surveilled sites in the world. In the film, there are frequent point-of-view shots that imply someone is watching Franny in the rearview mirror of a car. One of the Poems in Transit that Franny reads on her journeys across the city by subway is a Seneca song: 'It's off in the distance / It came into my room / It's here in the circle'. War, whether international or domestic terrorism, is close, and the paranoid response of Homeland Security brings it closer still.

'It came into my room' could be the tagline for Jennifer Reeves' contemporaneous New York (anti-)thriller *The Time We Killed* (2004), in which an agoraphobic writer thinks she hears a murder in the apartment across the lightwell from her. Like *In the Cut*, it reworks *noir* both by focusing on a female detective-protagonist, and by recasting the thriller's violence as a gendered war. Robyn (Lisa Jarnot),

Home Front: Women at War, Women against War

Fig. 14: Robyn trapped in her room, *The Time We Killed*

who has agoraphobia, is the opposite of risk-taking Franny, travelling only in her memories and imagination. Robyn could be seen as an avatar of the confessional individualism of US post-feminism and of US political isolationism in general. In Reeves's words, 'the horror of the US military "shock and awe" campaign brings to light the terrible cost of self-absorption and passivity, and shakes Robyn out of her self-made isolation'.[26]

Shutting herself away does not allow Robyn to shut herself off: the world comes into her room, in the same way that a murder takes place in the gardens under Franny's window at the start of *In the Cut*, entering her dreams and setting off the narrative connections (often poetic rather than rational) that will lead her to become a cop-killer. Both *In the Cut* and *The Time We Killed* are committed to killing the violent Father we carry in our heads and to releasing us into the world. They don't present an easy resolution of the 'return' of peace, but a recognition that US post-imperial wars are not specific, discrete and privileged above other narratives. Intersecting post-imperial wars and rape culture, they reveal that war is everyday and continuous, so we have to practice 'unwar' as we do non-violence. This is the realization reached by She (Joan Allen) in *Yes* (Sally Potter, 2004) when she returns to Belfast where she was raised by her aunt (Sheila Hancock) and sees the 'peace wall' topped with razor wire that still divides Protestant Shankill Road from Catholic Falls Road, despite a dismantlement clause in the 1998 Good Friday accord.

She is fleeing a dead marriage to a British politician (Sam Neill) and a passionate but complicated relationship with He (Simon Abkarian), a Lebanese political refugee living in London. He is in Beirut tracing bullet holes in walls while she is in Belfast; the film intercuts histories of colonial violence and their aftermath, a reminder that the immediate conflict that frames their relationship – the post-9/11 wars – are neither singular nor special. They are part of the long histories of imperialism. There is no peacetime in which to love, only the courage to step out into the risky public space of unwar, in which the divisions of rage persist. She fulfils her communist Aunt's dying wish, travelling to Cuba, where He meets her. Neutral ground – but for She, who is a US citizen, also a risk of losing her identity, a contravention of national rules. Indeed, the production had to relocate from Cuba to the Dominican Republic at the last moment, after Bush cracked down on US citizens such as Allen travelling to Cuba. As Giuliana Bruno comments in her 'virtual' letter to Potter, 'This form of cultural travel was not easy to achieve. You were shooting in times of war'.[27]

Through her relationship with He, She attempts to stand outside her privileged first world identity, and to stand in solidarity with those experiencing the fallout of Western imperialism, whether in Northern Ireland (an English colony), Lebanon or Cuba. A geneticist who works on embryology, She demonstrates that the feminist imperative for non-violent solutions arises through a political alignment with the vulnerable rather than through any essentialist claim to nurturing femininity. Insisting that we have always fought differently, these films negotiate a politics of non-violence that is never a policy of victimhood, never ceding our place in the narrative. As do Franny and Robyn, and like Makhmalbaf's Baktay, Potter's She learns that to travel, especially as a woman, is at once a necessity and a risk, a walk on dangerous and contested ground.

5

I Have No Country

British Cinema as a Runaway Girl

Leaving Home

She, the co-protagonist of Sally Potter's *Yes*, is not the only woman on the move in contemporary British cinema, and nor is she alone in the double significance of her journey. She may be fleeing within the context of multiple international wars, but, in returning to Belfast, She also runs *towards* a girlhood she had left behind. She reclaims herself as a girl who was fiercely loved by, and loved, her feminist, Communist aunt, rather than a daughter abandoned by her parents. Across contemporary British feminist cinema, women and girls are on the run, unsurprisingly, from abuse and poverty of opportunity, from domesticity and despair. But they are also running towards futures located in the reclamation of their pasts.

The displaced protagonists of the films considered in this chapter might be mouthy or silent, sexually exploratory or asexual, demanding visibility or privacy: as with water, it's their ambiguity and variety, their refusal to be pinned down to one meaning or being, that makes them strong. And their multiplicity makes them exciting. There is no one British feminist cinema in the twenty-first century. From Debbie Isitt's popular comedies to the experimental installations of Turner Prize winner Elizabeth Price and Jarman Prize winner Ursula Mayer, there is an unprecedented plethora of women moving, variously, through the spectrum of British cinema – and keeping it on the move. This unpindownability is in stark contrast to the usual unitary, stable, static meaning demanded of nationality and national cinema. As Maya Vitkova's Bulgarian state-of-the-nation satire *Viktoria* (2014) and Teodora Ana Mihai's Romanian observational documentary *Waiting for August* (2014) both differently demonstrate, the adolescent girl on the edge of flight may also be the new figure of East European national cinemas.

Women move, in part, because they are excluded from the closed-off definition of nation, both metaphorically and practically. The Women's Budget Group headlined their 2014 report 'Giveaways to men – paid for by women', stressing that austerity policies have hit women, particularly single mothers, hardest.[1] The Fawcett Society concurred, starting the Cutting Women Out protest campaign.[2] Andrea Luka Zimmerman's *Estate, A Reverie* (2015), bears this out, through documenting five years of work with the community on Haggerston Estate in East London as they await its demolition. The signs are there across the board that, in Britain, women don't count: pressure is mounting for an investigation into the sexual abuse of women detained as illegal immigrants at Yarl's Wood; the Metropolitan Police failed to charge undercover officers who had long-term sexual relationships with female activists; and domestic violence, including murder, is on the rise while funding for refuges and support services is slashed.[3]

It is hard not to see systemic sexual abuse and its investigations as British feminist cinema's 'frame of war'. Operation Yewtree, a Metropolitan Police investigation into sexual abuse by media personalities, has accrued the most media attention, but local and now governmental investigations have built up a picture of the systemic abuse of vulnerable girls, facilitated by a sexist, classist, racist police and judicial culture that led to allegations going unheard. Coverage of convictions in these operations led, in 2014, to the re-opening of Operation Rose, which investigated historic abuse in children's homes in Northumbria, and an Independent Inquiry into Child Sexual Abuse, covering all institutions in the UK, including the possible implication of the previous Conservative government in a high-level cover-up.[4]

It was at this highly charged moment that actor and filmmaker Samantha Morton gave an interview in which she spoke, for the first time, about being sexually abused while in foster care in Nottingham in the 1980s, and about the police's neglect of her case.[5] Morton openly describes *The Unloved* (2009), her first foray behind the camera, as an autobiographical reflection on her time in foster care. A spare film of unstinting intensity, it's characteristic of British feminist filmmaking in creating super-charged storytelling in difficult circumstances. The film was initially screened on Channel 4 as the centrepiece of a season called *Britain's Forgotten Children*, but critical plaudits led to a limited theatrical release in the UK, a rare event for a TV drama, as well as the BAFTA for Best Single Drama (television) in 2010.

At the end of the film, 12 year old Lucy (Molly Windsor) runs, but has nowhere to run to: both her homes – the family home and the foster home – are inadequate, disturbed, even punitive. Virginia Woolf famously said that 'The outsider will say, "in fact, as a woman, I have no country. As a woman I want no country. As a woman my country is the whole world".'[6] Lucy seems to have no home, no country, no

I Have No Country: British Cinema as a Runaway Girl

Fig. 15: Lucy reflected in the mall table, *The Unloved*

place at all, but we see the whole world through her eyes, through the rigorous cinematography by Thomas Townend that frames and colours her world of non-places with exacting attention.

Lucy is a displaced person within her own home, town and country. Through Morton's filmmaking, however, she can be read, in her lostness, as an uncomfortable part of national consciousness, a new symbol of a fragmentary, self-questioning, leftist Britishness. The films I discuss in this chapter concentrate on this figure of the young woman as social and cultural outsider, taking over from the adolescent male rebel of 1950s US cinema. The lost or displaced child has become an alternative figuration in postwar national cinema more broadly, as Stephanie Hemelryk Donald has traced in relation to Chinese children's cinema.[7] Emma Wilson writes in *Cinema's Missing Children*, that, through this figure, 'losses are relived, denied, obliterated, fictionalized without repair'.[8]

I Am Nasrine's titular protagonist, an Iranian migrant to Newcastle, is a reminder that the young woman, restless in the confines of an oppressive patriarchal society, is a common figure of national allegory in Iranian New Wave cinema. She particularly appears as such in the films of Jafar Panahi, such as transgressive transvestism drama *Offside* (2006), as well as those of the women of the Makhmalbaf family, discussed in chapter four. The experience of filmmaker Mania Akbari, star of Abbas Kiarostami's woman-on-the-move drama *Dah* (*Ten*, 2000), now living in exile in the UK, demonstrates that running is not always unambivalently joyous: 'I still love Iran. I am still fascinated by it. It gave me my creativity. But I had to leave'.[9]

The critique of Iranian government ideology in her films emerges out of her living body. 'With cinema, you can take your audience by their hands and guide them through your life… I carry with me every experience I've ever had'.[10] Her most recent film *From Tehran to London* (2013), shown in the BFI's retrospective of her work, ends abruptly by interrupting the domestic drama 'at home' in Tehran to reveal that Akbari can't finish the film, having fled to Britain.

Lost girls appear in New Labour state-of-the-nation British films such as *Last Resort* (Pawel Pawlikowski, 2000), *Children of Men* (Alfonso Cuarón, 2006) and *London to Brighton* (Paul Andrew William, 2006), as well as in Arnold's *Fish Tank* and the less well-known *Gypo* (Jan Dunn, 2005), the first accredited British Dogme 95 film. In *Gypo*, as in *Last Resort*, the teenage female protagonist is literally a displaced person; Natasha (Chloe Sirene) is a Romany Czech, doubly stateless because of her Roma identity. She finds a home with Helen (Pauline McLynn), an older Irish immigrant settled in Margate, Kent, which was also the setting for *Last Resort*. Eastern European migrants 'were dispersed to the Kent coast [in the 1990s] as a result of government efforts to "spread the burden" of what they claimed represented a massive influx of refugees and asylum-seekers into the country'.[11]

Dunn inverts viewer expectations concerning lost girls, as Natasha initiates a relationship with Helen, and appears to rescue her, rather than vice versa. As Rachel Lewis points out, 'in response to Helen's comment that, "you're so far from home and you're really vulnerable now", Natasha replies: "I don't feel vulnerable at all, but you seem to me the most vulnerable person I've ever met"'.[12] Similarly, Lucy's lostness in *The Unloved* is given context by her older roommate Lauren (Lauren Socha), who initially seems a tough veteran of the care system, guiding Lucy through both the foster home and urban space. But Lucy's watchful gaze and ethical sense becomes Lauren's only protection from sexual assault by care worker Shaun (Ben Parkinson).

Sisters by chance, Lauren and Lucy are a reminder of how often lost girls come in non-biological pairs, their relationship often fraught with tension but freighted with potential. At the climax of *Fish Tank*, Mia kidnaps Keira (Sydney Mary Nash), the young daughter of her mother's married boyfriend Connor (Michael Fassbender), who has also seduced Mia. Her hair-raising adventure with Keira, which appears on the surface as primarily intended to punish Connor, bears a striking similarity to Dorota Kędzierzawska's *Wrony* (*Crows*, 1994), in which a neglected girl steals a younger girl, hoping to become her surrogate mother. In *Fish Tank*, Mia has an unruly and contestatory relationship with her own younger sister Tyler (Rebecca Griffiths), and Keira represents a second chance. She contains all of Mia's wish-fears about being a sister, daughter, lover and mother;

unmanageably so, leading Mia into an act of unpremeditated violence. Keira survives her soaking in the sea, thus offering Mia the opportunity to change and the incentive to leave, having – in a sense – drowned herself and risen again.

Keira also echoes the white horse whom Mia futilely attempts to set free earlier in the film, a part of herself that longs for freedom and for justice, a transitional object that allows her to break out of the cycle of poverty of opportunity she foresees if she stays at home with her mother (Kierston Wareing). Arnold makes this lockstep palpable in Mia's final scene with her mother and Tyler, in which they dance, face to face, to Nas' 'Life's a Bitch'. Mia has been in motion, somewhere between dancing and running, since the first frame of the film. In Lucy Bolton's words, the 'camera picks up on her energy through its urgently unsteady hand-held motion and the accompanying sound of her exercised breathing... If it takes Mia a few minutes to get from one side of the estate to the other then it will take us a few minutes too'.[13]

Mia's mobility forms a stark contrast to the ending of Amma Asante's BAFTA-winning first film, *A Way of Life* (2004), which emerges from the same new social realist cinema of lost girls as figures for marginal communities as *Fish Tank*, *Nasrine* and *The Unloved*. Rage suffuses both the filmmaking and the protagonist, a rage against inequality that makes Asante's film kinetic and engaging even as her protagonist is stuck in the intersecting effects of poverty and gender the title condemns as 'a way of life'. Leigh-Anne (Stephanie James) is an incest survivor and a single mother, living in fear of social services. As she becomes complicit in both a rape and a racist beating, the film's title is also an important reminder of the vicious cycle of abuse, which she seems – possibly – about to exit at the end, as she breaks down and asks for help.

Leigh-Anne, like Mia, is represented not as the cause of the problem, but its potential solution. As Bolton adds, '*Fish Tank* may appear to suggest that Mia is a prime example of contemporary broken British culture, but it is a shot across the bows of such misperceptions, announcing that girls like Mia should not be dismissed or underestimated', although the failures of policing in Rotherham and Rochdale show how often they are.[14] The complexity and interconnection of the problems facing Leigh-Anne and Mia, and their perpetuation of them, are reminiscent of Morton's 2009 remark to Simon Hattenstone that, 'if she had included [in *The Unloved*] everything that had happened in her childhood, no one would have believed her... "Violence, sexual abuse, torture", she said, but refused to be drawn further'.[15]

All of these lost girls and women are a reference to one of the most famous figures in postwar British media, Cathy Ward (Carol White), the runaway protagonist of Ken Loach's television play *Cathy Come Home* (BBC, 1966), which led to massive public support for homelessness charity Shelter. On a smaller scale, Kim Longinotto's first documentary, a student project while she was at the National Film and Television School, *Pride of Place* (1976, co-directed with Dorothy Gazidis) did lead to the investigation and closure of her repressive former boarding school, the film's subject.

Longinotto has continued to document schools and organizations of all kinds, including her school's inverse in *Hold Me Tight, Let Me Go* (2007), about Mulberry Bush, an innovative British school and treatment centre for children with severe behavioural difficulties resulting from emotional trauma and abuse. Longinotto observes women and girls on the move globally, from Tehran (*Runaway*, 2001, co-directed with Ziba Mir-Hosseini) to Tamil Nadu (*Salma*, 2013). Her point of view, the lens that focuses on these breakaway spirits, may emerge from British class politics, but her deployment of it demonstrates that Morton's Lucy is part of a global network of young women running, even if they don't know where. While no single film described here has had the effect of *Cathy Come Home*, cumulatively they have created a culture in which Morton's story can now be heard and believed, by audiences if not by the justice system, creating the possibility of change.

Speaking Of

What saves *The Unloved* and its peers from unremitting bleakness is the love with which they are made and with which their characters are shaped. While Lucy is nothing like Tracy Beaker, the protagonist of Jacqueline Wilson's much-loved young adult novels about life in care, she shares Tracy's vulnerable, open heart. From the start of the film, we are in Lucy's aslant perspective, although we never fully gain access to her memories and perceptions. In this, she differs from the classic 'girl, interrupted', whom Anita Harris describes as an 'at-risk girl'.[16] In *Future Girl*, Harris observes that, post-Riot Grrrl, young women get divided up into 'at-risk' (working class) and 'can do' (middle class). Lucy is both 'at-risk' and 'can do', on her own terms, rather than the state's. She is opaque, resisting investigation by social workers, peers – and even the camera.

As Naomi Klein argues in *No Logo*, post-feminist 'can do' individualism allowed feminist tropes such as writing the self, whether via literary memoirs or taboo-busting zines, to be decontextualized, commodified and used as a method of control.[17] Confessional practices such as diaries, demonstrates Harris, are used by the state as the route from risk to achievement, as institutions and therapists assign and surveill self-reflection practices for at-risk girls. Yet Lucy, Mia, Nasrine and Leigh-Anne have been let down by the state; there is no incentive for them to offer up a narration of themselves to a state agent in order to be 'cured'. Instead, Lucy has to seek her own mode of survival that critiques the state and its 'can do' demands.

She's a companion to Tina (Kelli Hollis), who began her career shoplifting in Penny Woolcock's TV movie *Tina Goes Shopping* (Channel 4, 1999). Woolcock sums up her vision of working-class resistance in the title of the third film in the Tina trilogy, *Mischief Night* (2006). Rather than being adaptable, Tina (favourite phrase: 'end of') and her family are inventive anarchists for whom mischief is both subversion and survival. Woolcock's work has an ethical imperative that puts more conventional miserabilist British realism to shame: in developing her narratives with local actors and their communities in often deprived post-industrial areas where she films, she depicts and generates hard-won joy, love and community. There's a risky can do-ness of the kind that Lucy is beginning to explore.

Morton made her name with two similarly resistant roles in British feminist films, characters who draw the viewer in by virtue of their intense gaze rather than their to-be-looked-at-ness, girls whose selves are in their aslant point of view, not their legible confessional interiority. For many viewers, her most iconic role is as the eponymous protagonist of Lynne Ramsay's second feature, *Morvern Callar* (2002). Morton sweetly references Ramsay's adaptation of Alan Warner's novel in *The Unloved*, staging a headlit mini-rave that evokes the much-quoted dance scenes in *Morvern*. As for Morvie, so for Lucy: dance offers what Noël Carroll calls, with reference to Yvonne Rainer's films, 'moving and moving', embodied access to emotion, a joyous respite and euphoric natural high.[18]

Morvern is the originary runaway girl of twenty-first-century British feminist cinema, finding her place by chance as she drifts through the opportunities created by her boyfriend's suicide, from having the flat to herself (once she's coolly chopped up his body) to a trip to Ibiza with her best friend Lanna (Kathleen McDermott). Morvern's decision to submit her boyfriend's novel to a publisher under her name offers a smart, sly twist on both an emphasis on 'can do' confessionalism, and on Sue Thornham's argument for the feminist heroine's heroism as writing herself.[19] Through her strategic opacity, Morvern profits from her editors' classist and sexist assumptions. Impassive and/or profound: Morton and Ramsay move Morvern gracefully between hedonistic surface and deadpan depth.

If Morvern is a creature of chance, Rose, in *Under the Skin* (Carine Adler, 1997), is an animal of abandon. Morton is painfully alive as a daughter grieving her mother's death, out of place in her skin and the world as she wrestles with mortality and her lost status as daughter, until, once she has disposed of her mother's ashes, she can become fully herself. As Marcia Landy points out, *Under the Skin* represented a kind of torch-passing, via 'the presence of Rita Tushingham [as Rose's mother, which,] brief though it is, evokes memories… of Tushingham's portraits of off-beat femininity', particularly in *A Taste of Honey* (Tony Richardson, 1961), adapted from Shelagh Delaney's 1958 play.[20]

It's a signal of and to an aesthetic and ethic that grounds many contemporary British feminist films, most strongly Clio Barnard's *The Arbor*, about playwright Andrea Dunbar, whose first two plays were filmed as *Rita, Sue and Bob Too* (Alan Clarke, 1987). *The Arbor*, titled after the estate where Dunbar lived, is an utterly original hybrid that draws on the documentary tradition of social realism and contemporary verbatim theatre to suggest a very particular, strongly feminist mode of British realist cinema that is at once theatre and film, documentary and fiction, literary and vernacular, openly concerned with class and gender politics and deeply invested in investigating subjectivity.

Isabel Shapiro notes that Barnard's film threw documentary festival and award juries into quandaries. According to Shapiro, at a BFI panel,

> Barnard coolly countered: 'It's not a documentary, and I'm certainly not a documentary filmmaker, but part of what I wanted to do is explore what documentary is and isn't, and where it crosses over into fiction, that blurry line which is always there' (BFI Live: 2011). The instinct to theoretically and practically engage with these ideas has been shared with Barnard by several British artists and film-makers in recent years – all working from a similar premise that a claim to absolute authenticity is impossible, and certainly not imperative if, like *The Arbor*, there are alternative ways to narrate the 'true stories' of others.[21]

The Unloved shares Richardson's, Dunbar's and Barnard's commitments to this subjective social realism as a strategy of representational justice, and relates to their work's roots in documentary theatre.

Morton began working on the story of *The Unloved* at 16, just a few years older than Lucy, having left the last of several Nottinghamshire care homes in which she had grown up. Talking to Gilbert Gerard, she notes the film's roots in her personal experience, but also in British film history:

> I made this because I had something to say. It's a bit like the manifesto of the Free Cinema movement, that films can't be anything but personal, and this is what I had to say… I was attending the Television Workshop in Nottingham [at 16] and I said I wanted to

make a play about my situation and where I lived. So we devised a play and we performed it for a couple of nights.[22]

The Unloved was later developed in collaboration with screenwriter Tony Grisoni from her memories of that devised play. Morton's direction of Windsor and Socha, both of whom she cast from the Television Workshop in Nottingham where she had trained, enables them to channel her own performances in *Under the Skin* and *Morvern Callar*. All three films share a narration that could be described as 'first-person oblique', which sets them apart from the tradition of social realist cinema begun in Richardson's films. Their insistently subjective narration, via cinematography motivated by the girl-protagonist's watchful, intelligent gaze, loosens the hold of objective reality, while retaining a fierce political commitment.

Dreams of a Life (Carol Morley, 2011) enacts first-person oblique par excellence. Morley's docu-fiction, contemporaneous to *The Arbor*, also uses reconstruction to investigate, rather than document, its subject. An accompanying interactive web project created in collaboration with novelist A. L. Kennedy and photographer Lottie Davies is titled *Dreams of Your Life*, and works through the AnyWoman possibilities of the story that the film tells, rather than its exceptionalism.[23] Beyond classic identification or universalism, *Dreams of A Life* is an immersion in an unknowable life that, in order to know, we have to imagine inhabiting as ourselves.

Joyce Vincent died alone in 2003, aged 38, and it was three years before her remains were discovered. To tell Vincent's story, Morley draws on television, rather than engaging with theatre as Barnard does. The far-seeing medium hovers in the corner of domestic space like a crystal ball. Morley considers the paradox of the 'cool' medium's intimacy, its ability to conjure communion with the dead in the living room, as we see Joyce (Zawe Ashton) watch the documentary's interviewees talk about her 'on' her television. These inserts also re-evaluate whose life, how told, counts as news, particularly given the inclusion of local MP Lynne Featherstone as a participant. Morley's film gives to Vincent's life the attention that was only given to her in death, profoundly redressing the balance of representation, not least in the film's final scene, which locates a young Vincent in grainy video footage of the audience at a speech by Nelson Mandela: there she is, part of history, as we all are.

Ashton's graceful, inward-turned performance sets Joyce in motion. She is almost silent throughout, as the film scrupulously never puts words in Joyce's mouth or attempts to imagine her confession. Vincent left behind a few photographs, diaries, and address books and many questions. Although her story initially seems like one of total and abrupt stillness, what emerges, as Morley traces

Fig. 16: Joyce Vincent (left, turning towards the camera) at Nelson Mandela's talk, *Dreams of a Life*

her friends and acquaintances, is her restlessness. She moved from job to job, lover to lover, flat to flat, as if running from herself. Towards the end of the film, talking heads give voice to fears that Vincent had experienced an unknown childhood trauma, beyond the known facts that her mother died when she was at primary school, and that her father was distant. Others hint at the systemic trauma of racism and classism, discussing her attempt to change her accent, and the division of her life between her longest-term white partner and her participation on the fringes of the Black British music scene.

In the most moving moments, we hear recordings of Vincent's voice, sounding 'full of vibrancy', as one of her former acquaintances notes. If any identity emerges for Vincent, it is as a performer. For us as viewers, she is made of media, but even before her death, she seemed to come to life when singing and dancing, fashioning a self through performance: another kind of first-person oblique in which we can only read her through how she *acts*. It is, vividly, this personal-political aesthetics that moves us through the diegetic world of *Dreams of a Life*, centred, like *The Unloved*, on extraordinary embodiment.

Crossing Borders

There is a far higher percentage of female than male filmmakers internationally who begin their careers as performers: in contemporary Britain, that would include Asante (who appeared in TV drama *Grange Hill* [BBC, Phil Redmond, 1978–2008]) and Arnold (children's TV show *No. 73* [ITV, J. Nigel Pickard, 1982–1988]), as well as Sally Potter, who trained as a dancer and choreographer. In the twenty-first century, there has also been a noticeable trend for female playwrights and theatre makers to move into film, including Woolcock, who worked in community theatre, and Antonia Bird, whose parents were theatre professionals.

Screenwriters and directors who have moved into cinema include Bola Agbaje (*Gone Too Far* [Destiny Ekharaga, 2013]), Moira Buffini (*Byzantium* [Neil Jordan, 2012], *Jane Eyre* [Cary Fukunaga, 2011], *Tamara Drewe* [Stephen Frears, 2010]), Phyllida Lloyd (*Mamma Mia!* [2008], *Iron Lady* [2011]), Abi Morgan (*The Iron Lady*, *Brick Lane* [Sarah Gavron, 2007], *Shame* [Steve McQueen, 2011]), debbie tucker green (*Second Coming* [2014]) and Laura Wade (*The Riot Club* [Lone Scherfig, 2014]). As in Delaney's and Dunbar's eras, there is a strong commitment to new writing in British theatre. Since the invasion of Iraq, there has been a rekindling of political theatre accompanied by a drive for equality.[24] According to the Tonic Theatre Advance project on women in theatre, alas, it is delimited by the same financial and intersectional barriers as in film.[25]

Although the BFI Film Fund only announced a diversity policy in summer 2014, the UK Film Council had already sought to diversify the recipients of its funding. Successful artists from other disciplines were encouraged to make feature films, a strategy that has led to the emergence of gallery artists-turned-filmmakers McQueen, Sam Taylor-Johnson (formerly Taylor-Wood) and Gillian Wearing, and novelist Xiaolu Guo. Artists' film and video has an increasingly prominent profile in the UK via Film London's Jarman Award and the tireless work of LUX, supporting filmmakers such as Beck's Future winner Rosalind Nashashibi.

Nashashibi's Cairo-shot short 'This Quality' (2010), part of a LUX/ICO's touring programme, is a haunting juxtaposition of long takes showing the unveiled face of a thirtysomething woman looking directly at the camera, and of parked cars covered against the sun. It conjures an unheard conversation about visibility and invisibility, vulnerability in public space, and the quality of the female gaze. From Glasgow University where she studied ('University Library', 2004), to her family's home country of Palestine ('Dahiet Al Bareed, District of the Post Office', 2004), and travels on a cargo ship ('Bachelor Machines' parts one and two, 2007), Nashashibi's films roam widely.

So do Xiaolu's. Her second fiction feature *She, A Chinese* (2009) is so quintessentially a lost girl film, from its striking use of saturated colour details amid washed-out backgrounds to its release on Warp Films (whose parent company, Warp Records, provided the soundtrack for *Morvern Callar*), that it is almost pastiche. Li Mei (Lu Huang) travels from a remote Chinese village to the bleak out-of-season English seaside via various relationships with men that, at best, occur by coercive consent. Mei is affectless, drawn West by pop music and DVDs; she is more a cipher of globalization than a psychologically-realized character. What's beguiling about the film is that England, and London, do not offer a resolution to Mei's wanderlust, nor her salvation. At the end of the film, she is pregnant, arguing that identity begins in the body rather than in the world of nation-states.

Sara Ishaq's documentary *The Mulberry House* (2014), in which the Scottish filmmaker returns to her father's family in Yemen, offers a broadly similar argument from a different angle. We hear Ishaq, off-camera, engaging her father and younger sister in discussion about her determination to leave Yemen and study in the UK. We also feel, through the film's quality of attention, her palpable connection to her country of birth and her excitement about being there during its part in the Arab Spring. There is no simplistic equation, in either film, of Western European liberal democracy with perfection or closure; nor are these films haunted by the crises of identity that marked post-colonial literary fiction of the 1980s and 1990s. Hybridity and movement offer a secure and flexible origin for a new narrative point of view of valued complexity.

Ishaq and Xiaolu point to a refreshing strain of contemporary British cinema that crosses national as well as disciplinary and media borders. Leila Sansour's *Open Bethlehem* (2014) exemplifies this: the filmmaker remortgaged her London home to finance a documentary about returning to her father's home city. It shares its names with her campaign to link Bethlehem to international supporters through a Passport programme that allows anyone to declare their symbolic citizenship of the city.[26] The BFI Production Board of the 1970s, which funded Pratibha Parmar and Ngozi Onwurah among others, and Channel 4 (for whom Gurinder Chadha made her first film, the documentary *I'm British But...* in 1989) in the 1980s, together introduced a rich legacy of ethnic and transnational diversity into British filmmaking, which continues in the new century. Films by Akbari, Asante (*Belle* [2013]), Chadha (*Bend it Like Beckham* [2002], *Bride and Prejudice* [2004]), Ekaragha, Sally El Hosaini (*My Brother the Devil*, 2012), Gharavi, Ishaq ('Karama

I Have No Country: British Cinema as a Runaway Girl

Has No Walls' [2012]), Sansour, tucker green, Campbell X and Xiaolu explore bicultural heritages and the legacies of colonialism and post-colonialism.

Migration is central to Gavron's mainstream *Brick Lane*, adapted from Monica Ali's novel. Longinotto edits clips from Gavron's film into a tone-poem that forms the concluding fanfare of her BFI archival compilation documentary, *Love is All* (2014). The finale balances the film's earlier condensation of Anna May Wong's star turn as Shosho in British silent film *Piccadilly* (Ewald André Dupont, 1929). Although they couldn't be more different in tone or plot, both *Brick Lane* and *Love is All* centre on an Asian woman making her way in London, and Longinotto's quicksilver edits draw attention to the persistence of racism and sexism – but also to the continuous process by which the women's courage, desire, and determination have altered the city's and nation's social fabric towards openness. As Woolcock does in her BFI archival compilation documentary, *From the Sea to the Land Beyond*, Longinotto uses the idea of a national archive against itself, opening up the apparent lockbox to reveal a generous treasure trove. British cinema is revealed as a diverse vernacular, full of wit, passion, connection and change, all driven by female sexuality.

Woolcock, like Longinotto and Potter, is a white, middle-class filmmaker committed to representational justice; her most recent film project, documentary *One Mile Away* (2012), came about through her immersion in the disenfranchised communities whose stories she tells collaboratively. In 2009, Woolcock shot hip-hop musical *1Day* with non-professional actors from Birmingham, many of them semi-professional musicians. After it screened, Shabba, an MC who had participated in her research but not the film, asked to be put in contact with Dylan Duffus, who played the lead role of Flash; they belonged to the Burger Bar Boys (B21) and the Johnson Crew (B6) postcode crews respectively. Prompted by a rash of shootings, Shabba had decided to try to broker a truce in an unorthodox way: through Woolcock's observational camera. With an uncertain conclusion, *One Mile Away* comes close – like *1Day* – to being live, site-specific theatre.

Despite the men living one mile away from each other, hence the documentary's title, the need for a middlewoman was urgent. Woolcock told me:

> We were trying to do something that's just not in a filmmaker's brief: an attempt to actually change the reality that we were filming... The boys were risking their lives; and that made it a painful and stressful process. More so than for me, although I didn't sleep for a year from the stress. If I'd been killed, the killer would have been looking at 35 years. I'm a white, middle-class woman, it would have had relentless media coverage. But for the boys it was way more risky, and there's much less attention.[27]

On the film's release, Woolcock continued her commitment to the community's ownership of the film through the One Mile social enterprise. She turned to Kickstarter to raise funds for screenings in schools and prisons to reach the audiences to whom Shabba and Dylan wanted to speak directly, and who are often excluded by price, location, and élitist association, from accessing independent low-budget documentary.[28] Gharavi is currently using crowd-funding to support her Power to the Pixel-winning project. *From the Plantation to the Penitentiary* is a co-authored social justice documentary about the US prison-industrial complex that will be supported by a web platform where the online community can add material, re-edit and re-imagine the content.[29]

Gharavi's project, like Woolcock's, also points to an urgent new attention in British feminist cinema to disenfranchised young men. If the female protagonist is on the move – whether determinedly or displaced – these male protagonists are trapped. The title of Ekaragha's *Gone Too Far* says it all, metaphorically: it may be played for comedy, but the social and geographical gulf between Yemi (Malachi Kirby) and his brother Ikudayisi (O.C. Ukeje), more recently arrived from Nigeria, effectively captures meaningful tensions both within the British Nigerian community, and between them and their Caribbean neighbours in Peckham. Ekaragha's comedy resolves what Woolcock's documentary captures: the brutal colonialist logic of postcode wars in dividing and conquering young people who are potentially vectors of social change.

To this, El Hosaini's *My Brother the Devil* adds the new divide-and-conquer of homophobia and Islamophobia. *My Brother the Devil* has a double frame of war: in the distant background, the post-9/11 invasions and their fostering of Islamophobia; in the immediate foreground, the London protests sparked by the police shooting of Mark Duggan. This coincided with the film shoot, and meant the production had to 'confin[e] much of the action indoors' in claustrophobic stairwells and council flats.[30] Reminiscent of *My Beautiful Laundrette* (Stephen Frears, 1985), the Welsh-Egyptian El Hosaini's film illustrates how far backwards British cinema had gone post-9/11. In the 1990s, Ella Shohat and Robert Stam identified British cinema as positively post-colonial and cosmopolitan.[31] Whereas Hanif Kureishi's characters have what Shohat and Stam call 'lines out', for El Hosaini's protagonists, the only line out is near-tragedy.

For Rashid (James Floyd), as for Mia in *Fish Tank*, running away is the courageous option, but he comes to it through terrible violence, and with far more to lose. The film charts his incremental attempts to leave behind drug-dealing after the murder of his best friend, as he finds new interests and then love with Sayyid (Saïd Taghmaoui), a Parisian-Algerian former gang member. Rashid's involvement with

I Have No Country: British Cinema as a Runaway Girl

Sayyid threatens both the physical and psychic security of his younger brother Mo (Fady Elsayed), whose final rapprochement with Rashid sets up a telling contrast between the brother in flight (whose sexuality perhaps parallels him with lost girls) and the one left behind.

Both Woolcock and El Hosaini feature outspoken female characters – Taymar and Hanan (Amira Ghazalla) respectively – who call out the toxic, militaristic machismo inherent in gang culture. Woolcock told me:

> The hood is totally segregated, and the film reflects that. We made sure, with *One Mile Away*, they set up projects for women, and run by women for girls, because the women are part of that culture… I have written a script about the female side of hood life, but can't get anyone interested – I'm not giving up on it, though. There are a lot of really good female rappers I'd like to work with.[32]

Rebecca Johnson's Brixton-set *Honeytrap* (2014) takes the case of Samantha Joseph, who was imprisoned in 2009 for leading Shakilus Townsend into a fatal ambush, as its starting point to imagine the motivations and meanings of young women's lives in the hypermasculine world of gangs. Johnson observes that 'manhood has become idealized into a caricature of invulnerability. Boys must impersonate it, girls be desired by it – but to be respected they must impersonate it too'.[33] Unlike mainstream gang films, Johnson's, Woolcock's and El Hosaini's make a far-reaching gender critique central to their projects, as part of their commitment to the communities they are representing.

Like Woolcock, the directing duo Desperate Optimists (Joe Lawlor and Christine Molloy) began in community theatre, and have continued to work in uniquely collaborative ways, producing films for and with local councils and communities. Their first feature *Helen* (2008) takes a lost girl as a figure of the no-places created in British cities by postwar urban planning. Filmed across multiple cities, supported by multiple local councils and regional arts organizations, the film's production mirrors the utter displacement of their central character, Helen (Annie Townsend), who is in foster care like *The Unloved*'s Lucy.

Helen is even more profoundly not herself: she is about to leave the care system and school with no further support. In her dislocation, she is acting in a police reconstruction, wearing the jacket and walking the last steps of a missing girl called Joy. Helen becomes a tourist in Joy's middle-class world, in her family, in her subjectivity and in the brilliantly green copse of trees where her last known movements took place. Staring up at the night sky in the final shot, Helen is also the Helen of classical myth, whom Euripides says was transformed into a constellation. Through Helen, contemporary Britain becomes foreign to itself, a place of both utter poverty of opportunity and a starry wealth of possibility.

Imagining Otherwise

For all its social realism, contemporary British feminist cinema is an imaginatively liberating project. Like borders between nations, or the line between modes of film production, even the distinction between the real and the dreamed is shown to be part of the entrenchment of systemic hierarchy that has to be overcome. The films I've described here form a cinema that is pushing not only at the boundaries between documentary and fiction, or experimenta and narrative, or between nations, but also at those between past, present and future.

Maja Borg's *Future My Love* does this aesthetically by including clips from her earlier short 'Ottica Zero' (2007), which is about imagining a utopian future. In the short, actress Nadya Cazan rejects her opportunity for media celebrity, travelling to Venus, Florida, to seek out innovator and inventor Jacque Fresco, who has developed his resource-based economics over half a century. In *Future My Love*, Borg looks for the lost future that she and Cazan were planning to share, revisiting the Venus Project after their break-up. Along with *Perestroika*, Borg's film is part of a strikingly communitarian and cosmopolitan new British lesbian fiction feature cinema, represented by independent filmmakers Campbell X, Lisa Gornick (*Do I Love You?*, 2002), Shamim Sarif (*The World Unseen*, 2007; *I Can't Think Straight*, 2008) and Kanchi Wichmann (*Break My Fall*, 2011), one that entwines liberatory politics and liberated modes of filmmaking. Their films revivify the future the New Queer Cinema imagined, and their new sexual politics are central to chapter ten.

Like Fresco, Borg has devoted energy to imagining a future that is at once personal and political, and the film investigates what happens to these imagined futures when they go unrealized. Love, philosophy, engineering and popular science documentary flow together as forms that can conjure futures, and still contain them even when they don't come to pass. Borg's voiceover, which shares a poetic first-person oblique with Sarah Turner's in *Perestroika*, keeps *Future My Love* moving forward even as it oscillates back and forth through futures past.

In the same way that they use a first-person oblique narration or point of view, the films in this chapter also have a distinctive time signature that sets them apart from the linear continuities of previous social realism. It's obviously there in *Future My Love*, with its stated objective of understanding what happens to our imagination as futures pass us by; and similarly in *Perestroika*, as it likewise physically revisits the sites of memories, layering in archival footage. It's there in Longinotto's and Woolcock's archival jaunts, which take roughly chronological routes through the cinematic century, but also – like the beating of waves on a beach, or of the heart – have a rhythmic pulse that depends on graphic matches and thematic and musical repetitions to deroute any straightforward narrative of Progress.

It's there in *The Unloved*, where all time consists of waiting, flecked with hard, bright chips of painful memory, so that the past – where Lucy was with her parents – feels more real than the bland, washed-out present. It's there, differently, in the entwined temporalities of *Dreams of a Life*, in Joyce Vincent's dreamy Schrödinger's cat-like alive/dead simultaneity. It's not just that films like *The Arbor* are alive to the past, in the manner of skilful and moving historical dramas such as *Pride* (Matthew Warchus, 2014), as that, through their hybridity and ambiguity, the past is alive in them. Moreover, the films are alive with a particular, delicate and impassioned attention to the continual erasure of the stories of girls and women from the historical record.

When we think of stories of the Cuban Missile Crisis, we think of invasions, confrontations and war rooms: an historical set piece, populated by white male decision-makers. Potter's *Ginger and Rosa* (2012) considers the intimate impact of those global events on two teenage girls in London in 1962. Born in August 1945, when the US Army bombed Hiroshima and Nagasaki (an image of which opens the film), Ginger (Elle Fanning) and Rosa (Alice Englert) grow up intertwined with the Bomb. Although they are distant from any fall-out, albeit still surrounded by World War II bomb sites, Ginger feels both fear and responsibility. While the film is entirely set in London, it has the international(e) consciousness that marks Potter's oeuvre. And although linear, its temporality is as subtly diffuse as its geography. In Ginger's world, the Cuban Missile Crisis is not just an end-stopped historical non-event: it is the ongoing, daily prelude to the end of the world. Potter uses radio broadcasts and Campaign for Nuclear Disarmament (CND) meetings to connect Ginger to the rest of the world, and simultaneously to create the ominous and pervasive feeling that, just as teenage Ginger is discovering it, that larger world is about to be annihilated.

There is no reassuring invocation of the future, nor the knowing counter-historical machinations seen in the previous year's *X Men: First Class* (Matthew Vaughn, 2011), which climaxes with the Missile Crisis. Ginger lives, immediately, on the brink of erasure. At once a costume drama and a science fiction film, *Ginger and Rosa* captures a moment in which a global resistance embodied in individual courage dared to imagine otherwise – an otherwise that became our world today. It's a subtle use of both genres, and a slight but profound shift of both temporal and political consciousness. If the US and Russia did not fire nuclear weapons at each other from Cuba, then protest movements must work as Ginger believes they can, despite the discouraging note sounded in mainstream media. Our very existence aligns us with her and her political energy, towards changing the world.

Like Lucy, Mia, Nasrine, Joyce and the other runaway girls of British cinema, Ginger is an everygirl in everyday clothes. Her fisherman's sweater and jeans, blending into the London greys, contrast with the beautiful, finessed production and costume design of the contemporaneous *An Education* (Lone Scherfig, 2009), which pitches the 1960s as swinging and sheeny, even as it unveils their seamy side. Like Jenny (Carey Mulligan) in Scherfig's adaptation of Lynn Barber's memoir, Ginger's best friend Rosa gets involved with an untrustworthy bohemian older man (Ginger's father Roland [Alessandro Nivola]), a storyline that harks back to *A Taste of Honey*. But in Potter's film, the social realist attention to taboo subjects is a sideshow. Rosa's dilemma is filtered through Ginger's point of view, in which the bombshell her friend drops and the bombs hovering over the Americas are dual and related threats.

Arrested at a CND march, Ginger refuses to confess to the police and is left to meditate in her prison cell, in a series of shots reminiscent of medieval illuminations of saints, losing (herself in) time. When she is released, she tells her assembled alternative family (mother, father, gay godfathers, gay godfathers' poet friend) about Rosa and Roland. The bomb explodes – and is survived. In a meaningful sense, within the film's narration, Ginger's dramatic speaking of the truth – and her subsequent decision to ask Rosa's forgiveness – are the direct actions that prevent the Russian and American missiles from firing. Speaking out (not confession but declaration, on her own terms) and forgiveness can and do change the future.

Contemporary British feminist cinema is deeply concerned with trauma, not as a spectacle, but as a route to representational justice. These films are urgently seeking a survivable response that will allow their characters, and our culture, to recover without becoming 'can do'. Through their development of first person oblique narration, they offer a way to reclaim girlhoods without being contained by them, and to reclaim the night without being punished for doing so. A film such as *Ginger and Rosa* negotiates perceptively through the double binds of public/private and visible/invisible, not least through its attention to the secrets of the archive that allow for a thoroughgoing re-vision of historical girlhoods. It is an unsettled and unsettling cinema, a contrast to Britain's settler history, a postnational cinema that foregrounds a commitment to risk, to being in motion, to tending the edges, to dreaming across borders, to a necessary poetics of the everyday. It has ripped off the bodices of heritage drama in order to rewrite history.

6

All Dressed Up

Costume Drama Loosens its Corset

Belle

Despite all those post-modern girls on the move, British 'women's cinema' is still tied, as far as distributors imagine audiences, to the corset strings of what is variously called heritage, costume, period and/or historical drama. In 2014, it's still the face of British commercial cinema, too, but a changing one: the cover of the BFI Film Fund's Diversity Guidelines features Amma Asante's film *Belle*. Asante's second feature connects gorgeous dresses to social justice, and lavish British period drama to the slave-labouring empire that funded eighteenth-century leisure culture, which produced and enabled the novels whose adaptations form the backbone of British costume drama.

In a rousing speech to the International Women's Film Festival Network at the Berlinale in 2015, Asante counterposed an alternate source for historical drama in relation to her own history:

> Well, the Asantes [of the Kingdom of Ghana] had their very own warrior Queen – much like Boudica. Her name was Yaa Asantewaa. When the menfolk of the Asante tribe lost hope and failed to rise up against their colonialist oppressors, it was Yaa Asantewaa who stood up, roused the troops, got on her horse, and led the Asante men into battle in a bid to protect the Asante legacy and kingdom.
>
> So it is from her stock that I derive. I like to think that any woman who chooses to enter into a world that is predominantly male and traditionally not seen as the territory of the 'woman' is herself a warrior queen. Not because we are at 'war', but because our battle is in facing challenges that at times may seem insurmountable.[1]

Asante draws on the West African griot tradition of oral storytelling to relate her ancestry, connecting often-ignored pre-colonial African history to the anti-colonial struggle, both of which are continued in her work as a post-colonial filmmaker.

Post-colonial critique is the work of the feminist costume drama, which allows both for aesthetic commitment and rigorous politics and brooks no contradiction between them. Rachel Perkins' musical *Bran Nue Dae* (2010) is a wildly popular example: set in 1969, the film focuses on an Aboriginal community and critiques white racism and the Church, yet it entered the all-time top 50 Australian films at the national box office.[2] Although initially a male coming-of-age drama, it highlights Willie's (Rocky McKenzie) relationship with his mother Theresa (Ningali Lawford, a member of the original stage cast from 1989), and opens up a view of *her* 1950s girlhood. Like *Ginger and Rosa* and *The Arbor*, the films here imagine history's girlhoods, reclaiming history itself as feminist and female-identified. Historical drama is, of course, a powerful site for feminist genealogy, for making visible connections and legacies to suffuse the viewer with plenitude, where scarcity is usually the rule of the day. It often shows women joining together, even if this begins in conversations about men and matrimony, to create the changes that still resonate today.

Importantly, those changes are intersectional, striking at the whitewashed and upper-class presumptions of the mainstream heritage drama. On the BFI guideline's front cover, Belle (Gugu Mbatha-Raw) is (re)framed giving something offscreen the side-eye, presumably the persistent inequality in international filmmaking, including historical drama.[3] Asante's *Belle* was the first of three 2014 UK theatrical releases with Black British female directors, a banner year in a shameful history. Destiny Ekharagha (*Gone Too Far*) and debbie tucker green (*Second Coming*) became, respectively, only the third and fourth Black British women to have full-length features in theatrical distribution, after Asante (*A Way of Life*) and Ngozi Onwurah (*Welcome II the Terrordome*, 1995).[4]

The BFI's 'three tick' guidelines build on a diversity audit for funded productions that has led to the increase in women of colour behind the camera in the UK. Covering every aspect of film production – onscreen diversity (subject matter, lead character, prominent supporting characters); offscreen diversity (director, screenwriter, composer, DOP; all heads of department; crew; production company staff); opportunities and social mobility (*paid* internships; training and skills; progression) – they have been hailed internationally as a model for the development of a truly equal cinema.[5] This is representational justice in action, and *Belle* – in the person of Belle – is deservedly its icon.

It has particular implications for British productions of costume/heritage drama. As actor David Harewood intimated in a 2008 *Guardian* article that slowly led to talk of action on diversity in UK television in 2014, costume dramas remain prestige film and television productions, and they tend to favour all-white casts,

All Dressed Up: Costume Drama Loosens its Corset

Fig. 17: *Belle*, cover star of BFI Film Fund Diversity Guidelines

even when this is proven to be historically inaccurate.[6] Likewise, they tend to portray women as possessing only affective agency, in contradistinction to feminist historians' work, as described by Kameron Hurley, on recovering narratives of female and/or trans* and intersex soldiers and pirates, as well as female and/or trans* and intersex workers, artists and campaigners.

Contemporary British novels such as Jackie Kay's *Trumpet*, about an imagined female jazz trumpeter who lived, loved and worked as a man, or Ali Smith's *How to Be Both*, which imagines a similarly transvestite, queer life for artist Francesco della Cossa, both await their Sally Potter.[7] Rose Tremain's *Sacred Country*, with its sweeping account of postwar Britain on the coattails of swashbuckling Mary (who will be Martin), has found the perfect adapter in Jan Dunn, with support from actor Shirley Henderson, but the film is still at the fundraising stage.[8] Despite excitement online, rumours that Sofia Coppola would be adapting Sarah Water's *Tipping the Velvet* for the big screen with Beyoncé and Eva Longoria proved baseless.[9]

British plays exploring such histories have yet to receive the *History Boys* (Alan Bennett, 2004) screen treatment (Nicholas Hytner, 2008). Where are the film versions of *Mother Clap's Molly House* (Mark Ravenhill, 2001), set in an eighteenth-century London polysexual brothel, or *Her Naked Skin* (Rebecca Lenkiewicz, 2008), the first original play by a female writer to be presented on the largest stage at the National Theatre, about a suffragette in a lesbian relationship? European heritage drama zeroes in on a narrow class band in a narrow range of periods, tied to the emergence of the novel. Like the novel, it's predominantly addressed to a middle-class female audience. Yet, as Belén Vidal points out, heritage drama's 'relations with the past – as well as with its own generic past – is anything but static'.[10] Feminist filmmakers therefore might feel a specific charge to alter the costume drama, as well as a powerful charge in doing so.

Belle is a more than worthy talisman (and more than a worthy talisman) for both an emergent feminist historical drama and an emergent diverse British cinema. It is a film that tackles, at root, one of the most exclusionary – yet emblematic – national film genres. Its critique of the (mis)uses of history as nationalist propaganda emerges from the postcolonial project of rethinking European history. Asante points to the influence of Jamaican-born British cultural theorist Stuart Hall, telling Ashley Clark, 'It's the subtleties of a person like that existing. It's about the people he's empowered to speak about history in a manner that's creative and artistic. That spoke to me. He was like an uncle who just knows everything, who gives you self-esteem just by their existence'.[11]

In his article 'Cultural Identity and Cinematic Representation', Hall described the recovery of cultural identities through historical investigation as 'a very powerful and creative force in emergent forms of representation amongst hitherto marginalized peoples'.[12] He cites Frantz Fanon's account of what drives this force, a 'passionate research... directed by the secret hope of discovering beyond the misery of today, beyond self-contempt, resignation and abjuration, some very beautiful and splendid era whose existence rehabilitates us both in regard to ourselves and in regard to others'.[13]

Belle is a costume drama with a free eighteenth-century Black British woman in the lead role, a 'very beautiful and splendid' biographical subject who gives the lie to the wall-to-wall whitewash of historical dramas, rehabilitating the genre as she goes. The film premiered at Toronto in 2013 alongside *12 Years a Slave* (Steve McQueen, 2013). Kate Kellaway notes that, in terms of re-visioning history, *Belle* 'does what McQueen's film did not. It reminds us that the history of slavery belongs to Britain as well... In Georgian Britain, there were about 15,000 black people – mainly in London – and less than a third of that population was free'.[14]

Dido Belle Lindsay was the daughter of a freedwoman and a white aristocrat, and the adopted niece of Lord Mansfield (Tom Wilkinson), the Lord Chief Justice. At the centre of the film, Asante reflexively places the painting of a dual portrait, attributed to John Zoffany, of Dido and her cousin Elizabeth (Sarah Gadon), which is famously the first European painting to depict a person of colour on an equal eyeline with a white person.[15] Heritage drama is a supremely useful political animal because it catches our heritage – history, tradition, national narrative – in the act of being made.

The genre is also useful because its outline is so familiar, particularly to middlebrow female audiences. *Belle* had a highly successful independent release in the US, coming 'out of nowhere to manage a $10 million+ gross... all the more impressive because it came without the star power'.[16] Asante makes graceful, incisive use of every trope of the genre, from the costumes to the marriage narrative. In each instance, the trope is played and then shown to be played out. The film is a steely intelligence in a silk glove, a rigorous deconstruction of costume drama dressed up as a perfect example.

As Julianne Pidduck notes, 'many contemporary costume films... foreground the romantic desires and social aspirations of female protagonists against the constraints of convention, sexual repression and economic disadvantage'.[17] For Pidduck, this is the (post)feminist work that makes costume drama powerful: that it can render as history the intimate narrative of the novel, with its (often female) focus on subjectivity and affect. Emotional choices disrupt public personae: the stiff upper lip wobbles, and class myths are shaken.

To this end, *Belle* lives and breathes Jane Austen: Dido inherits her father's fortune, while Elizabeth is written out of her father's will; Elizabeth needs to marry well, Dido fears she will never marry at all. The cousins live in a world of women (some suspicious, some sustaining, all presented as rounded, motivated characters), chaperoned in public, subject to classed and gendered surveillance. *Belle* gives back political life and breath to Austen's economically-anxious heroines, who have been rendered safe entertainment by multiple chocolate-box adaptations, the edgiest of which is Emma Thompson's class-conscious screenplay for *Sense and Sensibility* (Ang Lee, 1995).

As if tackling the romantic heritage drama isn't enough, Asante places Dido's quest for full personhood in love within a broader drama. If you had seen the UK trailer you'd never know the film simultaneously covers Lord Mansfield's ruling on the case of the *Zong* massacre (1781), which is generally seen as the beginning of the end of British slavery. Mansfield nullified the insurance claim by the owners of the slave ship *Zong*, after it was revealed that the ship's crew had avoided taking on water and thrown living people overboard, on the reckoning that it was more cost-effective to claim insurance on their deaths than to keep them alive and sell them. Mansfield's ruling, historically, is read as being on the side of the insurers (and thus the market), rather than the drowned slaves.[18] Asante, however, makes the most of the opportunity to suggest that Mansfield's judicious phrasing in court is an attempt to satisfy his white, male, upper-class audience, but under the cover of a dry speech he is smuggling in the subversive intention true to his avuncular heart.

It is Dido who brings the testimony about the availability of water stations to her uncle's notice, after his clerk John Davinier (Sam Reid) shares the case papers with her. Love and justice entwine as Dido joins John and his radical abolitionist friends for debates in a pub in Kentish Town, then an insalubrious area of North London, transgressing class and gender decorum. Veiled hats, cloaks and carriages become Dido's spy/stealth-wear. The invisibility of her anomalous privilege allows her to move courageously around London, even as she works to undermine her own class, whose wealth rests – on this, the film is very clear – on plantation slavery and colonial expansionism.

'I have been blessed with freedom twice over, as a Negro and as a woman', Dido tells John. It is a statement of infinite power, because its meaning shifts as their working and romantic relationship progresses. When she proclaims it, during their walk along the grimy Regent's Canal behind the pub, it is in passionate defence of her good (economic) fortune, which has freed her from the social constraints of her skin colour and gender. But the statement resonates for John, as a working-poor second son of a churchman. It offers him an exhilarating realization: that it is *from* her marginalized position, not despite it, that she can live freedom fully. Belle's final, dramatic appearance in the courtroom where her uncle is sitting on the case, confirms this. She is the only woman present, and she takes her place in the public gallery rather than on the floor, foregoing prestige to stand in solidarity with freedmen, abolitionists and workers. It is this experience that leads her to ask John to marry her – reconfiguring the courtroom as a place of celebration and marriage as a route to freedom.

Before

Belle is a sister to Julie Dash's Riot Grrrl-era historical drama *Daughters of the Dust* (1991), the first feature film by an African American woman to be distributed theatrically in the USA. Her previous feature *Illusions* (1982), about an African American performer in 1940s Hollywood, was finally released on DVD in 2015. A dreamlike evocation of Gullah (creole) culture on the Sea Islands off Georgia in the early twentieth century, *Daughters* was nominated for the Grand Jury Prize at Sundance. Its making was the subject of a book co-written by Dash with bell hooks and Toni Cade Bambara, and Dash has recently revisited Gullah lands and history for *Travel Notes of a Geechee Girl*, a forthcoming documentary about Gullah-Geechee writer and activist Vertamae Smart-Grosvenor, who played the hair-braider in *Daughters* and was the inspiration for Bambara's play *The Johnson Girls* (1972).[19] *Daughters* marked the emergence of an African American feminist feature cinema immersed in remembering histories, which *Selma* continues, as Dash did with her TV film *The Rosa Parks Story* (CBS, 2002).

Asante's film bears close kinship with Dash's work, and realizes fully what's only hinted in the run of popular Riot Grrrl-era adaptations of canonical novels that followed Dash's lead: Potter's *Orlando*, Jane Campion's *The Portrait of a Lady* (1996), Patricia Rozema's *Mansfield Park* (1999), Mira Nair's *Vanity Fair* (2004) and most recently Andrea Arnold's *Wuthering Heights* and Chantal Akerman's cautionary anti-capitalist tale *Almayer's Folly* (2011). The protagonists of *Orlando* and *Vanity Fair*, in particular, are knowing subjects of the colonial era, post-colonially in on the genre joke. That intervention was taken up by English Civil War-set TV mini-series *The Devil's Whore* (Company Pictures/HBO/Power, Marc Munden, from a screenplay by Martine Brant and Peter Flannery, 2008), which flaunts its heroine Angelica's (Andrea Riseborough) feminist credentials by quoting shots from the closing scene of *Orlando*, in which the Angel (Jimmy Somerville) flies above a tree; and the post-credit scene of *The Piano*, showing Ada and Flora (Anna Paquin) landing on the beach.

Vidal argues that, although it is a nationalizing genre, heritage drama 'reconnect[s] British cinema to its European context'.[20] Within feminist cinema, the reconnection is global, via a critical address to European colonial history. There are strong references to colonialism in Dash's, Potter's, Rozema's, Nair's, Arnold's and Akerman's films and in Icelandic filmmaker Solveig Anspach's *Louise Michel: La Rebelle* (2010), in which the working-class Paris Communard, exiled to New Caledonia, joins the anti-colonial rebellion of the indigenous Kanaks. But it is in Deepa Mehta's *Earth* (1998) and *Water* (2005), and Sabiha Sumar's *Khumosh Pani* (*Silent Waters*, 2003) that the post-colonial costume drama fully takes form.

For all three films, the Partition of India and Pakistan in 1947 is the origin myth, as for Mira Nair's adaptation of *Midnight's Children* (2012). At once liberatory and traumatic, it shapes their female protagonists' stories. In *Water*, it offers a hopeful future to seven year old Chuyia (Sarala Kariyawasam), as I discuss later. *Earth* and *Silent Waters* are both concerned with protagonists whose identities and multicultural communities are shattered by Partition. Their use of dual time periods to reflect on its aftermath, in a telling formal conceit, questions the *post* in postcolonial. Both films use multiple time structures framed through the continuity of a female witness-narrator to reclaim the historical narrative. They don't obfuscate incidents of politicized violence but, instead of spectacularizing them, focus on their intimate impact and the possibility of survival.

In *Earth*, the adult voiceover narrator (Shabana Azmi) looks back nostalgically on her childhood in Lahore in 1947, while in the more complex 1979-set *Silent Waters*, Ayesha (Kiron Kher) has flashbacks. These are prompted by the arrival of a group of Sikhs in her Muslim village of Charki, in the Punjab, whose search for their families forces her to reveal to her son Saleem (Aamir Malik), a nascent *jihadi*, that she was raised Sikh and converted after being raped and imprisoned by a Muslim man after Partition. Ayesha commits suicide to save her son from shame, and her testimony about the violence of Partition is not carried into the present by Saleem. That role falls to Zubeida (Shilpa Shukla), who would have become Ayesha's daughter-in-law had Saleem not cast her aside. Zubeida's survival breaks the temporal fourth wall, placing Zubeida in our present, as Potter does with Orlando (Tilda Swinton). She is at once continuity and change: a transgenerational link to the violent events of Partition and, behind that, the British Empire; and a genealogical marker of the transformative impact of feminist courage *in extremis* such as Ayesha's.

What Zubeida offers within the diegesis of *Silent Waters* as a witness, Madeline Ivalu performed live at 2008 world premiere of *Before Tomorrow* (Marie-Hélène Cousineau and Madeline Ivalu, 2008) in Toronto. She took the stage in full ceremonial Inuit regalia, which she subsequently wore to collect the Telefilm Women in Film Award at the same festival in 2014.[21] Representing Arnait Video Productions, which grew out of the Women's Video Workshop of Igloolik, Ivalu – the film's co-writer, co-director and star – instantly made the audience aware that this would be an historical drama with a difference. The continuities between her costume for the premiere and her costume in the film challenge the way we traditionally think about not only costume drama, but history itself.

All Dressed Up: Costume Drama Loosens its Corset

Fig. 18: Madeline Ivalu and Marie-Hélène Cousineau, directors of *Before Tomorrow*, at Toronto International Film Festival, 2014

Even the phrase 'costume drama' suggests an ingrained and problematic distinction: costumes are what people (generally white, wealthy people) wore in the past; clothes are what we wear in the present. Ivalu's ceremonial stance acted as a dual reminder: firstly, that Inuit and other indigenous people are a living presence in contemporary culture; and relatedly, that there is a continuity between past and present, of which costume, performance, ritual and storytelling are all signs.

The third feature film to be shot in Inuktitut by Inuit filmmakers, *Before Tomorrow* was collaboratively adapted by the directors and Susan Avingaq from the Danish children's novel *For morgendagen* (*Before Tomorrow*) by Jørn Riel. Corinn Columpar notes that this is 'an act of pointed appropriation... refunctioning aspects of white authored contact narratives'.[22] In contrast to the 'contact' film by Arnait's brother production company Isuma, *The Journals of Knud Rasmussen* (Norman Cohn and Zacharias Kunuk, 2006), there are no white faces in *Before Tomorrow*. It is a more intimate film, focusing narrowly on the relationship between an elder, Ningiuq (Ivalu), and her grandson Maniq (played by Ivalu's real-life grandson Paul-Dylan Ivalu) as a small canvas on which to depict the coming of European colonialism around 1840 to what is now Nunavut, the federated Inuit territory of the Canadian High Arctic.

At the beginning of the film, Ningiuq and Maniq visit Apak (Peter Henry Arnatsiaq), who demonstrates his shiny new tool: a gleaming steel needle, which he says is far better for stitching skins than the old, brittle bone ones. Ningiuq is disquieted by the appearance of this and other strange objects, a premonition that is confirmed when she and Maniq return from an expedition to a remote island to find Apak and his entire community dead. As far as Ningiuq knows, she and Maniq are the last people alive in the world, and her time is running out.

Yet *Before Tomorrow*, in which Ningiuq retains screen presence and voice-over until the end, is not a simple, noble, cathartic *Last of the Mohicans* tragedy. It is tough, pragmatic and elegant, like Ivalu's regalia. Her appearance at TIFF to introduce the film confirms the survivance of Inuit community and culture through the determination of elders such as Ningiuq. For poet and theorist Gerald Vizenor (Anishinaabe), who appropriated the term from colonial legal jargon, 'Survivance is an active sense of presence, the continuance of native stories, not a mere reaction, or a survivable name. Native survivance stories are renunciations of dominance, tragedy and victimry'.[23] The film draws on and furthers Arnait's documentary work with women in Igloolik, collecting and recording the kind of traditional skills and stories Ningiuq passes on to Maniq, and through him, to the viewer. Survivance moves *through* the screen, transcending EuroWestern binaries of past and present, here and there, us and them. We are responsible to Ningiuq for carrying forward her family and her culture.

Belonging

That steel needle is seductive: it glints in the firelight as Apak (and later Ningiuq) wields it. It's also a reminder of one of the key metaphors for film spectatorship, suture. Suture, in cine-semiotics, is that which stops us noticing we are watching a film, particularly through editing that creates fixed relationships between shots, 'stitching' us into the diegetic world.[24] Feminist cinema has played with sewing since the 1970s, specifically in an attempt to make suture visible, and thus unstitch us from the cloth of conventional narrative cinema. Potter's *Thriller* (1979) is a radical costume drama in which we are asked to think, closely, about what it means that *La bohème*'s Mimi was a piece-worker, sewing flowers in an attic, her poverty romanticized by Giacomo Puccini and his contemporary counter-culture.

Before Tomorrow parallels the flashing needle with the gun, smallpox and alcohol as a weapon of colonialism – but one that, like the film camera, can be appropriated by a skilled and canny female elder. Mexican indigenous filmmaker Teofilia Palafox describes this practice, drawing a parallel between craft textiles (traditionally associated with women) and moving image technology: 'I am an artisan, I hand-weave, and I express my way of thinking in my weaving. We work with our hands like a woman film-maker does... That impulse makes us sense how to communicate using the medium we have at hand'.[25] Ningiuq's skill with the needle is a metaphor and reminder of the Arnait Collective's skill with the camera; at the same time, it boldly puts textile craft on a par with filmmaking as an art practice.

A textile cinema is palpable in Campion's *Bright Star*, set a world away (and yet connected via Empire) in late eighteenth-century London, firmly in Austenland. Hers is a story, however, in which our historical knowledge creates no expectation of marriage. Fanny Brawne (Abbie Cornish) takes pride in her millinery and dressmaking skills as equal to her neighbour John Keats' (Ben Whishaw) poetics – possibly, she implies, better, given that her skills can earn her a living. The needle is a flashpoint of female identity, a signifier of the conjunction of labour, craft and art, as well as a more abstract symbol, as in the Sleeping Beauty myth, of the implied risks of female sexuality. Fanny – as her flashing needlework implies – is in control of her sexuality, and the film suggests that it was this confident young woman who opened up a metaphorical and spiritual erotic dimension for the poet, leading him to his best work. She is more than the traditional Muse: she is a fellow artist, whose embroidery has to be read as a form of visual art, performance art, or even poetry itself.

Through Fanny's designs, *Bright Star* implies an aesthetic prehistory of feminist cinema in other media, using costume drama to construct a genealogy of feminist art practices that are absent from mainstream history, so that a feminist film history could stretch back through Fanny Brawne's patterns and Ningiuq's hides to the first cave-paintings, now thought to have been made by women.[26] While critiques of the costume drama often take aim at exactly those qualities of dress, design and decoration that are considered feminine or feminized, such accounts ignore how powerfully costume and its associated domestic arts shape our narratives of the past. Moreover, their pleasures are joyfully cinematic. As Elizabeth Watkins writes about Campion's *The Portrait of a Lady*, 'the staid surface of the film's generic costume drama codes is inflected by distractions. It is permeated by a myriad of reflections and fleeting impressions... while the musical score is threaded with tiny sounds and fragments, of leaves rustling, of the inhalation of breath, of fingers drumming'.[27] In creating fully realized sensoria, costume dramas can transport us into the embodied experience of our foremothers, reminding us of emotional and affective continuities even as they may recall for us how far we have come.

There aren't many well-known female visual artists available for the period drama biopic treatment. Agnès Merlet's *Artemisia* (1997) has a sensual appeal for its portrait of the artist as a young, vulnerable woman, although it depends for its drama on bodice-ripping rather than charcoal sketching. Gillian Armstrong's *My Brilliant Career* (1979) and Campion's *An Angel at My Table* (1990) set up the pioneering female writers who are their biopic subjects, Miles Franklin and Janet Frame, as analogies for filmmakers, offering fresh Antipodean correctives to the burden of history that often waylays European historical cinema.

In a similar vein, Julie Taymor's *Frida* (2002) set the screen on fire with a study of a postcolonial brilliant career. Frida Kahlo (Salma Hayek) was not only a female artist of colour, but notably bisexual, polyamorous, transvestite, disabled, Communist and allied to indigenous culture. Such a protagonist was a courageous statement in the USA in 2002; of course, Kahlo dies tragically, thus palliating conservative anxieties. Taymor and Campion opt for similar formal strategies to show their heroines moving through the world, connecting New Women on the move to the new technology of cinema. In *Portrait*, Campion shows Isabel's (Nicole Kidman) pre-marital travels as a black and white, under-cranked insert, while Taymor pastiches early and Surrealist film to trail Kahlo through Europe, rekindling the 'shock of the new' that accompanied Kahlo's innovative work on its first exhibition.

Taymor uses inventive techniques to explore Kahlo's self-portraiture and its relation to cinema, having Hayek under step into and out of the paintings, and – in an electrifying scene – hear Lila Downs sing a tango that acts as a soliloquy for her internal state. Kahlo's homosociality, including and beyond her sexual relationships with women, is vital. The women in the film, including Tina Modotti (Ashley Judd) and Josephine Baker (uncredited), are mirrors like her self-portraits, and correctives to the tokenist frame in which Kahlo and her international success are usually placed.

As with many biopics of female artists, Taymor's story is predicated on the duel between love and art, with a tension between Kahlo's relationships with women (including herself) and her lifelong affair with Diego Rivera (Alfred Molina). But the film celebrates the way in which she made art from her intellectual and affective struggles with monogamy and desire, heralding her as a modern(ist) woman. George Sand (Juliette Binoche) confronts a similar struggle, albeit from a more comfortable class position, in Diane Kurys' *Les enfants du siècle* (*Children of the Century*, 1999), while model Bettie Page (Gretchen Mol) navigates both class anxiety and a lack of love due to an abusive childhood in *The Notorious Bettie Page* (Mary Harron, 2006).

Harron's film is a powerful example of the centrality of costume and clothing in feminist historical films; in *Page*, famous for removing her clothes, Harron has the perfect figure to enquire into costume drama's fetishism of the female form and its trappings, Stella Bruzzi's 'sexual model [of heritage drama] that looks *at* clothes, privileging sexuality and eroticism'.[28] *The Notorious Bettie Page* is a costume drama turned inside out, in which the corset is kinky, but explicitly shown as worn for the pleasure of male viewers rather than the female subject. As with *Belle* and *Frida*, *The Notorious Bettie Page* navigates a double quandary in depicting a token woman with power, either social or cultural, who is simultaneously an object of the gaze.

Non-artist historical biopics have to confront the princess problem: the fact that the historical record, and thus historical drama, favours the white, wealthy and/or well-known. With *Marie Antoinette* (2006) and *The Countess* (2009) respectively, Sofia Coppola and Julie Delpy both chose historical 'bad girls' who (appear to) call the princess role into question. Marie Antoinette (Kirsten Dunst) was reviled for metaphorically doing what Countess Elisabeth Bathory (Delpy) was said to have done literally, sucking the lifeblood of the peasantry.

The most interesting element of *The Countess* is the presentation of Bathory as a canny businesswoman whose title refers as much to her concerns with accounting as her aristocracy. Whereas Moynan King's play *Bathory* (2000) draws a darkly sexy and poetic charge from playing the Countess as a Gothic lesbian heroine twisted by the youth-obsessed pressures of patriarchal culture, Delpy's film shies away from homoeroticism, suggesting that Bathory is obsessed instead with a young male lover. The film can just about be read as an allegory for the fears of a contemporary A-list performer, haunted by cautionary tales about female ambition and anxiety about ageing. In common with many post-feminist heroines, Bathory is a rebel without a well-defined cause, and with no female allies; she drives away her loyal servant Anna Darvulia, played by Annamaria Marinca, acclaimed for her performance as the loyal best friend in *4 Months, 3 Weeks and 2 Days* (Cristian Mungiu, 2007).

The Countess luxuriates in Gothic gloom, perhaps portending Bathory's eventual fate: being walled alive in her room. Delpy's film certainly erases the camp, hypersexual associations of previous B-movies concerning Bathory, but cannot find a fully complex narrative with which to replace it. Like Delpy, Coppola wants to have her cake and eat it with *Marie Antoinette*. These post-feminist films tell us that the legends of these girls' badness are true, but conflate their aristocratic excesses with a form of rebellion that accords more closely with contemporary feminism. Thus the wealthy, white protagonists elicit our sympathy through their run-ins with patriarchy, and their privilege is elided. Coppola dots the luxurious textures of the conventional costume drama with neon highlights: the cross-cutting between shoes and cakes to Bow Wow Wow's 'I Want Candy' is an indictment of how the acquisitiveness for which Marie Antoinette was beheaded has become part and parcel of our daily lives. At the same time it makes shopping and eating look really, really good. Complicitous critique is always present in Coppola's beautifully executed films, where a cool and withdrawn intelligence surveys the excesses, but thus also presents the seductions, of turbo-capitalism.

In *Annie Leibovitz: Life Through a Lens* (Barbara Leibovitz, 2006), we see the legendary photographer arranging a photoshoot at Versailles for *Marie Antoinette*. All the inherent post-feminist contradictions are on view, in the excitement of watching a female artist take power – but using it to celebrate wealth, whiteness, thinness and heteronormativity, as if having learned nothing from Marie Antoinette's fate. As Anna Backman Rogers notes, 'Coppola delineates how that body is harnessed and regulated via ritualistic processes: how it is turned into a spectacle and, by extension, a commodity to be owned by a patriarchal institution and, then, by the state'.[29] She observes that Coppola focuses on the pre-history of the Queen, a portrait of a young woman stripped (literally, as well as figuratively) of her self in order to serve the state. The film contains a powerful admonition about the continued reification and depersonalization of young women, and the isolation of being a white feminist glass ceiling-smasher. It demystifies the princess paradigm without quite de-glamorizing it.

Feminist costume dramas emerge between longing and belonging: a longing for a more expansive feminist genealogy, one in which historical belonging is less predicated on being wealthy, white, cis, straight and able-bodied. Cheryl Dunye sums up the longing (and her postmodern solution) at the end of her first feature *The Watermelon Woman* (1996). The closing credits state: 'Sometimes you have to create your own history'. The film follows an African American lesbian filmmaker called Cheryl (Dunye) as she does exactly that, including a visit to the (fictional) Centre for Lesbian Information and Technology (C.L.I.T.), a loving parody of the real Lesbian Herstory Archives, 'demonstrating the important place of the archive in the lesbian popular imaginary', as Ann Cvetkovich points out.[30] Cheryl discovers the hidden-in-plain-sight historical figure of Fae 'The Watermelon Woman' Richards (Lisa Marie Bronson), an African American lesbian actor of the 1940s. While Richards' director-lover Martha Page (Alex Juhasz) is loosely based on the historical figure of Dorothy Arzner, the Hollywood filmmaker whose rediscovery kicked off feminist film theory in the 1970s, Richards is an imagined figure, fusing hints from Hollywood history with the cultural history of African American lesbian life.

Belle and *Bright Star* deal with documented historical figures: Fanny walked on Hampstead Heath only a few decades after Dido, and may well even have seen her portrait at Kenwood House. Yet in each case, the documentation is minimal and external: we do not have Fanny's or Dido's diaries, letters or creative writing on which to draw. They belong in history, but it takes a feminist longing to place them there, stitching them in through both research and invention. While both films use classical film semantics such as seamless editing and linear narrative, they foreground the rustle and touch of textures and gestures in order to disrupt our easy assimilation of the story, and remind us that something new and different is taking place on screen. They insist that history is a stitch-up by the victors, and, simultaneously, that we have the power and the tools to refashion it to our own ends.

Beside

Kelly Reichardt's *Meek's Cutoff* takes its title from a geographical feature named after Stephen Meek, by himself, a conscious indicator that the film is immersed in the white European history of colonialism, and – like *The Piano* – is decolonizing history from a white feminist perspective. It sets out to 'Tell all the truth but tell it slant', as Emily Dickinson advised, in a poem written in the decades after the film's events.[31] Deadpan, the film uses Meek's claim in its title while undermining it by revealing him as a blundering bully who took credit for others' work. According to the film, the life-saving cutoff is located through an alliance between pioneer wife Emily Tetherow (Michelle Williams) and an unnamed Cayuse man (Ron Rondeaux), based an historical encounter recorded in trail diaries.

Reichardt worked with Kristen Parr, language instructor with the Confederated Tribes of the Umatilla Indian Reservation, who include the Cayuse, to shape Rondeaux's character and write his dialogue.[32] In the film's end credits, Reichardt also lists research material including women's diaries kept by regional women's history archives. There is a strong sense of the meeting-point – not necessarily in solidarity, but in negotiation – between these two erased histories: that of pioneer women, and that of the indigenous nations of the unceded West.

Reichardt framed the film's project as asking: 'What would John Wayne's character look like from [the perspective of] the woman that served his soup?'[33] She noted that, in contrast to male-dominated mainstream archival holdings, on the pioneer trail,

> women were the diary keepers and the diaries offer such a specific take on the history… [and] the loneliness women felt… The exceptions seemed to be the friendships the women formed with each other. You also get the sense that the diaries are the only thing besides the weather that mark the passing of time. The journey seems trance-like with each long day bleeding into the next.[34]

That diffuse temporality sets Reichardt's film apart from the majority of action-oriented westerns. As the men are mainly indolent, fractious and lost, the passing of time is relayed through the closely observed, repetitive tasks that are the women's responsibilities: cooking, sewing, praying and caring.

In its re-visioning of the western, it follows on from the brief revival of the genre after Clint Eastwood's *Unforgiven* (1992). Yet where *Bad Girls* (Jonathan Kaplan, 1994) became a post-feminist camp cult classic, the far more serious and interesting *The Ballad of Little Jo* (Maggie Greenwald, 1993) has all but disappeared. Greenwald uses the trope of the good woman from out East, but rather than a bride or schoolmarm who civilizes the pioneers, Josephine Monaghan (Suzy Amis) is sent out West after disgracing her family by bearing a child outside marriage. After a violent assault, she decides to live as a man in a frontier town. Having cut hir hair and stolen male clothes, Jo, an uncanny mash-up of hir 1993 costume drama contemporaries Ada and Orlando, initially attracts the attention of miner Percy (Ian McKellen, in his first out film role) and later lives with Tinman Wong (David Chung), a Chinese drifter who is as excluded by his ethnicity as Jo is by hir uncertain gender status.

Less post-modern in form than *The Piano* or *Orlando*, Greenwald's queering is perceived less as part of a radical engagement with Jack Halberstam's 'perverse presentism',[35] and more as part of a softly-softly alternative 'American Girl'-type history. Jocelyn Moorhouse's *How to Make an American Quilt* (1995) exemplifies this trend, with its historical inserts stitching together more than a century of women's interracial intimacy from the Freedom Railroad to the quilting circle of its present day. Reichardt and Greenwald, like Campion and Ivalu, choose to show the underside of history's stitching through a particularly quietist narrative mode, one in which feeling rather than action is the motor.

By contrast, *Deliver* (2008), Jennifer Montgomery's remake of *Deliverance* (John Boorman, 1972), jumps feet-first into the implications of physical violence and narrative spectacle as a response to the twenty-first-century's mediatized violence.

Montgomery shot the film on digital video on a micro-budget with a cast of older lesbian feminist filmmakers, including Peggy Ahwesh and Su Friedrich, taking the central (male) roles. In an interview with Penny Lane, Montgomery points to the post-9/11 hyper-militarized context for her project, exactly as Susan Faludi lays it out in *The Terror Dream*:

> We were at war when [James] Dickey wrote *Deliverance* [1970] and we are at war now. [His characters] were men heading towards middle age, and they're questioning their use value in wartime. Part of their trip out to nature was about reconfiguring or reclaiming their masculinity. The current wars in Iraq and Afghanistan are so pervasive that obviously it inflects contemporary art practice.[36]

Montgomery's punk aesthetic and immersion in radical lesbian experimental cinema bring her to strangely similar source material to Greenwald. The western remains the primary genre for understanding dominant US culture, a richly contradictory resource for its ability to surface stories of resistance by women, Native Americans, indentured Chinese labourers and queer and trans* people. Their glancing – but compelling – presence in mainstream versions of the narrative allows for these radical retellings.

Becoming

Although it's an historical drama grounded in primary sources, *Meek's Cutoff* feels like a premonition of the apocalyptic result of a toxic admixture of racist imperialism and misogynist fundamentalist Christianity that returned after 9/11. It could almost be read as at once a form of backstory for and a follow-up to Margaret Atwood's *The Handmaid's Tale* (filmed by Volker Schlondorff, 1990).[37] Like *Ginger and Rosa*, it is a tender take on history that, by challenging genre norms, displaces events from our expectations and untethers them from linear time. Emily Tetherow's experience could be a 'terror dream' of our future rather than our past, a warning about repeating forgotten history if the careful work of feminist archivists, theorists, historians and artists is once again neglected, devalued and obscured.

Margarethe von Trotta has made a career of such warnings, rendering the sub-genre of the biopic of the female political or intellectual radical her own. While not all prominent women, or indeed their biopics, are necessarily feminist (Margaret Thatcher in *The Iron Lady*, for example), von Trotta is always concerned to show the development of her subjects as political animals, particularly their intellectual processes as they think their way into public action. Theirs is a lonely life, however, in which solidarity is fleeting and often betrayed; their political formation is internal, disconnected. As Ania Ostrowska observes in her review of *Hannah Arendt* (2012), 'the act of thinking is suggested by the heroine's constant smoking, often combined with staring in space while lying on a day bed'.[38] This is perhaps because von Trotta's Arendt (Barbara Sukowa) is isolated. Despite powerful, intellectual female friends such as Mary McCarthy (Janet McTeer), 'Arendt rejected solidarity built on the fact of shared gender'.[39] As Arendt, Sukowa also carries the aura of an earlier performance as a Jewish intellectual for von Trotta, as Rosa Luxemburg (*Rosa Luxemburg*, 1986), of which Vincent Canby notes, 'The film is, surprisingly, most effective when Luxemburg is alone... Though she was a spectacular demonstration of the liberated woman, she had little interest in organized feminism'.[40] Von Trotta's lonely heroines have much of the Strong Female Character (SFC) about them, examining the paradox of the liberated woman who resists solidarity.

As in other genres, the solitary is more evident than solidarity, particularly for SFCs. While singular female achievers are acceptable even by Hollywood standards (especially if they are lonely or punished), fears of the 'monstrous regiment of women' haunts attempts to examine female solidarity and organizing. Morgan, who scripted *The Iron Lady*, wrote the screenplay for *Suffragette* (Sarah Gavron, 2015), a prestige production with BFI Film Fund support, permitted to shoot in Parliament.[41] Suffragettes have emerged as the acceptable face of feminist politics in conventional costume drama in the last few years, showing up as in HBO's *Iron Jawed Angels* (Katja von Garnier, 2004), a mini-series about US suffrage, and as comedic characters in the UK in *Parade's End* (BBC/HBO, Susanna White, 2012) and *Up the Women* (Baby Cow, Jessica Hynes, 2013).

There is proto-suffragism in the enjoyable but self-contradictory Edwardian romcom *Hysteria* (Tanya Wexler, 2011), a film about the invention of the vibrator that mocks and objectifies female sexuality. Wealthy reformer Charlotte Dalrymple (Maggie Gyllenhaal) makes marvellous firebrand socialist speeches within a film that, eventually, literally imprisons her. Its attempt to smuggle feminist rhetoric into the depiction of female-sexuality-for-laffs is reminiscent of the post-feminist argument made by girlfriends Atafeh and Shireen (Nikohl Boosheri and Sarah Kazemy) in *Circumstance* (Maryam Keshavarz, 2011). They claim that *Sex and the City* (Michael Patrick King, 2008) is more radical than *Milk* (Gus Van Sant, 2008) because it's more accessible and less likely to be censored.

Post-feminist heritage romcoms aside, there is an urgent, feminist intersectional commitment to recovering and restaging a people's living history that is

All Dressed Up: Costume Drama Loosens its Corset

within oral memory but whose contours are fading from view. Tanya Hamilton utilizes the classic US indie lovers-on-the-run genre for *Night Catches Us* (2010), which rehumanizes the demonized Black Panthers, as well as recovering women's involvement in radical African American politics. Ava DuVernay's *Selma* not only recentres women in the story of Martin Luther King Jr.'s organizing, but was released at a critical moment. The film's portrayal of the march on Selma responds to the repeal of the Voting Rights Act in 2013, but also, inadvertently, to the street protests in the face of police brutality in Ferguson, and elsewhere in the summer of 2014. DuVernay and her cast made that explicit when they wore iconic 'I Can't Breathe' T-shirts to the *Selma* New York premiere, days after a grand jury decided not to indict the NYPD officer who choked Eric Garner to death.[42]

Manohla Dargis visited the *Selma* set during the recreation of the first march from Selma on 7 March 1965, known as Bloody Sunday because of brutal police violence. Watching the filmmaker at work, she sees: 'A centrifugal force [who] rarely seemed to stop moving… it was thrilling to witness a female director bring this agonizing American story to life and, in the process, stake her own claim on our cultural history'.[43] DuVernay's claim does not only come through contemporary resonances, but through her precise realization of the time of the events. While detailed production design is crucial, it's the way in which she allows scenes to extend following the slow rhythms of King's delivery and movement that makes history. She uses slow motion only three times, in each case for a close up on a protestor subject to racist violence – the first being an older woman, Annie Lee Cooper (Oprah Winfrey). King and President Lyndon Johnson (Tom Wilkinson, assaying a similar role to his sympathetic power figure in *Belle*) constantly spar about who has the right to define time: the right time to pass a voting act, or how much time remains before events in Selma explode. The deadline of King's assassination hangs over the story; therefore DuVernay invites David Oyelowo to take up time, and invites the audience to take part in his time, to take his time into ours.

Feminist historical dramas engage not just with past facts but with the live present, and with histories of utopian potential that have yet to be actualized. *Water*, the conclusion to Mehta's elements trilogy despite being chronologically the earliest film, ends with a note of possible alteration to time itself. Mehta said of her chosen moment: 'I set the film in the 1930s but the people in the film live their lives as it was prescribed by a religious text more than 2000 years old. Even today, people follow these texts, which is one reason why there continue to be millions of widows'.[44] In the final sequence, the child widow Chuyia is taken to see Mahatma Gandhi arrive at the railway station in Varanasi, after the announcement of the repeal of laws concerning widows. The modern train and the ancient traditions co-incide and reshape each other on Indian, rather than Western, terms. Like Carol Morley's use of the footage of Joyce Vincent at Mandela's speech in *Dreams of a Life*, this scene is a powerful reminder that women have always been present in the making of history and liberated by their participation therein.

The very assertion of an active feminist presence is a suspension of received history, destabilizing both gender norms and national and transnational grand narratives. After 9/11, when history stopped ending, this became less a playful post-modern conceit (as it is in *Orlando*) and more a necessary, death-defying wager: there *has* to be a place for women in the past, so that there can be a place for them in our present and future. By constructing a counter-heritage cinema, filmmakers are building the filmic equivalent of the mysterious house at the centre of Shirin Neshat's *Zanan-e bedun-e mardan (Women without Men*, 2009), in which four outcast women create an anarchic anti-state within the state during and after the 1953 CIA-backed coup d'état in Iran. Neshat's film, adapted from the banned novel by Sharnush Parsipur (who lived in Neshat's garage when she was initially exiled to the USA), combines newsreel footage and floating girls to engender historical fantasy.[45] The house and its occasionally dead inhabitants may be subject to the symbolic logic of magic realism, but they are rooted in the historical.

History and fantasy are not – and for feminists, cannot be – distinct, as Joan Scott explores in *The Fantasy of Feminist History*.[46] Established histories tend to omit both what was and what could have been, insofar as it challenged the status quo, and thus we need to reimagine it. '#Filmherstory, a new Twitter hashtag started [in March 2015] by female critics and filmmakers Lexi Alexander, Miriam Bale, Shaula Evans, and Catrin Cooper, is providing a nice counterbalance to the ever-boring narrative of the biopic about a white guy who did something by highlighting a range of women across eras, countries, and ethnicities who led incredible lives'.[47]

Biopics of writer and activist Charlotte Perkins Gilman, poet and performer E. Pauline Johnson (Tekahionwake), or Lili'uokalani, first (and last) queen of Hawaii, could follow *Belle* in providing all the sensuous pleasures of costume drama while debunking the genre's insistence on a singular History. They would take us beyond what Vidal, reading *The Girl with a Pearl Earring* (Peter Webber, 2003), describes as 'participatory fantasies about the past' that 'cannot encompass the wider contextual, aesthetic or political reflection on the crucial historical periods represented'.[48] Rather than the fantasy of the Muse's inner life, feminist filmmakers (can) draw on fantasies of feminist history predicated on women's texts, retaining the 'what if', slant quality that Reichardt brings to *Meek's Cutoff*.

All Dressed Up: Costume Drama Loosens its Corset

Black British filmmaker Campbell X talked at Club des Femmes workshop 'Women are Writing Science Fiction' about her longterm ambition to adapt Octavia Butler's novel *Kindred*, in which African American writer Dana finds herself transported back and forth between 1976 and the plantation in pre-Civil War Maryland where her ancestors lived.[49] It's a paradigm of an intersectional feminist historical fantasy/fantastical history that demands imaginative and ethical engagement, and a suspension of disbelief in non-rational forces. Perhaps, as Potter identified with *Orlando*, the rich experimental terrain of slipstream and counter-historical science fiction and fantasy offers the best model (as well as a potent source) for a rejuvenation of historical and heritage drama. *Kindred* speaks directly to the ethics of doing (and learning) history, our responsibility to our ancestors: not to render an aspic for preservation, but to be the future they struggled to bring into being, as Ningiuq struggles in *Before Tomorrow*. As Marian Evans and Cushla Parekowhai argue, when a film attends to ancestors, it is also attentive to female community. They observe that in Mexican filmmaker Dana Rotberg's adaptation of Witi Ihimaera's novel *White Lies/Tuakiri Huna* (2013), 'a traditional Maori community is represented as successful, at ease in their land, a group not dislocated and dispossessed but positive, organised and determined. The film is 80% in te reo Maori, with subtitles. *White Lies/Tuakiri Huna* might also be New Zealand's first Bechdel Test narrative feature'.[50]

At the start of Inuit community documentary *Qallunaat! Why White People are Funny* (Zebedee Nungak and Mark Sandiford, 2007), Inuit scholar John Amagoalik theorizes about 'the people a long time ago who could see the future'. This is an entrancing and exacting way of conceiving the project of historical drama: that it's about telling the stories of our ancestors to give life to the futures they envisioned. Too often, historical dramas make a mockery of past attitudes for easy laughs (see *Hysteria*) while presenting present audiences as inevitably superior. Instead, feminist historical drama is committed to a genealogy in which learning goes both ways. These films step out of the thrall of dominant culture's writing of history, and of the negative association of the costume drama with the feminine. Instead, they recognize the genre as a necessary and generous site in which to correct the excesses and injuries of the textbooks. We, say projects such as *Kindred*, *Belle*, *Before Tomorrow* and *Silent Waters*, are worthy to be the fantastic future seen by the historical characters we portray.

7

Mirror, Mirror

Fairy Tales of the Feminist Fantastic

Frankenstein's Monster/Mother

Fantastical history meets historical fantasy meets the history of fantasy meets fantasies of history in the life and work of Mary Shelley. Often called the 'mother' of horror, science fiction, dystopian fiction and speculative fiction, Shelley drew her literary experiments from her lived experience. She is the presiding spirit of this chapter, which finds that fantasy is powerfully political. The daughter of political philosophers Mary Wollstonecraft and William Godwin, Shelley managed to shock her free-thinking father by running away with radical (and married) poet Percy Bysshe Shelley, with whom she lived precariously on the road, travelling through war-torn Europe in a complex relationship that included her stepsister Claire Clairmont. Beatniks and bohemians *avant la lettre*, both Shelleys transmuted political and emotional upheaval into literary art.

It's that skill that I seek here, in a rare chapter that testifies to a scarcity at the centre of feminist film, even if there is plenitude at the edge: the fairytale telefilms of Catherine Breillat offer what Hollywood cannot, and it is something we need urgently. Experimental cinema is more able to enter the unconscious, combining economic (relative) low risk with aesthetic high risk. Since Maya Deren's 'Meshes of the Afternoon' (1942) experimental feminist cinema has had the enthralling power of undoing thrall by stepping out into the dark. Artists' film and video such as Wangechi Mutu's mysterious serpentine 'Nguva' (2014) unlatch the mythical feminine from the coercive patterns of dominant narrative, re-presenting them so they can resignify. Similarly, Jennifer Phang animates the apocalyptic dreams of her protagonists in *Half Life* (2008), so that they are the main markers of the light futurism of the California in whose environmental collapse her characters live.

Abigail Child shot her Shelley biopic *A Shape of Error* (2012) on 16mm during her residency at the American Academy in Rome, casting her fellow artist-residents. She then remixed it as *UNBOUND* (2013), in which experimental form meets experimental content. Shelley (Eileen Ryan) comes vividly to life as a political animal thinking through the ethics of public and communal life through her relationships with Percy (Nick Wilding) and Claire (Aurelia d'Antonia). Using historically inflected modern dress for the Shelleys, Child places them in a suspended time between their historical moment and the future that, as radical socialists, they envisioned. She asks whether the future they imagined has yet come to be; and if not, whether we can, imaginatively, enter that utopian timespace in solidarity with them.

The fantasy of realism is suspended, but so are the technical tricks and tropes of the cinematic fantastic. Instead, Child alludes to the Surrealist cinema of Man Ray's *Emak Bakia* (1927) and its descendant Alain Resnais' *L'année dernière à Marienbad* (*Last Year at Marienbad*, 1961), as the events Mary remembers are repeated and rearranged, like a recurring dream. Time and space are both unstable; the piercing presence of Shelley's voice (often quoted from her letters and diaries) holds the film together, and the audience spellbound.

Curiously, there are two Hollywood biopics of Mary Shelley about to go into production, both helmed by non-American filmmakers making their Hollywood debuts: Saudi-Arabian pioneer Haifaa al-Mansour, who rewrote girlhood with *Wadjda*, and Coky Giedroyć, director of the Scottish runaway girl film *Stella Does Tricks* (1997), from a screenplay by A. L. Kennedy. Al-Mansour's *A Storm in the Stars*, from a screenplay by Emma Jensen, 'aims to tell of the tumult of first love of a young woman out of step with her time', following the contemporary standard of the feminist costume drama/biopic.[1] Elle Fanning is attached to al-Mansour's project as Mary, a role that brings together her genre cachet from *Maleficent* (Robert Stromberg, 2014, from a screenplay by Linda Woolverton), and – although this has gone unnoted in mainstream media coverage – her previous experience of playing a nascent writer as the young poet Ginger in *Ginger and Rosa*.

Giedroyć's film, *Mary Shelley's Monster*, will feature Sophie Turner and Taissa Farmiga, best known for, respectively, *Game of Thrones* (HBO, David Benioff and D.B. Weiss, 2011–) and *American Horror Story* (20th Century Fox, Brad Falchuk and Ryan Murphy, 2012–), tapping into cult/genre television fandom.[2] Both films have been mooted as portraits of the artist as a young woman in love who will go on to write *Frankenstein*. Fantastic fiction is suggestively entwined with romantic and erotic fantasy in this biopic model. Based on the filmmakers' previous work, it seems likely that they will overturn the internalized erotics of fantasy, predicated as they are on the objectification of women, albeit often framed as an 'ironic' tolerance of past mores in contemporary media. As Laurie Penny infamously wrote, in a piece that 'caused somewhat of a storm across the SFF blogosphere',[3] '*Game of Thrones* is racist rape-culture Disneyland with Dragons. To say that this series is problematic in its handling of race and gender is a little like saying that Mitt Romney is rich: technically accurate, but an understatement so profound that it obscures more than it reveals'.[4]

Penny's essay refuses the crumbs, while emphasizing that, as a literature that foregrounds the imaginative (whether called magic or technology) as a political force, the fantastic (science fiction, fantasy and horror) has great potential for representational justice. Feminist literary science fiction and fantasy has an outstanding seven-decade history in fiction, with precursors dating back to Shelley and Margaret Cavendish (1623–1673); Deren experimented with writing pulp science fiction short stories in an attempt to earn money. At around the same time as Laura Mulvey and Claire Johnston were changing film culture, writers such as Ursula K. Le Guin, Katherine V. Forrest, Octavia Butler, Pat Cadigan and Joanna Russ were revolutionizing the spaceman-dominated world of science fiction (SF).

Yet their work has had a limited role, either direct or indirect, in genre cinema – with the crucial and powerful exception of *Born in Flames*, and, to a more limited and controversial extent, Kathryn Bigelow's millennial dystopian thriller *Strange Days* (1995). Just as the radical left of the suffragette movement remains too controversial for cinema, so does the untrammelled politically radical imagination of SF female authors, often featuring women (and third-gendered, intersex, transgendered, polygendered, post-gender, non-binary, genderfluid and genderqueer characters) working together (and often sleeping together). As feminist science fiction is generally anti-colonial, these gender-diverse characters may be, or may act in solidarity with, aliens or monsters, rather than seeking to exterminate them.

At the heart of Child's *UNBOUND* is a vignetted film-within-a-film of *Frankenstein*, in which a secret history of feminism is revealed, one in which there is a resonance between the monster and Mary as vulnerable beings, rather than, as is usual, between Mary and the mad scientist as powerful creators. Played by an actor with modern facial piercings rather than the traditional bolts, the monster is suggestively a gender outlaw. His halting movements are a reminder that *Frankenstein* has been widely adopted within disability studies as well as feminist and queer theory. 'We do not often think of the monster in Mary Shelley's work as disabled, but what else is he?', as Lennard Davis asks.[5] A counter-cultural creature whose desires, like Shelley's, are unvoiceable within his historical time and place, the monster is rendered sympathetic in Child's vision. If the monster is a made creature, then so might the author be, as a woman and a writer, in line with Simone de Beauvoir's famous dictum on the social construction of gender, 'one is not born,

Mirror, Mirror: Fairy Tales of the Feminist Fantastic

Fig. 19: Frankenstein, *UNBOUND*

but rather becomes, a woman".[6] Child thus also addresses the persistent myth of the male-made Muse, represented in fantasy and science fiction films that draw on Pygmalion and Galatea, from *Metropolis* (Fritz Lang, 1927, from a screenplay by Thea von Harbou, adapting her own novel) onwards.

Child shoots the vignette in black and white, pastiching James Whale's 1931 adaptation (a history queered in *Gods and Monsters* [Bill Condon, 1998]). Her work has a long-standing fascination with pastiche and quotation of film history, and particularly its dramatization of embodiment, such as the play with silent melodrama in 'Perils' (1986) and the reappropriation of a silent lesbian porn film at the end of 'Mayhem' (1987), parts four and six respectively of her series *Is This What You Were Born For?*, a title that clearly tips its hat to de Beauvoir. Her micro-*Frankenstein* feels like another entry into the series, inquiring into what it means to be born into a society that genders you female, and renders that gendering monstrous. Rather than rocking the vote or campaigning for wage equality (although Child also made *B/Side* [1996], a documentary in solidarity with urban homeless people in New York), *Is This...* inhabits Jacqueline Rose's 'modern feminism [which] mess[es] with the idea of a cleaned-up politics by bringing sexuality to the table'.[7] For Rose, the unconscious is political, disrupting conventional politics' insistence on the rational, visible and recordable.

Sleeping Beauties (and Beasts)

Child's witty, disturbing short 'Subtalk' (2002) exactly takes on Rose's 'task... of exposing everything that is darkest, most recalcitrant and unsettling in the struggle for the better political futures we want'.[8] In Child's words, the short 'documents the heavy post-9/11 police presence in New York's subway system and imagines the [Metropolitan Transit Authority]'s "Subtalk" PSAs supplanted by Gertrude

Stein's [memoir of living in Occupied France] "Wars I Have Seen".[9] Her gesture is an uncanny precursor of Jane Campion's use of the MTA's 'Poetry in Transit' placards to give voice to Franny's post-9/11 unconscious in *In the Cut*. In Child's work, as in Campion's, 'confronting dark with dark might be the more creative path'.[10] Just as Child shows Shelley bringing her nightmare into her waking life and making art from it, Campion's film is about waking up but not forgetting the dark.

In the opening scenes, as Franny is half-sleeping, a petal shower in the garden outside her window prompts a recurrence of her dream about how her parents met. This romantic fantasy, in which her father proposed to her mother while skating on a pond, is repeated throughout the film, varying as Franny comes to understand the disturbing implications of his behaviour: dumping his fiancée for a woman he had just met; coercing her into marriage on his whim; abandoning her. Unlike her father, who repeats his behaviour endlessly with other women, Franny is able to perform what Luce Irigaray calls mimesis, or repetition with a difference, to work through and wake up from the nightmare of patriarchy that she had thought was a blissful dream.[11] While Sue Gillett has expertly unpacked many of the interconnected mythic and fairy tale female personae who appear throughout the film, she leaves aside the film's references to Sleeping Beauty.[12] Franny may fall into a dazed sleep beneath the killer's dead body, but she awakens herself, and then goes to wake her lover Malloy (Mark Ruffalo) with a kiss.

While *Maleficent* may be the first mainstream post-feminist cinematic take on the story, both Catherine Breillat (*La belle endormie*, 2010) and Julia Leigh (2011) released Sleeping Beauties this decade. Breillat's was a follow-up to her *Barbe bleue* (*Bluebeard*, 2009); her fairy tale telefilms are, like her other work, moral dramas with a mordant twist. She is fascinated by the strict logic of the fairy tale and the messy implications of the desiring unconscious it attempts to contain. For her, fairy tales are patriarchal texts that can be re-read by girls; literally, in *Bluebeard*, as two young sisters, Catherine (Marilou Lopes-Benites) and Marie-Anne (Lola Giovanetti), read the story to each other in a barn, each daring the other to be afraid of this cautionary tale of adult female sexual curiosity and excess.

As Manohla Dargis observes, 'Breillat puts a child at the center of *The Sleeping Beauty*, almost as if she wanted to get her hands on the girl (who can be seen as a stand-in for all girls) before the fairy tale has its way with her'.[13] Yet the girl Breillat foregrounds is not an innocent; she is a sexual being, full of agency fuelled by desire. Feral, scandalous, bad, for real: standing outside the social contract to which adults are resigned, the girl can more easily embody the rebellious feminisms I cited in chapter one. More easily, but also more transgressively.

Mirror, Mirror: Fairy Tales of the Feminist Fantastic

In 'Snow Canon' (2011), a short clearly influenced by Breillat, Mati Diop daringly explores the boundaries of permission. Vanina (Nilaya Bal) is a pre-teen Salome, testing her American babysitter Mary Jane (Nour Mobarak) as she experiences the power of her first crush. The 'canon' of the title is suggestive of repetition with a difference; time almost stands still in the snowed-in Alpine chalet where Vanina plays her games again and again, exploring her power in a way that is never sanitized, but also never spectacularized. Diop's other films are quasi-documentary, but she attests that Vanina is a semi-autobiographical character, a form of subjective or imaginative documentation of the artist in the process of becoming through desire. '"Snow Canon" is quite autobiographical. It is a film about the representation of the imaginary and the invention of the self during the lost hours of adolescence. As a child I could spend hours travelling in my head, making up stories, lives, characters'.[14]

In *The Sleeping Beauty*, Breillat's heroine finds herself 'travelling in [her] head'. Her self-willed finger-pricking – inspired by hearing the classic Charles Perrault tale – leads not to a coma, but to an adventure, which could be read as her fever-dream. Breillat meshes the Perrault story with that of a questing female protagonist, Gerda from Hans Christian Andersen's 'The Snow Queen' (1845), also the source text for *Frozen*. Within her adventure/dream, Anastasia's (Julia Artamonov) stepbrother is taken by the Snow Queen, and on her way to find him, she is befriended by a gypsy girl Véroutchka (Diana Rudychenko). Breillat hides a tale of female agency within the classic story of female passivity, displacing heteronormative love as a basis for female heroism. The territory of fantasy, with its risky encounters and uncontrollable forces, is a source of feminist power for Breillat, as for Rose in *Women in Dark Times*; both of them worry that feminism has ceded this territory in its urgent quest for legislative power and rational authority.

If Breillat's and Campion's films are structured around recurrent wake-up calls, Leigh's *Sleeping Beauty* (mentored by Campion) depends for its effect on one final, shocking awakening, in which Lucy (Emily Browning) realizes that she has been exploited, as the feminist viewer – alas for the film – has been all too aware from the offset. Leigh's brave but frustrating film exemplifies the princess problem: like *Frozen*, it wants to tell us 'that perfect girl is gone', but that necessitates the normative representation of a perfect girl. Lucy's whiteness is almost startling; she is dressed fetishistically in white underwear when she begins her career as a sex worker, contrasting with the more elaborate Gothic black underwear of the other female sex workers, some of them also darker-skinned.

Like Margarethe von Trotta's thinking women, Lucy is resolutely alone, untouched even by the fraught, often eroticized sisterhood experienced by

Breillat's girls. Blank-faced Lucy is a sister to post-feminist erotic adventurers (predominantly straight, white, cisgendered and able-bodied) such as Hannah (Lena Dunham) in *Girls*, whom Erika Price advocates for as 'neurotic, selfish female characters' in contrast to SFCs.[15] In a generous reading, we could consider these female characters as 'sleeper agents' whose violent awakening to their own internalization of patriarchy will wreak vengeance. Leigh's film suggests that this adventure in submission is a rite of passage, but the stark ending leaves Lucy's future up for grabs, with nowhere to go.

Red Riding Hoods and Wolves

Leigh won Best Director at the Sitges International Festival of Fantastic Film in 2011, following in the feminist fantasy footsteps of Best Film awards for female-centric films *The Company of Wolves* (Neil Jordan, 1984) and *Hard Candy* (David Slade, 2005), as well as *Orlando*. Sitges' definition of the fantastic is impressively broad, attentive to what could be called the 'everyday fantastic' of feminist cinema. Due to a combination of economics and politics, the feminist fantastic is generally set in the present, in a spare Brechtian evocation of a past, or in a low-budget near-future. It tends not to focus on spectacular technological innovation, either in the diegesis or in the filmmaking, instead obtaining its effects through mood and costume.

Sometimes, as in Leigh's film, it is a mood that infuses a seemingly realist story, as in Rebecca Miller's *The Ballad of Jack and Rose* (2005), a beguiling and haunting tale of a questing daughter, a missing mother, a capricious father, land politics, dreams of 1960s counter-culture, fire, water and the limits of love, which draws on the mood of the folk ballads that influenced the artists on its soundtrack. *The Company of Wolves*, adapted from Angela Carter's short stories and radio play, is more like classic fantasy on the surface: predominantly located in the all-white, ahistorical neverland of the Northern European forest, the film features a set of nested variations on Red Riding Hood. While its special effects are limited, its commitment to the imaginary is complete.

The fairy tales take place within a frame narrative, in which a modern teenage girl Rosaleen (Sarah Patterson) has fallen asleep in her family's rambling, isolated house, dreaming herself back into the forest. Even in 1984, atavistic fantasies of meeting the wolf remained the necessary substrate of the modern EuroWestern female adolescent imagination, the film implies, as we have few other available images for the powerful curiosity of emergent female sexuality. So powerful, in fact, that a veritable Red Riding Hood cycle emerged between Susan Faludi's

Backlash (1991) and her *Terror Dream*, offering cautionary tales about women alone in public space.[16] Both *Freeway* (Matthew Bright, 1996) and *Hard Candy* have been hailed as offering post-feminist Red Riding Hoods, played by Reese Witherspoon and Ellen Page respectively, who turn the tables on their respective wolves, predatory paedophiles in both cases.

The bulk of each film, however, works to inculcate dread in the female viewer, constantly implying the traditional narrative of gendered violence; conversely, each ends with an ambivalence towards its protagonist, asking the viewer whether she has gone too far in committing violence, effectively presenting a double bind in which neither of the protagonist's options – victim or hero – are permitted. *Ginger Snaps* (John Fawcett, 2000, from a screenplay by Karen Walton) seems more encouraging for women in dark times, with its wicked and funny werewolf sisters Ginger and Brigitte (Katharine Isabelle and Emily Perkins), who start the film by chanting 'out by 16 or dead on the scene, but together forever'. It is certainly more vivid and compelling than Hardwicke's *Red Riding Hood* (2011), part of a cycle of amped-up young adult genre films that predominantly thrill/thrall to dominatrix-lite bad mothers. Hardwicke's film, with Valerie (Amanda Seyfried) caught between a rich boy and a poor boy, is *Twilight* redux, in which Red primarily serves – *frisson* of threat again – as potential wolf-food.

Female power – that which, as Carter and Jordan argue in their final sequence, seduces the wolf of patriarchy and transforms him – retains its depiction as revenant and uncanny even in the modern era, in which some women hold political and economic power. Films such as *The Craft* (Andrew Fleming, 1996) score cult classic status because they offer the thrill of such world-making power, often from a loosely post-feminist perspective. Female friendship once again generates the fear of a monstrous regiment that has to be brutally contained. Most female viewers approach these films (*Maleficent*, *Freeway*, *The Craft*) with a version of bell hooks' 'oppositional gaze'.[17] We may be exhilarated by the set-up and then cauterize the ending, just as Willow (Alyson Hannigan) in *Buffy* 'always turns off the *Moulin Rouge!* [Baz Luhrmann, 2001] DVD at chapter 32 so it has a happy ending' (Fox, David Solomon, *Buffy the Vampire Slayer*, 'The Killer in Me', 7/13, 2003).

In *The Company of Wolves*, adapted as it is from Carter, the transformation is more thorough-going than an elective happy ending that ignores the economic and social situation of the female protagonist and the narrative tropes stacked against her. For Carter, the tale is altered by, and alters, its teller: male violence takes many forms, as Granny (Angela Lansbury) warns. Equally, uncanny, powerful female characters abound, including Granny and eventually Rosaleen herself, who transforms into a wolf.

If too few Red Riding Hoods get to undertake that transformation in contemporary cinema, there is another fairy tale political animal who speaks to gender fluidity and desire: the merperson. In particular, s/he speaks to queer, trans* and intersex desires and identities, to the erasure of the borderlines between human and animal, male and female, land and water. Before she left the film Sofia Coppola cast model Andreja Pejíc, who shifted in 2014 from identifying as genderfluid to transfemale, in her live action *The Little Mermaid* (2015).[18] Céline Sciamma's *Water Lilies*, a love (/hate) story set among synchronized swimmers 'recalls numerous images of nymphs and naiads', as Emma Wilson writes.[19] As in Lucrecia Martel's *La niña santa* (*The Holy Girl*, 2004) and *La mujer sin cabeza* (*The Headless Woman*, 2008) and Lucia Puenzo's *XXY* (2007) the transformation narrated tragically by Andersen is both reversed and reversible: girls become merfolk, but they do not go under.

Puenzo's Alex (Inés Efron, who also plays the languid lesbian swimmer Candita in *The Headless Woman*) exemplifies this fairy tale fluidity's real-world resonance. Alex, born intersex, raised female, is facing parental pressure to conform surgically to femininity. In hir bedroom, zhe has created a confident, fantastical visual idiolect of merfolk, amphibious creatures and modified doll bodies that reflect and shape hir identity. Zhe literally lives liminally, spending hir time on the beach near hir family's home; but when zhe claims it as a public space, zhe is met with violence by local teenage boys, a violence that the film explicitly reveals as suppressed desire.

Alex responds by becoming more hirself, as does Marie (Pauline Acquart) in *Water Lilies*, who defies the emotionally violent put-downs of her mean girl crush Floriane (Adèle Handel), captain of the synchronized swimming team, by taking to the water. Swimming belongs to and signals a girlhood aslant in Sciamma's *Tomboy* and Martel's *Holy Girl* too. The pool is a space charged with heteronormative conformity via the body fascism and hyper-visibility inherent in swimsuits, yet it also offers a suspension in the water that distorts and transforms the body/image.

While Dan Taulapapa McMullin's experimental short 'Sinalela' (2001) refers in a Samoan accent to what the filmmaker calls 'the Euro-Afro-Asian Cinderella story', it sends its fa'afafine (Samoan Two Spirit) protagonist out of the house and onto the shore, where she meets a handsome sailor with traditional Polynesian tattoos. Water suggestively analogizes the cinema screen; these queer bodies disrupt it. When Rosaleen becomes a wolf, she bursts through the narrative frame from the fairy tale woods into the house where her modern self still lies sleeping. It is merqueer films that are living up to this ferocious, unsettling and deeply feminist conclusion, in which Red Riding Hood transforms herself into a political animal: so political, in fact, that she can shatter the boundary between the imaginary and the real.

Cinderellas

Fairy tales have crossed over from the realm of the fantasy genre, particularly when it comes to post-feminist romantic narratives: *Enchanted* (Kevin Lima, 2007) is only the most obvious example. It's a fairy tale of New York, which provides a location for surprisingly similar fantasies in *Frances Ha* (Noah Baumbach, 2012, from a screenplay by Greta Gerwig), in which dancer/choreographer Frances (Gerwig) leaps through Manhattan in a single tracking shot, to David Bowie's 'Modern Love', a homage to Leos Carax's dystopian science fiction romance *Mauvais sang (The Night is Young*, 1986). Later on, as if emphasizing the fairy tale quality of the film, she spends her time at her alma mater Vassar walking the wooded grounds. Both the wander in the woods and the daring run through traffic typify the character, who is searching headlong for... *something*. Satisfyingly, it is not her prince; it may be herself. The film's climax is the first public performance of Frances' choreography, attended (as in a wish-fulfilment dream) by her ex-roommate/boyfriend, her former employer and her much-missed best friend Sophie (Mickey Sumner), with whom she reconnects.

It's a more hopeful moment than the end of Miranda July's *The Future* (2011), which forms a mirror to *Frances Ha*. July plays (another) Sophie, an underemployed choreographer who begins a dance-a-day YouTube project to deal with her feelings of frustration after adopting a cat with her partner Jason (Hamish Linklater). Yet this intriguing project is dropped in favour of unrelated games with cinematic time and narration. July's film explores multiple senses of fantasy, including monologues by the cat, Paw-Paw (voiced by July), and Sophie's liaison with another man. More worryingly, it suggests that both creativity and collective ecological action are fantasies with the same status and the same problematics as our erotic lives; all three are projects doomed to failure.

Both *The Future* and *Frances Ha* pay homage to the centrality of choreography and dance in the history of feminist film, and the dancer/choreographer as a figure of the feminist filmmaker. In particular, the New York setting of the latter summons Yvonne Rainer's *Lives of Performers* (1972) and, in its concern with gentrification and housing, *The Man Who Envied Women* (1985). Baumbach's film, like Lena Dunham's work, forms a bathetic contrast with the spiky re-visioning of New York in Madeline Olnek's strange, vibrant lo-fi B-movies *Codependent Lesbian Space Alien Seeks Same* (2011) and *The Foxy Merkins* (2014), the former an 'everyday fantastic' comedy in which monochrome, monotone aliens dance their way through the oddities of New York's lesbian dating scene. It's hard not to feel that Rainer's rigorous aesthetics and politics have been dislocated and appropriated as hipster reference points by a new, more privileged generation of critically lauded straight filmmakers, while filmmakers such as Olnek, who pay loving homage to no-wave, punk and New Queer Cinema, are pushed under the radar. Like Leigh's *Sleeping Beauty*, *The Future* and *Frances Ha* both feel like they end where they should begin, with the question of what comes next, once the princess has been awakened and is questioning the price of her privilege.

They form an instructive comparison with Claire Denis' *35 rhums* (*35 Shots of Rum*, 2008), in which Joséphine (Diop), like Frances, is moving towards independence in the big city; in this case, Paris. As Denis commented to Adam Nayman, Paris has been returned to the possibility of a realism, however sensuous and imaginative, that New York now lacks: 'When I go to New York, I'm not in the real New York: I'm in an imaginary place from photos and films'.[20] Post 9/11, New York has been objectified and re-romanticized in the very ways that Campion tries to undo in *In the Cut*, and as Denis does for Paris in *35 Shots* and her erotic fairy tale *Vendredi soir* (2002), which, like Campion's film, ends with a passionate woman walking through the dawn.

As so often in Denis' films, there is a scene of social dance in *35 Shots* that uses the filmmaker's 'rhythms of relationality', in Laura McMahon's words.[21] These rhythms tell wordless stories about the characters and emotions, coming to embody the power of film, and the particularity of place. The dance metaphorizes the patriarchal exchange of women: Jo initially dances with her father Lionel (Alex Descas); when the Commodores' song 'Nightshift' begins, their rich landlord Noe (Denis stalwart Grégoire Colin) cuts in, and Lionel takes up with the café owner (Adèle Ado) who has let them shelter from the rain. For McMahon, 'the intimate logic of the same upon which the relation between father and daughter is tenderly built opens to encounters with others'.[22]

The end of the film, in which Jo uses Noe's crush on her as a way to set herself and her father free from their co-dependent stasis, is less cutesy than that of *Frances Ha*, in which Frances folds up the nametag for her new apartment's mailbox, thus renaming herself from Halladay or Haliday to Ha. Imdb gives both, but I read it as Halflady, a joke on her (and the film's) incompleteness. That's partially because of the economic rationale behind Jo's choice; her father is a just-retired train driver, and, unlike Frances, she doesn't have the luxury of playing at being poor. In Denis' film, Cinderella meets new versions of the harsh economic realities out of which Marina Warner argues surviving versions of fairy tales arose.[23]

Amazons

If Cinderella has yet to be fully employed as a story about austerity in mainstream cinema (and Kenneth Branagh's 2015 lavish live action version is the exact opposite), then it's perhaps no wonder that the pacifist Wonder Woman has been recast as a warrior in her most recent incarnation, to be played by Gal Gadot as a third wheel in *Batman vs. Superman: Dawn of Justice* (Zack Snyder, 2016). So far, Snyder's interpretation of the character is primarily a costume, images of which were released shortly after Gadot uploaded a pro-IDF image to Facebook (receiving over 200,000 likes) during Operation Protective Edge.[24] There is a sour resonance between the new hardbody suit of armour worn by the princess of peace and Gadot's militant views. For Melissa Silverstein, the follow-up *Wonder Woman* feature will be 'a high-stakes gig… one of the highest-profile, if not THE highest-profile, gig[s] a woman director has ever gotten'.[25]

What Patty Jenkins, succeeding Michelle MacLaren who left in April 2015 over 'creative differences', will be able to do in *Wonder Woman* (2017) with the character as (re)conceived by Snyder remains to be seen. She will probably not be able to answer Crunk Feminist Collective's call for a film that honours the feminist origins of the character and her meaning for women of colour, where the Amazons are 'women of all races, ethnicities, abilities, ages and sizes… who appear out of the sky to support their sister and *wreck* shit, because the evil dwellers messed with the wrong Amazon'.[26]

In the meantime, there are two US documentaries that reveal the 'real' Wonder Woman. Jeannie Epper, Lynda Carter's stunt double for *Wonder Woman* (Warner Bros., Stanley Ralph Ross, 1975–79), is the co-star of Amanda Micheli's *Double Dare* (2004), along with Zoë Bell, Lucy Lawless' stunt double for *Xena Warrior Princess* (MCA, John Schulian and Robert G. Tapert, 1995–2001). Bell moved to LA and, under Epper's mentorship, was hired for Quentin Tarantino's *Kill Bill Vol. 1* (2003). Micheli's film is a wonderful meditation on the strength, discipline and carefuless of Bell and Epper. Behind the thrilling fight scenes, it's revealed, are highly-trained, physically adept performers who avoid damaging contact at all costs. *Double Dare* turns the action genre inside out, allowing us to appreciate the skills of the performers while deconstructing the violent fantasies they portray.

Wonder Woman also appears in the foundational feminist film *Penthesilea: Queen of the Amazons* (Laura Mulvey and Peter Wollen, 1974), in which a stage production of Heinrich von Kleist's 1808 play about the Amazon queen is followed by a flick through a 1970s issue of the comic in which the cartoon Amazon fights street harassment. Kristy Guevara-Flanagan's documentary *Wonder Women! The*

Fig. 20: Stretch Goal Reached! Storm art for 'Rain', Maya Glick

Untold Story of American Superheroines (2014) captures the character's 1970s heyday, when she appeared on the front of the first issue of *Ms.* magazine, but it also considers her meaning to multiple generations of American women of diverse ethnicities, embodiments and sexualities. *Wonder Women!* also follows independent comic book stores who use Women of Wonder Day to raise awareness and funds around domestic violence.[27] The Kickstarter backing for the film testifies, likewise, to the feedback cycle between the comics/genre fan community and diversity activism, which is starting to produce films as well as fundraising. Maya Glick's 'Rain', a short fan film about *X Men* character Storm, not only reached its fundraising goal, but drew such support from keen fans that it was able to reach its 'stretch goal', an extension that allows more work on a project, such as more special effects.[28]

Storm is notable as a rare woman of colour in the superhero universe. Documentaries such as *American Outrage* (Beth and George Gage, 2008), about sisters Carrie and Mary Dann, Western Shoshone women fighting for their ranch against the US government, and Kim Longinotto's *Pink Saris* (2010), about the Gulabi Gang, anti-sexual violence vigilantes based in Uttar Pradesh (also the subject of Nishtha Jain's *Gulabi Gang* [2012]), and their extraordinary leader Sampat

Pal, are striking reminders of the absence of women of colour in Amazonian narratives. This is contrary to the reality often unaddressed by both feminist and anti-racist activists; as Kimberlé Crenshaw notes, women of colour remain at the greatest risk of state and personal violence.[29]

Particularly in *American Outrage* there is a reminder that the classic conception of Wonder Woman is not only as a physical warrior, but on a spiritual path. Films that emphasize spiritual power tend, like 'A Red Girl's Reasoning', to emerge from and/or be embedded in, or draw on, non-Euro western imaginaries. *Baksy* (*Native Dancer*, 2008) is the second feature by Kazakh director Gulshat (Guka) Omarova, who was the Assistant Director on her co-writer Sergey Bodrov's prestige historical epic *Mongol* (2007), tasked with overseeing the epic horseback battle at his film's climax. The *baksy* (healer) of her film is grandmother Aidai-Apa (Nesipkul Omarbekova), who dies early on, after the corrupt police remove her from her land, which is taken over a local mafioso. After her death, the film fractures into temporal discontinuity, with the flow of time only returning when Aidai-Apa is found, having played dead and returned to her home town.

Aidai-Apa is, like Maleficent, both a witch and a warrior, fighting with magic and with a big stick. The similarities end there; *Native Dancer* is not concerned with moral judgements on women's power, but with its actualization as, and at, a political hotspot. Most importantly, the film believes in her power. Rather than depicting it through showy CGI, it makes it the optic of the film. We enter the healer's visionary point of view on several occasions when she performs rituals. Cinema is recast as shamanic, in contrast to the thriller/western subplot that Omarova uses in order to discard. Aidai-Apa is a rare powerful female protagonist in the fantasy genre who is not young, slender, able-bodied, straight, cisgendered and white.

That's why Maja Borg's 2030-set short 'We the Others' (2014) prominently features a princess; fantasy tropes persist in the science fictional imagination. Part of *Dazed & Confused*'s Visionaries project, Borg's film shares its name with *Noi.Gli Altri*, the European festival of disability cinema, and its protagonist is played by Tove Boström who, like all members of the cast, has Down syndrome. In a statement that resonates with feminist/queer merfolk and werewolves, Borg says of the film's cast, 'Feared by all as the "others", "they" are in fact most of us'.[30] Reshaping the fantasy genre towards representational justice began with Borg's questions about reproductive justice, when she was required to have an amniocentesis during her pregnancy. She imagined a future in which people with Down had been almost wiped out. Thus her film is the ultimate in the 'everyday fantastic', starting, as Shelley's did, in the lived experience of pregnancy.

Boström's unnamed protagonist embodies many fairy tale archetypes, first appearing in a sunlit wood dressed in a long gown, with a traditional, conical 'princess' hat whose gauzy veil floats aloft as she dances. In subsequent scenes, Boström puts on make-up and takes her wig on and off, solving the princess problem by revealing that 'princess' is performative, a metaphor that can be taken up by anyone. It is a symbol of self-worth and self-definition, rather than of external hierarchies. Borg shot on distressed black and white 16mm in order to rewrite the history of cinema to include Boström's embodiment of the princess: this is cinema as becoming-girl, and becoming-girl as cinema, as in Child's *UNBOUND*. Dominant cinema strives to control the unconscious and the fantastic because they are ripe for radical re-visioning.

Focusing on a female-helmed *Wonder Woman* studio movie risks limiting our imaginations. We need to look at experimental cinemas that reconceive the genre as well as the narratives. We need to heed Ava DuVernay, tweeting a photograph of Bree Newsome, the activist who removed the South Carolina statehouse's Confederate flag, with the words: 'Yes. I hope I get the call to direct the motion picture about a black superhero I admire. Her name is Bree Newsome.'[31] We need more films like Frances Bodomo's 'Afronauts' (2014), about 17-year-old albino Matha (Diandra Forrest), sent to the moon by the Zambian Space Programme in 1969 to form a post-colonial alliance with (other) aliens. We need to attend more to projects where 'groups of unrelated people are suddenly coming together everywhere', connected by their identification with 'bare life', as in Melanie Gilligan's post-apocalyptic online video series and gallery installation *Popular Unrest* (2010).[32] Through the transformative magic of film, Boström's closing dance – like Shelley's kinship with the monster – becomes the cinematic fantasy we have always had, the becoming we have always dreamed.

8

Girl 'Hood

A Body, a Room and a World of One's Own

Her Name Is

One of the most powerful feminist fantasies is writing the self in a room of one's own, even if that room is a forest and writing a dance, as for Tove Böstrom in 'We the Others'. In staking that claim, feminist cinema creates a new place, which I name the girl 'hood. As I discussed in chapters four and five, the war film and current British arthouse cinema have placed women, differently, in unexpected places, from the Pentagon to constant motion. The concept of girl 'hood names the continuum of environments through which women move and in which they act. Girls take up space, but also change it to serve themselves, and connect different places in unexpected ways.

Girls are figures of vulnerability in dominant culture. Their access to public space is highly policed and often curtailed through the inculcation of fearful fantasies. This gives rise to cautionary tales about the pleasures and dangers of straying from the path to grandmother's cottage. Such protagonists are generally young, straight, white women entering risky territory within a cultural framework that is, broadly, safe; *An Education* and *Fifty Shades of Grey* bring this story to the multiplex. Alternately, there are films about 'go[ing] outside', in Ava DuVernay's phrase, in order to forge families in which to belong and become. Such films exhibit an expanded definition of girlhood, including queer and trans* narratives, that redefine these categories against pathology and towards positive grounds for identity. Girl 'hood is that ground.

In *The Punk Singer*, Kathleen Hanna notes that girls are always making art in their bedrooms; what's needed is a way to distribute it economically, effectively and encouragingly. That's palpable in *The Diary of a Teenage Girl* (Marielle Heller, 2015) where for 15 year old Minnie (Bel Powley), alternative comics offer a way out as her drawings infiltrate the screen; later, she sets up as an artist on the boardwalk.

Phoebe Gloeckner's autobiographical, 1970s-set graphic novel charts her difficult route to self-expression; its current adaptation by Heller and continued readership is evidence of her success in entering a network of alternative distribution, spurred by the abusive atmosphere in which she grew up. The bedroom can be a site of terror, as it is for Lucy and Lauren in *The Unloved*; but, as Morton, Gloeckner, Heller and Hanna all show, art as activism is rooted in the determination to reclaim the bedroom as a private space. Beyond the concept of 'a room of one's own' is the formation of an entire world as your girl 'hood – a world that begins in the skin, extends through that room, out into the world.

Few recent films have undertaken the relation between the becoming-girl and finding (or making) one's place as strikingly as *Elle s'appelle Sabine* (*Her Name is Sabine*, 2007), actor Sandrine Bonnaire's filmmaking debut, which won the International Critics' Prize at Cannes in 2007. Sabine is Sandrine's younger sister; home movie footage included in the documentary reveals their similarities and differences as teenagers. Several critics have noted that Sabine's idiosyncratic body language and interactions, framed by her autism-related struggles with socialization, may have formed the basis for Sandrine's career-defining roles as Suzanne in *À nos amours* (*To Our Loves*, Maurice Pialat, 1983) and as Mona Bergeron in Agnès Varda's *Sans toit ni loi* (*Vagabond*, 1985). *Vagabond* is cited as a major influence on their bold, runaway girls by both Carol Morley and Penny Woolcock, an alternative to the Red Riding Hood narrative that prioritizes sexual transgression with older men as an expression of female rebellion.[1] Invoking Mona in Sabine, Sandrine's documentary is thus a double study of young women in formation on-, off- and between screens, challenging our expectations of lived and cinematic girlhood.

As Judith Gould and Jacqui Ashton Smith note, autism is itself a challenge to dominant conceptions of gender, such that 'girls are less likely to be identified with ASD [autism spectrum disorder], even when their symptoms are equally severe. Many girls are never referred for diagnosis and are missed from the statistics'.[2] The rare mainstream films that address psychological and physical disabilities for female characters often do so in such a way that strongly genders the disability, sometimes to the extent of implying that either physical impairments or psychological states are manifestations of identifying as female, whether essentialized as 'hormonal' or seen as a tragic product of vulnerability to oppression. When Nathan Rabin coined the term 'manic pixie dream girl', he used disablist language in referring to the character who inspired it as 'psychotically chipper'.[3] The fantasized free-thinking, free-loving alternative to and for the male protagonist is often similarly crudely associated, by both films and critics, with psychological and/or mental health diagnoses, or even just throwaway insults, as if to rationalize her eventual capture, containment or removal.

Like Jane Campion's *An Angel at My Table*, which depicts writer Janet Frame's survival of an incorrect diagnosis with schizophrenia, which almost resulted in a lobotomy, *Her Name is Sabine* is a rare film that tells the story the other way around. Examining the particular premium on correctly gendered behaviour for women, it explores how any divergence from normative femininity is pathologized. In her late twenties, feeling isolated from her Paris-based siblings after the death of her older brother prompted her mother's move to the countryside, Sabine was institutionalized and heavily medicated based on an incorrect diagnosis. Sandrine was compelled to make the film by Sabine's maltreatment in state institutions, and to agitate for the roll-out of versions of the group home where Sabine is recovering some of her earlier adolescent competence and self-awareness. The film reached large and appreciative audiences in France, and thanks to its influence, Bonnaire told the *Observer*, 'I am being invited to all the political meetings, with the right people.'[4] The home in Charentes seen in the film, which provides one-to-one care, was initially opened due to Sandrine's intervention, based on her knowledge of a similar centre.

A psychologist at the home defines autism for Sandrine as a loss or lack of bodily limits; the first girl 'hood that Sabine reclaims is the space of her own embodiment. As I'll explore in this chapter, girl 'hood is a space that bridges the inside and outside of institutional contexts through the body. Whether in a family, a school, a sports club, or a group home, there is a pervasive tension between the individual and the institution, accompanied by an ambivalence about the desire to belong, to be *somewhere*, versus a resistance to conformity.

Like the British films discussed in chapter five, *Her Name is Sabine* investigates the possibility of a first-person oblique narration or point of view. Although the title speaks in third person, it suggests the centrality of Sabine and her commitment to naming herself. Sabine is not a passive documentary subject but an occasional co-director from in front of the camera, deeply involved in, intrigued by and fully cognizant of the filmmaking process. When another resident of the group home starts throwing and biting, Sabine tells Sandrine kindly that if it's too much for her, she can leave.

Sabine's sharp intervention, in which she suggests that it is not she but Sandrine who has a limited emotional capacity, contrasts strongly with claims about autism, and with earlier footage of a non-verbal, disengaged Sabine after her institutionalization. It also forms a telling contrast with one of the film's most powerful and disturbing scenes in which Sandrine and Sabine watch a home movie of the teen sisters' trip to New York on Concorde, when Sandrine used her film earnings to

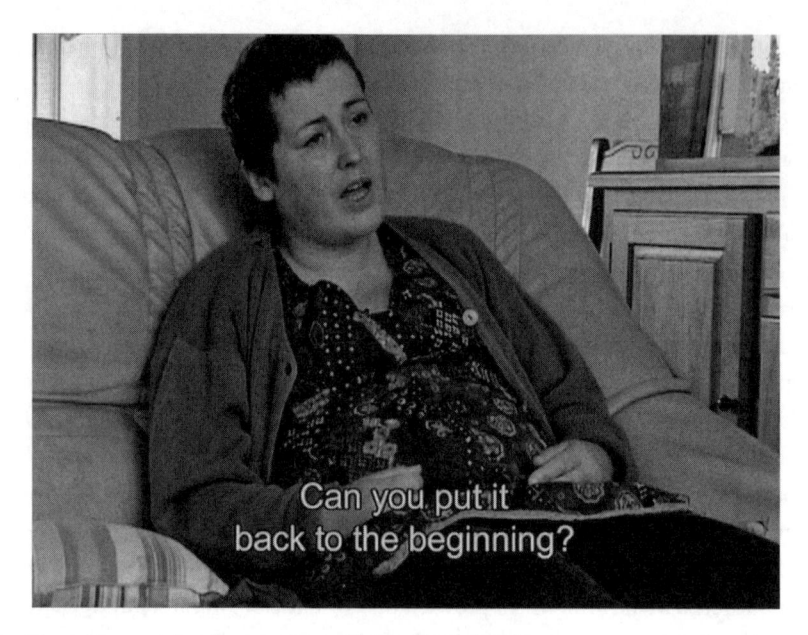

Fig. 21: Sabine watches her younger self, *Her Name is Sabine*

grant her sister's greatest wish. The fairy tale flight and destination are a cue for a terrible mourning that demonstrates Sabine's returning self-awareness, and a howl of rage against her institutionalization. That grief belongs, differently, to both sisters, but – implies the film – can only be given voice by the more affectively perceptive Sabine, who asks Sandrine to rewind the tape, collaboratively recapturing and redoing her girlhood.

Both self-documentation and sisterly co-operation, in which a documentarist collaborates with her subject, are prevalent in contemporary feminist cinema. Elle-Maíjá Tailfeathers' follow-up to 'A Red Girl's Reasoning' is a short documentary co-directed with filmmaker Terreanne Derrick that begins with a reflexive voice-over about their friendship and working relationship. 'Hurry Up, You Stupid Cripple' (2013) takes its defiant, provocative name from a game that Derrick, who has cerebral palsy, played with her siblings in the supermarket, hanging back deliberately until, at her insistence, one of them would shout the title phrase. This mischievous childhood memory is made more poignant as the film reveals that Derrick's long-term memory and communication skills have been badly affected by a car crash in which her mother was killed. 'It shapeshifted everything', she tells Tailfeathers, the mythological verb implying the co-directors' shared indigeneity and overlapping belief systems; Derrick is Gitxsan, Tailfeathers Blackfoot and Sami.

The power of trauma is reconceived through their collaboration and from an indigenous feminist perspective: it literally has the power to reshape the world. Derrick explains that she had to relearn to tell stories, and the film works with her narrative style rather than insisting on linearity, using extensive close-ups, jump cuts and low-angle shots to reorient the viewer's experience of the world and bring them close to Derrick's alternate view as she tours us around her girl 'hood.

Boy I Am

While Derrick is frequently shown actively in motion – walking, riding, talking, wheeling – the film in no way subscribes to a 'can do' attitude, or what Stella Young and other disability activists have called 'inspiration porn'.[5] Borrowing the title of Young's TEDX talk, Sandra Alland has curated the *I'm Not Your Inspiration* film series, documenting queer and trans* deaf and disabled Scottish artists.[6] Their work, like 'Hurry Up', uses the difference of disability to both question and change social space. Judith Butler and Sunaura Taylor, an artist who uses a wheelchair, offer a similar riposte during their freewheeling conversation about what bodies can do in *Examined Life*. Importantly, Taylor and Derrick are shown as part of social formations, in contradistinction to the usual representation of people with disabilities as an exception, and as lonely. Likewise, Sabine is shown to have become reconnected to her sister, her family, her community at the group home, and – through the film – to the audience, rather than being isolated, as she was when hospitalized.

Community is the core of girl 'hood, although from *Mean Girls* (Mark Waters, 2004, from a screenplay by Tina Fey) to *The Bling Ring* (Sofia Coppola, 2013) it's the tensions and status contests that tend to propel the drama of post-feminist variations on the girl group narrative. Coppola's last film has been unfairly derided as being as vacuous as the characters it depicts and the celebrity culture that obsesses them. Its total commitment to their world, however, offers an almost-documentary incisiveness about how adolescent status anxiety mirrors the adult world that condemns and dismisses adolescents as immature. As in *Marie Antoinette*, what's sad about the film is how willingly the young female characters participate in the capitalist culture that objectifies them, and how little escape they have.

By contrast, Marieme (Karidja Touré) in Céline Sciamma's *Bande de filles* (*Girlhood*, 2014) both enjoys and questions the stakes in being one of the gang. *Girlhood* is very much a film about the 'hood, an unusual representation of contemporary urban space and its post-colonial subjects as female. The *filles* are banded together by their shared location in the *banlieus* of Paris, with all that that means socially and economically. Marieme is one of Sciamma's watchful, thoughtful, powerful leads, defining herself through interaction with a magnetic group of peers led by Lady (Assa Sylla). When Lady renames Marieme 'Vic. Vic as in victory' it empowers her to a classic girl 'hood triumph, when she leaves home (particularly her violent older brother) and enters into the larger, adult world of grey-market Paris.

Sciamma suggests that this world is Marieme/Vic's home writ large, as she exchanges control by her brother for a demanding older male boss. As Mallory Andrews observes:

> Even her moment of becoming is staged almost as a superhero origin story. While doing dishes, she discreetly pockets a knife similar to one wielded by Lady. Framed from behind, she grips the edge of the counter backlit by the light over the sink, fully committing her allegiance to 'Vic'.[7]

As she rebels against her boss' orders, the masculine abbreviation of Vic marks a possible gender transition. In the final section of the film, Vic binds their chest to pass as one of the guys, identifying where the power is, but also in contrast to the demand that they dress high femme to deliver drugs to wealthy clients. For Sciamma: 'In the last shot of the film, Marieme wears the braids of childhood, the makeup of a diva, and the clothing of a boy. She's possibly everything or none of those'.[8] Dressed down in a hoodie in the closing sequence, Vic suggests a line of flight from gendered conventions, a final move made possible by the endless fluidity of girl 'hood.

Feminist filmmakers apply a similarly critical lens to boyhood, particularly concerning young men of colour, as with Woolcock's *One Mile Away*. Anita Doron's adaptation of *The Lesser Blessed* (2012) focuses on Dogrib teenager Larry (Joel Nathan Evans) who has to come to terms with killing his abusive father in self-defence, and also (through) his status as beta male to best friend Johnny (Kiowa Gordon) who turns out, like his father, to be an asshole. Turning away from the normative lessons of manhood is critical in Annemarie Jacir's *Lamma shoftak* (*When I Saw You*, 2012), as 11 year old Tarek (Mahmoud Asfa) becomes a mascot to a group of guerrilla fighters in a refugee camp, to his mother's dismay. These films share with Cherien Dabis' *Amreeka* (2009), a Palestinian 'coming to America' drama, a moving attention to mother-son relationships that are at once protective and jagged. Both *Amreeka* and *Lesser Blessed* feature rebellious female adolescent characters who act as the male protagonists' bolder selves.

Boyhood is as complex as girlhood, particularly at their intersection. Girls are now expected to play hard; that is, to be more normatively masculine. Brunei's first

Girl 'Hood: A Body, a Room and a World of One's Own

film in half a century, martial arts drama *Yasmine* (Siti Kamaluddin, 2015) uses sport as a metaphor at once for its female protagonist's rebelliousness, and for the strictures surrounding gendered behaviour. Recent films about girls in sport, from *Girlfight* (Karyn Kusama, 2000) and *Bend it Like Beckham* to *Kicks* (Lindy Heymann, 2009), *Fast Girls* (Regan Hall, 2012) and *She Monkeys*, as well as documentaries such as Florence Ayisi's *Zanzibar Soccer Queens* (2008), enter this difficult terrain. Like films about women on the military frontline, these films consider the pros and cons of entering what is still seen as a masculine world and its impact on girls' becoming, often getting entangled in vexed questions about gender and sexuality.

Frequently, the difficulty of the terrain is expressed through an outdated and pejorative association of sporty women, and all-female spaces, with lesbianism. Maria Govan's *Rain* (2008), the first Bahamian-made feature, addresses it head-on, as teenage runner Rain (Renel Brown) learns that her coach Ms. Adams (CCH Pounder) is a lesbian. The film openly critiques, rather than playing up, the expectation that Ms. Adams' investment in Rain's talent is in any way erotic, but also allows Ms. Adams to have a fully-fledged sexual identity. Filmmaker Bette Gordon praises the way in which Kusama handles the complexity in *Girlfight*, as boxing has 'the intimate nature of a sport where two nearly naked opponents have agreed to fight each other – focusing on a physicality that is so intense as to be hypersensual'.[9]

Kusama allows Diana (Michelle Rodriguez) to inhabit the black femme identity that Kara Keeling argues is too often invisible, and whose visibility is so potent; 'the black femme', she concludes, 'might restore a critical belief in the world by revealing that alternatives persist within it'.[10] Diana dates a male boxer, although he is ultimately threatened by her commitment to the sport; but her heterosexuality is uncompromised by the stereotypical association of sporting women. At the same time, the film does not shy away from the ring's intense homosociality, nor does it punish it. Kusama told Gordon that she took up the sport on the advice of lesbian filmmaker Sande Zeig.[11]

Elissa Washuta titles her memoir *My Body is a Book of Rules*, an apt and chilling description of what sport films exemplify but all girl 'hood films narrate.[12] The girl punks in *Vi är bäst!* (*We Are the Best*, Lukas Moodysson, 2013) compose their protest anthem 'Hate the Sport' exactly to critique such institutional discipline. Creative resistance to rules is especially apparent in a small, very recent trend for films about trans* childhoods, including first person documentaries such as *Boy I Am* (Sam Feder, 2006) and *She's a Boy I Knew* (Gwen Haworth, 2007) and features such as Mariana Rondon's unstraight hair-straightening comedy *Pelo Malo* (*Bad Hair*, 2014). In Sciamma's *Tomboy*, Mikäel (Zoé Héran) takes advantage of the summer holidays to introduce himself to his local peers before being forced to assume his official identity as Laure when school begins. The institution is a threatening presence in abeyance here, its strictures echoed by the anxiety of Mikäel's parents. Like the threat of a special unit hanging over Mia in *Fish Tank*, it fuels rebellion rather than containing it, forging a crisis point. Mikäel/Laure's closing encounter with his crush Lisa (Jeanne Disson) suggests that love and friendship can provide a counter-space in which to formulate his identity.

In its generational contrasts, *Tomboy* echoes an earlier French film *Ma vie en rose* (Alain Berliner, 1997). Berliner's well-received late New Queer Cinema classic shares with Chelsea McMullan's documentary *My Prairie Home* (2013) a celebration of the performative as a mode of alternative becoming: where Ludovic (Georges du Fresne) dresses up and dreams of entering the world of her favourite Barbie-like TV show *Le monde du Pam*, non-gender binary singer Rae Spoon stages their life as a musical in collaboration with McMullan. What is candy-coloured wish-fear in *Ma vie* is a carefully negotiated and beautifully recorded lived experience in *My Prairie Home*. Moving between choreographed music video, live performance, interview and voiceover, McMullan scrapbooks Spoon's story. As in 'Hurry Up', there is a sense of co-authorship, almost of the filmmaker bringing her subject's internal visions to life. The film appropriates and resignifies the iconic (often highly masculinized) attributes of the prairie home Spoon loves, including moose, long-distance bus rides and hikes in the snow. Spoon owns, and is owned by, their prairie home.

Erica Tremblay's documentary *In the Turn* (2014) also takes on rural Canadian prejudices, speaking to them through the national/masculine interest in skating rather than on Spoon's musical slant. The film combines a narrative of enforced socialization in a bad institution with a narrative of becoming in a good alternate family. Crystal, growing up transfeminine in rural Canada, is accepted at church but bullied and excluded at school, having to give up the sports she loves because gender-segregated school teams deny her entrance. We see Crystal's hard-won self-defined embodiment being erased by her geographical community. Online, she and her mother discover Los Angeles-based queer and trans* roller derby collective the Vagine Regime, who stage a fundraiser to bring Crystal to California for a roller derby training camp. The connection also broadens the documentary into a portrait of a range of queer and trans* embodiments among the adult team members, and – unlike *Girlfight* or *Bend it Like Beckham* – foregrounds a sport whose rules have been written by and for the feminist and queer communities. It's less about fitting in and more about making your own world.

Its narrative contours of sporting empowerment are a familiar North American trope, not least from Drew Barrymore's directorial debut, *Whip It* (2009), in which Riot Grrrl Bliss (Ellen Page) finds a place to belong via roller derby. *In the Turn* uses the tropes unabashedly, simultaneously to draw in a broad audience and to change the script. Crystal fits in with the Vagine Regime and with her fellow skaters at camp, but, while previous queer cinema has stressed California as *the* queer and trans 'hood, Tremblay uses the international Vagine Regime collective to show that girl 'hood is really a network, a republic of heaven that can – and has to – be made where you are.

Revolution Girl Style Here!

Roller derby emerged as a feminist force from the cultural constellation of Riot Grrrl music, zines and 1990s feminist film and cultural theory. New Queer Cinema, part of the same matrix, has reawoken in the US, kicking off with *Pariah* (Dee Rees, 2011). Rees' debut hews close to the 'coming of age' narrative template, but the dapper style it brings to telling a familiar story is thrilling. The film, like its protagonist Alike (Adepero Oduye), has swagger, bringing the viewer with immediacy and confidence into African American lesbian Brooklyn youth culture. A student of Spike Lee, Rees shares her mentor's ability to capture the energy of a highly specific time and place. The opening club scene, in which AGs (aggressives/butches) flirt with femme performers is a compelling rush: you are right there. Jamilah King argues that 'one of the Rees's biggest achievements [is…] turning what was once taboo (openly gay teens) into something that's painfully ordinary (kids struggling to fit in)', using that narrative framework as a map to unfamiliar territory.[13]

Alike faces familiar struggles such as her parents' conflict and the tension between her education and her social life, but from the new and nuanced position of a queer woman of colour, which enables her to change the situation. The ending, in which Alike gets a scholarship to Berkeley, suggests that she will be enmeshing her learning and partying in the queer capital of the USA, but also that, having chosen a school known for social activism as well as queer theory, she will go on to be an agent of change through her writing.

Alike's scholarship is also a nod towards the foundations and programmes that support independent queer cinema. *Pariah*, like *Circumstance*, was shaped by participation in Sundance Institute labs, and was a beneficiary of the Adrienne Shelly Foundation Women Filmmakers' Grant, an award honouring the director of *Waitress* (2006) and star of Hal Hartley's New American Indie films, who was killed in 2006.[14] The grants and scholarships in Shelly's name are an example of grassroots feminist organizing for diversity in film, alongside the Sarah Jacobson Film Grant. A smaller sum, it is awarded annually to female, trans* or genderqueer filmmakers 'whose work embodies some of the things that Sarah stood for: a fierce DIY approach to filmmaking, a radical social critique, and a thoroughly underground sensibility'.[15] Winners include *KUSAMA: Princess of Polka Dots* (Heather Lenz, 2012) and *Grrrl Love and Revolution: Riot Grrrl NYC* (Abby Moser, 2011), whose footage Sini Anderson quotes in *The Punk Singer*.

The 1990s phenomenon of girl-made media thus persists into the new century, using all the tools available. Grassroots, self-organized and self-documenting formations such as DIY music festival Ladyfest have been joined by Reel Grrls, which can be seen in action in *Wonder Women!*. A media arts and leadership programme for teenagers that aims to create representational justice on and offscreen, Reel Grrls formalizes the kind of collaborative, intersectional practices already being realized ad hoc. Rees encouraged *Pariah* viewers to share their stories of adolescent exclusion and becoming on the *Pariah* YouTube stream.[16] She joins directors such as Tailfeathers and Bonnaire in finding ways of 'shapeshifting' cinematic vision towards a collaborative girl 'hood point of view.

Blame It On

Such projects, alongside the mass experiment in democratization (or exploitation) seen on YouTube and Vine, are increasing access to technical skills while also producing their own conformities. Few grrrl filmmakers apart the from Makhmalbaf sisters or Sadie Benning, who shot her films including 'Girl Power' (1992) on a Fisher-Price camera, have achieved widespread distribution for their films while still in their teens. Independently of their considerable filmmaking skill, both Benning and the Makhmalbafs are also the daughters of well-known male filmmakers (James Benning and Mohsen Makhmalbaf). Samira's first film *The Apple* tells a story that is the absolute opposite of her own experience of leaving school to study with her father, but may reflect unconscious ambivalence about intersecting a master-apprentice relationship with a father-daughter one. But Samira's success also opened a door to distribution for subsequent Muslim-world girl 'hood films by adult filmmakers, such as *Persepolis*, *Wadjda* and *Sepideh* (Berit Madsen, 2014).

Madsen's documentary won fans at Sundance, not least for its focus on an ambitious young Iranian scientist. Conveyed via gorgeous time-lapse photography of the night sky, Sepideh's dream of being an astronaut goes beyond the 'can do' narrative of post-feminist advertizing described by Natalie Baker as 'fempowerment'.[17] In *Persepolis*, Satrapi offers a primer on Iranian feminisms and counter-cultures, a

Girl 'Hood: A Body, a Room and a World of One's Own

girl 'hood that never seems to find a place to be itself. This is never truer than when teenage Marjane (voiced by Chiara Mastroianni) confronts a double whammy in exile in Vienna: the nihilist punk culture at her school and the domineering nuns at her boarding house.

The latter put the morality police in Tehran into context, a reminder that surveillant control of adolescent behaviour is not specific to one religion, as Heidi Ewing and Rachel Grady's terrifying documentary *Jesus Camp* (2006) makes clear. There are few scenes in contemporary cinema more horrific than a small girl having her mouth taped over in preparation for an anti-abortion protest, as an adult male voice offscreen says 'Doesn't she look beautiful?'. Ewing and Grady capture the way in which fundamentalist religion, while asserting control over all children, is most visceral in its girl-training.

In *Wadjda*, sport is freedom, and the classroom the site of stifling girl-training based on the Qu'ran, echoing the filmmaker's experience. Haifaa al-Mansour has described the experience of shooting street scenes in Riyadh while hidden in a van, a Kafkaesque irony given that the film is about a young woman's demand for access to public space and mobility. Dan Zak sums up the irony when he states that al-Mansour 'misses being in the van, she says, then clarifies herself. It's not that she misses being in the van. She misses her mind-set when she was in the van', the mind-set of a ground-breaking, working filmmaker.[18]

The film shows both Wadjda (Waad Mohammed) and her mother (Reem Abdullah), who is working because she knows her husband is about to leave her, still struggling for basic freedoms. Wadjda's craftiness in getting the bicycle she desires is not purely 'can do', nor is her daring coded as 'risky'. Al-Mansour wittily has her proto-easy rider earning her rebellion by excelling at Qu'ranic recitation rather than robbing banks. She is clearly a figure of the filmmaker as rebellious daughter, her bike a stand-in for al-Mansour's camera-van. Imaginatively, al-Mansour remakes her adolescence into a filmmaking girlhood, one in which she took her place in public and told her story.

Made with the imprimatur of King Abdullah and financial support from Prince Alwaleed bin Talal, *Wadjda* also reflects on the delicate balance, and often patronage, necessary for such filmmaking enterprises. Julie Gavras' *La faute à Fidel!* (*Blame it on Fidel*, 2006), like Samira Makhmalbaf's *Apple*, is torn between gratitude to and frustration with parental figures of support and inspiration. Although the film is adapted from an autobiographical novel by Domitilla Calamai, the film's father-figure Fernando (Stefano Accorsi) is clearly a portrait of Gavras' filmmaker father Costa-Gavras. Having left Greece under the Generals to study film in France, Costa-Gavras was blacklisted from university and from a US visa because of his father's suspected Communism.[19] The film smuggles a detailed account of leftist fervour and thought in early 1970s Paris into a wide-eyed coming-of-age drama.

Anna (Nina Kervel-Bey) is heartily sick of her parents' sudden political conversion and its impact on her life, including a rotating carousel of refugee nannies from leftist hot spots, getting dragged on marches and her parents fighting about her mother (Julie Depardieu) signing the infamous Manifesto of the 343, publicly declaring her support for abortion rights. Known as *le manifeste des salopes* (bitches or sluts), its real-life signatories included French film feminists Catherine Deneuve, Marguerite Duras, Delphine Seyrig and Agnès Varda.

At the end of the film, Anna defiantly changes allegiance, choosing to leave her beloved Catholic school for a public one, in solidarity with her parents' politics. She also establishes her independence and suggestively exchanges her biological family for the alternate family of schoolfriends, with whom she will shape her own, twenty-first century-inflected political trajectory. 'Gavras's final shot is a quietly ravishing visual metaphor for Anna's path to political consciousness: In the schoolyard's hustle and bustle, she strikes up a friendship with a group of students playing "Ring Around the Rosie".'[20] In place of the strident dogmatism of her parents' political rhetoric comes a performative, musical, joyful and embodied solidarity.

An artist parent seeking to recapture the romance of her political days is also an ambivalent figure in Maria Saakyan's *Alaverdi* (*I'm Going to Change My Name*, 2012). Sona's (Maria Atlas) lonely daughter Evridika (Arina Adju) finds her girl 'hood online on a suicide fantasy website, where she posts imaginative animations and music. But it is Sona's ex Pyotr (Evgeniy Tsyganov) who is the unsettling force; reappearing, he distracts Sona further while being romanced by Evridika's suicidal fantasies. It is through a risky encounter with Pyotr that Evridika works out how to save herself and begin again. Saakyan's eerie film is one of the best representations to date of adolescent online self-fashioning. For Evridika, the threat of suicide is leverage, one of the few powerful tools available to her as a teenage girl in an isolated small town in post-Soviet Armenia.

A self-willed Eurydice, she both enters and survives the myth without a need for an Orpheus. In *Female Perversions*, the only feminist cultural theory book to have been adapted as a feature film (Susan Streitfeld, 1996), Louise J. Kaplan talks about self-cutting as a creative act, one that both crafts the body and asserts control over it.[21] Lauren Greenfield's documentary *Thin* (2006) subtly explores the possibility that anorexia might be a perverse form of resistance to body fascism as well as an escape from oppressive families. Suicidal ideation is at once creative and terroristic,

Girl 'Hood: A Body, a Room and a World of One's Own

Fig. 22: Billie and James connect online and offline, *52 Tuesdays*

an imaginative space charged with intense poetic emotions that is also a demand for attention, a demand that the film, in lieu of Evridika's mother, answers.

Sophie Hyde's *52 Tuesdays* (2014) takes a more positive view of parental support for self-fashioning, as well as exploring the increasing similarities between parents and teenagers generated by digital second lives. James (Del Herbert-Jane) announces to daughter Billie (Tilda Cobham-Hervey) that he has decided, finally, to live as the man he has always known he was, telling her he will need time alone, and distance on motherhood, to fashion himself; suggestively, to enter a second adolescence of sexual becoming. Billie goes to live with her father, agreeing to see James for dinner every Tuesday evening. Both parent and daughter turn to digital video as a way to understand the changes in their lives; James becomes part of an online community of people transitioning, sharing documentation of physical and psychological stages of the process. When it turns out he is adversely affected by testosterone, he switches off the camera, the internet and his relationship with Billie.

This allows Billie to enter further into her own digital documentary daring, filming the sexual play of Jasmin (Imogen Arthur) and Josh (Sam Althuizen), a cool older couple from her school. After she falls out with Jasmin, she edits her films together with news footage and her own video diaries, and presents a DVD to Jasmin, who has not consented for the filming sessions to be used as part of an art project. Her distress prompts an intervention by all three teens' parents, although it is the young people who resolve their friendship bonds together. While Billie's project is censored within the diegesis, it becomes a frame for our viewing, as her video diaries meditating on time, change, political upheaval and identity appear metronomically throughout the film. Through its frankness, the film holds a space that reshapes the home, the hospital, the school and the screen.

Hyde has said: 'I feel upset that we as a culture have decided that naked children are pornographic… As the mother of a child I feel we are suggesting that her body is shameful and I'm frustrated by that'. In the same interview, Cobham-Hervey asserted that 'If it felt scary I would just say "Sophie, this feels scary"'.[22] While this collaborative practice is rare in the mainstream, Hollywood high-grosser Catherine Hardwicke started her film career by co-writing the low-budget *Thirteen* (2003) with its teenage co-star Nikki Reed. Reed plays Evie, the bad girl next door who leads Tracy (Evan Rachel Wood) astray. Melanie (Holly Hunter), Tracy's mother, is a compelling representation of a working-poor single mom whose struggles with her daughter are fraught with economics as well as the generational divide. Wood's performance as Tracy is genuinely risk-taking, most notably in the scene in which she terrorizes her mother with the chant 'No bra, no panties', embodying Kaplan's female perversion.

It's no accident that the film is set in Los Angeles; Tracy and Evie are, suggestively, products of the entertainment industry's girl-training in the post-feminist era and milieu recounted in Ariel Levy's *Female Chauvinist Pigs* (2006). Levy notes in the introduction: 'As former adult film star Traci Lords put it to a reporter a few days before her memoir hit the best-seller list in 2003 [the year *Thirteen* was released], "When I was in porn, it was like a back-alley thing. Now it's everywhere"'.[23] While I disagree with Levy's blanket dismissal of pro-sex feminism, it is undeniable that the hyper-sexualization of young women by celebrity and commodity culture became a prominent element of Anglophone girl-training in the late 1990s. *Thirteen* is the perfect cautionary tale of that moment, in which girl 'hood explicitly begins to negotiate with an everywhere that is pornified.

To My Sister(s)

Catherine Breillat prefigured Hardwicke's film with her scintillating and disturbing *À ma soeur* (*Fat Girl*, 2001). Desiree Akhavan described it to me as the progenitor of the new wave of sexually-open feminist cinema:

> When I saw that film, it was such an incredible moment of thinking: 'This is what filmmaking is, this is how you fuck with the medium'. I see the way that sex is depicted in films as a feminist pursuit of mine... and that's something Breillat has done in all her work.[24]

As Kay Armatage describes, the film was banned in Canada, but a successful legal challenge to the ban not only led to the film's release, uncut, but to the closing of the Ontario Censor Board.[25] Breillat's film literally opened up possibilities for feminist cinema in Canada.

Western European cinema has been, in general, more open to the risky girl. For Molly Haskell, in her essay on Bonnaire in *À nos amours*,

> The teenage girl on the cusp of sexual awakening is a beloved icon of French cinema... But over the years, as one transfixing newcomer after another, barely out of braces and backpacks, embarks on the *vita sexualis*, we have to wonder, whose sexuality is it, exactly? Is this the way they see themselves, are these their yearnings, or is this precocious sensuality a projection of the guilty desires and fears of directors old enough to be their fathers?[26]

Haskell's question remains relevant. We can ask 'whose sexuality is it, exactly?' of cismale-directed films such as *La vie d'Adèle* (*Blue is the Warmest Colour*, Abdellatif Kechiche, 2013) or *Jeune et jolie* (François Ozon, 2014), both of which have won plaudits and brickbats in equal measure from feminist viewers for their fantasies of adolescent female desire/ability.

The *frisson* carried by the rebellious schoolgirl as a figure of transgression is frequently put to work by European feminist filmmakers. Jessica Hausner's *Lovely Rita* (2001), Katell Quillévéré's *Un poison violent* (*Love Like Poison*, 2010), Rebecca Zlotowski's *Belle épine* (2010), Alice Rohrwacher's *Corpo Celeste* (2011), Muriel d'Ansembourg's short 'Good Night' (2012), Frances Lea's *Strawberry Fields* (2012) and Agnès Troublé's *Je m'appelle Hmmm...* (*My Name is Hmmm...*, 2013): European female auteures appear to establish themselves with first films that centre on these descendants of Suzanne and Mona, vagabonds of desire, whose girl 'hood consists of testing boundaries. In Franco-Lithuanian filmmaker Alanté Kavaïté's Sundance winner *The Summer of Sangaile* (2015), gravity itself is tested by wannabe pilot Sangaile (Julija Steponaityte), where her loop-the-loops parallel the intense bodily experience of first love and sex with her girlfriend Auste (Aiste Dirziute).

Adolescent female sexuality provides a narrative motor of risk, often in relation to older male figures of wish-fear, and likewise in counter-formation to the

Catholic Church as girl-training institution. Yet these narratives are often implicitly framed as hagiographies in which the adolescent girl's body is the site of spectacular torture to prove her faith/heroism (and provide a legitimate turn-on). Małgorzata Szumowska's Silver Bear-winning *Ciało* (*Body*, 2015) makes dark comedy from the ways in which the Church legitimates and eroticizes images of extreme embodiment. Twenty-year-old anorexic Olga (Justyna Suwala), according to Szumowska, 'hates her body, which she sees as something useless. She wants to be free, to be void of its corporeality. She is a victim of this contemporary chase for an ideal body which in the end doesn't exist at all'.[27] Juxtaposing Olga's group therapy sessions with her father's police work, Szumowska shows how Olga resists girl-training under the Law of the Father, although she chooses a dangerous method.

Like Szumowska's film, Troublé's *My Name is Hmmm...* is compelling in that, unlike the others, it is premised on the reality of adolescent girls' behaviour and experiences, rather than on Electra fantasies. Céline (Lou-Léila Demerliac) renames herself Hmmm after she runs away on a class trip, determined not to return home to her sexually abusive father. In what could be read as her fantasy, a truck driver called Peter Ellis (Douglas Gordon) takes care of her. Peter's truck is festooned with fairy lights, op art curtains and sparkly horses, a clear sign that he is Hmmm's invention, a willed manifestation of a safe girl 'hood that is at once a bedroom and on the move.

Troublé's film, like Tailfeathers' and Derrick's 'Hurry Up', is an essay on how trauma alters perception. Peter and Hmmm encounter Butoh dancers, a bonfire, a dancing windsock and street art, moments of abstract joy that enable Hmmm to rebuild herself in her idiosyncratic strangeness, reflected by the film's odd temporality and point of view. It shares this strangeness, on the edge of fantasy or allegory, with *Innocence* (2004), Lucile Hadžihalilović's sinisterly dreamy adaptation of Frank Wedekind's novella, *Mine-Haha, or On the Bodily Education of Young Girls* (1903). *Innocence* is a beautiful film, and a film about beauty, in which young women attend a fantastical boarding school they cannot leave. As its title suggests, that beauty is intensified by a sense of fragility, and the film's overwhelming saturated colour becomes a kind of violation.

Hadžihalilović described her static camera as akin to 'pinning butterflies in a box', its fixed framing creating an additional discomfort around the question of what lies beyond the school garden's high wall.[28] The filmmaker told film phenomenologist Vivian Sobchack that 'the further the story progresses without giving any answers, the more the anxiety builds'.[29] *Innocence* is a problematic for

Hadžihalilović, something from which her characters need to break free, in a stark contrast to Hollywood's insistence on virginal teens.

In the final scene, emergence is conflated with meeting young men, suggesting that innocence belongs specifically to the discarded all-female world of the Gothic girls' school. Just as the risky-girl film admits and is ambivalent about its schoolgirl *frisson*, so too the Gothic girls' school, in which the risk is not just female sexuality but homosociality, often figured as (murderous) hysteria. The unstable lesbian makes an appearance in Mary Harron's *The Moth Diaries* (2011), which attempts to adapt a novel by Rachel Klein that is utterly dependent on an unreliable first-person narrator. Harron struggles to find a cinematic equivalent, having to commit to the psychological reality of Rebecca's (Sarah Bolger) perceptions, be they of vampires or queer desire. The book's delicate conjuration of grief and its traumatic effects on perception are lost as the film adopts familiar horror tropes that appear to address both a heteropatriarchal fetishization of adolescent girls, and the same audience's anxiety about what those girls get up to alone, together.

Jordan Scott's *Cracks* (2009) makes a better attempt at capturing the ambiguous intensity of boarding school friendships and their fallout, adapting Sheila Kohler's novel.[30] The film's 1950s English setting, transposing the novel from South Africa, draws attention to the framing of girl 'hood within oppressive social strictures. There's a slim suggestion that the girls' attentive bonding is a nascent proto-feminism that is formed by classism and racism as well as misogyny. Yet the film also shades into lesbophobia, particularly with relation to Miss G (Eva Green), cast initially as a catalyst and then, once her 'secret' is revealed, as a predator. Yet the St. Agnes' Eve scene, in which the girls dress and make each other up, across a range of gender roles, is palpably, tenderly erotic: a door that the film then slams shut.

Léa Poole's *Lost and Delirious* (2001) also curtails its central lesbian relationship, but makes clear that it is classism and homophobia that leads to tragedy. Adapted, once again, from a novel (Susan Swan's *The Wives of Bath*, based on her own boarding school years), Poole's film updates Swan's novel from the 1950s.[31] Yet the conventions of the Gothic girls' school are so powerful that there are few signs of the 1990s bar a long take in which Paulie (Piper Perabo) sobs convulsively to Ani DiFranco over the end of her relationship with Tori (Jessica Paré). Paulie's Shakespeare-quoting, fencing and hawking are at once bold adoptions of traditionally masculine pursuits, and a sad mimicry of Tori's class status. While the film eschews the novel's daringly grotesque ending, in which Paulie murders a man and glues his penis to her pelvis in an attempt to win back Tori, it is clear that possessing the mobile phallus (in the form of the fencing foil, 'pale, stale, male' quotation, or bird of prey) cannot be the solution, whatever the *frisson* it allows.

THEM AND US

Carol Morley's *The Falling* (2014) adopts the ruse of a Gothic girls' school drama, amping up the horror cues with flash inserts, called 'subliminals' by the filmmaker.[32] These often show body parts or bloody hands, accompanied by a buzz drone, dramatizing the mass hysteria (now called mass psychogenic illness) sweeping through a private girls' school in Oxfordshire in 1969. Like *Innocence*, *The Falling* associates female adolescence with the natural world, but here it is autumn rather than spring, with massive trees both decaying and deceptive as their reflections tremor in the lake. Girls, suggests the film, are still waters beneath whose reflective surfaces are dark depths. The film leaves the cause of the mass illness ambiguous, invoking grief, desire, rage, historical change, ley lines, hormones, performance and suggestibility. It moots what I call patriarchal affective disorder, transmitted from the state via the school and the family, as the real cause.

'IT'S THEM AND US, TITCH', shouts the protagonist Lydia Lamont (Maisie Williams) (aka Lamb, a reference to Blakean innocence) at her sceptical friend Titch (Rose Caton), who refuses to accept that Lydia's fainting has a biological cause. Morley has her fainting schoolgirls interrogated by a disbelieving psychiatrist (Simon Paisley Day), whose questions show the limits of medical science. Indeed, the girls resist him with silence or, in Lydia's case, a sharp assertion that he is patronizing her. Although the film shares with *The Moth Diaries* and *Lost and Delirious* an unrequited lesbian love story at its centre, the focus of the plot is not how Lydia goes uncontrollably mad after the death of her best friend Abbie (Florence Pugh), but how she very much goes sane. While her intelligence is engaged by the damaging double standard and her vision shapeshifted by trauma, she cannot articulate her new knowledge in words because she is pierced to the core by loss. Fainting – and Lydia's compulsive relationship with her brother Kenneth (Joe Cole), who had briefly been Abbie's lover – are the expressive female perversions that get her through.

In a device hauntingly similar to Morley's short 'Stalin My Neighbour' (2004), in which Annie (Alicya Eyo) answers questions about a past trauma she wants to forget as asked by an offscreen documentary-maker who turns out to be imaginary and internal, the psychiatrist in *The Falling* is initially represented solely as an adult male voice offscreen. It is only Lydia who is able to re-embody this voice of God, through cuts between her twitchy gaze and medium close-ups of a foot, a calf and finally a face. Whereas the psychiatrist remains a powerful authoritative voice to the others, to Lydia's frank gaze he is just a man (in bits).

Her realizations about how the world works are painful and maddening, but powerful, as her teachers learn when they attempt to isolate her from her friends. Morley is generous to the teachers, particularly the melancholy Miss Mantel (Greta Scacchi), who sees herself as a trembling ghost reflected in the classroom window. When she tells Abbie that she, too, will be 'living history' it's hard not to hear her name as a reference to celebrated novelist Hilary Mantel, and to imagine a different future for this thwarted woman, who is painfully prompted by Abbie's death to remember the girl she once was. Yet these private glimpses (including near-hysteria fostered between Miss Mantel and headmistress Miss Alvaro [Monica Dolan] about being middle-aged and misunderstood) do not disrupt keeping up appearances: it is Them and Us.

Lydia contests this closed front, standing up in her final school assembly and declaring, 'You all know something is wrong. Are you not going to fight for the truth?… Kill the system! It's killing you!' She calls for solidarity in the face of systemic oppression, and her friends all back her, telling her she is not crazy, even as she punches into the crumbling plaster wall of the school toilets, determined to find the 'something' that is poisoning her life. She finds it not at school, but at home, with her agoraphobic and emotionally distant mother Eileen (Maxine Peake). Or rather: she finds it between the two, at the oak tree that was hers and Abbie's special place.

Above all, girl 'hoods are made in spaces and places where girls come together, either physically, or technologically, or imaginatively. Evridika and Billie demonstrate that the internet is as powerful a site of girl 'hood as the sports field or the malls where Marieme/Vic and the Mean Girls roam. These often temporary spaces, used against their purpose, might offer a place a girl can call home, where she can come to inhabit her body (or, in the case of trans*, non-binary or intersex characters, also his, hir or their bodies). Flung up in the branches of an oak tree, almost a girl in the moon, Lydia pulls herself out of the institutions of school and the nuclear family. She creates a new kind of girl 'hood, a fragile night-time space that incorporates the transgenerational, the queer, the elemental, the spiritual and the performative; a displaced place in which she can become.

9

Haunted Houses
Reclaiming 'Women's Cinema'

Safe as Houses

Girl 'hood, as Carol Morley shows in *The Falling*, is intimately entwined with questions of maturity and maternity, including a mourning for the lost possibilities of mother-daughter relationships. The film ends with a reconciliation between Lydia and Eileen: when Lydia jumps/falls into the mere beneath the oak tree at the peak of her grief, her mother Eileen braves everything to come after her. As Eileen pulls her out of the water, Lydia sees (her mother as) her best friend Abbie, eliding the two most potent women in her life. Lydia positions Abbie as a second mother, her pregnant, sexually more mature friend who nurtured her and inducted her into adult life; but she also realizes that her mother was once Abbie, a beautiful and brave young woman trapped by patriarchy.

Crucially, this realization and reconciliation happens outside a major patriarchal trap: the family home. There's a telling scene in which Lydia folds herself into the bottom shelf of a wardrobe, mimicking her mother's agoraphobia. The films discussed here are simultaneously wedging themselves into that womb-like space and working themselves out of it, dealing with both the longing and the visceral anxiety provoked by the thought of the domestic, maternal home. Rebecca Solnit borrows the phrase 'the faraway nearby' from letters by Georgia O'Keeffe to describe her relationship with her mother.[1] I borrow it here in turn as a powerful descriptor for how feminist cinema approaches maternity and domesticity: something so intimate it requires distance to be approached.

Dodie Bellamy, another San Francisco-based writer, uses her love of *E.T.* (Steven Spielberg, 1982) to frame an essay about caring for her mother while she had cancer. From its title onwards, 'Phone Home' evokes the daughter's simultaneous alienation from the domestic and her longing to return, and the subsequent strangeness of her location in the maternal home as an adult, via the film as viewed on TV. 'As we watch *E.T.* fragments coalesce and point in one direction: Home. Home is a place of perfect belonging, wholeness. Home is an instinct, a yearning that has never, ever been satisfied'.[2]

Televisions conjoin the interlinked yet fractured familial spaces in Lucrecia Martel's first film *La Ciénaga* (*The Swamp*, 2001). Martel's film won the Golden Bear at Berlin, 'mark[ing] what might be the most auspicious debut of a woman cineaste so far this century'.[3] Patricia White describes the film as a 'deconstructed, oneiric melodrama', a drift through the history of the melodramatic 'women's film' and its Latin American equivalents.[4] As in a *telenovela*, there are thwarted quasi-incestuous romances, sororal rivalries, wounded bodies, a hidden pregnancy, languid heat, rebellious daughters, lost dresses, a final symbolic disaster, lots of early afternoon drinking – and an apparition of the Virgin. It's this latter that forms the televisual substrate of the film, one which blurs the medium and its message as monstrous matriarch Mecha (Graciela Borges) and her sprawling family (children, sister, nieces and nephews, domestic workers) catch ongoing news reports about the apparition on the water tower of a nearby house.

The first characters in the film to 'see' the Virgin are Mecha's youngest daughter Momi (Sofia Bertolotto) and the family's younger domestic worker Isabel (Andrea Lopez), a young indigenous woman on whom Momi has a desperate crush. They are lying in a tangle of limbs watching TV as a reporter interviews a woman called Nilda whose daughter Miriam saw the Virgin on the tank that looms on stilts above their small house. Television can't capture the Virgin's image: we can see only a rusting water tank and then a shy young woman who struggles to find the words to describe her experience once it is mediatized. Television is doubly a home invader, first as the doorstepping camera, and then as the screen in the corner. Visuality – and particularly televisuality – are paralleled with the European colonizers, who have brought the faraway nearby.

Mecha even fears her own telephone, forcing her indigenous domestic workers to answer it. Telephones link there to here, creating dangerous cracks in the self-sufficiency of each location and speaker. Several scenes in the film consist of one side of a phone conversation in which information circulates between the various domestic spaces, infecting them. Sound, which leaks and connects, creates the palpable mood of threat: the film opens with the sound of thunder and closes, over the end credits, with the sound of a car door slamming and a radio playing mariachi, then losing its tuning as the thunder encroaches.

These noises off are explicitly linked to the indigenous community when Mecha's extremely sound-sensitive sister Tali (Mercedes Morán) complains vehemently about 'their' noise in the street, which sounds to her like a protest. It's a

Fig. 23: Isabel and Momi in Isabel's room, *The Swamp*

carnival, and there is a thread that links the music in the street to the final music on the radio, and to the rumble of thunder, as a premonition of an indigenous resurgence or revolution in the face of the European invaders. *The Swamp*, as do Martel's subsequent films, raises the faint possibility that it's the daughters who may escape the monstrous middle-class home via loving allegiance with other young women, particularly indigenous women.[5] After Isabel, who is pregnant, leaves Mecha's house, Momi goes to see the Virgin.

Although the Virgin never (re)appears, there's something supernatural and haunting about *The Swamp*. Martel told Haden Guest that all her film titles 'seem like B-movie titles, and I love that'.[6] With no special effects or direct scares, *The Swamp* is a horror film, with Mecha and Tali's late bedridden mother as, suggestively, the ghost who haunts the decaying house – and even as the house itself. Mary Ann Doane argues that in women's films such as *Rebecca* (Alfred Hitchcock, 1940), 'the house becomes an analogue of the human body, its parts fetishized by textual operations'.[7] In contemporary animated children's films such as *Monster House* (Gil Kenan, 2006) and *Up* (Pete Docter and Bob Peterson, 2009), the suburban home is haunted by – and in the former, literally possessed by – a dead housewife.

House Wives

The angel in the house, to use Virginia Woolf's phrase, continues to haunt even avowedly liberal feminist cinema: the latest wave of female-helmed indies from the USA is still in thrall to the malaise identified in Betty Friedan's *The Feminine Mystique* (1963). Canadian director Tara Johns' *The Year Dolly Parton Was My Mom* (2011) at least sets its depiction of an oppressed housewife in 1960s suburbia, and tackles divorce and adoption as well. Rebecca Miller adopts a similar strategy in *The Private Lives of Pippa Lee* (2009), which roots its eponymous protagonist's (Robin Wright) marital discontent in memories of her working-class 1950s childhood. But unhappy marriages abound, and heteropatriarchal capitalism is rarely mooted as the cause.

Contemporary white, well-educated, middle-class housewives may try to throw off the shackles of discontent via elective sex work (*Concussion*, Stacie Passon, 2013), adopting a homeless sex worker (*Afternoon Delight*, Jill Soloway, 2013), or having an affair (*The Kids Are All Right*, Lisa Cholodenko, 2010) in current 'edgy' female-helmed comedies. All of these solutions seem patently borrowed from *le cinéma du papa*; we could call them the *Belle du jour* (Luis Buñuel, 1988), *Boudu sauvé des eaux* (*Boudu Saved from Drowning*, Jean Renoir, 1932) and bleeding obvious models. Jules's (Julianne Moore) affair may be with her sperm donor, cheating on her female partner Nic (Annette Bening), but Cholodenko's film wears its social politics so lightly it's hard to tell whether the cliché is being deployed knowingly to satirize the smug middle-class marrieds who have left queer politics behind, or it's just a witty twist.

And witty these films are: well-crafted, well-acted, well-made and well-received, prompting debate and fandom in equal measure. Yet the comedy of awkwardness often only touches on hot-button issues. Moreover, as when Rachel (Kathryn Hahn) invites McKenna (Juno Temple) into her home in *Afternoon Delight*, these films use the outsider as a step in their normative protagonists' recovery programs. Why, five decades after Friedan's book, are so many women whose mothers read it still caught in the home trap? Bright, white, privileged ciswomen, the protagonists of these films are trying to be good *and* to have it all.

Soloway's online series *Transparent* has the insightful twist of having transwoman Maura (Jeffrey Tambor) wrestling with the burden and duties of the liberal American Jewish *paterfamilias*. After coming out and moving into a queer community block, she slips the question of selling the family home by giving it to her oldest child, Sarah (Amy Landecker), who has left her heteronormative marriage to reunite with her college girlfriend Tammy (Melora Hardin). Maura's youngest daughter Ali (Gaby Hoffmann) then goes on a hot date with transman Dale (Ian Harvie). He may over-determinedly ask her to call him Daddy, but all the (straight) father figures have disappeared and (queer) mothers proliferate, attached umbilically to Maura's mid-century modern California dream house.

Nicole Holofcener comes the closest to blowing the whistle on these home/bodies, with Catherine Keener as her muse. She is a restless, discontented presence in *Lovely and Amazing* (2001), where her character Michelle's tiny furniture is surely the wellspring for Lena Dunham's so-titled film (2010). In *Friends with Money* (2006), *Please Give* (2010) and *Enough Said* (2013), Keener is indeed *keener*: both sharper and more elegiac in her portrayals of women on the edge. Michelle is an artist and stay-at-home mom who initiates a relationship with teenage Jordan (Jake Gyllenhaal), ending in a make-out session fatally undermined when she notices that his mom (Lee Garlington) has the same dressing gown that she does. As Claire Perkins observes, 'Keener's distracted fixation on the mother's robe may mock middle-class values and behavior, but it does not reduce female experience to a caricature of malaise'.[8] It's her no-bullshit bond with her youngest sister Annie (Raven Goodwin), an African American girl recently adopted by her white English mother Jane (Brenda Blethyn), that is most hopeful – not least because the film closes with Annie rearranging her mother's pillows in a scene that both suggests she's found a home, and that she now holds the point of view.

Even Holofcener's and Keener's sharp-tongued anti-heroines can't escape the house/wife double helix. It's there too in Joanna Hogg's *Exhibition* (2013), in which artist D (Viv Albertine) finds that the aesthetically stunning space she had thought was her 'room of one's own' is both a difficult child and a sterile trap, an aesthetic project that remains coextensive with her physical and affective body. Straight marriage and middle-class bohemian life have frustrated and etiolated her: can she break free? As Kim Longinotto's documentary *Salma* (2013) shows, the trap of the home/body is not just metaphorical for many women outside the over-developed world. 'It's so hard to know the full scale of the suffering', she notes, 'because it happens behind closed doors, in secret, in the family'.[9]

Longinotto writes that, 'Salma's mother was like her jailer – refusing to let her go out or go to school', on the instruction of her husband; yet once her daughter married and began writing poetry, 'she helped her escape by smuggling out the poems in the dirty laundry'.[10] Salma, now a celebrated poet and politician, makes clear, however, that her rebellion is within the context of a continued connection to her family and village, not a rejection. In 'My Ancestral Home – 2', Salma speaks unsparingly about her mother's hysterectomy and the loss of her first home:

> The excitement pouring forth
> from the center of my heart
> that bit of flesh, where
> my life had once found shelter
> turns later into enormous grief.[11]

The poem speaks to the complex emotional and practical bonds between mother and daughter, flesh and feeling, home and world.

The home – and its associations with motherhood, family, domestic labour and the economic – is thus both hymned and horrorized in feminist cinema. In particular, the middle-class white mother seems caught in the double bind. As Tammy Oler writes in 'The Mommy Trap', Stewart Thorndike's low-budget horror *Lyle* (2014) 'is *Rosemary's Baby* [Roman Polanski, 1968] meets [Sheryl Sandberg's book] *Lean In*: a horror film that takes the idea of sacrificing your children for your career to its logical yet horrible extreme'.[12] Jennifer Kent's international hit *The Babadook* (2014), which is where Oler starts her review of the trope, has renewed discussions about the possibility of a feminist horror cinema. It joins Lynne Ramsay's critically-acclaimed adaptation of Lionel Shriver's novel *We Need to Talk about Kevin* (2011) in the small canon of feminist films about maternal disquiet, violent and vivid expressions of the everyday mutual love-hate that binds mother and child under patriarchy.[13]

Like *The Falling*, *The Babadook* is motivated by ambivalence about the family home as safe space. In *The Falling*, Eileen's home contains (in both senses) the rape by which she conceived Lydia, but also the traumatic loss of her husband through divorce or separation. Amelia's (Essie Davis) home in *The Babadook* similarly contains deep grief for the loss of a husband, a grief that she can't move through. In both cases, the mothers project their own traumatic, melancholic relation to the absent fathers onto their eldritch children. *The Babadook* commits totally to its genre semantics, gleefully and chillingly reworking the psychological horrors of the maternal dyad latent in films such as *Carrie* (Brian De Palma, 1976, and remade by Kimberley Peirce, 2013). In Kent's film, paternity is the repressed, in Freudian terms, that returns through son Samuel (Noah Wiseman) as medium. That's audible in the very title of the film: Peter Bradshaw may hear it as 'perhaps baby-talk for baby's book, or mama's book', but the babadook is clearly the dadda-book.[14] The house is haunted by the controlling narrative of the nuclear family in which the mother and child are lost without the father.

Horror and science fiction have long exploited the alien anxieties of pregnancy, motherhood and the family home, an association identified by Sigmund Freud when he defined the uncanny in relation to the womb and female genitals.[15] Bodies and buildings that are supposedly 'safe as houses' are overrun with supernatural or interstellar beings, generally as a comment on the fearful Otherness with which patriarchy regards ciswomen and their (in)ability to conceive (and choice to do so or not). Being a mother equates, in the patriarchal imagination, to being a bad mother, who ended the dyad and will not allow the subject to re-enter the womb.

There is no way out of the double bind: pregnant women and mothers are monsters, childfree ciswomen are unnatural.

Chika Anadu's *B for Boy* (2013) shows the impact of these deep-seated wish-fears on Amaka (Uche Nwadili), a post-modern Igbo Lagosian 'have it all' working mother with a loving and beloved husband and beautiful daughter. But her husband, influenced by his traditional mother, wants a son. When Amaka miscarries, she turns to Joy (Frances Okeke), a surrogate involved in a con. Joy is pregnant, broke and has run away from her partner in the scam; Amaka agrees to support Joy if she can adopt Joy's son. The women bond precariously, riven by the demands of a patriarchal and capitalist society that sets them against each other, resulting in a provocative ending. Imperious, entitled and haunted, Amaka is as complex and ambivalent a character as Eva (Tilda Swinton) in *We Need to Talk About Kevin*, while Joy – like McKenna in *Afternoon Delight* – is opaque, her motivations unknowable to the viewer as they are to Amaka. Through Amaka's false pregnancy belly, her mother-in-law's village rituals, and the strange apparitional and transferable pregnancy, Anadu mobilizes the tropes of Nollywood horror within a realist film.

For Jax (Nadine Marshall) in debbie tucker green's *Second Coming*, her perimenopausal, possibly pregnant body and her family home are entwined as sites of anxiety through a similar combination of the realist and the fantastic. She has vivid nightmares (initially coded as waking hallucinations) in which torrential rain falls on her in her bathroom, as her husband and son sleep. Again, social realism and horror semantics are fused, with the film never settling the question of paternity, or even of her pregnancy's reality. tucker green takes a bold risk in exploring the association of maternity, menopause and madness, wielding a powerful combination of authenticity and genre-inflected ambiguity towards an ending that privileges Jax's perceptions and experiences as a woman and a mother.

House Call

While horror is the genre of (bad) motherhood, the police thriller is currently being used, by feminist filmmakers, as a genre of displaced motherhood, one that examines the conflict between career and parenting, and points to the state as bad father. In particular, feminist procedurals offer a powerful site for critiquing the nuclear family's secrets and abuses, and effecting alternate, elective families predicated on mutual respect borne of shared survival of trauma.

Amy Taubin writes of July Jung's *Dohee-ya* (*A Girl at My Door*, 2014) that 'Jung's indictment of Korean machismo is as unsparing as her depiction of the confusion of identification, desire, and guilt in the policewoman's rescue fantasy'.[16] Unsurprisingly, a film in which Young-Nam (Doona Bae), an alcoholic lesbian policewoman, attempts to redeem herself by rescuing Dohee (Sae-ron Kim), a brutally, systematically abused teenage girl who – on realizing she has inadvertently sent her protector to prison – sets up her father to be arrested for rape, has proven controversial. The final shot, of Young-Nam watching Dohee sleep in the rain-spattered car, suggests that she has re-inscribed the work of policing from upholding state justice (which is corrupted by patriarchal norms) to caring immediately and intimately.

A growing number of cisfemale onscreen cops are tackling gendered violence, as in Maïwenn's ensemble drama *Polisse* (2011). Undercover anti-corruption officer He Yanhong/An Xin (Zhao Wei) in Ann Hui's *Goddess of Mercy* (2003) is an unusual exception. Writers and filmmakers want to foreground investigations into sexual violence, but at the same time, female detectives are pigeonholed into those roles and/or given traumatic backstories that not only justify but naturalize their commitment to their jobs. This is true of Robin (Elisabeth Moss) in Jane Campion's *Top of the Lake*, but it's one of the many clichés that Campion explores in order to expose.

As Anne Helen Petersen notes in her 'incomplete list of all the shit Robin Griffin has to deal with', Campion shows Robin as embedded in rape culture rather than a tragic exception. Her investigation of herself and her gang rape as a teenager is the loose thread that unravels the entire weave of the home town to which she has returned. What sets Robin apart from recent televisual detectives, argues Petersen, is 'her desperate desire to save the next generation of women from her own fate. Lots of characters try to save their daughters, but the wide-eyed, wordless Tui embodies something broader than blood connection'.[17] Robin, who is a child offences officer, finds herself, like Young-Nam, protecting one particular girl, Tui (Jacqueline Joe), the mixed-race daughter of smalltown crime lord Matt (Peter Mullan) and his ex-wife Kimmie (Michelle Ang).

In particular, Robin trails Tui when she goes missing via photographs, texts on her cell phone and a video clip, whose author is indeterminate: possibly a local man who is on the sex offenders' register; possibly Tui's best friend Jamie (Luke Buchanan). Robin's job is to rescue Tui from being or becoming the cinematic artefact that these traces imply, one more (di)splayed dead girl, contained and punished for leaving home, like those on concurrent British television shows as observed by Fiona Sturges.[18] Robin grasps these tools, the trail of breadcrumbs that Tui leaves for her, in order to crack the case, finally pointing her cellphone camera, balanced on her gun, at the members of paedophile ring responsible for the rape of Tui and other teenagers in the town.

Campion uses the multi-part, ensemble nature of the TV mini-series to conjure the eerie over-closeness of a small town whose supposed safety acts as a cover for the depredations of corrupt police chief Al (David Wenham). It is in Al's house that Robin discovers and reveals that it is the paternal state, which polices women, that is itself commissioning violence against them. Home, here, is too close for comfort. By trusting her intuition and rejecting the police hierarchy, Robin finally forges an unconventional family of her own with her lover Johnno (Thomas M. Wright), Tui and Tui's son Noa, all four of them posited as Matt's children at one point or another, and now all of uncertain paternity. They are living on what was once Matt's land, known as Paradise, whose sale to a female commune was the prompt for many of Matt's irrational actions (including murder). Matt's story about the land's name, which relates it ironically to the murderous European colonizers who first appropriated it, makes clear the show's attempt to foreground the connection between colonial and sexual violence. In a transitional unhome on this contested land Robin, like Young-Nam stopped in a car between two places, begins to reconcile her traumatic experiences and career ambitions with the demands of family.

Home Work

Among the other terrible things with which Robin Griffin has to deal is her mother Jude's (Robin Nevin) suffering and death from cancer, which brought her back to Laketop from Sydney. Emerging into maturity requires a reckoning with being a daughter in feminist home/body cinema. In *The Swamp*, Mecha and Tali may not be mourning their mother, but they are certainly compelled by her memory. Martel says that her 'love of storytelling comes from oral tradition, the stories from my grandmother and conversations with my mother. The world is full of discussions of condensation, drifts, misunderstanding, repetition. These are the materials I work with. My debt is to these women'.[19] Domestic labour and the haunted house unite in the oral tradition.

As Marina Warner notes, 'Cinderella is a child in mourning for her mother, as her name tells us; her penitential garb is ash… the sign of loss, the symbol of mortality'.[20] Warner points out that the upper-class men who wrote the story down, Giambattista Basile and Charles Perrault, both explain her name through an association with housework and her status as a domestic worker. Cinderella, grey among the ashes, stands for all invisible and undervalued domestic labour, as described by Silvia Federici in her still-searing pamphlet *Wages against Housework* in 1975. She argued that 'housework been imposed on women, but it has been transformed into a natural attribute of our female physique and personality, an internal need, an aspiration, supposedly coming from the depth of our female character'.[21]

Haunted Houses: Reclaiming 'Women's Cinema'

Claudia Llosa's *La Teta Asustada* (*The Milk of Sorrow*, 2009) resurfaces the filial grief for which this essentialized domestic labour is a cover story. Her film's title literally means *The Frightened Breast*, which shares a B-movie quality with Martel's titles (*The Terrified Tit*, maybe). Llosa also followed Martel in winning the Golden Bear at Berlin, as well as an Academy Award nomination for Best Foreign Film, Peru's first ever. The film opens with Llosa's regular collaborator, Quechua actor and singer Magaly Solier, listening to an older woman sing, in Quechua, a litany of her rape and torture, which will be part of the film's larger indictment of sexual violence by European-ancestry men against indigenous women.

Perpetua (Bárbara Lazón) is dying. Her daughter Fausta (Solier) tends to her mother's body, suggesting that the true fairytale labour of a daughter among the ashes is mourning for the lost mother, who also stands for and carries in herself the loss of indigenous land rights and culture. Jules Koostachin's beautiful short documentary 'PLACEnta' (2014) narrates the inverse of this, as Koostachin seeks the correct spot for a traditional Cree Nation placenta ceremony after her son's birth. On the way, she (and we) learns from elders and young women who are reviving and carrying forward the traditions, repairing not only family bonds, but the larger social bonds damaged by colonialism.

Without these resources, Fausta, like Amelia in *The Babadook*, remains arrested in her grief. According to her uncle, Fausta suffers from 'frightened breast', which he describes as a transgenerational inheritance common to Andean children born during the 'time of terror' (1980–1992, during the conflict between the government and Shining Path). The breast referred to is at once Perpetua's, as she transmitted her trauma to her daughter through breastfeeding, and Fausta's, naming her fear of intimacy, particularly sexual. Fausta learned from her mother to keep a potato (emblematic of the Andes, where the tuber originated) in her vagina as a rape prevention method. Fausta carries herself as Andean earth into her domestic work in Lima. Her employer Señora Aída (Suis Sánchez) bribes her to sing traditional musical notes with pearls, which Fausta collects to pay for her mother's burial. Meanwhile, Aída creates a concert performance based, unattributed, on her employee's music in a veritable Faustian pact. Pearls, drops of milk, potatoes, even musical notes: there is a fairy tale-like exchange of spherical objects that are at once associated with fertility and with pain to their host vessels.

As in Martel's film, there is a movement between houses and home bodies: Fausta's body means something different in the rural lean-to she shared with her mother and in Aída's glossy metropolitan apartment. The poor, often brown-skinned, working-class women – who enable middle-class women to resist tradition in ways approved and earned by white liberal feminism (family planning, white collar jobs) – are only very gradually taking centre stage in feminist cinema. Rahel Zegeye's *Beirut* (2011) is the first feature made by a migrant domestic worker, about migrant domestic workers. She told Beti Ellerson:

> Most media and organizations working to help migrant domestic workers in Lebanon portray the worker as a helpless victim, her fate ruled by evil agencies and bad madams. Although this often does happen and is definitely an issue that needs attention, reality is much more complicated. I want to shed light on the inner lives and thoughts of a domestic worker, an aspect which is usually hidden from the Lebanese and foreign public.[22]

Fausta and Isabel are part of a trend identified by White, whereby 'the tension between white women and indigenous domestic workers has risen to the fore in recent Latin American films'.[23]

In Alicia Scherson's *Play* (2005), the point of view rests with Cristina (Viviana Herrera), a young Mapuche woman who has moved to Santiago from her tribal land in the south of Chile in order to work as a carer. Cristina's desire drives the film, as Fausta's does, albeit in a more light-hearted way. She finds the briefcase of wealthy, recently separated architect Tristan (Andres Ulloa) after it's been stolen, and develops an obsession with him. Cristina breaks into Tristan's house, dressing up as his wife in a feminist reworking of both *Vertigo* (Alfred Hitchcock, 1958) and moral panic films about the 'other' woman such as *Fatal Attraction* (Adrian Lyne, 1987). Cristina tries on the role of wealthy white housewife in the house of, notably, an architect, even pursuing the convention of an affair with the couple's working-class gardener Manuel (Juan Pablo Quezada). Cristina's ease of movement and masquerade contrasts with Fausta's, as does her relationship to her work as carer for Milos (Franscisco Copello), a frail Hungarian émigré. Her breast is not frightened by her desire for Manuel and/or Tristan, which becomes polymorphous when she starts sniffing strangers' necks on public transport. Tristan meanwhile, has taken his romantic and physical wounds (from the theft of his briefcase and his separation) back to his mother's house.

It's telling that Scherson began work on *Play* while away from Santiago, studying on a Fulbright in Chicago.[24] For Cristina, the question of home is not one of literal but cultural maternity and its loss. She reads to Milos from a National Geographic article about the genocidal displacement of an Amazonian tribe, and makes sad phone calls home. Pun (Arkaney Cherkam) makes similar phone calls in *Jao nok krajok* (*Mundane History*, 2009), Anocha Suwichakornpong's first feature. Pun is a professional nurse who has migrated for work to Bangkok, leaving his family in the provinces. He is taking care of Ake (Phakpoom Surapongsanuruk), a spoilt upper middle-class teenager who has been paralyzed in a car crash. Ake's mother (as in a fairy tale) is dead, and his father is not only distant, but possibly so distracted, uncaring or resentful that, a flashback implies, he caused the crash that injured Ake.

Sounds off and news footage locate the film during the red-shirt anti-government protests in Bangkok in spring 2009, and Ake's father is clearly a figure of the state and/or government. As in the films of her mentor Apichatpong Weerasethakul, Anocha uses medical metaphors to allegorize the relationship between state and citizen in a country where even indirect criticism of the royal family risks prison. Ake, who figures the urban/middle-class citizenry, gradually mellows under Pun's care. Films about carer-patient relationships usefully displace gender essentialism and allow for an examination of class and ethnic tensions in intimate situations. Even within the white middle-class milieu of Tamara Jenkins' *The Savages* (2007), these tensions arise, particularly through Wendy's (Laura Linney) blunderingly liberal relationship with her father's nurse Jimmy (Gbenga Akinnagbe), an economic migrant to the USA.

In Hui's *Tou ze* (*A Simple Life*, 2011), caretaking roles are reversed in a profound comment on the gender and class of caring. Ah To (Deanie Ip), an elderly maid, retires to an old people's home after a life in service to one Hong Kong Chinese family, and forms a mutually sustaining relationship with sole surviving family member Roger (Andy Lau), in a story based on the experience of Hui's producer. Like *Mundane History*, *A Simple Life* is a national allegory: Ah To was orphaned in the Japanese invasion of Manchuria, and her relationship with Roger operates as a comment on the relationship between Hong Kong and China.

Anocha's film goes further, finding in its national allegory a cosmic dimension. Pun takes Ake to visit the Bangkok planetarium, in which they first see a diorama with models of Stonehenge and other prehistoric sites considered to have an astronomical function, before entering the dome. Through Pun, Ake is once again at home in the world – a world enlarged by care beyond the bedroom, the house and even the nation-state. Like Fausta and Cristina through their indigenous inheritance, he is reconnected to a spiritual and historical continuum that is at once outside the home, and a home in itself.

House Music

The housing and unhousing of grief threads through Milagros Mumenthaler's *Abrir Puertas y Ventanas* (*Back to Stay*, 2009). Albeit somewhat sunnier, it shares with Martel's work its lassitude, its intense sound world and its loving attention to young women. In a setting at once fairy tale and Chekovian, there are three sisters who have to decide what to do with the house of the grandmother who raised them, using the odd but beautiful approach of playing through her record collection. Like *Milk of Sorrow*, *Back to Stay* formulates feminist genealogy through music. In *The Acoustic Mirror*, Kaja Silverman suggested that sound is feminized in mainstream cinema, and therefore offers feminist filmmakers a site to intervene for representational justice. Nonverbal sound is intimately linked to our first home; Silverman draws on Julia Kristeva's conception of the *chora*, the embryonic soundspace that 'figures the oneness of mother and child'.[25]

Nowhere is that more profoundly felt than in a transcendent central scene in Francesca Comencini's *Lo spazio blanco* (*The White Space*, 2009), adapted from Valeria Parrella's novel. Maria (Margherita Buy) becomes pregnant after a one-night stand and decides to carry to term, albeit with considerable anxiety about how having a child will change her life. The child is very premature, and Maria's home shifts from her dark, messy flat to the neon-lit hospital, specifically its hushed neonatal ward. Under the even, dimmed lighting, against the pallor of the walls, time appears to stop, holding Maria and her baby in a precarious and fraught unity. It only seems certain that Maria wants to be a mother when she performs, along with other parents in the ward, a dreamlike ballet of holding, rocking and cradling to Cat Power's 'Where Is My Love'. The singer's love is faraway nearby, both carried towards her on galloping horses and in her arms, a painfully acute description of Maria's relationship with her child, whose survival is not guaranteed.

The gentle sound of the song softens the 'white space' of panic in which Maria has been since discovering the pregnancy. Music offers a similar, brief connection and emotional release in *Villa Touma* (Suha Arraf, 2014). While the film was listed as stateless at Toronto and London due to a dispute with the Israeli Ministry of Culture about its funding grant, the home for which the film is named is emphatically Palestinian, in Ramallah: a film with(out) a home, for a homeland whose film culture has been severely circumscribed.[26] Like Mumenthaler, Arraf appeals to the fairy tale figure of three sisters: aristocratic Christians Juliette (Nisreen Faour), Violet (Ula Tabari) and Antoinette (filmmaker Cherien Dabis). They take in Badia (Maria Zreik), the orphaned daughter of their beloved younger sister who eloped with a Muslim. Badia is a Boudu, shaking the house up with her (terrible) piano playing, and even inducing the youngest, prettiest sister Antoinette to play a record and dance.

When Badia meets Khaled (Nicholas Jacob), a handsome wedding singer, it seems inevitable that she will follow her mother's path. Imprisoned in the house after her aunts discover she is pregnant by Khaled (who dies in an attack by Israeli soldiers), Badia is a potent figure for the trapped Palestinian nation. So potent that the film, like her aunts, isn't sure what to do with her: in the end, the house and the three sisters endure – and a baby's soft cry sounds from a hidden crib.

For Marina (María Canale), Sofía (Martina Juncadella) and Violeta (Ailín Salas) in *Back to Stay*, their grandmother is an auditory ghost, (dis)embodied by her record collection of English and American psychedelic folk – the film takes its English title from a John Martyn song the sisters listen to. Somehow LPs by Martyn, Bridget St. John and Linda Perhacs have made their way to Buenos Aires, a counter-cultural sound that could be read as able 'to open doors and windows' (to translate the Spanish title) during the *junta*, and represents the sisters' passage from abandoning themselves to grief to re-entering social life. The hothouse atmosphere of the film, which is almost entirely contained (like *Villa Touma*) within four walls, the sense of a lost *chora* that is both soothing and (s)mothering, is related through the nostalgic, fragile music.

Musical performance – like the home – provides a particular site to examine the politics and pragmatics of women's choices. Feminist filmmakers have documented the lives of beloved female singers who – particularly in the Middle East – are metonyms for a public, sexually, intellectually and expressively liberated womanhood. Didem Pekün's documentary *Tulay German: Years of Fire and Cinders* (2010) features the singer-as-revolutionary, throwing off her parents' middle-class expectations to emerge as the performer who invented Anatolian pop and became the voice of the Turkish community in France, while in a relationship with an exiled Marxist writer.

As part of *Profession: Documentarist* (2014), an omnibus project by seven Iranian female documentarians, Farahnaz Sharifi made a short film about legendary singer Googoosh, who was banned after the Revolution and stands as a symbol of liberation and modernity. The opening text screen proclaims that: 'We, Iranian documentary directors, have movies that can only be made in our minds. Sometimes, we tell them to each other'. Sharifi thus poetically tells her film, describing, foregrounding and resisting her inability to include any footage of Googoosh singing under censorship codes in Iran.

In the USA, a wave of female-helmed biopics of African American musicians emphasises the female voice as a site of resistance and possibility. Whitney Houston (*Whitney*, Lifetime, Angela Bassett, 2015), Nina Simone (*Nina*, Cynthia Mort, 2015) and Bessie Smith (*Bessie*, HBO, Dee Rees, 2015) are presented as working performers, iconic self-made artists whose lives testify to the interconnection of political, emotional and aesthetic struggles. Although Allison Anders switched from a chilly film industry to a welcoming TV industry this century, her last two films, *Grace of My Heart* (1996) and *Sugar Town* (1999, with Kurt Voss), are celebrations of female musicians and indictments of the music industry. Anders maintains a blog chronicling her listening adventures through Greta Garbo's record collection,[27] and her films convey clear parallels between the music biz and the film industry, which puts a provocative reading on Jane (Frances McDormand), the boob-flashing, daughter-in-law seducing rock producer in Cholodenko's *Laurel Canyon* (2002). Callie Khouri's return to public view also focuses on women in the music business, although where Anders tackles New York's Brill Building in the 1960s and LA's rock scene in the 1990s, Khouri is focused on the megabucks, media-friendly, female-fandom-oriented world of mainstream country in *Nashville* (ABC, 2012–).

In the show's opening scene, Rayna James (Connie Britton) is stressing about the mortgage on her house, bought with her music earnings and mortgaged to support her husband's business. Anxieties about downsizing, property prices and home ownership – also seen in *Boyhood* (Richard Linklater, 2014) – are indexed to the 2008 financial crash, but also reflect, as in *Boyhood*, an anxiety about good-enough mothering, particularly about working mothers and mothers in the public eye. Rayna, whose first name means 'queen', is still grieving for her mother's death in a car accident when she was a teenager. She is both a biological mother (to two daughters who want to be musicians) and, as the show goes on, a professional mother to young female talent, remortgaging her house to start her own boutique record label. In Season 3, she and the show openly identify a crisis in mainstream country music, currently dominated by male singers; Rayna frequently evokes both her own coming-up in the 1990s and her mother's singing career in the 1970s as lost golden eras for talented female artists.

Her commitment to feminist genealogy – including supporting wild child pop musician Juliette Barnes (Hayden Panettiere) – can't but be read through the lens of the scrutiny applied to the Dixie Chicks, as documented in Barbara Kopple and Cecila Peck's *Shut Up & Sing* (2006). What started as a straightforward tour doc became a record, at once dazzling and searing, of the profound misogyny and gendered violence fostered by right-wing politics and media in the USA. Kopple comments that, 'we all came to see this experience of the Dixie Chicks as a lens through which to see the current political climate in America'. She adds that she 'also filmed with their families in intimate moments', including IVF treatment, capturing the difficulty of balancing life as a working musician and mother.[28]

The title *Shut Up & Sing* quotes a comment from a death threat letter to the band, referring to verbal silence, but there is an uncanny echo of the women 'shut up' in Villa Touma. If music is the sound of the *chora*, the powerfully unsettling bond between mother and child that contests patriarchal authority, then when it's made public, it makes trouble. When Dixie Chicks' lead singer Natalie Maines declared on stage in London in 2003 that she was ashamed to be from George W. Bush's home state of Texas, it was an out-loud sign of dissent from a supposedly conservative milieu, as was the band's subsequent album. It began the recuperation of country as a feminist genre, showing that genres discounted as feminized by dominant culture can harbour resistance all the more powerful for being unexpected.

Home Movies

At the centre of Sarah Polley's documentary *Stories We Tell* (2012) is a short piece of black-and-white footage of a poised blonde woman – Polley's mother, Diane – singing 'Ain't Misbehavin'', written by Fats Waller in 1929 when he was in prison for non-payment of alimony. It's a painfully apposite soundtrack, as inserts are intercut relating the story of Polley's mother Diane's divorce, which led her to lose custody of her children to her wealthy husband. It's also ironically apposite to the arc of the film in general, which tells the story of Polley's discovery that a persistent family joke was true: she was not her father Michael's biological daughter. Her mother had been 'misbehavin'', and Polley set out to discover with whom.

As Polley and her three parents are media figures, and the personal story was broken in the Canadian media, *Stories We Tell* represents Polley's determination to bring the narrative back 'in house'.[29] She also sets out to reclaim it for her mother: although Michael and possible paternal figure Harry Gulkin have an almost overwhelming presence in the film, its purpose is not to adjudicate between their claims. Through their stories, Polley sets out to rediscover Diane, who died when she was eight, and to reforge their bond.

The black-and-white audition footage is the only cinematic evidence we see of Diane's career in theatre and as a casting agent. The majority (60 per cent) of the home movies seen in the film were staged by Polley using over 20 Super 8 cameras provided by the Canadian National Film Board. Her producer Anita Lee commented that the team 'literally searched through people's basements for the right Super 8 camera', putting the 'home' in home movies, in a neat parallel to Polley's excavation of her family's memory-basements.[30] While the diegetic revelation of Polley at work directing these scenes unsettled many viewers, it provides a still all-too-rare cinematic image of a female filmmaker at work and an uncanny revelation of the family house as constructed set.

Fig. 24: Sarah Polley and cinematographer Iris Ng making a home movie, *Stories We Tell*

Polley also uses the pull-back to stage a scene in which we see her talking, unheard under the non-diegetic musical soundtrack, to Rebecca Jenkins, the actor playing Diane in the reconstructions. She is most likely giving direction, but film allows the illusion that the grown-up Polley has travelled back in time to talk to her mother as she was before her birth. She is at once completing her mourning and reconciling with the mother she lost doubly: once to death, and the second time to a revelation that changed her sense of self, both the fact of her paternity, and that her mother considered aborting the pregnancy. These tasks are accomplished through her work as filmmaker, as the moment onscreen with Jenkins shows. She has done what Diane could not and successfully entered the film industry, taking charge of the story.

As Michelle Citron argues in her essential book *Home Movies and Other Necessary Fictions*, not only are all home movies fake to some extent, as edited versions of family life, but they implicitly suggest a man (the father) behind the camera.[31] Both assumptions are exposed by the book in its consideration of Citron's germinal experimental feminist documentary 'Daughter Rite' (1978), in which optically printed home movies provide a 'faraway nearby' through which to think about her mother and her childhood home. In her multimedia project *Mixed Greens* (2004) Citron revisits both her family's various homes as they migrated from Dublin to a working-class Boston neighbourhood, and the home movies she discusses in *Home Movies* – particularly the first one she shot, on returning from college with her fiancé and the woman on whom she had a crush.[32]

This first home movie as director acts as the fulcrum between the documentary chapters of her extended familial autobiography and a series of staged 'home movies'. These recreate American lesbian life and community from the 1950s to the 2000s through era-appropriate media, from tinted stills that evoke the covers of lesbian pulp fiction to developing Polaroids that prefigure the cellphone selfie. Biological, adoptive, elective and rejective families are part of this herstory, which itself intersects with and draws on other parts of Citron's overarching *Queer Feast* project. Its final 'course' *Leftovers* (2014),[33] is an intense and careful archival documentary about baseball players Norma and Virginia, who lived together for 45 years amid boxes of the lesbian subcultural ephemera that Ann Cvetkovich describes as 'an archive of feelings'.[34]

For Cvetkovich, the official record of history is utterly lacking because it dismisses home/bodies and their intimate memories, often encoded in small or friable objects, clothes, craft projects, oral storytelling and home movies. These are the things that Polley has to invent, setting them against paternal writing (both Michael and Harry write to her copiously about Diane), in order to reconnect her mother's life to history. Judith Butler remarks that one effect of revolutionary discourse is that:

> politics is no longer defined as the exclusive business of public sphere distinct from a private one, but it crosses that line again and again, bringing attention to the way that politics is already in the home, or on the street, or in the neighbourhood.[35]

The home/body is always already a political animal, connected outwards through media, labour, music and the politics of class and race as well as gender.

She is also, always, the affective origin of our politics and our aesthetics, as she is of the selves we carry through the world. We may not literally adopt Fausta's potato method, but these films argue that we cannot leave our mother (earths) behind. Like Robin, Young-nam and Fausta, we may also find that opening ourselves to the broad spectrum of maternal (non-essentialized) caring labour enables us to find a critical distance from the state, while still taking up public space. Diane Polley's divorce made the news pages of the *Toronto Star*; in the 1990s section of Citron's *Mixed Greens*, a mixed-race lesbian couple announce their commitment ceremony in the newspaper. These facts, grounded in the domestic and affective, are the material of public discourse, and thus of political change.

10

Come Together
Love, Justice and a New Sexual Politics

Shaken and Stirred

Shonali Bose's *Margarita, With a Straw* (2014) could be the twenty-first-century chapter of Michelle Citron's twentieth-century American lesbian history *Mixed Greens*: Laila (Kalki Koechlin) arrives in New York from Delhi, and literally sweeps Khanum (Sayani Gupta) off her feet at a protest against police brutality. When they're teargassed, Laila pulls Khanum onto her lap and scoots them out of danger on her motorized wheelchair, the perfect meet-cute getaway vehicle. The film was made with the support of Indian disability rights advocacy organization ADAPT, and Laila is undoubtedly a film first: a romantic heroine with cerebral palsy. Bose's cousin Malini Chib has cerebral palsy, and her mother Dr. Mithu Alur established ADAPT, the first organization of its kind in India.[1]

Focused on Laila's relationship with her mother, it's a family film in more ways than one. Equally, it's one with a confident sense of home turf: although Bose now lives in California, she views the film as Indian and is looking forward to its home reception, telling Leslie Felperin, 'I'm so confident about the Indian audiences accepting the film because it's fast-moving and emotional… We tested it on a lot of mainstream viewers – people who are not interested in disability or gay rights – and after 10 minutes they got drawn in'.[2]

Margarita is a film about getting drawn in: about how love and friendship and family bring us together. Khanum is Laila's first lover, but not her first love; their relationship – which Laila brings home to Delhi – gives her the impetus and courage to come out as bisexual to her mother (Revathi). Laila is Indian and Hindu, Khanum Pakistani and Muslim, but, as much as their mutual desire, it's the protest that brings them together. 'Justice is what love looks like in public', to take up one of Cornel West's favourite riffs; love, it turns out, is also what justice looks like in private, for feminist cinema.

Come Together: Love, Justice and a New Sexual Politics

Fig. 25: Laila and Khanum meet cute, *Margarita, With a Straw*

So rather than talk about romcoms and their white liberal feminist twists here, I'm entwining love, justice and togetherness in multiple ways, to argue that feminist cinema re-integrates what dominant culture separates. Erotic and romantic love, familial love, friendship, solidarity: these ways of being in the world come together even where one might least expect it; for example, in feminist pornography. Rather than the dyad held sacred by the romance, I sing a love song to the network – not the 'social' one, but its original sense of a 'work of net', a mesh in which every knot has been tied by hand. The characters in the films I discuss are the knots, but also the workers making the net to catch the utopian future they are dreaming.

In the course of *Margarita*, Laila moves from Delhi to New York and back again; sends her mother home and moves from her student apartment to Khanum's apartment; and has sex with fellow student Jared (William Moseley). She even finds time to watch internet porn, go to college, and – after her return to Delhi – switch roles to become her mother's caregiver. The complex intersections of familial and erotic love, desire and curiosity, political activism and dating add up to a full life. Mobility is the film's key theme: across borders, across identities and for the protagonist. Laila is not, however, one of British cinema's runaway girls; she is working towards positioning in the streets/in the sheets as holistic rather than contrasting, creating a network of places where she can be at home in her full self.

The central couple in Desiree Akhavan's *Appropriate Behavior* (2014) illustrate the movement from the feminist and queer rejection of (and by) the family home (and often of the mother) to a more complex mutual recognition of home. Maxine (Rebecca Henderson) has been cut off by, and cut herself off from, her Midwestern family after coming out as a lesbian. She is frustrated with her girlfriend Shirin (Akhavan), who refuses to come out to her Persian-American middle-class family. Shirin, like Laila, is bisexual; like Laila, Shirin does eventually come out to her mother, who elects to see her daughter as confused.

Laila's conversation with her mother comes as part of a process of separation and a declaration of maturity and independence, despite or because of involving comic use of voice technology Siri. Shirin, however, comes out as her mom is bandaging her burns, caused by her leaping-before-looking approach to the firepath at a Nowruz party. Shirin's mother reads her declaration of bisexuality as the sexual equivalent of living in a grungy flatshare, pursuing filmmaking and teaching kids on a short-term contract; her precariat lifestyle is unrecognisable to her successful, professional parents. What makes the film more touching than the other recent 'hot mess' female-helmed and -centric comedies with which it has been compared (including *Girls*, in which Akhavan has had a role) is Shirin's attachment to her parents and to Persian culture. She wants to be her whole self, whether she's teaching five year olds to make films, or at lavish Iranian parties in New Jersey, or in the bedroom.

This holism, in all its complexities, is summed up by Audre Lorde:

> I cannot separate my life and my poetry. I write my living, and I live my work. I am a Black Woman Poet Lesbian Mother Lover Teacher Friend Warrior, and I am shy, strong, fat, generous, loyal, and crotchety, among other things. If I do not bring all of who I am to whatever I do, then I bring nothing of lasting worth, because I have withheld some piece of the essential.[3]

Family, romance, friendship, community, pedagogy, creativity: relationship with a range of others (including the creative self) intersect and enmesh for Lorde, something that Akhavan's and Bose's films fight for and express. Even as they speak to EuroWestern LGBTQIA politics of recognition and visibility, they are also arguing for something more: something that recognizes all intimacies and relationalities as interlinked, and as the place where 'the essential' that is being a political animal happens.

Chela Sandoval, a contemporary and comrade of Lorde, calls this '"democratics"… a "zeroing in" that gathers, drives, and orients' the ways in which marginalized communities and individuals challenge dominant culture, 'with the intent of bringing about not simply survival or justice, as in earlier times, but egalitarian social relations, or… "love" in a de-colonizing, postmodern, post-empire world'.[4] Shirin and Laila affirm that love can be an anxious, hopeful, delicious and political oscillation (to paraphrase Miranda July's 2005 film title) between me and you and every body we are.

With a Twist

'"I love to you" is more unusual than "I love you", but respects the two more: I love to who you are, to what you do, without reducing you to an object of my love'.[5] This is one of Luce Irigaray's many insights into the central question of relationality in her 2002 book *The Way of Love*. She's part of group of feminist thinkers to have turned to love as a way of thinking in the twenty-first century, including Lauren Berlant, bell hooks, Laura Kipnis and Gillian Rose. 'Women's cinema' has long been invested in the question of why love hurts; just as Nicole Holofcener is the mistress of the discomfiting home truth for the white middle-class, so she is their agony aunt. Fellow US indie filmmakers Lynn Shelton, Josephine Decker and July have followed suit, with small-scale dramedies that offer visions of modern love, often disquieting and disjunctive. Dangerously so, in Decker's *Butter on the Latch* (2014), where female friendship, heterosexual eroticism and sexual jealousies are entangled, fracturing the film's narrative and form.

Deadly dyads persist, despite tantalizing offers of escape: Shelton plays a minor character offering one of the protagonists escape in her film *Humpday* (2009). Monica (Shelton) has an open relationship with her girlfriend Lily (Trina Willard), but their sexual flexibility and playfulness scares off dudebro Andrew (Joshua Leonard), who can't find it in his heart (or, really, his cock) to challenge his narrow and conformist heteronormativity, even if it means hot sex. Half-sisters Iris (Emily Blunt) and Hannah (Rosemary DeWitt) create a more hopeful outcome in their accidental menage à trois with Jack (Mark Duplass), in Shelton's follow-up *Your Sister's Sister* (2011), but it's predicated on a pregnancy as the tie that binds.

Perhaps unsurprisingly, queer cinema – where love is often fought for as a right – has gone further in saying 'I love to you'. As Shamim Sarif said on the simultaneous release of her films in April 2009: 'My aim is to get people to see *I Can't Think Straight* and *The World Unseen* as just love stories. I think the next step for integration and acceptance, where it's not an issue any more to be gay, is to not have it be an issue in art'.[6] Sarif's films foreground women of colour in lesbian relationships, staking a claim to the intimate drama that has long been the privilege of straight white cisfemale able-bodied protagonists and viewers. For her, the existence of her films is enough as an active extension and challenge to the simple formula 'I love you'.

But Irigaray goes on to argue that love proceeds through the verb, a part of speech that 'marks out paths, builds scaffolding, provides for transports' between people and in the world.[7] Maybe that's why queer filmmakers are particularly drawn to making films where love and justice meet (cute) in action and activism, where the central couple's path may not be smooth, but it builds scaffolding for their whole community, and provides for transport over borders.

Jamie Babbit's *Itty Bitty Titty Committee* (2007) focuses on protest group Clits in Action. CiA make pub(l)ic protest art, guerrilla feminist culture-jamming that first bewilders and then energizes 18-year-old Anna (Melonie Diaz), who is stuck in stasis with no college place and no interest in marriage or motherhood. While Anna's relationship with the charismatic CiA leader Sadie (Nicole Vicius) is the film's central thread, their path is both active and collective, bringing together CiA and threatening to blow it apart. There's a range of feminist, lesbian and trans* characters and embodiments on show, and a similar range of lesbian culture in-jokes, with a cast including Melanie Lynskey and Clea Duvall of Babbit's break out film *But I'm a Cheerleader!* (1999), Daniela Sea and Jenny Shimizu of *The L-Word* fame, and (of course) *Go Fish*'s Guinevere Turner.

The ensemble nature of its cast also extended to the communitarian vision of its production and content. *Itty Bitty* was the first feature film produced by Professional Organization of Women in Entertainment Reaching Up (POWER UP), and Babbitt received permission to use the Guerrilla Girls' slogans and artwork in the film.[8] The film is the change it wants to see in the world, and its multiple love stories – including the activist love that bonds the group – are part of the vehicle for that change. *Itty Bitty* gives us an alternative kind of sociality, a way of being together that is also a way of *doing* together.

When *The Real L-Word* performer Anna Margarita Albelo made her first film, it seems almost inevitable that it would focus on a lesbian filmmaking collective shooting a micro-budget, all-dyke version of *Who's Afraid of Virginia Woolf?*. Albelo's film is deliciously layered, not least as it riffs on *HOOTERS!* (2010), her own behind-the-scenes mock-guerrilla documentary for Cheryl Dunye's *The OWLS* (2010), a murder mystery about queer women behaving badly. Like Akhavan, Albelo plays a version of herself onscreen: 'a character I'd never seen before: a Cuban-American Latin 40-year-old lesbian filmmaker'.[9] Albelo's *Who's Afraid of Vagina Wolf?* (2013) shares both its post-modern parody and 'let's put on a show' energy with *Itty Bitty* and *OWLS* – and, of course, Guinevere Turner.

As *Vagina Wolf* exemplifies, collective feminist filmmaking tends to happen at the margins, for a number of reasons. It is concentrated in low/no budget work because, on the one hand, there is minimal risk to the experiment, and, on the other, collaboration – from fully sharing artistic labour to in-kind donations of services – makes micro-budget filmmaking possible. It also tends to concentrate in filmmaking modes where the filmmakers and their audiences belong to a shared community (one that, in the digital era, might be global or hyper-local). Unlike Anna's disastrously over-budget film within the film, *Vagina Wolf* ran a successful Indiegogo campaign to create a 'Wolf Pack' of supporters that helped it reach 92 per cent of its $25,000 goal.[10]

Crowdfunding is a radical new model of collective filmmaking, particularly in cases where donors have the option (albeit economically determined) to become associate producers, or – as with *Vagina Wolf* – to receive script notes from the film's screenwriter. It raises questions about the sustainability of independent cinema, but also highlights the diffusion of gatekeeping power to audiences. Ariel Dougherty argues that crowdfunding platforms:

> put the makers of feminist media in the driver's seat when it comes to raising funds… Second and more revolutionary is the new, dynamic role of members of the audience or "media users."… Engaged as backers of a project, they are invested and can become the best agents to draw in more backers. The power of the many – even if many of these backers make small, individual contributions – can actually bring about change.[11]

There is a compelling reflection between the collective politics of Riot Grrrl described in *The Punk Singer* and its Kickstarter campaign, which raised 150 per cent of its funding almost solely through perks up to $50 and $100.[12]

Similarly, co-directors Colette Ghunim and Tinne Van Loon have funded *Banat an-Nas* (*The People's Girls*), their documentary about street harassment in Cairo, through a crowd-funding model that echoes both the mobilization of protestors in Tahrir Square and their global mobilization of a viral audience for the initial video 'Creepers on the Bridge' (2014).[13] Also forthcoming is Attiya Khan's *A Better Man*, executive produced by Sarah Polley, which raised 148 per cent of its goal by building a community in support of the film that mirrors the community the film hopes to build, in order to end violence against women.[14] As Frances Negrón-Muntaner notes with regard to her community videographic practice in the mid to late 1980s, 'it is not an accident that we tend to use the term [community] when we speak of groups of people who have a certain disempowered relationship to dominant power structures'.[15]

Albelo's collective filmmaking ideology relates joyously to the work of feminist community documentary videographers such as Negrón-Muntaner, and also Alexandra Juhasz, who supported and collaborated with Dunye on *The Watermelon Woman*. This reflective communitarian model, in which a film is funded by the audience it is setting out to reflect onscreen, is exemplified by *Stud Life*, directed by *OWLS* collaborator Campbell X: crowdcast at open auditions as well as crowdfunded, it features diegetic YouTube videos in which Black British stud JJ (T'Nia Miller) sets forth her thoughts on queer politics and on filmmaking, getting the viewer in on the action. *Stud Life* also reworks the pair-bondage romantic comedy as a communal genre, as JJ and Elle (Robyn Kerr) fall in lust through a series of LGBTQIA weddings; their relationship is bound together by, and binds, their community. Hot sex and community politics are shown as complementary.

As Negrón-Muntaner points out, '"communities" are also composed of other "communities" which have different power relationships within'.[16] JJ and her best friend Seb (Kyle Treslove) live and work on a council estate; their queer community is embedded in a diverse, working-class East London. Likewise, Kanchi Wichmann's *Break My Fall*, a love/hate story as punk as a knuckle tattoo, was shot on location, mostly in Hackney, East London in three weeks, for a budget of under £50,000, and featured local bands. It's a document of a time, place and emergent social formation (the queer artist precariat) wrapped around a romance, a tribute in its way to the no-wave, lesbian-centric, proto-New Queer Cinema of 1980s New York that B. Ruby Rich flags up.[17]

Dunye also shot a segment of the freewheeling multi-director adaptation of Michelle Tea's memoir *Valencia* (2013) (with the protagonist played by a different actor, not all female-identified, in each segment). It depicts pre-dot-com 1990s queer countercultural life on the eponymous street in San Francisco, in all its precarity and *joie de vivre*, underlining the economics that Rich notes made New Queer Cinema possible. *OWLS* collaborator Sarah Schulman's recent study *The Gentrification of the Mind* underlines the increasing economic and political erasure of opportunities, within North American and Western European urban areas, to work in the ways that Albelo's, Dunye's, Tea's, Wichmann's and X's films depict.[18]

Wu Tsang's *Wildness* (2011) is an incisive insight into the meeting point of the new queer precariat, who are often the forerunners of gentrification, and a previous generation. It captures the tensions and potential as a group of young trans* and genderqueer artists start a performance night at historical drag bar the LA Silver Platter. 'Tsang moves from being the party's co-host to an engaged political organizer exploring new forms of activism surrounding health, economics and safety issues' within the diegesis, and outside the frame, hands the narration to the Silver Platter itself, through a voiceover delivered and co-written by Guatemalan-American transgender actress and Silver Platter performer Mariana Marroquin.[19]

Shushan, an unusual gay bar in Jerusalem (now closed), whose customers include both young Palestinians from Ramallah and 'Orthodykes', is the site for a fascinating negotiation of Middle East politics in Yun Suh's documentary *City of Borders* (2009). Bar owner Sa'ar Netanel, the first openly gay politician in Jerusalem, says in the film: 'When I read in the Bible that I could be killed for being gay, I understood what it was like to be Palestinian'. Shushan was not only a rare space where the LGBTQIA community could express itself in increasingly Orthodox-controlled Jerusalem, but one of the few in the city that was also integrated. Mixed-race lesbian couple Samira and Navit demonstrate how love and sex bring *everything* to the table, not just for themselves as a couple, but in their self-aware reflections on the political situation in their countries.

Screaming Orgasm

Gay bars are not the only unlikely site for feminist political solidarity. Love is a verb for collective action, too, in feminist and queer pornography. Feminist film's initial stance on porn was expressed in the landmark documentary *Not a Love Story* (Bonnie Sherr Klein, 1981), an exposé of exploitation in the porn industry, produced by Studio D, the women's studio of Canada's National Film Board. Later in the 1980s, conflicts arose as anti-porn feminists and counter-cinema advocates clashed over films such as no-wave NY cult classic *She Must Be Seeing Things* (Sheila McLaughlin, 1987), which featured lesbian role-playing and BDSM, and Abigail Child's 'Mayhem', which used found footage from an early amateur porn film in which a male burglar 'surprises' a lesbian couple.

Influenced by these filmmakers as well as by Ulrike Ottinger's and Monika Treut's work in New German Cinema, New Queer Cinema boasted a rare sex-positive vision in Anglophone narrative cinema. NQC put sexual desire and sexuality at the heart of narrative and motivation, while not making them the sole definition of character. Scenes such as Daria's (Anastasia Sharp) 'trial' for straight sex in *Go Fish* interrogated the silencing and judgementality surrounding desire.

But while sexually explicit gay male cinema continues to thrive in the twenty-first century, entering the indie mainstream with *Brokeback Mountain* (Ang Lee, 2005) and world arthouse with the films of Apichatpong Weerasethakul and Tsai Ming-Liang, lesbian and/or feminist sex cinema had fallen quiet. Even sex-positive pioneer Monika Treut played it safe with the haunting but oblique

Ghosted (2009). Films such as *Blue is the Warmest Colour* and Peter Strickland's *The Duke of Burgundy* (2014) have attracted some negative responses from lesbian and feminist audiences not (only) for their male-gaze oriented depiction of lesbian sex, but because the prestige and attention visited on their films as 'lesbian' films erases, rather than opening up, space for lesbian filmmakers.

The same could be said for *Fifty Shades* as a depiction of heterosexual female desire: regardless of its quality, it takes up all the space. Jane Campion's *In the Cut* was part of a small group of explicit female-helmed films, along with Catherine Breillat's satirical *Anatomie de l'enfer* (*Anatomy of Hell*, 2004), Claire Denis' charming *Vendredi soir* and Penny Woolcock's dark *The Principles of Lust* (2003), which features, unusually, a bisexual male character involved in a love triangle. Breillat is the doyenne of a Sadeian feminist cinema, in which the erotic and the philosophical are as entwined as the bodies she depicts performing sex as an absurdist demonstration of the limits of gendered behaviour under patriarchy. Rebecca Zlotowski's *Grand Central* (2013), about workers at a nuclear power plant entering into a dangerously unstable affair, suggests a mainstreaming of Breillat's Brechtian approach, a return of explicit eroticism to European women's cinema.

Things are changing, as seen in the sexual carnival of the final ten minutes of Sarah Polley's *Take this Waltz* (2011) – and the change is coming from Scandinavia, famed for its sexual liberalism at least since *Jag är nyfiken* (*I am Curious [Yellow]*, Vilgot Sjöman, 1967). Ester Martin Bergsmark's *Nånting måste gå sönder* (*Something Must Break*, 2014) is – I'm fairly sure – the first film screened during the main London Film Festival to feature a protracted anal fisting scene. Yet the explicitness is matter-of-fact rather than spectacular: the particularity of the sex act tells us about the characters engaged in it – Sebastian/Ellie (Saga Becker), who is transitioning to female, and Andreas (Iggy Malmborg), who identifies as straight and cismale. It is Sebastian/Ellie who controls this encounter, and penetrates Andreas, dramatizing the questions of identity, power and desire at the heart of the story.

Bergsmark's work is rooted in a sex-positive feminist moment in Sweden; his short 'Fruitcake' (with Sara Kaaman), was part of Mia Engberg's film anthology *Dirty Diaries* (2009). Engberg's initial short 'Come Together' (2008), which collages together shots of women's faces, including hers and her girlfriend's, as they masturbate, was initially made for the Mobile Movies competition. The outraged and outrageously sexist and homophobic reactions to her film led her to conceive of *Dirty Diaries* in order to throw down the gauntlet to viewers upset by her short's lack of the conventional signifiers of heteronormative masculine pornographic fantasies. She raised funds from the Swedish Filminstitut and loaned the Nokia N93 cameraphone she'd been given by the festival to 11 Swedish feminist colleagues. Like many feminist filmmakers before her, she then penned a manifesto, whose fourth point is that, 'the porn industry is sexist because we live in a patriarchal, capitalist society. It makes profit out of people's needs for sex and erotica and women get exploited in the process. To fight sexist porn you have to smash capitalism and patriarchy'.[20]

In her essay '"Every time we fuck we win"', *Dirty Diaries* contributor Ingrid Ryberg roots the project in the joyfully explicit American feminist aesthetics of the 1970s, 'in the artwork of Judy Chicago and Carolee Schneemann and in the films by Barbara Hammer and Anne Severson'.[21] Chicago and Hammer both lived and worked in feminist collectives, although their names appear on their work as an auteurial signature. Their visions were part of the background to the social and artistic formations pursued by Negrón-Muntaner and Juhasz, and emerged out of nineteenth-century Utopian movements as described by Susan Sontag in her novel *In America*, many of which embraced and asserted free love, women's emancipation and homo-positivity as part of their core beliefs.[22]

The project of feminist porn could be seen as part of a larger engagement in remembering and refiguring these movements, which have often been written out of dominant history, and even feminist histories. Documentaries such as *Lesbiana – A Parallel Revolution* (Myriam Fougère, 2012) and *She's Beautiful When She's Angry* (Mary Dore, 2014) are re-integrating the wilder, witchier, sexier outlands of feminist organizing into the record. Love-as-justice operates through this unexpected ability of sex – that ephemeral act – to reinscribe lost histories through the storied bodies it brings together.

Make Mine a Double

Experimental filmmakers such as Hammer and Child have questioned the very grammar of 'I love you', particularly the hierarchy of subject and object that is all too often gendered with a masculine active speaker. Trinh T. Minh-Ha's *A Tale of Love* (1995) is a playful and thoughtful adaptation of a classical Vietnamese poem cycle by nineteenth-century poet Nguyen Du, framed within a narrative in which modern-day Kieu (Mai Huynh), named for the poem's heroine, works as an artist's model to fund her own writing. Trinh told Deb Verhoeven that:

> there's no cinema – only entertainment, document, information, technique, for example – if there's no love. On the other [hand], the entire history of narrative cinema is a history of voyeurism, and no matter what form it takes, the art of narrative cinema is unequivocally the art of resurrecting and soliciting love.[23]

Trinh suggests, even in the title of her film, that there is an irreducible connection between *love* and *story*, that you cannot have one without the other. By locating Kieu as the author of her own romance, one whereby she comes to self-love and a connection to her poet-ancestor through a typically fraught heterosexual relationship, Trinh 'resurrect[s]' love. As she puts it, 'I'm not so much interested in Shakespeare as I am in the figure of Juliet and her love relationship with Romeo', which she refers to in *A Tale*.[24]

Leticia Tonos Paniagua, the first Dominican female filmmaker, recasts Shakespeare's play for her second film *Cristo Rey* (2013), a Dominican-set mixed-race romance that brings out the faultlines of difference in the play, embedding love in social justice issues of racism, narcopolitics, poverty and violent machismo. And the play's tropes underscore Aurora Guerrero's garlanded debut feature *Mosquita y Mari* (2012), in which the star-crossed lovers are both Latina, but separated by their class backgrounds. Guerrero points to a particular tension between romantic choices and community that is present in Shakespeare's narrative, and also in her film.

> For Latinos, the majority of us are part of an indigenous culture and the indigenous cultures that you see are part of a community and community living, in familia... I think that's a good thing, a beautiful thing. But there is the other side of that. There is the weight that we carry when there is this expectation to live up to of your family and their ideas of what you need to do.[25]

Warwick Thornton uses the story similarly and powerfully within an Australian Aboriginal community in *Samson and Delilah* (2009). Even *Romeo and Juliet*, the quintessential EuroWestern patriarchal love story (one that, as with Cathy and Heathcliff, teenage girls are socially conditioned to idealize), can be transformed into a story of feminist self-love, or love-and-justice, or love within a community.

Susanne Bier's *Efter brylluppet* (*After the Wedding*, 2006) takes a core Eurowestern romantic narrative – the wedding – and threads it through with questions of social justice and international politics. This determination to reinvent and reclaim love can be seen, as well, in Polley's *Away from Her* (2006): both films move between romantic/sexual relationships and institutional caring settings – an orphanage in Bier's film; and a residential elder care centre in Polley's. In each case, memory, bodily fragility, interdependence and a particular masculine melancholia – a privileged sense of exclusion from the processes of living, dying and feeling – pervade the film, through the respective central performances of Mads Mikkelsen and Gordon Pinsent. Helene (Sidse Babett Knudsen) and Fiona (Julie

Christie and Stacey LaBerge) are muse figures, at a slight remove from the film's centre, both of them differently oblique and inaccessible to the protagonists. Fiona is the more spirited of these lost loves, crafty and cunning in her use of encroaching dementia to dispense vengeance and forgiveness, like a female King Lear.

In both cases, the film plays on the status of Knudsen and Christie as stars, elusive objects of desire, thus offering subtle new grammars of cinema that displace and dispel film's voyeurism. They are rigorous and spare studies of the loss of (the myth of) love, but also oblique national and political allegories. Helene distracts Jacob (Mikkelsen), one of Bier's 'male sojourners' in Belinda Smaill's term, from his overseas NGO work, in a slanted but spiky comment on contemporary Danish politics, something also palpable in Bier's *Hævn* (*In a Better World*, 2010).[26]

Tinatin Kajrishvili's *Patardzlebi* (*Brides*, 2014) offers a strategically and stringently oblique comment on Georgian politics: Goga (Giorgi Maskharashvili) is in prison for an unspoken crime connected to his writing; Nutsa (Mari Kitia) takes care of their children with the supportive interference of her mother. Modern young Europeans, Goga and Nutsa are unmarried; prison regulations force them into a paper marriage so that Nutsa can visit. Instead of making passionate love during her one visit, Goga and Nutsa make common cause with the neighbouring couples, whose female partners Nutsa knows through meeting in queues, searches, waiting rooms and even the wedding ceremony. They share their forbidden chewing gum, and sing together through the bars as the light fades. From Goga and Nutsa's difficult and tense love, a community comes into being.

In US cinema, two recent films have contrasted the dyadic romance with the bonds of prison to striking effect: *Sherrybaby* (Laurie Collyer, 2006) is an aftermath story, focusing on Sherry (Maggie Gyllenhaal), staying in a halfway house as she reconnects with her young daughter, coming together and unravelling as she confronts a history of sexual abuse. Ava DuVernay's second feature *Middle of Nowhere* (2012) won her Best Director at Sundance for its stunning critique of respectability politics in the central character of Ruby (Emayatzy Corinealdi) as she structures her life around visiting her husband in prison, risking trapping her imagination and spirit there.[27] Both films renew women's stories as family stories, love stories, and self-love stories, and simultaneously political stories about the state and its violence.

On the Rocks

Prison provides an analogy for conventional society (including marriage), but also a way to deconstruct it. Before *Orange is the New Black* presented viewers with its diverse ensemble of queer women of colour making survival relationships, Dunye's HBO movie *Stranger Inside* (2001) not only depicted contemporary life in prison, but used 1930s and 1940s prison blues on the soundtrack to historicize the experience of African American women in the prison-industrial complex. The politics of collectivity play differently in prison, particularly for Treasure (Yolonda Ross), whose birth mother Brownie (Davenia McFadden) is the house mother of a prison 'family', in which she takes the paternal role. Like Laila and Shirin, like Mosquita and Mari, Treasure finds herself caught between erotic and familial love, although Dunye's film de-essentializes and demythologizes motherhood as much as it does the collective. Treasure forms a friendship network of women closer to her age that is more horizontal than her mother's 'family', and there are multiple kinds of love – sexual, familial and self-love – on display in the film.

Stranger Inside is itself an act and tale of love, bespeaking Dunye's determination to bring the stories of African American LGBTQIA women to the screen, and the rigorous respect and ethics with which she does so. As Frann Michael writes:

> Dunye has described her early films and videos as 'dunyementaries', works in which she integrates 'documentary and fiction'. ... Dunye workshopped the script with women prison inmates, and many of the extras in the film were former inmates, as were some of the participants in the unrehearsed group therapy sessions that punctuate the film.[28]

The idea of social realism as a form of witnessing, an ethical act of love, presents a powerful a challenge to the 'tale of love' described by Trinh.

It accords with feminist documentary ethics: Kim Longinotto's latest film *Dreamcatcher* (2015) follows sex work survivor Brenda Myers-Powell, who, like Treasure, has run up against the racism and sexism of the prison-industrial complex. The indomitable founder of the Dreamcatcher organization for Chicagoan women looking to exit street-based sex work, she is campaigning, person-to-person, to break the apparently unbreakable connections between a fragile education system, systemic poverty and racism, sex work, drugs and the prison-industrial complex. Like many of the central subjects of Longinotto's documentaries, Myers-Powell creates a network of love rooted in hard-won self-love – and she ends the film singing to her at-risk high school students' workshop to celebrate their connection before she takes a break for surgery. It's a classic Longinottan moment, reminiscent of spirited pre-teen Fouzia in *The Day I Will Never Forget* (2002), who co-opts the filmmaker as support and witness when she performs the poem that gives the film its title, demanding that her mother spare her younger sister from the process of female genital mutilation that she has undergone.

It's exactly that connection between the loving network of witness and solidarity and its expression in performance that drama therapist and documentarian Zeina Dacacche facilitates through her prison work. *Scheherazade's Diary* (2012) takes its name from the play that Dacacche devised with the inmates of Baabda prison in Beirut. Many are serving time for crimes commissioned or reported by male partners; adultery, even an unsubstantiated accusation, carries a jail sentence for women in Lebanon. Dacacche's film gives a curious real-life framework to Nadine Labaki's anti-war musical fantasia *Et maintenant on va où?* (*Where Do We Go Now?*, 2011), in which the women of a small, mixed-faith Lebanese town team up with each other, and with some visiting Russian dancers. They perform an escalating series of pranks and performances designed to distract their husbands from joining the latest hostilities.

Labaki's film riffs on Aristophanes' *Lysistrata*, while Daccache's draws on *Alf layla wa-laylah*, the folk tale collection known as *One Thousand and One Nights*, and its framing device, in which the king's young wife Scheherazade must keep herself – and all the remaining women of Persia – alive by telling stories. It is within this conventional tale of love (as femicide) that the Scheherazades in the film tell their stories, to the camera and the audiences, both at the play and watching the film. 'After seeing the play and witnessing the tough living conditions at Baabda, audience members offered legal assistance and social support, helped improve hygiene facilities and even gave jobs to women leaving the prison', according to Janey Stephenson.[29]

As in *Stranger Inside*, group therapy sessions create an opportunity for an ensemble to cohere and contest, but it is through the stylized, rehearsed and heightened verbal and gestural language of the play that the film truly makes its point. The same is true of the final dramatic (in both senses) performance in Pelin Esmer's rural community theatre documentary *Oyun* (*The Play*, 2006), as rehearsals reveal hidden tensions and dreams within the village's female community. Dacacche's coup is to conjoin the structure of the 'let's put on a show' film with a closed-space documentary, to show the women taking action within the limits of the prison walls, and through dramatic action coming to value and love themselves.

Sex on the Beach

Daccache's film draws its energy and power from its loving attention to people not often seen on screen, or even in society. She weaves the imprisoned women into the network of the live and film audiences, as Scheherazade wove her listeners into her stories, so our lives are entangled. That attention to the unseen or underseen as a way of weaving together the world has been a key part of the work of two inspiring elders: Grace Lee Boggs and Agnès Varda. As Varda reveals in *The Beaches of Agnès*, she left home immediately after World War II, and found herself making and mending nets for fishermen in Corsica. *Beaches* is full of images of nets, whether strung under trapeze artists, holding colourful holiday debris, or even woven out of the celluloid of Varda's old films.

Varda also weaves herself into a community she documents in her short film 'Les veuves de Noirmoutier' ('The Widows of Noirmoutier', 2004), which is excerpted in *Beaches*. Here, 15 (other) widows, who all live on the rocky Bréton island where Varda and Jacques Demy had a home, talk directly to the camera about their experience of widowhood. As in *Scheherazade's Diary*, there is a sense of revelation, as those who are expected to be silent speak about that which is expected to remain unspoken. There is an added air of mutuality, as the widows know they are speaking to a widow (Demy died in 1990): this puts us, as the audience, in the dual state of discovering what it means to be widowed as we are simultaneously in the position of a widow. First shown as a 16 screen installation, *Widows* is an affecting testimonial that connects back to Varda's political documentaries such as 'Black Panthers' (1968) and 'Réponse de femmes' ('Women Reply', 1975), making widowhood as political a stance or space as girl 'hood – even more so, perhaps, given the invisibilization against which it has to fight.

Varda's bittersweet short finds a saucier echo in Adèle Tulli's 'Rebel Menopause' (2014), a short film about Parisian feminist Thérèse Clerc, now 85 and still part of a thriving transgenerational community of women at the wonderfully named Baba Yaga House – like *Scheherazade's Diary*, a nod to the sustaining power of such mythic archetypes. For Clerc, the house and its conversational (and occasionally choral) community is as important an expression of her feminist politics as marches, debates and protests. Tulli's short screened at Sheffield Doc/Fest 2014, where I detected 'a secret thread of feminist elders' in the selection, which included Nancy Kates' *Regarding Susan Sontag* (2013), Sam Feder's *Kate Bornstein is a Queer and Pleasant Danger* (2013), same-sex marriage tribute *Living in the Overlap* (Mary Dalton and Cindy Hill, 2013) and *Croc-a-Dyke Dundee*

(Fiona Cunningham-Reed, 2013) – as well as Grace Lee's outstanding *American Revolutionary: The Evolution of Grace Lee Boggs*.[30]

The younger Lee met her older namesake (now 100) while making a documentary about her many namesakes, *The Grace Lee Project* (2005), which became a rich history of Asian American immigration, integration and activism. She and Boggs developed a conversational relationship, out of which the PBS documentary emerged. The film transmits transformative hope, rooted in love-as-justice. Highlights including Boggs and her husband, labour organizer James Boggs, being interviewed for primetime television by Ossie Davis and Ruby Dee, supportively and knowledgeably, about their communist politics. The Boggs' love story is central to the documentary, not as a romantic tale, but as an example of collaborative activism, shared politics and a lifetime of debate. Boggs prefers evolution to revolution, grounding growth in a constant turning-over of ideas between friends, lovers, colleagues and students, an audience of whom she tells, 'All of you clapping, do more thinking!' Love is not an easy, sweet panacea for Boggs, in any of her relationships (and she continues to build networks among young volunteers in Detroit today): it is a rigorous, testing and tested engagement, a joyous form of work.

Love as protest rather than deference, as constant growth rather than stasis, is palpable in Varda's *Beaches* too. In her mourning for Demy, one senses that she mourns the lost opportunity to continue working together, informing each others' new projects, challenging each other. She talks about *Jacquot des Nantes* (1991), her film about Demy's childhood, as a labour of love, but that love suffuses all of her cinema, and particularly her late, great documentaries: *Beaches* and *The Gleaners and I*. To glean, she reveals in that film, is to love what is discarded, and to love among those who are discarded, summed up in the gleeful pun of a children's recycling project she discovers: 'Poubelle ma belle' (My Beatiful Bin).

Varda's 'gleaning' ethic changes the meaning of the film frame, knowingly inverting Roland Barthes' famous dictum that photography equals death, taken up brilliantly with regards to the transition from film to digital cinema by Laura Mulvey in *Death 24x a Second*.[31] Although Varda is visibly moved to tears in *Beaches* by her photographic exhibition in Avignon, where she lays roses for each of her lost friends, the (digital) film's attention to the exhibition revivifies the dead. This is a feminist move: in *Camera Lucida*, Barthes reaches his conclusion based on looking at photographs of his late mother taken before his birth. His instance of maternal mourning is reconfigured into a feminist genealogy by Varda, a transgenerational connection that may include both mourning and celebration.

Fig. 26: Lovers on the beach behind nets, *The Beaches of Agnès*

There's something similar at work in Kirsty Macdonald's *Assume Nothing* (2008), a documentary about the work of New Zealand photographer Rebecca Swan, whose portraits of trans*, intersex and non-binary people of Maori, Samoan and Pakeha descent brings a world into being. Swan's conversations with intersex educator Mani Bruce Mitchell, in particular, make space for mourning – for a medicalized childhood, for the trauma of both internal and external scars created by prejudice – but for also a joy in becoming.

As in Varda's earlier documentary *Daguerréotypes* (1976), punning on the people ('types') who live on her street in Paris (Rue Daguerre), photography in *Beaches* and *Gleaners* is the work of love, a bringing-together of different times and spaces so that images, ideas and people can cross the frame. Love is not (just) what's depicted on screen, but the frame itself. It's the motive force of Varda's cinema, as it is of Daccache's and Dunye's. Across their work, as in Trinh's, rewriting the love story offers the possibility of reinscribing a feminist self, doing justice not only to the world but to and through the complex, multiple subject, who is not de-eroticized in order to be taken seriously.

Sex-positivity and curiosity opens us, as audience, to a diversity of embodiments. *Beaches* is not a chapter of *Dirty Diaries* by any measure, but it has a striking and lovely frankness about sexual desire, including a deliberately eye-popping shot of an erection. Since her cult classic *Lions Love* (1969), a hippy threesome starring Warhol muse Viva, Varda has been busting cinematic taboos, championing the joys of embodiment and consensual sexuality. *Beaches*, like 'Rebel Menopause' and *American Revolutionary*, gives a feminist twist to the problematic 1960s promise that free love and political freedom might be interconnected. This is how the net works: love catches us and holds us. In that connection the desire to make change – together – is born.

Conclusion

An Open Letter

Pasts

The 2014 European Film Awards might have thought they were paying obeisance to an adorable grandmother when handing a lifetime achievement award to Agnès Varda. But Varda gleaned the opportunity to raging feminist purpose, stating:

> What I have noticed is that it is very sweet to receive this award but when I see the nominees here, I feel there are not enough women. I think more women should be included. I know a lot of very good female directors and women editors and I would like them be more represented and helped by the European film academy.[1]

Her speech echoes the 2012 open letter demanding more female presence penned by the feminist collective La Barbe to Thierry Frémaux, the director of the Cannes Film Festival.

So far it's had little material result bar Jane Campion's appointment as jury president in 2014, a lack that emphasises its truth. It ended: 'Women, mind your spools of thread! And men, as the Lumière Brothers did before you, mind your film reels! And let the Cannes film festival competition forever be a man's world!'[2] What's open about this letter is not just its public address – published in *Le Monde* and the *Guardian* – but its exposure of that which heteropatriarchy keeps hidden, the persistence of insidious misogyny cloaked in claims of aesthetics or commerce.

Lexi Alexander broke the silence surrounding the operations of Hollywood cinema by going public about her industry experiences via her blog and *Women and Hollywood*, offering evidence for her statement that:

> Gender discrimination in Hollywood goes far beyond women simply not getting the gig. It is reflected in movie budgets, P&A budgets, the size of distribution deals (if a female director's movie is lucky

enough to score one), official and unofficial internship or mentorship opportunities, union eligibility, etc. Women in Hollywood have no male allies.[3]

Editor Melissa Silverstein introduces Alexander's post with a note that: 'This is a woman director standing up for herself and other women directors. She does this at great peril'. Alexander's courage in coming forward, Silverstein's support, the huge supportive response to her post, the negative experiences she describes, and the lack of any concrete change so far, all speak to the current media landscape in which sexism and feminist responses thereto are both hyper-visible. The open letter continues to open our eyes.

'Women Reply': Varda's cinema has been an open letter since at least this short essay film of 1975. A collective portrait of women as a political, rather than biological, category, 'Women Reply' speaks both to and from women, starting a conversation rather than making a statement. While conversations about tests, stats and quotas persist, I want to close *Political Animals* by arguing that such measures are finally like Virginia Woolf's 'room of one's own', no more than a place from which to begin doing the work. As Isabel Coixet says, 'we need action. I think all these statistics are good to have, but I think it's [a] very dead end'. Asked about statistics at a press conference, she demanded that financiers take action to end the circular discussion.[4]

But even this argument for the free market is limited. Lake Bell's *In a World* (2013) offers a perfect example: when Carol (Lake Bell) finally wins the contract to record the voiceover for *The Amazon Games* trailer, her moment of triumph (over her father, no less, heir apparent to the voiceover crown) is soured by a conversation in the ladies' room. The film's producer Katherine Huling, knowingly played by feminist media institute founder Geena Davis, tells Carol that her casting wasn't meritocratic, but opportunistic, with a cynical eye on the film's young, female audience. It's a bittersweet reflection on the industry; the film ends with a productive tension between knowing Bell is succeeding behind the camera, and seeing Carol drop out of the voiceover industry. *In a World* says that we need to do more than take the studio's crumbs. We have to speak out, assertively, in our own voices.

It may sound counterintuitive, but for me the conclusion has to be where I say 'over to you', an opening for the next wave. The strategies that I note here for enlarging the production, exhibition and preservation of feminist film are those that are similarly open. There's the open approach and invitation to participate of queer femme film curators Club des Femmes (CdF), who programme shorts, mini-festivals, weekenders and workshops in London. And there's the openness to a new way of making film of Hope Dickson Leach's community group Raising Films (RF). Inspired by films such as *Dagurréotypes* and *52 Tuesdays*, both made around caring for young children, RF reflects on a practice all too rarely accessible or visible.[5] Dickson Leach writes of pre-production for her film *The Levelling*:

> Last year I found myself jealous and frustrated by not being able to leap into this movement of no-budget filmmakers because having a family meant I couldn't just sleep on someone's sofa for six months and not worry about rent. But after sleepless nights I realised that microbudget cinema might be the thing that allows me to work with the family commitments I have.[6]

As she explores, RF is not just an issue that affects straight ciswomen, although historically they have been more affected by it; due to women's cultural association with caring, it remains 'gender-poignant'. But it could, and should, be a site where filmmaking, as in Wanuri Kahiu's vision in chapter three, actually contributes to a 'humane society of sorts'.

As I've worked to shape *Political Animals* to reflect the work done by the films it discusses, I've had to be open, out there and engaged, not least as a member of both CdF and RF. I'm grateful for the opportunities to see filmmaking and exhibition from the inside, in all its challenges. Film criticism can seem hermetic and hermitic compared to the collaborative and discursive work of curation – but, for me, the charge of my critical practice is in connection. That might be with filmmakers for interviews or audiences at panel discussions, or debating issues in film and feminism with my colleagues, particularly my co-curators Selina Robertson, Alex Thiele, Sarah Wood and Campbell X, my co-editors Corinn Columpar and Elena Oroz, and my editors Frances Morgan at *Sound on Film* and Ania Ostrowska at *The F-Word*.

What I've discovered is that feminist film *is* an 'open letter': not only in the sense of Varda's 'Women Reply' but as a mode of practice. Onscreen and off, it's communitist, inclusive and concerned with address (who is speaking, who is listening). It's at once chaotically futurological and passionately historical, offering utopian visions that draw its audience into action. That R-A-G-E I spelled out in the introduction has become a rage *for* and *towards*, located in the oppression we may have experienced individually and collectively because of our race/religion, age/ability, gender and sexuality and/or economic class. It becomes – as Belle says in *Belle* – our source of intellectual and personal freedom.

That's not to say that every feminist film or film event is Platonically intersectional by any means. As Marta Owczarek reports, a discussion at the 2012 London Feminist Film Festival following a screening of *Lesbiana* was disrupted when a panellist, Julia Long, asked non-cisfemale audience members to leave the screen.[7] Long's request, not cleared with the organizers, generated discomfort and anger at the event and immediate debate online, pointing to an actively engaged community, one for whom transparency and inclusion remains crucial. It also makes visible that the event itself was open and so was the audience: a packed house of all genders brought together by an interest in the documentation of alternative social histories.

Post-Occupy, there is a hunger for evidence that another way is possible – and feminist cinema is addressing it. There is an activist cinema that ranges from features such as Maria Sadowska's whistle-blowing drama *Dzien kobiet* (*Women's Day*, 2012), in which one working mother takes on capitalist corruption, to Mona Eldaief and Jehane Noujaim's *Rafea: Solar Mama* (2012), an extraordinary documentary about the impact of an NGO education programme, the Barefoot College, for one Bedouin woman and her community. Leena Manimekalai's incendiary *Rape Nation* (2014), a dramatized response to the rape and murder of Jyoti Singh, offers an informed and impassioned on-the-ground perspective, in contrast to Leslee Udwin's prominent campaigning documentary *Daughters of India* (2015), which has been called out for its 'white saviour' complex.[8] *Women's Day*, *Rafea* and *Rape Nation* all highlight the flourishing of feminist cinemas engaged with local specificities that speak to a global audience.

Political, they are also proudly personal, maintaining the core belief of second-wave feminism, but focusing it confidently outward, as in Chai Jing's lecture-style documentary *Under the Dome: Investigating China's Smog* (2015). Chai is an experienced reporter who has covered climate change issues, but – unlike Al Gore in the film that's clearly her model, *An Inconvenient Truth* (Davis Guggenheim, 2006) – she has proclaimed an immediate personal connection, after discovering her baby was carrying a benign tumour linked to smog pollution.[9]

Elena Oroz and I were proud to foreground the slogan 'The personal is political/Lo personal es politico' as the title of our feminist documentary programme and anthology at Punto de Vista in 2011. Celebrating feminist genealogies in action, we paired Alina Marazzi's animated history of Italian feminism, related through women's diaries from postwar to post-punk, *Vogliamo anche le rose* (*We Want Roses Too*, 2007) and Cecilia Barriga's protest vérité 'Granada 30 años despues' ('Granada 30 Years On', 2010). These two recent films document and democratize the joyous labour of feminist organizing from the personal through the political and back again, opening the possibility to anyone watching that they could take up the banner.

As I've shown throughout, the work of love that is feminist cinema cares for the past, the present and the future, and above all for their interconnection, for each time's need for the other. The feminist struggle has been proceeding, differentially across the globe, for generations if not centuries. I'm not totally committed to the definition of 'waves' (particularly because they're largely limited to Anglophone feminism), but it's a useful metaphor because, among other things, it points to the troughs, the backlash moments when the work of a previous generation is forgotten, erased, banned, or simply not cared for by dominant culture. Hence Clarissa Jacob is crowd-funding a documentary on *Women & Film*, the first feminist film magazine.[10] She argues that, 'in the midst of the current, apparent fourth wave, this legacy becomes especially important as feminists once again begin to scrutinize the cinema and ask questions about women's place on and off the screen'.[11]

Curation, at root, means taking care (from Latin *cūra*, care): we need to take care of the incredible film culture recorded here (and all the films, filmmakers, film critics, film theorists and film festivals I can't fit into the inelastic bonds of the codex form). It's amazing how fast it can disappear. The Museum of Modern Art in New York held the first celebration of the work of the Women's Film Preservation Fund in 2015, pairing popular films such as *Desperately Seeking Susan* (Susan Seidelman, 1985) with forgotten films preserved by the fund such as *Will* (1981), directed by Jessie Maple, the first African American woman member of the New York branch of IATSE, Moving Picture Technicians, Artists and Allied Crafts.[12]

In summer 2014, CdF and the University of Kent hosted the first ever feminist film Wikipedia edit-a-thon at the ICA in London. Eighteen participants created 26 articles on filmmakers, films and film collectives that were absent from the site, with subjects including Michelle Parkerson (herself the author of many crucial documentaries of African American womanist and lesbian culture), Campbell X and even the classic experimental film *Riddles of the Sphinx* (Laura Mulvey and Peter Wollen, 1977), only released by the BFI on DVD in 2013.[13] Wikipedia is a crucial site for intervention, as it dominates the circulation of information online. Like all such dominant sites, it is also frustratingly constructed (albeit unconsciously, like Cannes) to exclude feminist content.[14]

As I learned working on Sally Potter's digital archive SP-ARK, new media offer an incredible resource for digitizing, cataloguing, posting, sharing and contextualizing all kinds of archival material that may otherwise be unseen, and for democratizing access to industry and institutional information.[15] At the same time, as Astra Taylor notes in *The People's Platform*, to:

> understand why the most idealistic predictions about how the Internet would transform cultural production and distribution… have not come to pass, we need to look critically at the current state of our media system… and recognize the forces that are shaping the development and implementation of technology – economic forces in particular.[16]

They are the same forces that have persistently narrowed the cinematic frame. Taylor's vision of 'strategies and policies for an age of abundance' alludes to the claim I made in the introduction: that, when it comes to non-dominant cultural production of all kinds, we need to change the narrative framework from scarcity to plenty.[17] New modes of exhibition and circulation are necessary not just as revenue streams (although, as Taylor argues, filmmakers such as Laura Poitras can hardly work for free), but for representational justice, so that the next generation has to hand the materials for which we have had to search in order to make our work.[18]

While the internet may be a vexed question, as far as taking care is concerned feminist filmmaking is deeply committed to digital possibility. Lynn Hershman Leeson, ever a technological innovator, has used both film and the web for the major project that is *!Women Art Revolution* (2010), a documentary that overspills the frame through its online components.[19] Maria Binder has created something similar, yet *sui generis*, with her documentary project *Trans X Istanbul* (2014), which combines a personal essay (by the filmmaker, who identifies as cisfemale) about a community of trans* women in Istanbul with a growing online anthology of films made by the documentary subjects and their community.[20] Films themselves act as archives: documentarians such as Sini Anderson (*The Punk Singer*), Sam Feder (*Kate Bornstein is a Queer and Pleasant Danger*), Shola Lynch (*Free Angela*), Grace Lee (*American Revolutionary*) and Pratibha Parmar (*Alice Walker: Beauty in Truth*, 2013) are recording feminist icons' lives in action, as Nancy Kates (*Regarding Susan Sontag*) and Dagmar Schultz (*Audre Lorde: The Berlin Years 1984–1992*, 2012) have done through archival materials for the recently departed.

The list is dominated by US filmmakers and icons, which speaks to a continuing cultural hegemony, but also to four decades of persistent, generous taking-care by distributor and funder Women Make Movies in building an appetitive audience

Fig. 27: Kate Bornstein with *My Gender Workbook*, *Kate Bornstein is a Queer and Pleasant Danger*

for feminist film.[21] Feder's documentary about Bornstein offers a metatextual parallel between writer and trans* activist Kate Bornstein's development of her passionate audience through performances, reading tours and Twitter, and the film's journey through the LGBTQIA festival circuit.

The necessity of intertwining counter-strategies for production, distribution, exhibition, promotion and curation for non-dominant cinemas goes back to the very beginning of feminist film. Maya Deren was not only a pioneer in her film language, but in her tireless work to reach (and indeed, invent) audiences. Theresa Geller writes that, although other historians have seen Deren's screen work and her promotional work as separate: 'Cutting across Deren's innovations as a filmmaker and an activist... is a coherent "chamber" aesthetic formed as a critical response to the sexual division of public and private space'.[22]

The 'chamber' is an exact parallel for Woolf's 'room of one's own'; Deren shot and edited films in her Greenwich Village apartment, and even exhibited them there. But she also developed a touring circuit of US college campuses, wrote about her own and others' films for publications from mimeographed newsletters to *Esquire*, and founded the first US funding foundation for film, supporting the work of Shirley Clarke among others. In her time, Deren's work was an open letter arguing for a counter-cinema; immediately after her death in 1961, it was lost as the male-dominated counter-cinema that she had nurtured took shape.

Conclusion: An Open Letter

With the coming of second-wave feminism in the 1970s, her work was sought out as a rare example of a precursor female filmmaker. Deren described her creative practice as:

> like a crack letting the light of another world gleam through. I kept saying to myself, 'the walls of this room are solid except right here. That leads to something. There's a door leading to something. I've got to get it open because through there I can go through to someplace instead of leaving by the way I came in'.[23]

It was exactly a 'light of another world' that Deren shone for Barbara Hammer when she studied film in the 1970s, as 'Meshes of the Afternoon' was the only film by a woman on her course.[24] Four decades later, Hammer repaid the honour with 'Maya Deren's Sink' (2011), an experimental exploration of Deren's living spaces in LA and New York – and, moreover, an invocation of the filmmaker's living presence. While Deren has also been the subject of the monumental *Legend of Maya Deren* print anthology and Martina Kudlacek's documentary *In the Mirror of Maya Deren* (2002), Hammer's personal essay – an open letter from and to Deren's physical addresses – demonstrates how, from kitchen table to kitchen sink, feminist film takes care of itself and its community.[25]

Presents

From the vantage of the mid-1990s, looking back on the first 20 years of feminist film culture, B. Ruby Rich hoped for the moment 'when the cinematic/videographic telling of history catches up finally with my moment of living it and arrives on the doorstep of feminist film. Perhaps then we will be able to claim and honor [sic] some of the women... mentioned here'.[26] That moment has arrived, as Feder's film *with* Bornstein shows (and she is very much an active participant in its construction) – and yet.

The documentaries I've mentioned still struggle for funding and exhibition. Parmar, a globally-celebrated filmmaker for her three decades of documentary-making about queer women of colour, had to fundraise on Indiegogo to complete a documentary on one of the most significant living US writers, and *Alice Walker: Beauty in Truth* never received theatrical distribution.[27] I'm fairly sure that Steven Spielberg had an easier time funding his adaptation of *The Color Purple* (1985). With that independence, however, Parmar was able to reshape the bio-doc subtly, interweaving a portrayal of the artist-activist with a portrait of Walker as gardener, living the truth and beauty of her writing through her interconnected nurturing of the land and community.

Both production and exhibition are costly; as I noted looking at the statistics in chapter one, feminist film gets stopped wherever the buck stops. As Hammer writes in her memoir:

> a film rests in a can until it's screened but a book can be opened at any time by anyone in any country. It doesn't require a darkened room, a special location or equipment. I thought a book could be a portal to my films. Perhaps my films, a life's work, could reach a new audience through the words and stories of my life.[28]

But *Hammer!* is more than a memoir; it's also a work of feminist film theory and history. And Hammer is not alone in asserting her auteureship in book form to reach audiences that cannot reach the films. Chantal Akerman, Abigail Child, Michelle Citron, Julie Dash, Virginie Despentes, Cheryl Dunye, Marguerite Duras, Kim Longinotto, Sally Potter, Yvonne Rainer, Martha Rosler, Hito Steyerl, Trinh T. Minh-Ha and Agnès Varda have all published books that collect and blend critical and autobiographical writing, at once asserting their presence as filmmakers, and the interconnection of art, thought and life.[29]

Again the list is predominantly North American, and largely white, albeit with a strong lesbian presence. These are filmmakers who, like Deren, have built a precarious connection to academic film studies as well as general audiences, through teaching and campus exhibition. They are also predominantly post-modernists whose cinematic work is concerned exactly with the question of documenting the self as a feminist practice. As Corinn Columpar notes with reference to *The Tango Lesson* (Sally Potter, 1997), this means that their films often risk being called narcissistic where a male filmmaker would be saluted as an auterial genius, because they foreground women's lives and often destabilize claims to both authorship and self.[30] The auteure is a feminist filmmaker for whom narrating (from) the self is an open letter, a call to others not through sameness but for conversation and continuance.

In her study of women's life writing, philosopher Adriana Cavarero argues that socialization creates a difference in male and female self-documentation: for her, a female memoirist 'is a narrator, not an author'.[31] Cavarero compares the position of the feminist self-narrator to Scheherazade, whose stories within stories keep the storyteller and all the women she knows alive. Self-documentarians such as Mai Masri (*Beirut Diaries: Truth, Lies and Videos*, 2006) and Sonali Gulati (*I Am*, 2011) have renewed second-wave Anglophone feminist cinema's

Conclusion: An Open Letter

commitment to foregrounding female lives, in their non EuroWestern contexts. Rather than asserting originality or individuality in closed texts sealed with an authorial signature, Masri's and Gulati's films resound with community building, moving through the self towards conversation and engagement. Cavarero adds that 'there is an ethic of the gift in the pleasure of the narrator… [who] gives to the protagonists of his/her story their own stork': that is, becomes the agent of delivery or witness.[32]

Potter's *Naked Cinema: Working with Actors* emerges exactly from this ethics of the gift, democratizing one of the most mystified and mystificatory aspects of the filmmaker's craft – and, given that it's about relating to others, of being human. It's a book about building a community, albeit a temporary one, through taking care and being open. The book itself is a community, comprising interviews with many of Potter's actors – from Julie Christie (*The Gold Diggers*, 1982) to Elle Fanning and Christina Hendricks (*Ginger and Rosa*) – whom she allows, as in her films, to take centre stage. Potter's strategies, on- and offscreen, always 'highlight the very gestural, ephemeral, and unfinished aspects of communication in self-reflexive [cinematic] meditations on authorship' that, for Cecilia Sayad, enable such work to 'compete with the traditional attributes of control, authority, and permanence expected from "legitimate" artists'.[33]

By removing the pedestal from beneath the auteure, *Naked Cinema* resonates with Potter's radically democratizing films and invites us to engage in new readings thereof. Feminist film culture's circulation in print is crucial and we need to value it – like Deren's exhibition strategies – as central and contiguous, rather than supplementary, to the work of filmmaking. At the same time, it's critical to want all of these writer-filmmakers to keep producing and circulating films. Alexandra Hidalgo is developing a unique video book project that is at once a documentary of and a textbook for ethical feminist filmmaking, and also an argument for hands-on audiovisual work as a critical practice.[34] Hammer's current practice combines critical autobiography in 'A Horse is Not a Metaphor' (2009) (which, like Rainer's feature *MURDER and murder* [1996] is a rare unsentimental consideration of breast cancer) and critical feminist art histories such as *Lover Other: The Story of Claude Cahun and Marcel Moore* (2006). Non-binary Surrealist artist Cahun has also been the subject of an experimental documentary, *Magic Mirror* (2013), by British filmmaker Sarah Pucill.

Hammer, Potter and Rainer – as well as Mania Akbari, Rakhshan Bani-Etemad, Věra Chytilová, Yoko Ono, Lis Rhodes and Joyce Wieland – have all been the subject of retrospectives in London in the last decade, primarily at the British Film Institute (who also hosted Elinor Cleghorn's Maya Deren film programme). The

London Lesbian and Gay Film Festival (now BFI Flare) has, additionally, held retrospectives for Dorothy Arzner, Su Friedrich, Ulrike Ottinger, Tejal Shah and Monika Treut. With Tate Modern, the ICA and LUX, the BFI has been part of fostering attention to experimental and artist filmmakers, areas in which women tend to feature more prominently than in mainstream feature filmmaking.

Films by Clarke, Deren, Pucill, Hammer, Wieland and Margaret Tait are also slowly becoming available on DVD, testament to the work of dedicated scholars such as Sarah Neely (on Tait) and the renewed interest their scholarship has generated – but also to decades of neglect.[35] It took Tait until she was 74 to secure the funds to make her first feature, *Blue Black Permanent* (1992), a semi-autobiographical auteure-ist study of a female poet, and it's taken another 23 years for it to become available on DVD. Project Shirley, from Milestone Films, had to raise release funds on Kickstarter for Clarke's *Portrait of Jason* (1967), a film ranked joint thirty-seventh in *Sight & Sound*'s 2014 poll of the best documentaries of all time.[36]

Here is where the argument for feminist filmmaking as curation comes full circle. Whereas in the art world it has become a form of authorship that dominates rather than invites, *feminist* curation can be, as Cavarero suggests, narration, returning agency to the artists being curated. That's increasingly important for the kind of films that will never be on Netflix and need a 'people's platform'. Feminist and LGBTQIA film festivals have proliferated in London in recent years, with the emergence of Birds Eye View (2002–2014), the London Feminist Film Festival (2012–), Underwire (2010–), FRINGE! (2011–), Wotever DIY Film Festival (2011–), the London Transgender Film Festival (2008–) and the London Sex Worker Film Festival (2011–), as well as curators CdF, Jemma Desai's I am Dora, Joanna Hogg's and Adam Roberts' À Nos Amours (opening with an Akerman retrospective), Corrina Antrobus' Bechdel Test Fest and Kate Hardie's A Woman's Work.

Hardie summed up the impetus for feminist curating in this cultural moment:

> The main objective was to get people thinking seriously and regularly about the awful statistics for women working in film whilst also being entertained by their diverse work, past and present... Hopefully one day we won't need specialist events about women and cinema but whilst we do: the more the merrier![37]

Outside London, Holly Tarquini of the Bath Film Festival is pioneering the F-rating for films that are female-helmed or have female leads; the Brighton Festival 2015, curated by Ali Smith, showcased Varda's films and installation work; and, in Glasgow, the Film Theatre teamed up with the Women's Library for a women in science fiction programme in 2014, while in 2015 the CCA played host to the first

Conclusion: An Open Letter

GLITCH festival, showing films by and about queer, trans* and intersex people of colour, and Scottish Queer International Film Festival (SQIFF) is coming.

In the USA, events such as the Bluestocking Film Series and the Athena Film Festival highlight the continuing need to promote women's cinema outside the conventional festival network, as does Barbara Ann O'Leary's global Directed by Women fortnight.[38] Both Toronto and London felt moved to celebrate their inclusiveness in 2014, having reached a truly equitable 1:4 ratio of films by female- and male-identified filmmakers. As Clare Stewart, Head of Festivals for the BFI, told me when I interviewed her in 2014,

> it's incredibly exciting to see that as a burgeoning area… but there's still work to do; we're not at parity: none of our galas are directed by women. But festivals are much more likely to be a home for women filmmakers than the marketplace, and we want to do more to welcome them.[39]

Stewart has been true to her word: *Suffragette* opened the 2015 festival, the first female-helmed gala since *In the Cut* in 2003. A healthy film ecology would include parity at headline festivals, and also a diversity of local, specific, communitarian festivals fostering emerging filmmakers, short films and experimental multimedia practices. In the 1980s and 1990s, women's film festivals in the US became incorporated into the headline festivals, which was seen as a sign of progress; but mainstreaming changed both audiences and programming. It shouldn't be a case of either/or: if *Political Animals* demonstrates anything, it's that there's more than enough powerful, original, engaging films to go around, both contemporary and historical.

And there will be more. Interventions such as La Barbe's open letter, Stacy L. Smith's MDSC statistical reports and Kathryn Bigelow's Oscar win have led to the major studios investing in gender-specific talent campuses and training programmes, whose effectiveness may be compromised by working inside a system that needs to be changed. Davis' Bentonville Film Festival initiative for 2015 may be focused on cinematic diversity, but it's co-funded by Walmart, subject to the largest class action gender discrimination lawsuit in US history.[40] As Tina Gharavi provocatively named her response to what she called yet another 'meaningless, toothless diversity scheme': Thanks But We're Good.[41]

Grassroots initiatives such as the Chicken and Egg Films documentary funding programme; the Director List, a news site for female-helmed films; the Bitch Pack, a screenwriting website promoting intersectional cinema (all US); Australian women's plans for 'dinosaur-frightening', in the words of Marian Evans; and Germany's

Pro Quote Regie, a group of filmmakers advocating for gender quotas in state funding similar to Anna Serner's 50/50 success story in Sweden, are more compelling.[42] Similarly, the re-emergence of feminist film collectives is a welcome development. They may come from a very different political place to the Third Cinema-inspired Cine de Mujer collectives of the 1970s, but groups such as Danis Goulet's Embargo Collective, New York's Film Fatales and Ingrid Veninger's Femmes Lab (funded on the spot, as Veninger announced it, by Melissa Leo) represent both plenitude and solidarity, as well as giving the lie to the heteropatriarchal fostering of competition amongst women.[43]

Through her aptly-named production company pUNK Films, Veninger has produced a number of inspiring low-budget features, including *i am a good person/i am a bad person* (2011), in which she plays a filmmaker touring a film around festivals accompanied by her daughter – shot as Veninger toured her film *Modra* (2010) to European festivals. As Allan Tong remarks, 'I don't even think John Cassavetes took personal filmmaking this far'.[44] Like *52 Tuesdays*, *i am a good person* is a remarkable example of family-friendly filmmaking that shows its working as a film about parenthood, and the productive tensions between life and art.

Like Deren, Veninger is a filmmaker-as-curator, extending her creative practice to fostering other talents and visions. That extension beyond the self is as necessary to feminist politics as the documentation and exploration of the self; they travel in tandem. Selina Robertson, co-founder of CdF with Sarah Wood, writes of the group's curatorial practice:

> We consciously look outside our own experiences, to champion the old, the classic or the under-appreciated, the misunderstood, the sidelined, the flawed, the edges. We want to promote new processes of thought, ones that come from outside a white heteronormative viewpoint. We like outsider films because we are outsider curators too. We are not interested in the mainstream. We want elsewhere. Changing. The future.[45]

Futures

Lucy Bolton concludes her book about thinking women on film with a wish for female-identified characters 'with histories, memories and – crucially – futures'.[46] In that relation of history, memory and future is a rejection of the tired model of 'progress'. As the Gay Straight Alliance's Make it Better project (2010–2012) for LGBTQIA teens argues, the narrative that 'it gets better' is doubly problematic, suggesting that suffering in the present will magically win pleasure in the future – and all without effort or systemic change.[47] The films I've discussed here believe in *making* it better: in healing the present and past as aspects of taking care, and in working towards a better future – even if (and maybe because) it has to be imaginary. As Ali Smith writes in *Artful*, 'the notion of offer involves hope, a certain flexibility around acceptance or rejection, and the likelihood of both… we only much more rarely think about the generosity implicit in response to what's offered, in acceptance'.[48] Like the characters they create and document – whether Elsa in *Frozen*, Lucy in *Wendy and Lucy*, Laila in *Margarita, With a Straw*, or Walker in *Beauty in Truth* – feminist film filmmaker/curators work with open hands, both giving and receiving.

The future of feminist cinema lies in your hands. One of the great truths told by non-dominant art is that it's the audience who have the power. If there's any expertise at all in how I've researched and written *Political Animals*, it's the expertise of the viewer, particularly a viewer who doesn't often see the films she cares about covered in the media. A growing sense of complicity in this structuring absence led to my own open letter to *Sight & Sound* in 2014, with 80 female-identified signatories, calling on the magazine to include more feminist voices covering feminist work.[49] You – we – need to know what films are on release and being made, because we are the first, foremost and final curators.

In an open letter calling out lack of media support for her film *Beyond the Lights* (2014), Gina Prince-Bythewood animates the social, cultural and political argument that Taylor sums up in the phrase 'the people's platform':

> I want us to look up on screen and see a black woman fighting to find her voice, find her authentic self and be brave enough to live an authentic life. I want us to look up on screen and be inspired to want more for ourselves, to want to love, and to love ourselves.[50]

The film went straight to DVD in the UK, despite its Brixton beginnings, due to the continuing prejudice against black films identified by Simran Hans; the Bechdel Test Fest's screening at the Ritzy in Brixton sold out, evidence of an audience that distributors ignore and feminist curating can tap into.[51]

Our choice of what ticket to buy or link to click on (re)shapes the media, not simply as an economic tick that flickers on an executive's spreadsheet, but because it changes *us*, psychically and affectively, and thus changes our community. Choosing a feminist film can be an act of love, for the film and for ourselves. The films we see enter our imaginations, our intimate and political fantasies; they shape our interactions, our conversations, possibly even our revolutions. They

Fig. 28: Crystal, with the star on her helmet, joins the Gnarlies youth team for her first jam, *In the Turn*

become part of *our* story: they are the storks that deliver us, and we can be the storks that deliver them.

If feminist film is an open letter because it's addressed to a possible future, it's also open because, in order to bring that future into being, it has to go beyond the merely invitational. 'They were just… so… welcoming', says Crystal to her mother at the end of Erica Tremblay's *In the Turn*, after her first skate with roller derby youth team the Gnarlies. There is a dazed wonder in her voice at the very possibility of *being* welcomed after her experience of transphobia at school. The Gnarlies and the Vagine Regime (which includes filmmaker Tremblay, who skates – and fundraises – as Go Go Gidget) don't just issue Crystal an invitation: they insist on her presence by raising funds for her flight. Gnarlies' coach Killo Kitty insists that Crystal set aside her nerves and get skating in the mixed-age, mixed-ability, ethnically diverse pack.

Roller derby is far from the parodic model of fluffy pseudo-feminist homogeneity and 'equality': instead, it celebrates difference, determination and playing hard. It offers multiple subject positions that make it a powerful analogy for being part of the feminist film community: on the rink, there are lead jammers and 'the pack', but also referees shaping the game and queerleaders giving it spirit, as well as the encircling fans, all contributing to the alternative derby world. Jamming is the art of finding gaps in the opposing team's pack so that you can move ahead and score points, and jammer is a mobile role transferred from player to player. It relies on both individual skill and intense teamwork, and it's a great metaphor for feminist film as it weaves and curves exhilaratingly through the available gaps in dominant culture.

I argued, in chapter two, that animals on screen are important because they represent 'bare life', the raw basics of embodiment and vulnerability. They also represent a *joyful* embodiment that is often denied to the bodies of the 99 per cent, a promise that we can be muscles and nerves and movement through the world, towards it and part of it. Representational justice is about not standing still but – as Ava DuVernay's *Selma* shows historically and reflects for the present – marching, dancing, wheeling, falling and getting up again, keeping the message moving because of, not despite, the forces arrayed against us. At the end of *Frozen*, Elsa pulls Anna onto the ice to skate, ending the film with spirals of movement rather than the traditional closed-in kiss. Provisional and precarious as ice, this final dance suggests that feminist film's work is not done, it is *doing*. Feminist cinema is, in Asta's words about Anna, 'always trying', always on the move, always active, always activist, always open – and always inviting us to join in. Girls to the front: let's go.

Notes

All URLs accessed 1 September 2015, except where noted.

Introduction: Girls to the Front

1 Lynskey, Dorian, '*Frozen*-mania: How Elsa, Anna and Olaf conquered the world', The *Guardian*, 13 May 2014, available online, http://www.theguardian.com/film/2014/may/13/frozen-mania-elsa-anna-olaf-disney-emo-princess-let-it-go.
2 Griffith, Nicola, and Kelley Eskridge, 'War machine, time machine', in W. G. Pearson, V. Hollinger and J. Gordon (eds), *Queer Universes* (Liverpool: Liverpool University Press, 2008), available online, http://nicolagriffith.com/2008/12/02/war-machine-time-machine/.
3 Rodriguez, Amanda, '*Frozen*: Disney's first foray into feminism', *BitchFlicks*, 2 December 2013, http://www.btchflcks.com/2013/12/frozen-disneys-first-foray-into-feminism.html Access date needed.
4 Shelley, Maureen, 'Disney, disability and *Frozen*', *The Word*, 9 January 2014, http://thecopycollective.blogspot.co.uk/2014/01/disney-disability-and-frozen.html; Orsborn, Sarah Sweatt, 'Watching *Frozen* with my daughters: Disability as superpower and the power of sister love', *Huffington Post*, 7 April 2014, http://www.huffingtonpost.com/sarah-sweatt-orsborn/watching-frozen-with-my-daughters_b_5105525.html.
5 Ussir, Embi and Molly Horan, 'Disney's *Frozen* whitewashing controversy', *Know Your Meme*, http://knowyourmeme.com/memes/disneys-frozen-whitewashing-controversy.
6 Senior, Antonia, 'The pernicious pinkification of little girls', *The Times*, 29 May 2009, available online, http://www.thetimes.co.uk/tto/law/columnists/article2048920.ece.
7 Smith, Stacy L., 'Gender disparity on screen and behind the camera in family films: The executive report', available online, http://seejane.org/wp-content/uploads/full-study-gender-disparity-in-family-films-v2.pdf.
8 Bradshaw, Asta, interview with writer, 19 September 2014. With thanks to Rebekah Polding for overseeing the interview (and thoughts on Hans), and to Bo Bradshaw for insights into Olaf.
9 hooks, bell, *Reel to Real: Race, Sex and Class at the Movies* (London and New York: Routledge, 2008), p. 107.
10 Johnson, Chloé Hope, 'Becoming-grrrl: The voice and videos of Sadie Benning', in C. Columpar and S. Mayer (eds), *There She Goes: Feminist Filmmaking and Beyond* (Detroit: Wayne State University Press, 2010), pp. 172–82.
11 Rich, B. Ruby, 'The New Queer Cinema', *Sight and Sound* 2/5 (1992), pp. 30–34; reprinted with notes in Rich, *New Queer Cinema: The Director's Cut* (Durham NC: Duke University Press, 2013), pp. 16–32.
12 Mulvey, Laura, *Death 24x a Second: Stillness and the Moving Image* (London: Reaktion Books, 2006), p. 23.

13. Roman, Shari, 'Agnès Varda', *Digital Babylon: Hollywood, Indiewood & Dogme 95* (Los Angeles: iFILM, 2001), pp. 178–82.
14. Westwell, Guy, *Parallel Lines: Post 9/11 American Cinema* (London: Wallflower Press, 2014).
15. Khan, Shahnaz, 'Afghan women: The limits of colonial rescue', in R. L. Riley, M. B. Pratt and C. T. Mohanty (eds), *Feminism and War: Confronting US Imperialism* (London: Zed, 2008), p. 161.
16. Dorsey, Xochitl. 'Women Make Movies responds to hate', Women Studies Quarterly 30/1-2 (Spring-Summer 2002), pp. 221–226.
17. White, Patricia, *Women's Cinema, World Cinema: Projecting Contemporary Feminisms* (Durham NC and London: Duke University Press, 2015), pp. 8; 14. With many thanks to Patricia for generously sharing her ms. before publication.
18. *Camera Obscura* 19 3/57 (2004) Special Issue: Todd Haynes: A Magnificent Obsession; Dempsey, Anna, 'Women's stories and public space in Iranian new wave film' in L. Khatib (ed), *Storytelling in World Cinemas: Contexts* (New York: Wallflower, 2013), pp. 122–32.
19. Whedon, Joss, quoted in Avni, Sheerly, 'MoJo Audio: Joss Whedon', audio recording, *Mother Jones* (November/December 2008), http://www.motherjones.com/media/2008/10/mojo-audio-joss-whedon.
20. Bourke, Joanna, *Wounding the World: How Military Violence and War Play Invade Our Lives* (London: Virago, 2014), p. 216.
21. Grant, Catherine, 'A long hard look at Slow Cinema studies', *Film Studies for Free*, 23 April 2013, http://filmstudiesforfree.blogspot.co.uk/2013/04/a-long-hard-look-at-slow-cinema-studies.html.
22. 'Shannen Koostachin DC comic heroine', *Remembering Our Sisters Everywhere*, April 5, 2014, http://www.rememberoursisterseverywhere.com/photo/shannen-koostachin-dc-comic-heroine.
23. Bordwell, David, 'The viewer's activity' in *Narration in the Fiction Film* (Madison, WI: University of Wisconsin Press, 1985), pp. 30–47.
24. Dolan, Jill, *The Feminist Spectator in Action* (New York: Palgrave Macmillan, 2013).
25. Tay, Sharon Lin, *Women on the Edge: Twelve Political Film Practices* (Basingstoke & New York: Palgrave Macmillan, 2009), p. 24.
26. Longinotto, Kim, quoted in Cousins, Mark and Kevin MacDonald, 'The burning question', in M. Cousins and K. MacDonald (eds), *Imagining Reality: The Faber Book of Documentary* (London: Faber & Faber, 2006), p. 443.
27. Davis, Angela Y., 'A vocabulary for feminist praxis: on war and radical critique', in Riley, Pratt and Mohanty (eds): *Feminism and War*, p. 20.
28. Wilson, Emma, '"The sea nymphs tested this miracle": *Water Lilies* (2007) and the origin of coral', in C. Brown and P. Hirsch (eds), *The Cinema of the Swimming Pool* (Bern: Peter Lang, 2014), p. 203.
29. Schneemann, Carolee, quoted by Hoffman, Alison, 'The persistence of (political) feelings and hand-touch sensibilities: Miranda July's feminist multimedia-making', in Columpar and Mayer (eds): *There She Goes*, p. 20.

30 Potter, Sally, 'Barefoot filmmaking', 6 February 2009, http://sallypotter.com/barefoot-filmmaking/, and reprinted in Potter, Sally, *Naked Cinema: Working with Actors* (London: Faber and Faber, 2014), pp. 138–39.
31 Barlow, Melinda, 'Toward a feminist Coney Island of the avant-garde: Janie Geiser recasts the cinema of attractions', in Columpar and Mayer (eds): *There She Goes*, p. 61.
32 Rich, *Chick Flicks: Theories and Memories of the Feminist Film Movement* (Durham NC: Duke University Press, 1998), p. 381.

1. Ain't about the (uh) Cha-Ching, Cha-Ching: Framing the New Feminist Cinema

1 DuVernay, Ava, quoted in Dargis, Manohla, 'Making history', *New York Times*, 3 December 2014, available online, http://www.nytimes.com/2014/12/07/movies/ava-duvernay-makes-a-mark-with-selma.html.
2 Brouillette, Sarah, 'Paranoid subjectivity and the challenges of cognitive mapping: How is capitalism to be represented?', *e-flux*, 12 March 2015, http://conversations.e-flux.com/t/paranoid-subjectivity-and-the-challenges-of-cognitive-mapping-how-is-capitalism-to-be-represented/1080/9.
3 Kang, Inkoo, 'Selma crosses $50 million at domestic box office', *Women and Hollywood*, 3 March 2015, 'http://blogs.indiewire.com/womenandhollywood/selma-crosses-50-million-at-domestic-box-office-20150303.
4 http://www.boxofficemojo.com/movies/?id=frozen2013.htm.
5 Handy, Bruce, 'Women-centric films out-gross male-centric films on average: twist!', *Vanity Fair*, 16 March 2014, available online, http://www.vanityfair.com/online/daily/2014/03/women-films-out-gross-male-films.
6 https://twitter.com/Lexialex; Alexander, Lexi, quoted in Renee, Kimberley, 'Cinema in Noir' podcast, 14 December 2014, http://www.blogtalkradio.com/cinemainnoir/2014/12/14/cinema-in-noir-qa-with-lexi-alexander.
7 Child, Ben, 'Women fare better in independent films than in Hollywood, study finds', *The Guardian*, 23 January 2013, available online, http://www.theguardian.com/film/2013/jan/23/women-independent-film-sundance-survey.
8 Smith, S.L., quoted in Silverstein, Melissa, 'Geena Davis Institute new research shows that girls and women are missing onscreen and behind the scenes worldwide', *Forbes.com*, 22 September 2014, http://www.forbes.com/sites/melissasilverstein/2014/09/22/geena-davis-institute-new-research-shows-that-girls-and-women-are-missing-onscreen-and-behind-the-scenes-worldwide/.
9 Goulet, Danis, 'Welcome to the Embargo Collective II blog!', *imagineNATIVE Blog*, 30 April 2014, http://www.imaginenative.org/wordpress/2014/04/welcome-to-the-embargo-collective-ii-blog-intro-by-danis-goulet/.
10 Perry, Grayson, 'The rise and fall of Default Man', *New Statesman*, 6 October 2014, available online, http://www.newstatesman.com/culture/2014/10/grayson-perry-rise-and-fall-default-man.
11 Younge, Gary, 'Ferguson, *Selma* and a mood for change', The *Guardian*, 29 January 2015, available online, http://www.theguardian.com/film/2015/jan/29/what-selma-means-now.

12 Reiniger, Lotte, 'Film as ballet: A dialogue between Lotte Reiniger and her familiar', in A. Lant and I. Periz (eds), *Red Velvet Seat: Women's Writing on the First Fifty Years of Cinema* (London & New York: Verso, 2006), p. 170.
13 Johnston, Claire, *The Work of Dorothy Arzner: Towards a Feminist Cinema* (London: British Film Institute, 1975).
14 Mulvey, 'Visual pleasure and narrative cinema', *Screen* 16/3 (1975), pp. 6–18.
15 McDonough, Jill, 'SUBMITATHON! as applied feminist epistemology: Rejecting models of scarcity, believing in plenty', *VIDA*, 13 September 2014, http://www.vidaweb.org/submitathon-applied-feminist-epistemology-rejecting-models-scarcity-believing-plenty/.
16 http://blogs.indiewire.com/womenandhollywood/; http://africanwomenincinema.blogspot.co.uk; http://wellywoodwoman.blogspot.co.uk.
17 http://www.joansdigest.com; http://cleojournal.com.
18 Kelly, Gabrielle, 'Summary', in G. Kelly and C. Robson (eds), *The Celluloid Ceiling* (Twickenham: Supernova, 2014), pp. 380–83.
19 http://www.theshowroom.org/research.html?id=1738.
20 White: *Women's Cinema*, p. 33.
21 Columpar, Corinn, 'The dancing body: Sally Potter as feminist auteure', in J. Levitin, J. Plessis and V. Raoul (eds), *Women Filmmakers: Refocusing* (Vancouver: University of British Columbia Press), pp. 108–16.
22 See Further Reading 1.
23 Chaudhuri, Shohini, *Feminist Film Theorists: Laura Mulvey, Kaja Silverman, Teresa de Lauretis, Barbara Creed* (Abingdon & New York: Routledge, 2006), p. 123.
24 See Further Reading 2; Ramanathan, Geetha, *Feminist Auteurs: Reading Women's Films* (London, Wallflower, 2006); Butler, Alison, *Women's Cinema: The Contested Screen* (London: Wallflower, 2002).
25 White: *Women's Cinema*, p. 103.
26 Hodal, Kate, 'Brunei shoots for the stars with trailblazing first commercial film' The, *Guardian*, 18 October 2013, available online, http://www.theguardian.com/world/2013/oct/18/brunei-trailblazing-first-commercial-film-yasmine-silat.
27 Bloom, Harold, *The Anxiety of Influence: A Theory of Poetry* (New York: Oxford University Press, 1973); Gilbert, S. M., and S. Gubar (eds), *The Madwoman in the Attic: The Woman Writer and the Nineteenth-Century Literary Imagination* (New Haven: Yale University Press, 1979).
28 Irigaray, Luce, quoted in Bolton, Lucy, *Film and Female Consciousness: Irigaray, Cinema and Thinking Women* (Basingstoke: Palgrave Macmillan, 2011), p. 44.
29 Anders, Allison, quoted in Willmore, Alison, 'Lifetime's *Ring of Fire* director Allison Anders: How to be an indie filmmaker in a TV world', *Indiewire*, 24 May 2013, http://www.indiewire.com/article/television/allison-anders-lifetime-ring-of-fire.
30 http://theslopeshow.com/episodes/; http://awkwardblackgirl.com; http://www.ackeeandsaltfish.co.uk/.
31 July, Miranda, quoted in Day, Elizabeth, 'Miranda July: "I had some rough episodes when I was younger"', *The Observer*, 8 February 2015, available online,

http://www.theguardian.com/books/2015/feb/08/miranda-july-had-some-rough-episodes-when-i-was-younger-first-bad-man-interview

32. Davis, Therese and Belinda Smaill, 'Introduction: The place of the contemporary female director', *Camera Obscura: Feminism, Culture, and Media Studies* 29 1/85 (2014), pp. 1–3.
33. Porter, Dawn, 'Here's why we need more women and minority filmmakers', *Indiewire*, 2 October 2014, http://www.indiewire.com/article/heres-why-we-need-more-women-and-minority-filmmakers-20141002 Access date?
34. Faludi, Susan, *The Terror Dream: What 9/11 Revealed about America* (London: Atlantic, 2008).
35. Cochrane, Kira, *All the Rebel Women: The Rise of Fourth Wave Feminism* (London: Guardianshorts, 2013).
36. Rainer, Yvonne, 'Mulvey's legacy', *Camera Obscura* 21/3 (2006), p. 168.
37. Lesage, Julia, 'Women's fragmented consciousness in feminist experimental autobiographical video', in D. Waldman and J. Walker (eds), *Feminism and Documentary* (Minneapolis: University of Minnesota Press, 1999), pp. 309–37.
38. James, Nick, 'The equalizers', *Sight & Sound* 24/11 (November 2014), available online, http://www.bfi.org.uk/news-opinion/sight-sound-magazine/comment/equalizers.
39. http://www.unwomen.org/en/news/stories/2014/9/geena-davis-study-press-release.
40. Robinson, Tasha, 'We're losing all our Strong Female Characters to Trinity Syndrome', *The Dissolve*, 16 June 2014, http://thedissolve.com/features/exposition/618-were-losing-all-our-strong-female-characters-to-tr/.
41. Sarkeesian, Anita, 'The Bechdel Test for women in movies', *Feminist Frequency*, 7 December 2009, http://www.feministfrequency.com/2009/12/the-bechdel-test-for-women-in-movies/.
42. Gay, Roxane, 'The solace of preparing fried foods and other quaint remembrances from 1960s Mississippi: Thoughts on *The Help*', *Bad Feminist* (London: Corsair, 2014), pp. 207–17.
43. Hill, Natalie, '*Miss Representation*: A critical review', *The F Word: Feminist Media Collective*, 3 November 2011, http://www.feminisms.org/3922/miss-representation-a-critical-review/. Access date?
44. Smith, S. L., Marc Choueiti, Dr Katherine Pieper, Tracy Gillig, Dr. Carmen Lee and Dylan DeLuca, 'Inequality in 700 popular films: Examining portrayals of gender, race and LGBT status from 2007-2014'. Media, Diversity and Social Change Initiative, August 2015, available online, http://annenberg.usc.edu/pages/~/media/MDSCI/Inequality%20in%20700%20Popular%20Films%208215%20Final%20for%20Posting.ashx.
45. Chaiworaporn, Anchalee, 'Moving up: Women directors and South-East Asian cinema', in Kelly and Robson (eds): *Celluloid*, p. 169.
46. Gatewood, Tara, 'Shifting views with *Drunktown's Finest*', *Native Peoples Magazine* (March-April 2014), available online, http://www.nativepeoples.com/Native-Peoples/March-April-2014/Shifting-Views-with-Drunktowns-Finest/.

47 Freeland, Sydney, introduction for *Drunktown's Finest*, BFI Southbank, 28 March 2015.
48 Keeling, Kara, *The Witch's Flight: The Cinematic, the Black Femme, and the Image of Common Sense* (Durham, NC: Duke University Press, 2007), pp. 41–44.
49 Pérez, Miriam Zoila, 'An open letter to the *New York Times*: Race and the reproductive rights movement', *Colorlines*, 31 July 2014, http://colorlines.com/archives/2014/07/an_open_letter_to_the_new_york_times_race_and_the_reproductive_rights_movement.html.
50 Campbell, Deragh, quoted in 'Outside of the box: A roundtable on Gillian Robespierre's *Obvious Child*', *cléo: a journal of film and feminism* 2/2 (August 2014), http://cleo-journal.com/2014/08/21/outside-of-the-box-a-roundtable-on-gillian-robespierres-obvious-child/; Mayer, Sophie, 'A choice not that obvious', *The F-Word: Contemporary UK Feminism*, 29 August 2014, http://www.thefword.org.uk/reviews/2014/08/obvious_child_review.
51 http://vesselthefilm.com/#host; Benzine, Adam, 'Terror attack at *Vessel* screening in Sweden', *Realscreen*, 9 December 2014, http://realscreen.com/2014/12/09/terror-attack-at-vessel-screening-in-sweden/.
52 Guerin, Orla, 'Mutilated Pakistani woman rebuilds her life', *BBC News*, 2 August 2012, available online, http://www.bbc.co.uk/news/world-asia-18595834.
53 Rose, Jacqueline, *Women in Dark Times* (London: Bloomsbury, 2014), p. 1.
54 Macnab, Geoffrey, 'Amour Fou developing films with Nobel prize-winner', *Screendaily*, 22 January 2015, http://www.screendaily.com/5082239.article.
55 http://www.cornerhouse.org/art/art-exhibitions/sophia-al-maria-virgin-with-a-memory.
56 Clover, Carol, *Men, Women and Chainsaws: Gender in the Modern Horror Film* (Princeton: Princeton University Press, 1993).
57 Marcos, Subcomandante, quoted in Klein, Naomi, 'The unknown icon', The *Guardian*, 3 March 2001, available online, http://www.theguardian.com/books/2001/mar/03/politics.
58 Bronfen, Elisabeth 'Nocturnal embodiments: Gendering allegories of the night', *Edda* 4 (2004), p. 312.
59 Faludi, *The Terror Dream*: pp. 1–18, 199–286.
60 Hamad, Hannah, 'Save the cheerleader; save the males: Resurgent protective paternalism in popular film and television after 9/11', in K. Ross (ed), *The Blackwell Handbook of Gender, Sexualities and the Media* (Malden, Ox.: Blackwell, & New York: Wiley, 2011), pp. 157–73.
61 Makhmalbaf, Samira, quoted in Said, S F, '"This girl behaves against it": An interview with Samira Makhmalbaf', in Columpar and Mayer (eds): *There She Goes*, p. 167.
62 Sebastian, Meryl Mary, 'Even our name is banned in Iran: An interview with Hana Makhmalbaf', *The Big Indian Picture*, August 2013, http://thebigindianpicture.com/2013/08/even-our-name-is-banned-in-iran/.
63 Ritman, Alex, 'Egypt court sentences editor of Oscar-nominated *The Square* to three years in prison', *Hollywood Reporter*, 27 October 2014, http://www.hollywoodreporter.com/news/egypt-court-sentences-editor-oscar-744086.

64　Badawi, Hend, quoted in Steavenson, Wendell, 'Two revolutions', *The New Yorker*, 12 November 2012, available online, http://www.newyorker.com/magazine/2012/11/12/two-revolutions-2.

65　Tharoor, Ishaan, 'Oscar nominated documentary *The Square* takes on a political life of its own', *Time*, 27 February 2014, http://world.time.com/2014/02/27/the-square-oscars-egypt-kiev/.

66　Butler, Judith, 'Bodies in alliance and the politics of the street', *Transversal* (October 2011), http://www.eipcp.net/transversal/1011/butler/en.

67　https://www.youtube.com/user/PussRiot.

68　http://www.feministfrequency.com.

69　https://twitter.com/helenlewis/status/233594800908169217

70　http://everydaysexism.com; *Feral Feminisms*, http://feralfeminisms.com; *GUTS Canadian Feminist Magazine*, http://gutsmagazine.ca; *HYSTERIA*, http://www.hystericalfeminisms.com; https://twitter.com/rgay.

71　Yee, J. (ed), *Feminism FOR REAL: Deconstructing the Academic Industrial Complex of Feminism* (Ottawa: Canadian Centre for Policy Alternatives, 2011).

72　Taylor, Astra, *The People's Platform: Taking Back Power and Culture in the Digital Age* (London: HarperCollins, 2014).

73　McKenzie, Mia, 'Am I a bully? One angry black woman's reflection', *Black Girl Dangerous*, 17 September 2013, http://www.blackgirldangerous.org/2013/09/am-i-bully-one-angry-black-womans-reflection/.

74　http://feministkilljoys.com.

75　Ahmed, Sara, 'Feminist killjoys and other willful subjects', *The Scholar and Feminist Online* 8/3 (Summer 2010), http://sfonline.barnard.edu/polyphonic/print_ahmed.htm.

76　http://feministgodzilla.tumblr.com.

2. Not in Kansas: Animal Selves and Becoming-Girls

1　Reichardt, Kelly, quoted in Brown, Sophie, 'Kelly Reichardt on smashing the system sustainably', *Dazed & Confused*, February 2014, http://www.dazeddigital.com/artsandculture/article/18455/1/kelly-reichardt-on-smashing-the-system-sustainably.

2　Berman, Jillian, 'Nearly half of American households are one emergency away from financial disaster, report finds', *Huffington Post*, 30 January 2013, http://www.huffingtonpost.com/2013/01/30/financial-emergency-report_n_2576326.html.

3　Tirado, Linda, *Hand to Mouth: Living in Bootstrap America* (New York: Putnam, 2014).

4　Haraway, Donna, *Companion Species Manifesto* (Prickly Paradigm Press, 2003), p. 2.

5　Collis, Stephen, 'Notes towards a manifesto of the biotariat', *Beating the Bounds*, 25 July 2014, http://beatingthebounds.com/2014/07/25/notes-towards-a-manifesto-of-the-biotariat/.

6　'Her Yer Taksim! Feminist and LGBTQI engagement in the Gezi Park protests', Association for Women's Rights in Development, 26 July 2013, http://www.awid.org/news-and-analysis/her-yer-taksim-feminist-and-lgbtqi-engagement-gezi-park-protests.

7 de Luca, Tiago, 'Dead time: Animals, contingency and death in Carlos Reygadas's *Japón* and Lisandro Alonso's *Los Muertos*', in T. de Luca and N. Barradas Jorge (eds), *Slow Cinema* (Edinburgh: Edinburgh University Press, 2015). With thanks to Tiago for sharing his essay before publication.
8 http://confusedcatsagainstfeminism.tumblr.com.
9 http://catsonfilm.net.
10 Armatage, Kay, *The Girl from God's Country: Nell Shipman and the Silent Cinema* (Toronto: University of Toronto Press, 2003).
11 Diski, Jenny, 'Under our skin', *What I Don't Know About Animals* (London: Virago, 2010), pp. 163–92.
12 *Feral Feminisms*, http://feralfeminisms.com/about/.
13 Deren, Maya, quoted in *Esquire*, December 1946; reprinted in Neiman, Catrina, VèVè A. Clark, and Millicent Hodson (eds), *The Legend of Maya Deren*, Vol. 1 pt. 2, (New York: Anthology Film Archive/Film Culture, 1998), p. 331.
14 *Wendy and Lucy* EPK, available online, http://www.wendyandlucy.com/press_images/wal_pressnotes.pdf.
15 Harb, Shuruq, 'Film review: *Summer 2006, Palestine*', Electronic Intifada, 28 March 2007, http://electronicintifada.net/content/film-review-summer-2006-palestine/3513.
16 Pick, Anat, *Creaturely Poetics: Animality and Vulnerability in Literature and Film* (New York: Columbia University Press, 2011), p. 5.
17 http://dogwoof.com/documentary/blog/post/the_blackfish_effect_seaworld_profits_drop_84/29163.
18 Rose, Steve, '*Attenberg, Dogtooth* and the weird wave of Greek cinema', The *Guardian*, 27 August 2011, available online, http://www.theguardian.com/film/2011/aug/27/attenberg-dogtooth-greece-cinema.
19 Ibid.
20 Agamben, Giorgio, *Homo Sacer: Sovereign Power and Bare Life*, trans. Daniel Heller-Roazen (Stanford: Stanford University Press, 1998).
21 Solnit, Rebecca, *Motion Studies: Time, Space and Eadweard Muybridge* (London: Bloomsbury, 2003).
22 Barnard, Clio, quoted in Sarhimaa, Jutta, 'Heavy metal: Clio Barnard on junkyards, heroes, and fairytales in *The Selfish Giant*', *cléo: a journal of film and feminism*, 2/2 (Summer 2014), http://cleojournal.com/2014/08/21/heavy-metal-clio-barnard-on-junkyards-heroes-and-fairytales-in-the-selfish-giant-2/.
23 Haraway: *Companion Species*, p. 2.
24 Sicinski, Michael, '*Wendy and Lucy* [review]', *Cineaste* 34/2 (2009), available online, http://www.cineaste.com/articles/emwendy-and-lucyem. Accessed 1 September 2014, no longer functional. *Cineaste's* archive is currently under reconstruction.
25 Gately, Andy, 'Trainhopping: A round-up of hobos on film', *I Love Mike Litt*, http://www.ilovemikelitt.com/2010/04/trainhopping-a-round-up-of-hobos-on-film/.
26 Reynaud, Bérénice, 'For *Wanda*', *Senses of Cinema* 22 (Oct 2002), http://sensesofcinema.com/2002/feature-articles/wanda/; Duras, Marguerite, *Green Eyes: Reflections on Film by the author of* The Lover (1980), trans. Carol Barko (New York: Columbia University Press, 1990), pp. 151–74.

27 Paley, Tony, 'London film festival puts a trailblazing film called *Wanda* back on the road', *The Guardian*, 17 October 2011, http://www.theguardian.com/film/filmblog/2011/oct/17/london-film-festival-wanda-loden.
28 Novak, Matt, 'Oregon was founded as a racist utopia', *Gizmodo*, 21 January 2015, http://gizmodo.com/oregon-was-founded-as-a-racist-utopia-1539567040.
29 Tagaq, Tanya, quoted in MacNeil, Jason, 'Tanya Tagaq talks missing and murdered aboriginal woman [sic], PETA in CBC National interview', 29 September 2014, *Huffpost Music*, http://www.huffingtonpost.ca/2014/09/29/tanya-tagaq-missing-murdered-aboriginal-women_n_5899980.html.
30 Grant, Catherine, 'A fishy little curio: Lucrecia Martel's *Pescados* (2010), with subtitles in English', *Mediático*, 27 January 2014, http://reframe.sussex.ac.uk/mediatico/2014/01/27/a-fishy-little-curio-lucrecia-martels-pescados-2010-with-subtitles-in-english/.
31 Pick: *Creaturely Poetics*, p. 15.

3. Water Rites: Ecocinema's New Earth Mothers

1 Mies, Maria and Vandana Shiva, *Ecofeminism* (London: Zed Books, 1993); Shiva, *Water Wars: Privatization, Pollution, and Profit* (Boston: South End Press, 2002).
2 http://water.org/country/kenya/.
3 Kahiu, Wanuri, quoted in Seibel, Brendan, 'Kenyan sci-fi short Pumzi hits Sundance with dystopia', *Wired*, 22 January 2010, http://www.wired.com/2010/01/pumzi/.
4 Kermeliotis, Teo, 'Wanuri Kahiu: "In Kenya, I'm a hustler"', *CNN: Screening Room*, 30 March 2010, http://edition.cnn.com/2010/SHOWBIZ/Movies/03/26/wanuri.kahiu.pumzi/.
5 Kahiu, quoted in Seibel: 'Kenyan sci-fi'.
6 http://en.wikipedia.org/wiki/Recent_African_origin_of_modern_humans.
7 James, Diana, 'Re-sourcing the sacredness of water', in K. Lahiri-Dutt (ed), *Fluid Bonds: Views on Gender and Water* (Kolkata: Stree, 2006), pp. 85–6.
8 Tay: *Women on the Edge*, p. 193.
9 Rich, 'Queering the social landscape', *New Queer Cinema*: pp. 167–82.
10 Wilson: '"The sea nymphs"', p. 204.
11 Ibid. p. 204.
12 Davis, Geena, 'Two easy steps to make Hollywood less sexist', *Hollywood Reporter*, 11 December 2013, available online, http://www.hollywoodreporter.com/news/geena-davis-two-easy-steps-664573.
13 Pilkington, Ed, 'Top kill meets *Titanic*: James Cameron enters fight against oil spill', The *Guardian*, 2 June 2010, available online, http://www.theguardian.com/film/2010/jun/02/james-cameron-underwater-oil-spill.
14 Morris, Courtney Desiree, 'Why misogynists make great informants: How gender violence on the left enables state violence in radical movements', *make/shift* 7 (Spring/Summer 2010), available online, http://inciteblog.wordpress.com/2010/07/15/why-misogynists-make-great-informants-how-gender-violence-on-the-left-enables-state-violence-in-radical-movements/.

15 http://www.cmsimpact.org/fair-use/related-materials/codes/code-best-practices-sustainable-filmmaking.
16 'Age of Stupid premiere: The green carpet treatment', photostory, The Guardian, 16 March 2009, available online, http://www.theguardian.com/environment/gallery/2009/mar/16/the-age-of-stupid-climate-change#/?picture=344648730&index=0.
17 Murray, Leo, 'Maldives pledges to go carbon-neutral in ten years', Spanner Films, 16 March 2009, http://www.spannerfilms.net/news/maldives_become_carbon_limbo_world_champions.
18 Zeitoun, Mark, *Power and Water in the Middle East: The Hidden Politics of the Palestinian-Israeli Water Conflict* (London: I.B.Tauris, 2008).
19 Butler, Judith, *Frames of War: When is Life Grievable?* (London: Verso, 2010), p. 170.
20 Reeves, Jennifer, quoted in Mayer, '"The skin, the aging, the imperfection, the colour, the beauty"', *Vertigo* 4/2 (Winter/Spring 2009), available online, http://www.closeupfilmcentre.com/vertigo_magazine/volume-4-issue-2-winter-spring-20091/the-skin-the-aging-the-imperfection-the-colour-the-beauty/.
21 Marks, Laura U., *The Skin of the Film: Intercultural Cinema, Embodiment and the Senses* (Durham NC: Duke University Press, 2000).
22 Morrison, Toni, 'The site of memory', *What Moves at the Margin: Selected Non-Fiction* (Jackson: University Press of Mississippi, 2008), pp. 65–80.
23 Elie, Lolis Eric, 'Kimberly Rivers Roberts, the woman behind *Trouble the Water*', Inside Treme, 12 November 2012, http://www.inside-treme-blog.com/home/2012/11/12/kimberly-rivers-roberts-the-woman-behind-trouble-the-water.html.
24 Solnit, *A Paradise Built in Hell: The Extraordinary Communities that Arise in Disaster* (New York: Penguin, 2009), p. 7.
25 Mayer, 'Dirty pictures: Framing pollution and desire in "new New Queer Cinema"', in A. Pick and G. Narraway (eds), *Screening Nature: Cinema Beyond the Human* (Oxford & New York: Berghahn Books, 2013), pp. 145–61.
26 Millares Young, Kristen, 'Misty Upham: The tragic death and unscripted life of Hollywood's rising star', The Guardian, 30 June 2015, available online, http://www.theguardian.com/global/2015/jun/30/misty-upham-native-american-actress-tragic-death-inspiring-life
27 http://www.samaqan3.ca.
28 Gutiérrez, Chus, quoted in Walsh, David, 'An interview with Chus Gutiérrez, director of *Return to Hansala*', *World Socialist Web Site*, 24 September 2008, http://www.wsws.org/en/articles/2008/09/guti-s24.html.
29 Ibid.
30 Gilroy, Paul, *The Black Atlantic: Modernity and Double Consciousness* (London: Verso, 1993).
31 Farhat, Maymanah, 'Finding a sense of home in *Salt of This Sea*', *Electronic Intifada*, 15 April 2009, http://electronicintifada.net/content/finding-sense-home-salt-sea/8184.
32 Ellerson, Beti, '*Barakat!* by Djamila Sahraoui', *African Women in Cinema Blog*, http://africanwomenincinema.blogspot.co.uk/2010/09/barakat-by-djamila-sahraoui.html.

33. Dallas, Paul, 'Children of the revolution', *Filmmaker*, 6 December 2013, http://filmmakermagazine.com/82776-children-of-the-revolution-director-narimane-mari-on-her-award-winning-bloody-beans/.
34. Lahiri-Dutt, 'Introduction' in Lahiri-Dutt (ed): *Fluid Bonds*, p. xv.

4. Home Front: Women at War, Women against War

1. Butler, J., *Precarious Life: The Power of Mourning and Violence* (London: Verso, 2006).
2. Makhmalbaf, Hana, interview in EPK, available online, http://www.wildbunch.biz/movie/buddha-collapsed-out-of-shame/.
3. Butler, J., *Frames of War*, p. ix.
4. White: *Women's Cinema*, p. 16.
5. Mohanty, Pratt and Riley, 'Introduction: feminism and US wars – mapping the ground', in Riley, Pratt and Mohanty (eds): *Feminism and War*, p. 2.
6. Hurley, Kameron, '"We have always fought": Challenging the "women, cattle and slaves" narrative', *A Dribble of Ink*, 20 May 2013, http://aidanmoher.com/blog/featured-article/2013/05/we-have-always-fought-challenging-the-women-cattle-and-slaves-narrative-by-kameron-hurley/.
7. White: *Women's Cinema*, p. 2.
8. Barrett, Emma, 'Women at war', BBC Radio 4, 8 October 2013, http://www.bbc.co.uk/programmes/b03c3dx1; Austen, Ian, 'Armed forces in Canada resolved issue long ago', *New York Times*, 24 January 2013, available online, http://www.nytimes.com/2013/01/25/world/americas/armed-forces-in-canada-resolved-issue-long-ago.html.
9. Freeman, Beth, email to author, July 20, 2014.
10. Hutcheon, Linda, *The Politics of Postmodernism* (1989), 2nd edition (London & New York: Routledge, 2001), pp. 24–25.
11. Lebow, Alisa, 'The unwar film', in A. Juhasz and A. Lebow (eds), *A Companion to Contemporary Documentary Film* (West Sussex: Wiley Blackwell, 2015), p. 456.
12. Hedges, Chris, *War is a Force that Gives us Meaning* (New York: Random House, 2003), p. 3.
13. Whitsitt, Sam, '"Come back to the humvee ag'in Will honey," or a few comments about the sexual politics of Kathryn Bigelow's *The Hurt Locker* (2009)', *Jump Cut* 52 (Summer 2010), http://www.ejumpcut.org/archive/jc52.2010/whitsittHurtLocker/index.html.
14. Washuta, Elissa, 'Violence against indigenous women: Fun, sexy, and no big deal', author's blog, 25 August 2014, http://washuta.tumblr.com/post/95744773341/violence-against-indigenous-women-fun-sexy-and-no.
15. Columpar, *Unsettling Sights: The Fourth World on Film* (Carbondale and Edwardsville: Southern Illinois University Press, 2010).
16. Stuart, Tessa, '*Manhunt* sets the *Zero Dark Thirty* record straight', *BuzzFeed*, 29 January 2013, http://www.buzzfeed.com/tessastuart/manhunt-sets-the-zero-dark-thirty-record-strai#b1ctyw.

17 Bazelon, Emily, 'Does *Zero Dark Thirty* advocate torture?' *Slate*, 11 December 2012, http://www.slate.com/articles/arts/culturebox/2012/12/zero_dark_thirty_and_torture_does_kathryn_bigelow_s_bin_laden_movie_make.html.
18 Kaye/Kantrowitz, Melanie, 'Feminist organizing in Israel', in Riley, Pratt and Mohanty (eds): *Feminism and War*, p. 243.
19 http://www.notinvisible.org/about.
20 Cioca, Kori, quoted in Guzman, Natasha, '"I really thought I was the only one: Q&A with military rape survivor Kori Cioca', *Bitch Magazine*, 19 June 2013, http://bitchmagazine.org/post/i-really-thought-i-was-the-only-one-qa-with-military-rape-survivor-kori-cioca.
21 Susskind, Yifat, 'What will it take to stop Isis using rape as a weapon of war?' The, *Guardian*, 17 February 2015, available online, http://www.theguardian.com/global-development/2015/feb/17/disarm-isis-rape-weapon-war.
22 Drakulić, Slavenka, *S. A Story about the Balkans*, trans. Marko Ivic (New York: Penguin, 1999).
23 http://www.un.org/en/globalissues/briefingpapers/endviol/.
24 Asibong, Andrew, 'Marie NDiaye', *Centre for the Study of Contemporary Women's Writing*, http://modernlanguages.sas.ac.uk/centre-study-contemporary-womens-writing/languages/french/marie-ndiaye.
25 Lebow: 'Unwar film', pp. 460–61.
26 Reeves, Jennifer, '*The Time We Killed*', author's website, http://www.jenniferreevesfilm.com/pages/artpage_1.php?page=4.
27 Bruno, Giuliana, '*Yes*, it's about time: A "virtual" letter to Sally Potter from Giuliana Bruno', *Journal of Visual Culture* 7 (April 2008), p. 29.

5. I Have No Country: British Cinema as a Runaway Girl

1 http://www.wbg.org.uk/2014-assessments/.
2 http://www.fawcettsociety.org.uk/2013/03/cutting-women-out/.
3 Townsend, Mark, 'Serco whistleblower's Yarl's Wood claim', The *Guardian*, 24 May 2014, available online, http://www.theguardian.com/uk-news/2014/may/24/serco-whistleblower-yarls-wood-pressure-immigration; Jones, Owen, 'Women need protection from undercover officers', The *Guardian*, 25 August 2014, available online, http://www.theguardian.com/commentisfree/2014/aug/25/cps-police-spies-sexual-relations-under-cover-women-activists; Bates, Laura, 'Women are being assaulted, abused and murdered in a sea of misogyny', The *Guardian*, 12 September 2014, available online, http://www.theguardian.com/lifeandstyle/womens-blog/2014/sep/12/women-being-assaulted-abused-murdered-misogny.
4 The '*Guardian* view on child sex abuse: this time it really must be never again', The *Guardian*, 4 February 2014, available online, http://www.theguardian.com/commentisfree/2015/feb/04/guardian-view-child-sex-abuse-this-time-really-never-again.

5. Hattenstone, Simon, 'Samantha Morton: Rotherham brought back memories of my own sexual abuse', The *Guardian*, 12 September 2014, available online, http://www.theguardian.com/film/2014/sep/12/samantha-morton-interview-rotherham-sexual-abuse.
6. Woolf, Virginia, *Three Guineas* (New York: Harcourt Brace Jovanovich, 1966), p. 109.
7. Donald, Stephanie Hemelryk, *Little Children: Children's Film and Media Culture in New China* (Lanham, MD: Rowman and Littlefield, 2005).
8. Wilson, *Cinema's Missing Children* (London & New York: Wallflower, 2003), p. 10.
9. Akbari, Mania, quoted in Seymour, Tom, 'Iranian film-maker Mania Akbari: "Cinema threatens the government"', The *Guardian*, 15 July 2013, available online, http://www.theguardian.com/film/2013/jul/15/iranian-filmmaker-mania-akbari.
10. Akbari, quoted in Seymour: 'Iranian film-maker'.
11. Lewis, Rachel, 'Towards a transnational lesbian cinema', *Journal of Lesbian Studies*, 16/3 (2012), p. 283.
12. Lewis: 'Towards', p. 285.
13. Bolton, Lucy, 'Mia in *Fish Tank*: Being a modern girl in modern Britain', in F. Handyside and K. Taylor (eds), *International Cinema and the Girl: Local Issues, Transnational Contexts* (London: Palgrave Macmillan, 2015). My thanks to Lucy for sharing the essay with me before publication.
14. Bolton: 'Mia'.
15. Hattenstone: 'Samantha Morton'.
16. Harris, Anita, *Future Girl: Young Women in the Twenty-First Century* (London: Routledge, 2004), p. 14.
17. Klein, Naomi, 'Patriarchy gets funky: The triumph of identity marketing', *No Logo* (New York: Picador, 2000), pp. 107–126.
18. Carroll, Noel, 'Moving and moving', *Millennium Film Journal* 35/36 (Fall 2000), available online, http://www.mfj-online.org/journalPages/MFJ35/MovingandMoving.htm.
19. Thornham, Sue, *What If I Had Been the Hero? Investigating Women's Cinema* (Basingstoke & New York: Palgrave Macmillan, 2012).
20. Landy, Marcia, '*Under the Skin*', Screenonline, http://www.screenonline.org.uk/film/id/493153/.
21. Shapiro, Isabel, 'Beyond borders: The enactment of ethics in contemporary British documentary', M.Phil. dissertation, unpublished, p. 2. My thanks to Isabel for sharing her dissertation.
22. Morton, Samantha, in Gilbert, Gerard, 'Look back in anger: Samantha Morton makes her directorial debut', The *Independent*, 16 May 2009, available online, http://www.independent.co.uk/arts-entertainment/films/features/look-back-in-anger-samantha-morton-makes-her-directorial-debut-1685742.html.
23. http://lookspring.co.uk/games/dreams-of-your-life.
24. Edgar, David, 'Enter the new wave of political playwrights', The *Guardian*, 28 February 2010, available online, http://www.theguardian.com/stage/2010/feb/28/david-edgar-new-political-theatre.
25. Ellis-Petersen, Hannah, 'Theatre's leading female figures gather to shine a spotlight on the gender gap', The *Guardian*, 22 September 2014, available online, http://www.theguardian.com/stage/2014/sep/22/theatre-female-figures-gender-gap.

26 McGrath, Nick, 'My hymn to Bethlehem', The *Guardian*, 6 December 2014, available online, http://www.theguardian.com/lifeandstyle/2014/dec/06/my-hymn-to-bethlehem-documentary-film; http://www.openbethlehemcampaign.org.
27 Woolcock, Penny, quoted in Mayer, 'How far is one mile', *The F-Word: Contemporary UK Feminism*, 4 April 2013, http://www.thefword.org.uk/reviews/2013/04/how_far_is_one_mile.
28 https://www.kickstarter.com/projects/313414227/one-mile-away.
29 https://www.indiegogo.com/projects/from-the-plantation-to-the-penitentiary--2.
30 Robey, Tim, '*My Brother the Devil*', *The Telegraph*, 8 November 2012, available online, http://www.telegraph.co.uk/culture/film/filmreviews/9664711/My-Brother-the-Devil-review.html.
31 Shohat, Ella and Robert Stam, *Unthinking Eurocentrism: Multiculturalism and the Media* (London: Routledge, 1994), p. 42.
32 Woolcock quoted in Mayer: 'How Far'.
33 Johnson, Rebecca, *Honeytrap* press notes.

6. All Dressed Up: Costume Drama Loosens its Corset

1 Asante, Amma, quoted in Kang, 'Amma Asante on channeling the warrior queen to make *Belle*', *Women and Hollywood*, 17 February 2015, http://blogs.indiewire.com/womenandhollywood/amma-asante-on-channeling-the-warrior-queen-to-make-belle-20150217.
2 Tseng, Ada, 'Starting up a *Bran Nue Dae*: Interview with director Rachel Perkins', *Asia Pacific Arts*, 11 September 2010, http://www.asiapacificarts.usc.edu/w_apa/showarticle.aspx?articleID=15634.
3 'BFI Film Fund: Diversity Guidelines for Production', July 2014, http://www.bfi.org.uk/news-opinion/news-bfi/announcements/bfi-obligates-supports-lottery-funding-recipients-reflect-diversity-uk.
4 Clark, Ashley, 'Portrait of a lady', *Sight & Sound* 24/7 (July 2014), p. 33.
5 Kang, 'BFI Film Fund's new requirements promote diversity on and off screen', *Women and Hollywood*, 8 July 2014, http://blogs.indiewire.com/womenandhollywood/bfi-film-funds-new-requirements-promote-diversity-on-and-off-screen-20140708; Evans, Marian, 'The BFI greenlights diversity', *Wellywood Woman*, 19 September 2014, http://wellywoodwoman.blogspot.co.uk/2014/09/the-bfi-greenlights-diversity.html.
6 Harewood, David, 'Why do we black actors have to go the US to be taken seriously?', *The Guardian*, 9 May 2008, available online, http://www.theguardian.com/commentisfree/2008/may/09/race.usa.
7 Kay, Jackie, *Trumpet* (London: Picador, 1998); Smith, Ali, *How to be Both* (London: Hamish Hamilton, 2014).
8 https://www.indiegogo.com/projects/sacred-country/x/3553981.
9 Waters, Sarah, *Tipping the Velvet* (London: Virago, 1998); Alexander, Bryan, 'Eva Longoria: I'm not starring in lesbian movie', *People*, 13 November 2006, http://www.people.com/people/article/0,26334,1558912,00.html.

10 Vidal, Belén, *Heritage Film: Nation, Genre and Representation* (London and New York: Wallflower Press, 2012), p. 1.
11 Asante, quoted in Clark: 'Portrait', p. 33.
12 Hall, Stuart, 'Cultural identity and cinematic representation', in R. Stam and T. Miller (eds), *Film and Theory: An Anthology* (Oxford; Malden, MA: Blackwell, 2000), p. 705.
13 Fanon, Frantz, *The Wretched of the Earth* (1961) trans. Constance Farrington (Harmondsworth: Penguin, 1967), p. 168, quoted Hall: 'Cultural identity', p. 705.
14 Kellaway, Kate, 'Amma Asante: "I'm bi-cultural, I walk the division that Belle walked every day"', The *Observer*, 18 May 2014, available online, http://www.theguardian.com/film/2014/may/18/amma-asante-belle-bicultural-ghanaian-british-director-grange-hill.
15 Clark: 'Portrait', p. 32.
16 Knegt, Peter, 'The eleven biggest winners at the summer indie box office', *Indiewire*, 2 September 2014, http://www.indiewire.com/article/the-11-biggest-winners-at-the-summer-indie-box-office-20140902.
17 Pidduck, Julianne, *Contemporary Costume Film: Space, Place and the Past* (London: BFI, 2004), p. 1.
18 Thorpe, Vanessa, 'Dido Belle: the slave's daughter who lived in Georgian elegance', The *Guardian*, 4 May 2014, available online, http://www.theguardian.com/film/2014/may/04/dido-belle-slaves-daughter-who-lived-in-georgian-elegance.
19 Dash, Julie, bell hooks, and Toni Cade Bambara, *Daughters of the Dust: The Making of an African American Women's Film* (New York: New Press, 1992); http://travelnotesofageecheegirl.com.
20 Vidal: *Heritage Film*, p. 3.
21 Staff, 'Nunavummiut on the red carpet', *Nunatsiaq News*, 5 September 2014, http://www.nunatsiaqonline.ca/stories/article/65674photo_nunavummiut_on_the_red_carper/.
22 Columpar: *Unsettling Sights*, p. 182.
23 Vizenor, Gerald, *Manifest Manners: Narratives on Postindian Survivance* (Lincoln: University of Nebraska, 1999), p. vii.
24 Silverman, Kaja, 'Suture', *The Subject of Semiotics* (Oxford: Oxford University Press, 1983), pp. 194–236.
25 Palafox, Teofilia quoted in Meier, Annemarie, 'Cine de mujer. Individualismo y colectividad', in N. Iglesias and R. L. Fregoso (eds), *Miradas de Mujer: Encuentro de cineastas y videoastas mexicanas y chicanas* (Tijuana: El Colegio de la Frontera Norte & Davis CA: University of California, 1998), p. 77; translated by Mar Diestro-D'opido and reprinted in S. Mayer and E. Oroz (eds), *Lo personal es politico: feminismo y documental* (Pamplona: INAAC, 2011), p. 108.
26 Hughes, Virginia, 'Were the first artists mostly women?', *National Geographic*, 8 October 2013, available online, http://news.nationalgeographic.com/news/2013/10/131008-women-handprints-oldest-neolithic-cave-art/.
27 Watkins, Elizabeth, 'Color and fluid: The (in)visibility of *The Portrait of a Lady*', in Columpar and Mayer (eds): *There She Goes*, p. 201.
28 Vidal: *Heritage Drama*, p. 93, paraphrasing Bruzzi, Stella, *Undressing Cinema: Clothing and Identity in the Movies* (London: Routledge, 1997).

29 Backman Rogers, Anna, 'The historical threshold: Crisis, ritual and liminality in Sofia Coppola's *Marie-Antoinette* (2006)', *Relief* 6/1 (2012), p. 82.
30 Cvetkovich Ann, 'In the archives of lesbian feelings: Documentary and popular culture', *Camera Obscura* 49 17/1 (2002), p. 108.
31 Dickinson, Emily, 'Tell all the truth but tell it slant', F1263, available online, http://www.poetryfoundation.org/poem/247292.
32 Rastogi, Nina Shen, 'What's the Native American man saying in *Meek's Cutoff*?', *Slate*, 18 April 2011, http://www.slate.com/content/slate/blogs/browbeat/2011/04/18/what_s_the_native_american_man_saying_in_meek_s_cutoff.html.
33 Reichardt: Sundance 2011 'Q&A: *Meek's Cutoff*', 22 January 2011, available online, http://cs.entertainmentcareers.net/blogs/filmfest/archive/2011/01/22/q-amp-a-meek-s-cutoff.aspx.
34 Reichardt, quoted in Kathryn, 'Diaries as film source in *Meek's Cutoff*, Archives and Auteurs, 1 May 2011, http://archivesandauteurs.blogspot.co.uk/2011/05/diaries-as-film-source-in-meeks-cutoff.html.
35 Halberstam, Jack, 'Perverse presentism', *Female Masculinity* (Durham: Duke University Press, 1988), pp. 45–73.
36 Lane, Penny, 'Interview with Jennifer Montgomery', *Incite: Journal of Experimental Media*, 4 January 2011, http://www.incite-online.net/montgomery.html.
37 Atwood, Margaret, *The Handmaid's Tale* (Toronto: McLelland & Stewart, 1985).
38 Ostrowska, Ania, 'Thinking is a lonely business', *The F-Word: Contemporary UK Feminism*, 7 October 2013, http://www.thefword.org.uk/reviews/2013/10/Hannah_Arendt.
39 Ibid.
40 Canby, Vincent, '*Rosa Luxemburg*: New light on an early leftist', *New York Times*, 1 May 1987, available online, http://www.nytimes.com/movie/review?res=9B0DEFDB1130F932A35756C0A961948260.
41 '*Suffragette* to be filmed on location in House of Commons', UK Parliament website, 7 March 2014, http://www.parliament.uk/business/news/2014/march/suffragette-to-be-filmed-on-location-in-house-of-commons/.
42 Halperin, Moze, 'Ava DuVernay and *Selma* stars wear "I Can't Breathe" t-shirts to New York premiere, *Flavorwire*, 15 December 2014, http://flavorwire.com/newswire/selma-stars-wear-i-cant-breathe-t-shirts-to-new-york-premiere.
43 Dargis: 'Making history'.
44 Mehta, Deepa, quoted in Levy, Emmanuel, 'Mehta *Water*', 24 April 2006, http://emanuellevy.com/interviews/mehta-iwateri-6/.
45 Neshat, Shirin, response to author, Q&A, Barbican, London, 5 December 2008.
46 Scott, Joan, *The Fantasy of Feminist History* (Durham NC: Duke University Press, 2011).
47 Donnelly, Elisabeth, '#FilmHerStory: 10 female biopics that desperately need to happen', *Flavorwire*, 4 March 2015, http://flavorwire.com/507694/filmherstory-10-female-biopics-that-desperately-need-to-happen.
48 Vidal: *Heritage Film*, pp. 120; 119.
49 Ex, Campbell, workshop, Hackney Picturehouse, 22 November 2014; Butler, Octavia, *Kindred* (New York: Doubleday, 1979).

50 Evans and Parekowhai, Cushla, 'Dana Rotberg and *White Lies/Tuakiri Huna*', *Wellywood Woman*, 23 June 2013, http://wellywoodwoman.blogspot.co.uk/2013/06/dana-rotberg-and-white-liestuakiri-huna.html

7. Mirror, Mirror: Fairy Tales of the Feminist Fantastic

1 Kit, Borys, 'Elle Fanning to star as Mary Shelley in *A Storm in the Stars*', *The Hollywood Reporter*, 30 July 2014, http://www.hollywoodreporter.com/news/elle-fanning-star-as-mary-722334.
2 Yamato, Jen, '*Game of Thrones* Sophie Turner set for *Mary Shelley's Monster* opposite Jeremy Irvine, Taissa Farmiga', *Deadline*, 12 August 2014, http://deadline.com/2014/08/mary-shelleys-monster-sophie-turner-jeremy-irving-taissa-farmiga-818269/.
3 West, Cel, 'On criticising *Game of Thrones*', *There is No Alternative: Politics, Speculative Fiction & Pop Culture* blog, 6 June 2012, http://noalternative.org/2012/06/06/184/.
4 Penny, Laurie, '*Game of Thrones* and the Good Ruler complex', *The New Stateman*, 4 June 2012, http://www.newstatesman.com/blogs/tv-and-radio/2012/06/game-thrones-and-good-ruler-complex.
5 Davis, Lennard, *Enforcing Normalcy: Disability, Deafness and the Body* (London: Verso, 1995), p. 144.
6 de Beauvoir, Simone, *The Second Sex*, 1949, trans. H.M. Parshley (New York: Avon, 1972), p. 267.
7 Rose: *Women*, p. x.
8 Ibid.
9 Child, Abigail, 'Subtalk', http://www.abigailchild.com/index.php?/films/subtalk/.
10 Rose: *Women*, p. xii.
11 'Luce Irigaray: Mimesis', *Internet Encyclopaedia of Philosophy*, http://www.iep.utm.edu/irigaray/#SH4a.
12 Gillett, Sue, 'Engaging Medusa: Competing myths and fairytales in *In the Cut*', *Senses of Cinema* 31 (April 2004), http://sensesofcinema.com/2004/feature-articles/in_the_cut/.
13 Dargis, Manohla, 'No sleep for a beauty who seeks adventure', *New York Times*, 7 July 2011, available online, http://www.nytimes.com/2011/07/08/movies/sleeping-beauty-from-catherine-breillat-review.html.
14 Diop, Mati, quoted in Cruz, María Palacios, 'Mati Diop: *Snow Canon*', *Vdrome*, http://www.vdrome.org/diop.html.
15 Price, Erika D., 'All hail the neurotic selfish female character', author's blog, 22 October 2013, http://erikadprice.tumblr.com/post/64787950454/all-hail-the-neurotic-selfish-female-character.
16 Faludi, *Backlash: The Undeclared War against Women* (London: Vintage, 1991).
17 hooks, 'The oppositional gaze: Black female spectators', *Black Looks: Race and Representation* (Boston: South End Press, 1992), pp. 115–31.
18 Tsjeng, Zing, 'Andrej[a] Pejíc Joins Sofia Coppola's *The Little Mermaid* Cast', *Dazed Digital*, June 2014, http://www.dazeddigital.com/artsandculture/article/20308/1/andrej-pejic-joins-sofia-coppolas-the-little-mermaid-cast.

19. Wilson: '"The sea nymphs"', p. 205.
20. Denis, Claire, quoted in Nayman, Adam, 'Claire Denis', *Reverse Shot*, June 26, 2009, http://www.reverseshot.com/interviews/entry/395/claire-denis.
21. McMahon, Laura, 'Rhythms of relationality: Denis and dance', in M. Vecchio (ed), *The Films of Claire Denis: Intimacy on the Border* (London: I.B.Tauris, 2014), pp. 175–87.
22. Ibid.
23. Warner, Marina, *From the Beast to the Blonde: On Fairy Tales and their Tellers* (London: Vintage, 1995).
24. Selby, Jenn, 'Wonder Woman Gal Gadot on Israel-Gaza: Israeli actress's pro-IDF stance causes controversy', *The Independent*, 1 August 2014, http://www.independent.co.uk/news/people/wonder-woman-gal-gadot-on-israelgaza-israeli-actresss-proidf-stance-causes-controversy-9643412.html.
25. Silverstein, 'It's official: Michelle MacLaren will direct *Wonder Woman*', *Women and Hollywood*, 25 November 2014, http://blogs.indiewire.com/womenandhollywood/its-official-michelle-maclaren-will-direct-wonder-woman-20141125.
26. Crunkista, 'Bringing back Wonder Woman', *Crunk Feminist Collective*, 23 May 2013, http://www.crunkfeministcollective.com/2013/05/23/bringing-back-wonder-woman/.
27. https://www.facebook.com/pages/Wonder-Woman-Day/152248224786224.
28. https://www.kickstarter.com/projects/rainfilm/rain-a-fanfilm-about-storm-finishing-funds.
29. Crenshaw, Kimberlé, 'Mapping the margins: Intersectionality, identity politics, and violence against women of color', *Stanford Law Review* 43/1241 (July 1991), pp. 1241–99.
30. Borg, Maja, 'Maja Borg's outsider manifesto', *Dazed Digital*, 2014, http://www.dazeddigital.com/artsandculture/article/19405/1/maja-borgs-downs-syndrome-outsider-manifesto-others-film.
31. Lewis, Hilary, 'Ava DuVernay supports Bree Newsome in tweet alluding to *Black Panther* rumors', *The Hollywood Reporter*, 27 June 2015, available online, http://www.hollywoodreporter.com/news/bree-newsome-removes-confederate-flag-805571
32. http://popularunrest.org.

8. Girl 'Hood: A Body, a Room and a World of One's Own

1. Facebook discussion on author's wall, 19 February 2015.
2. Gould, Judith, and Jacqui Ashton Smith, 'Women and girls on the autism spectrum', *The National Autistic Society*, May 2011, http://www.autism.org.uk/about-autism/introduction/gender-and-autism/preparing-girls-for-adulthood.aspx.
3. Rabin, Nathan, 'The Bataan Death March of Whimsy case file #1: *Elizabethtown*', *A.V. Club*, 25 January 2007, http://www.avclub.com/article/the-bataan-death-march-of-whimsy-case-file-1-emeli-15577.

4   Bonnaire, Sandrine, quoted in Marriott, Edward, 'Saving Sabine', The *Observer*, 15 June 2008, available online, http://www.theguardian.com/lifeandstyle/2008/jun/15/family-andrelationships.healthandwellbeing.
5   Young, Stella, 'We're not here for your inspiration', *The Drum*, 3 July 2012, http://www.abc.net.au/news/2012-07-03/young-inspiration-porn/4107006.
6   https://vimeo.com/album/2551082.
7   Andrews, Mallory, '(Be)coming-of-age film: Céline Sciamma's *Girlhood*', *Movie Mezzanine*, 30 January 2015, http://moviemezzanine.com/becoming-of-age-film-celine-sciammas-girlhood/.
8   Sciamma, Céline, quoted in Nastasi, Alison, '*Girlhood* director Céline Sciamma on reclaiming childhood, casting her girl gang, and how her film mirrors *Boyhood*', *Flavorwire*, 30 January 2015, http://flavorwire.com/502100/girlhood-director-celine-sciamma-on-reclaiming-childhood-casting-her-girl-gang-and-how-her-film-mirrors-boyhood.
9   Gordon, Bette, 'Karyn Kusama', *BOMB* 73 (2000), available online, http://bombmagazine.org/article/2337/karyn-kusama.
10 Keeling: *Witch's Flight*, p. 145.
11 Kusama, Karyn, quoted in Gordon: 'Karyn'.
12 Washuta, *My Body is a Book of Rules* (Pasadena: Red Hen Press, 2014).
13 King, Jamilah, '*Pariah* proves there's an audience – and a hunger – for real stories', *Colorlines*, 3 January 2012, http://colorlines.com/archives/2012/01/pariah_film.html.
14 Wood, Gaby, 'The unbelievable truth', The *Observer*, 15 July 2007, http://www.theguardian.com/film/2007/jul/15/features.review1.
15 http://www.freehistoryproject.org/sarah-jacobson-film-grant/.
16 Rees, Dee, 'Share your story', YouTube video, posted to *Pariah* [official site], 17 November 2011, http://www.focusfeatures.com/pariah/news?bid=dee_rees_wants_your_story.
17 Baker, Natalie, 'Is "girl-power" advertising doing any good?', *Bitch Media*, 28 July 2014, http://bitchmagazine.org/post/is-girl-power-advertising-doing-any-good.
18 Zak, Dan, '*Wadjda* director Haifaa Al Mansour gives female perspective of life in Saudi Arabia', *The Washington Post*, 19 September 2013, available online, http://www.washingtonpost.com/lifestyle/style/wadjda-director-haifaa-al-mansour-gives-female-perspective-of-life-in-saudi-arabia/2013/09/19/ff9b15f6-1bd5-11e3-8685-5021e0c41964_story.html.
19 French, Philip, '*Blame it on Fidel*' [review], The *Observer*, 21 October 2007, available online, http://www.theguardian.com/film/2007/oct/21/drama.worldcinema1.
20 Schrodt, Paul, '*Blame it on Fidel*' [review], *Slant*, 27 July 2007, http://www.slantmagazine.com/film/review/blame-it-on-fidel.
21 Kaplan, Louise J., *Female Perversions: The Temptations of Emma Bovary* (New York & London: Doubleday, 1991), pp. 369–72.
22 Gruber, Fiona, '*52 Tuesdays*: "I was up for gender being a fluid term"', The *Guardian*, 1 May 2014, http://www.theguardian.com/film/australia-culture-blog/2014/may/01/52-tuesdays-i-was-up-for-gender-being-a-fluid-term.
23 Levy, Ariel, '*Female Chauvinist Pigs*', http://www.ariellevy.net/books.php?article=2.
24 Akhavan, Desiree, in Mayer, 'Desiree Akhavan: It matters which stories we tell', *The F-Word: Contemporary UK Feminism*, 28 February 2015, http://www.thefword.org.uk/features/2015/02/desiree_akhavan_interview.

25 Armatage, Kay, 'Material effects: Fashions in feminist programming', in Columpar and Mayer (eds): *There She Goes*, pp. 102–103.
26 Haskell, Molly, '*À nos amours*: The ties that wound', *Criterion.com*, 5 June 2006, http://www.criterion.com/current/posts/426-a-nos-amours-the-ties-that-wound.
27 Szumowksa, Małgorzata, quoted in '*Body*: An interview with director Małgorzata Szumowska', *The Upcoming*, 10 February 2015, http://www.theupcoming.co.uk/2015/02/10/body-an-interview-with-director-malgorzata-szumowska/.
28 Hadžihalilović, Lucile, quoted in Graham, Daniel, 'Extras [interview]', *Innocence* (France: Artificial Eye, 2004), DVD.
29 Hadžihalilović: quoted in Sobchack, Vivian 'Waking life: Vivian Sobchack on the experience of *Innocence*', *Film Comment*, 1/6 (2005), p. 48.
30 Kohler, Sheila, *Cracks* (London: Bloomsbury, 2009).
31 Swan, Susan, *The Wives of Bath* (London: Granta, 1993).
32 Morley, Carol in Mayer, 'Things fall apart', *Sight & Sound* 25/5 (May 2015), pp. 28–31.

9. Haunted Houses: Reclaiming 'Women's Cinema'

1 Solnit, *The Faraway Nearby* (London: Granta, 2013), p. 108.
2 Bellamy, Dodie, 'Phone home', in B. Pera and M. Tupitsyn (eds), *Life As We Show It: Writing on Film* (San Francisco: City Lights Books, 2009), p. 105.
3 White: *Women's Cinema*, p. 44.
4 Ibid.
5 Mayer: 'Dirty pictures'; Mayer, '"*Gutta cavat lapidem*": The sonorous politics of Lucrecia Martel's swimming pools, in Brown and Hirsch (eds), *Swimming Pool*: pp. 191–202.
6 Martel, Lucrecia, quoted in Guest, Haden, 'Lucrecia Martel', *BOMB* 106 (Winter 2009), available online, http://bombmagazine.org/article/3220/lucrecia-martel.
7 Doane, Mary Ann, 'The "woman's film": Possession and address', in C. Gledhill (ed), *Home Is Where the Heart Is: Studies in Melodrama and the Woman's Film* (London: BFI, 1987), p. 288.
8 Perkins, Claire, 'Beyond Indiewood: The everyday ethics of Nicole Holofcener', *Camera Obscura: Feminism, Culture, and Media Studies* (2014) 29 1/85 (2014), p. 138.
9 Longinotto, Kim, 'Filming *Salma*' in Rajathi Salma and Kim Longinotto, *Salma: Filming a Poet in Her Village* (New York & London: OR Books, 2013), p. 31.
10 Ibid., p. 30.
11 Rajathi Salma, 'My ancestral home – 2', trans. Kalyan Raman, in Salma and Longinotto, *Salma*: p. 26.
12 Oler, Tammy, 'The mommy trap', *Slate*, 24 November 2014, http://www.slate.com/articles/arts/culturebox/2014/11/horror_movies_about_mothers_and_children_the_babadook_lyle_and_other_films.html.
13 Shriver, Lionel, *We Need to Talk about Kevin* (London: Serpent's Tail, 2003).
14 Bradshaw, Peter, '*The Babadook* [review]', The *Guardian*, 23 October 2014, available online, http://www.theguardian.com/film/2014/oct/23/the-babadook-review-chilling-freudian-thriller.

15. Freud, Sigmund, 'The "uncanny"', 1919, trans. Alix Strachey, in E. Jones (ed), *Collected Papers*, Vol. 4 (London: Hogarth Press, 1934), pp. 398–99.
16. Taubin, Amy, 'Dog days', *Film Comment* (July/August 2014), available online, http://www.filmcomment.com/article/cannes-2014-amy-taubin.
17. Petersen, Anne Helen, 'A tribute to *Top of the Lake*'s Robin Griffin, made of china and steel', *The Hairpin*, 24 December 2013, http://thehairpin.com/2013/12/a-tribute-to-top-of-the-lakes-robin-griffin-made-of-china-and-steel.
18. Sturges, Fiona, 'Another day, another TV heroine brutalised', The *Independent*, 7 July 2013, available online, http://www.independent.co.uk/voices/comment/another-day-another-tv-heroine-brutalised-8692536.html.
19. Martel, quoted in Hernandez, Eugene, '*Headless Woman* director Lucrecia Martel: My love of storytelling comes from oral tradition', *Indiewire*, 20 August 2009, http://www.indiewire.com/article/lucrecia_martel_interview.
20. Warner: *From the Beast*, p. 206.
21. Federici, Silvia, *Wages against Housework* (Bristol: Power of Women Collective and Falling Wall Press, 1975), p. 2.
22. Ellerson, Beti, 'International Migrants Day, 18 December: A tribute to Rahel Zegeye, Ethiopian migrant worker/filmmaker', *African Women in Cinema*, 18 December 2014, http://africanwomenincinema.blogspot.co.uk/2014/12/international-migrants-day-18-december.html.
23. White: *Women's Cinema*, p. 195.
24. Knipp, Chris, 'Festival favorites: Two from the San Francisco International Film Festival', *CineScene* (2006), http://www.cinescene.com/knipp/sfiff.htm.
25. Silverman, *The Acoustic Mirror: The Female Voice in Psychoanalysis in Cinema* (Bloomington and Indianapolis: University of Indiana Press, 1988), p. 102.
26. Newton, Creede, '*Villa Touma*: The world's first stateless film', *Middle East Eye*, 16 October 2014, http://www.middleeasteye.net/in-depth/reviews/villa-touma-worlds-first-stateless-film-489386955.
27. http://gretasrecords.tumblr.com.
28. Kopple, Barbara, quoted in Brooks, Brian, 'Barbara Kopple, co-director of *Shut Up & Sing*', *Indiewire*, 24 October 2006, http://www.indiewire.com/article/indiewire_interview_barbara_kopple_co-director_of_shut_up_sing.
29. Polley, Sarah, '*Stories We Tell*: A post by Sarah Polley', *NFB Blog*, 29 August 2012, http://blog.nfb.ca/blog/2012/08/29/stories-we-tell-a-post-by-sarah-polley/.
30. Lee, Anita, quoted in *Stories We Tell* press pack, EPK available online, http://onf-nfb.gc.ca/medias/mediakit/STORIES%20WE%20TELL%20press%20kit.pdf.
31. Citron, Michelle, *Home Movies and Other Necessary Fictions* (Minneapolis: University of Minnesota Press, 1998).
32. http://queerfeast.com/mixedgreens/.
33. http://queerfeast.com/leftovers/.
34. Cvetkovich, Ann, *An Archive of Feelings: Trauma, Sexuality, and Lesbian Public Cultures* (Durham NC: Duke University Press, 2003).
35. Butler, J.: 'Bodies in Alliance'.

10. Come Together: Love, Justice and a New Sexual Politics

1. http://www.adaptssi.org/founderchairperson.html.
2. Bose, Shonali, quoted in Felperin, Leslie, 'Margarita, with a Straw', The *Guardian*, 23 October 2014, available online, http://www.theguardian.com/film/2014/oct/23/margarita-with-a-straw-shonali-bose-cerebral-palsy-india.
3. Lorde, Audre, 'Poetry makes something happen', in R. P. Byrd, J. B. Cole and B. Guy-Sheftall (eds), *I Am Your Sister: Collected and Unpublished Writings of Audre Lorde* (Oxford & New York: Oxford University Press, 2009), p. 184.
4. Sandoval, Chela, 'New sciences: Cyborg feminism and the methodology of the oppressed', in J. Wolmark (ed), *Cybersexualities: A Reader on Feminist Theory, Cyborgs and Cyberspace* (Edinburgh: Edinburgh University Press, 1999), p. 250.
5. Irigaray, Luce, *The Way of Love*, trans. Heidi Bostic and Stephen Pluháček (London & New York: Continuum, 2002), p. 60.
6. Scott, Rachael, 'Having a gay old time', The *Guardian*, 2 April 2009, available online, http://www.theguardian.com/film/2009/apr/02/shamim-sarif.
7. Irigaray: *Way*, p.60.
8. Foxx, Luna B., 'Who you callin' itty bitty?', *GO Magazine*, 10 July 2008, http://www.gomag.com/article/who_you_callin_itty_bitty/.
9. Albelo, Anna Margarita, quoted in Taylor, Trey, 'Who's Afraid of Vagina Wolf?', *Dazed*, 25 October 2014, http://www.dazeddigital.com/artsandculture/article/20700/1/who-s-afraid-of-vagina-wolf.
10. https://www.indiegogo.com/projects/who-s-afraid-of-vagina-wolf.
11. Dougherty, Ariel, 'A crowdfunding primer: Feminist media producers engage a community of backers', *On the Issues: A Magazine of Feminist, Progressive Thinking*, http://www.ontheissuesmagazine.com/hot_topics/article/59.
12. https://www.kickstarter.com/projects/1558491775/the-punk-singer-the-documentary-about-kathleen-han.
13. https://www.kickstarter.com/projects/tinnevl/anti-harassment-documentary-the-peoples-girls.
14. https://www.indiegogo.com/projects/a-better-man.
15. Negrón-Muntaner, Frances, quoted in Meier: 'Cine de Mujer', p. 78.
16. Ibid.
17. Rich, 'Before the beginning: Lineages and preconceptions': *New Queer Cinema*, pp. 3–15.
18. Schulman, Sarah, *The Gentrification of the Mind: Witness to a Lost Imagination* (University of California Press, 2012).
19. Macaulay, Scott, '25 new faces of independent film 2012: Wu Tsang', *Filmmaker Magazine*, http://filmmakermagazine.com/people/wu-tsang/#.VJLR8FYWGy0.
20. Engberg, Mia, 'Manifesto', http://www.dirtydiaries.org/#!manifesto/cyuu.
21. Ryberg, Ingrid, '"Every time we fuck, we win": The public sphere of queer, feminist, and lesbian porn as a (safe) space for sexual empowerment', in T. Taormino, C. Penley, C. Parrenas Shimizu and M. Miller-Young (eds), *The Feminist Porn Book: The Politics of Producing Pleasure* (New York: The Feminist Press, 2013), p. 144.

22 Sontag, Susan, *In America* (New York: Farrar, Strauss, Giroux, 1999).
23 Trinh T. Minh-Ha, 'A scenography of love', *Cinema Interval* (New York & London: Routledge, 1999), pp. 5–6.
24 Ibid.
25 Guerrero, Aurora, quoted in Fuchs, Ellise, 'Most of us don't need to put labels on it: An interview with Aurora Guerrero', *PopMatters*, 5 December 2012, http://www.popmatters.com/feature/164954-interview-with-aurora-guerrero/.
26 Smaill, 'The male sojourner, the female director, and popular European cinema: The worlds of Susanne Bier', *Camera Obscura* 85 29/1 (2014), pp. 4–31.
27 Lucca, Violet, '*Middle of Nowhere* [review]', *Film Comment*, 10 October 2014, http://www.filmcomment.com/entry/middle-of-nowhere-2012-ava-duvernay.
28 Michael, Frann, 'Eating the (m)other: Cheryl Dunye's feature films and black matrilineage', *Rhizomes* 14 (Summer 2007), http://www.rhizomes.net/issue14/michel/michel.html.
29 Stephenson, Janey, '"A peaceful, constructive riot": how prison theatre is changing policy in Lebanon, *New Internationalist*, 8 May 2014, http://newint.org/features/web-exclusive/2014/05/08/prison-theatre-lebanon/#sthash.P1nxopkp.dpuf.
30 Mayer, 'Sheffield Doc/Fest 2014: a secret thread of feminist elders revealed', *The F-Word: Contemporary UK Feminism*, 22 July 2014, http://www.thefword.org.uk/reviews/2014/07/sheffield_docfest_2014_review.
31 Barthes, Roland, *Camera Lucida: Reflections on Photography*, trans. Richard Howard (New York: Hill & Wang, 1981); Mulvey: *Death 24x*.

Conclusion: An Open Letter

1 Varda, Agnès, quoted in Ellis-Petersen, Hannah, 'Agnès Varda hits out at European cinema's failure to recognise women', *The Guardian*, 14 December 2014, available online, http://www.theguardian.com/film/2014/dec/14/agnes-varda-european-film-awards.
2 La Barbe and signatories, 'Men of the Cannes film festival, keep defending those masculine values', *The Guardian*, 15 May 2012, available online, http://www.theguardian.com/commentisfree/2012/may/15/cannes-film-festival-men-open-letter.
3 Alexander, Lexi, 'An Oscar-nominated director gets real about how women are treated in Hollywood', *Women and Hollywood*, 14 January 2014, http://blogs.indiewire.com/womenandhollywood/an-oscar-nominated-director-gets-real.
4 Coixet, Isabel, quoted in Eidelstein, Eric, 'Berlin: *Nobody Wants the Night* director Isabel Coixet won't ever work with your studio', *Indiewire*, 6 February 2015, http://www.indiewire.com/article/berlin-nobody-wants-the-night-director-isabel-coixet-wont-ever-work-with-your-studio-20150206.
5 http://www.clubdesfemmes.com; www.raisingfilms.com.
6 Dickson Leach, Hope, 'iFeatures and beyond: Fast, cheap & good – a film can be all three', *Women in Film and Television*, 17 November 2014, http://www.wftv.org.uk/resources/reports-and-statistics/ifeatures-and-beyond-fast-cheap-good-film-can-be-all-three.

7 Owczarek, Marta, 'How a feminist debate was derailed by asking all men to leave', The *Guardian* Comment is Free, 3 December 2012, http://www.theguardian.com/commentisfree/2012/dec/03/asking-men-to-leave-feminist-film.

8 Krishnan, Kavita, 'Nirbhaya film: Solidarity is what we want, not a civilising mission', *Daily O*, 3 March 2015, http://www.dailyo.in/politics/kavita-krishnan-nirbhaya-december-16-indias-daughter-leslee-udwin-mukesh-singh-bbc/story/1/2347.html; Singh, Sunny, 'It is India's fearless women revolutionaries who are being silenced, not the BBC', *Media Diversified*, 8 March 2015, http://mediadiversified.org/2015/03/08/it-is-indias-fearless-women-revolutionaries-who-are-being-silenced-not-the-bbc/; Islam, Asiya, 'Indian women are not the world's daughters', *The F-Word: Contemporary UK Feminism*, 12 March 2015, http://www.thefword.org.uk/reviews/2015/03/leslee_udwin_delhi_doc.

9 Tran, Mark, 'Phenomenal success for new film that criticises China's environmental policy', The *Guardian*, 2 March 2015, available online, http://www.theguardian.com/world/2015/mar/02/china-environmental-policy-documentary-under-the-dome-chai-jing-video.

10 https://www.kickstarter.com/projects/1571695840/the-women-and-film-project.

11 Jacob, Clarissa, '*Women & Film*: The first feminist film magazine', *Feminist Media Histories* 1/1 (Winter 2015), p. 162.

12 http://www.moma.org/visit/calendar/films/1551.

13 http://en.wikipedia.org/wiki/Wikipedia:SHE_MUST_BE_WIKI:_Feminist_Film_Wiki-a-thon.

14 Beck, Laura, 'Wikipedia's editors are 91 percent male because citations are stored in the ball sack', *Jezebel*, 25 January 2013, http://jezebel.com/5978883/wikipedias-editors-are-87-percent-male-because-citations-are-stored-in-the-penis.

15 http://www.sp-ark.co.uk.

16 Taylor: *People's Platform*, p. 4.

17 Ibid., p. 232.

18 Ibid., pp. 39–41.

19 http://womenartrevolution.com/index.php.

20 http://www.transxistanbul.com/index_en.php.

21 http://www.wmm.com/about/general_info.shtml.

22 Geller, Theresa L., '"Each film was built as a chamber and became a corridor": Maya Deren's film aesthetics as feminist praxis', in Columpar and Mayer (eds): *There She Goes*, p. 80.

23 Butler, A., *Maya Deren: The Politics of Self-Representation*, MA thesis, unpublished, (London: 1984), p. 8.

24 Hammer, Barbara, *Hammer! Making Movies out of Sex and Life* (New York: Feminist Press, 2010), p. 62.

25 Neiman, Hodson and Clark (eds): *The Legend*.

26 Rich: *Chick Flicks*, p. 384.

27 https://www.indiegogo.com/projects/alice-walker-beauty-in-truth.

28 Hammer: *Hammer!*, p. 232.

29 See Further Reading 3.
30 Columpar: 'The dancing body', 109–10.
31 Cavarero, Adriana, *Relating Narratives: Storytelling and Selfhood*, 1997, trans. Paul A. Kottman (London: Routledge, 2000), p. 2.
32 Cavarero: *Relating*, p. 3.
33 Sayad, Cecilia, *Performing Authorship: Self-Inscription and Corporeality in the Cinema* (London: I.B.Tauris, 2013), p. xxi.
34 Hidalgo, Alexandra, 'A more ethical lens: An argument for feminist film and video production in the classroom', HASTAC, 28 May 2015, conference presentation
35 Tait, Margaret, *Poems, Stories and Writings*, S. Neely (ed) (Manchester: Fyfield/Carcanet Press, 2012).
36 https://www.kickstarter.com/projects/870959691/portrait-of-jason-film-restoration; http://www.bfi.org.uk/sight-sound-magazine/greatest-docs; Clark, A., 'Portrait of Shirley [DVD review]', *Sight & Sound* 25/4 (April 2015), pp. 96–97.
37 Hardie, Kate, email to author, 9 January 2015.
38 http://directedbywomen.com/en/.
39 Stewart, Clare, quoted in Mayer, 'Knocking on the celluloid ceiling: movies directed by women in the London Film Festival 2014', *Sight & Sound* [web exclusive], 10 October 2014, http://www.bfi.org.uk/news-opinion/sight-sound-magazine/comment/festivals/london-film-festival-2014-preview-films-women.
40 Reed, Amanda, 'Walmart and sex discrimination', *National Organization of Women*, 6 June 2013, http://now.org/blog/walmart-and-sex-discrimination/.
41 http://shitpeoplesaytodiversefilmmakers.tumblr.com
42 Evans, 'The activist complex female protagonist goes for it, in Ausutralia', *Wellywood Woman*, 11 June 2015, http://wellywoodwoman.blogspot.co.uk/2015/06/the-activist-complex-female-protagonist_11.html?spref=tw; Kang, Inkoo, 'Swedish Film Institute achieves 50/50 funding distribution for male and female directors', *Women and Hollywood*, 29 May 2015, http://blogs.indiewire.com/womenandhollywood/swedish-film-institute-achieves-50-50-funding-distribution-for-male-and-female-directors-20150529. http://thedirectorlist.com; http://www.thebitchpack.com; http://www.proquote-regie.de.
43 http://www.filmfatalesnyc.com; Barnard, Linda, 'Oscar-winner Melissa Leo funds Canadian female screenwriting project', *The Toronto Star*, 15 January 2014, available online, http://www.thestar.com/entertainment/movies/2014/01/15/oscarwinner_melissa_leo_funds_canadian_female_screenwriting_project.html.
44 Tong, Allan, 'TIFF: *i am a good person/i am a bad person*', *Filmmaker*, 18 September 2011, http://filmmakermagazine.com/30516-tiff-i-am-a-good-personi-am-a-bad-person/#.VJRYxKC0L8.
45 Robertson, Selina, email to author, 15 December 2014.
46 Bolton: *Film and Female*, p. 203.
47 https://www.youtube.com/user/MakeItBetterProject.
48 Smith, A., *Artful* (London: Penguin, 2013), p. 157.
49 Mayer, Ostrowska, and signatories, 'An invitation is not enough', *Sight & Sound* 25/1 (Jan 2015), p. 111, available online, http://www.bfi.org.uk/news-opinion/sight-sound-magazine/comment/invitation-not-enough

50 Prince-Bythewood, Gina, quoted in Davenport, Leigh, 'Film director Gina Prince-Bythewood pens open letter to encourage support for her low grossing *Beyond The Lights*', *The Urban Daily*, 5 December 2014, http://theurbandaily.com/2014/12/05/gina-prince-bythewood-open-letter-to-encourage-support-for-her-beyond-the-lights/.

51 Hans, Simran, 'British cinemas need to do better for black audiences', *BuzzFeed*, 29 June 2015, http://www.buzzfeed.com/simranhans/black-lives-on-the-big-screen

Further Reading

Sections 1, 2, and 3 are the most exhaustive English-language bibliographies that I could compile; sections 4, 5, and 6 refer exclusively to titles cited in the book.

For details of all films referred to in the book, as well as a list of my interviews and reviews relevant to the films, see fuckyeahfeministcinema.tumblr.com/filmography

1. Books on Feminist Filmmakers and their Films, Listed by Filmmaker

Chantal Akerman

Foster, Gwendolyn Audrey, *Identity and Memory: The Films of Chantal Akerman* (Trowbridge, Wilts.: Flicks Books, 1999).

Margulies, Yvonne, *Nothing Happens: Chantal Akerman's Hyperrealist Everyday* (Durham, NC: Duke University Press, 1996).

Schmid, Marion, *Chantal Akerman* (Manchester: Manchester University Press, 2010).

Gillian Armstrong

Collins, Felicity, *The Films of Gillian Armstrong* (St. Kilda, Vic.: ATOM, 1999).

Andrea Arnold

Journal of British Cinema and Television 12/4 (forthcoming, Oct 2015).

Dorothy Arzner

Johnston, Claire, *The Work of Dorothy Arzner: Towards a Feminist Cinema* (London: British Film Institute, 1975).

Mayne, Judith, *Directed by Dorothy Arzner* (Bloomington: Indiana University Press, 1994).

Kathryn Bigelow

Jermyn, Deborah and Sean Redmond (eds), *The Cinema of Kathryn Bigelow: Hollywood Transgressor* (London: Wallflower, 2003).

Further Reading

Keough, Peter (ed), *Kathryn Bigelow: Interviews* (Jackson, MS: University Press of Mississippi, 2013).

Dara Birnbaum

Demos, T. J., *Dara Birnbaum: Technology/Transformation: Wonder Woman* (London: Afterall, 2010).

Lizzie Borden

Women & Performance: A Journal of Feminist Theory Special Issue: *Born in Flames* 23/1 (2013).

Catherine Breillat

Keesey, Douglas, *Catherine Breillat* (Manchester: Manchester University Press, 2009).

Mabel Cheung Yuen-Ting

Ford, Stacilee, *Mabel Cheung Yuen-Ting's* An Autumn Tale (Aberdeen and Hong Kong: Hong Kong University Press, 2008).

Jane Campion

Cheshire, Ellen, *The Pocket Essential Jane Campion* (Harpenden, Herts.: Pocket Essentials, 2000).
Coombs, Felicity, and Suzanne Gemmell, *Piano Lessons: Approaches to* The Piano (Sydney: John Libbey, 1999).
Gillett, Sue, *Views from Beyond the Mirror: The Films of Jane Campion* (St. Kilda, Vic.: ATOM, 2004).
Margolis, Harriet (ed), *Jane Campion's The* Piano (Cambridge: Cambridge University Press, 2000).
McHugh, Kathleen, *Jane Campion* (Urbana & Chicago: University of Illinois Press, 2007).
Polan, Dana, *Jane Campion* (London: BFI Publishing, 2001).
Radner, Hilary, Alistair Fox and Irene Bessiere (eds), *Jane Campion: Cinema, Nation, Identity* (Detroit: Wayne State University Press, 2009).
Tincknell, Estella, *Viewing Jane Campion: Angels, Demons and Unsettling Voices* (London: Palgrave Macmillan, 2013).
Verhoeven, Deb, *Jane Campion* (London & New York: Routledge, 2009).
Wright Wexman, Virginia (ed), *Jane Campion: Interviews* (Jackson, MS: University Press of Mississippi, 1999).

Sofia Coppola

Backman Rogers, Anna, *Sofia Coppola* (Oxford: Berghahn Books, forthcoming).

Claire Denis

Beugnet, Martine, *Claire Denis* (Manchester: Manchester University Press, 2004).
Mayne, Judith, *Claire Denis* (Urbana & Chicago: University of Illinois Press, 2005).
Vecchio, Marjorie (ed), *The Films of Claire Denis: Intimacy on the Border* (London & New York: I.B. Tauris, 2014).

Maya Deren

Jackson, Renata, *The Modernistic Poetics and Experimental Film Practice of Maya Deren (1917–1961)* (Lewiston & Lampeter: Edwin Mellen, 2002).
Keller, Sarah, *Maya Deren: Incomplete Control* (New York: Columbia University Press, forthcoming).
Neiman, Catrina, VèVè A. Clark, and Millicent Hodson (eds), *The Legend of Maya Deren*, Vol. 1 pts. 1 & 2 (New York: Anthology Film Archive/Film Culture, 1998).
Nichols, Bill (ed), *Maya Deren and the American Avant-garde* (Berkeley & London: University of California Press, 2001).
Rhodes, John David, *Meshes of the Afternoon* (Basingstoke: Palgrave Macmillan, 2011).
Sullivan, Moira, *An Anagram of the Ideas of Filmmaker Maya Deren: Creative Work in Motion Pictures* (Stockholm, Sweden: Stockholm University, 1997).

Marguerite Duras

Günther, Renate, *Marguerite Duras* (Manchester: Manchester University Press, 2002).
Williams, James S. (ed), *Revisioning Duras: Film, Race, Sex* (Liverpool: Liverpool University Press, 2000).

Ann Hui

Yue, Audrey, *Ann Hui's Song of the Exile* (Aberdeen and Hong Kong: Hong Kong University Press, 2010).

Joan Jonas

Morgan, Susan, *Joan Jonas: I Want to Live in the Country (And Other Romances)* (London: Afterall, 2006).

Further Reading

Diane Kurys

Tarr, Carrie, *Diane Kurys* (Manchester: Manchester University Press, 1999).

Jennie Livingston

Hilderbrand, Lucas, Paris is Burning: *A Queer Film Classic* (Vancouver: Arsenal Pulp, 2013).

Lucrecia Martel

Martin, Deborah, *Lucrecia Martel* (forthcoming).

Deepa Mehta

Ghosh, Shohini, Fire: *A Queer Film Classic* (Vancouver: Arsenal Pulp, 2010).
Jain, Jasbir (ed), *Films, Literature and Culture: Deepa Mehta's Elements Trilogy* (Jaipur, New Delhi, Bangalore: Rawat, 2007).

Márta Mészáros

Portugues, Catherine, *Screen Memories: The Hungarian Cinema of Márta Mészáros* (Bloomington: Indiana University Press, 1993).

Kira Muratova

Taubman, Jane, *Kira Muratova* (London & New York: I.B. Tauris, 2005).

Mira Nair

Muir, John Kenneth, *Mercy in Her Eyes: The Films of Mira Nair* (New York: Applause, 2006).

Alanis Obomsawin

Lewis, Randolph, *Alanis Obomsawin: The Vision of a Native Filmmaker* (Lincoln: University of Nebraska Press, 2006).

Further Reading

Ulrike Ottinger

Rickels, Laurence, *Ulrike Ottinger: The Autobiography of Art Cinema* (Minneapolis: University of Minnesota Press, 2008).

Sally Potter

Fowler, Catherine, *Sally Potter* (Urbana & Chicago: University of Illinois Press, 2008).
Mayer, Sophie, *The Cinema of Sally Potter: A Politics of Love* (London: Wallflower, 2009).

Yvonne Rainer

Green, Shelley, *Radical Juxtaposition: The Films of Yvonne Rainer* (Metuchen, NJ & London: Scarecrow Press, 1994).
Wood, Catherine, *Yvonne Rainer: The Mind is a Muscle* (London: Afterall, 2007).

Lynne Ramsay

Kuhn, Annette, *Ratcatcher* (Basingstoke: Palgrave Macmillan, 2008).

Patricia Rozema

Mendenhall, Julia, I've Heard the Mermaids Singing: *A Queer Film Classic* (Vancouver: Arsenal Pulp, forthcoming).

Nell Shipman

Armatage, Kay, *The Girl from God's Country: Nell Shipman and the Silent Cinema* (Toronto: University of Toronto Press, 2003).

Margaret Tait

Todd, Peter and Benjamin Cook (eds), *Subjects and Sequences: A Margaret Tait Reader* (London: LUX, 2004).

Julie Taymor

Blumenthal, Eileen, *Julie Taymor: Playing with Fire: Theatre, Opera, Film* (New York: Harry N. Abrams, 1995).

Further Reading

Liv Ullmann

Long, Robert Emmet (ed), *Liv Ullmann: Interviews* (Jackson MS: University Press of Mississippi, 2006).

Agnès Varda

Bénézet, Delphine, *The Cinema of Agnès Varda: Resistance and Eclecticism* (New York: Wallflower Press, 2014).
Kline, T. Jefferson (ed), *Agnès Varda: Interviews* (Jackson, MS: University Press of Mississippi, 2014).
Orpen, Valerie, *Cléo de 5 à 7* (London & New York: I.B. Tauris, 2007).
Smith, Alison, *Agnès Varda* (Manchester: Manchester University Press, 1998).
Ungar, Steven, *Cléo de 5 à 7* (Basingstoke: Palgrave Macmillan, 2008).

2. Books on National and Continental Feminist Cinemas

Ellerson, Beti, *Sisters of the Screen: Women of Africa on Film, Video and Television* (Trenton, NJ: Africa World Press, 2000).
Harper, Sue, *Women in British Cinema: Mad, Bad and Dangerous to Know* (London & New York: Continuum, 2000).
Knight, Julia, *Women and the New German Cinema* (London: Verso, 1992).
Laviosa, Flavia (ed), *Visions of Struggle in Women's Filmmaking in the Mediterranean* (New York: Palgrave Macmillan, 2010).
McFadden, Cybelle H., *Gendered Frames, Embodied Cameras: Varda, Akerman, Cabrera, Calle, and Maïwenn* (Teaneck, NJ: Fairleigh Dickinson: 2014).
Nair, Parvati, and Julián Daniel Gutiérrez-Albila (eds), *Hispanic and Lusophone Women Filmmakers: Theory, Practice and Difference* (Manchester: Manchester University Press, 2013).
Rashkin, Elisa J., *Women Filmmakers in Mexico: The Country of Which We Dream* (Austin: University of Texas Press, 2001).
Schuhmann, Antje, and Jyoti Mistry (eds), *Gaze Regimes: Film and Feminism in Africa* (Johannesburg: University of Witwatersrand Press, 2015).
Tomsic, Mary, ' "We *will* invent ourselves, the age of the new image is at hand": Creating, learning and talking with Australian feminist filmmaking', *Australian Feminist Studies* 22/53 (Summer 2007), pp. 287–306.
Wang, Lingzhen (ed), *Chinese Women's Cinema: Transnational Contexts* (New York: Columbia University Press, 2011).

3. Books by Feminist Filmmakers

Akerman, Chantal, Catherine David and Michael Tarantino, *Bordering on Fiction: Chantal Akerman's* D'Est (Minneapolis: Walker Art Center, 1995).

Child, Abigail, *This is Called Moving: A Critical Poetics of Film* (Tuscaloosa: University of Alabama Press, 2005).

Citron, Michelle, *Home Movies and Other Necessary Fictions* (Minneapolis: University of Minnesota Press, 1998).

Dash, Julie, Toni Cade Bambara and bell hooks, Daughters of the Dust: *Making of an African American Women's Film* (New York: The New Press, 1992).

Deren, Maya, *Essential Deren: Collected Writings on Film* (Kingston, NY: Documentext, 2005).

Despentes, Virginie, *King Kong Theory*, trans. Polly McLean (London: Serpent's Tail, 2009).

Dunye, Cheryl and Zoe Leonard, *The Fae Richards Photo Archive* (San Francisco: ArtSpace Books, 1996).

Duras, Marguerite, *Green Eyes: Reflections on Film by the Author of* The Lover, trans. Carol Barko (New York: Columbia University Press, 1990).

Hammer, Barbara, *Hammer! Making Movies out of Sex and Life* (New York: Feminist Press, 2010).

Longinotto, Kim and Salma Rajathi, *Salma: Filming a Poet in Her Village* (New York: OR Books, 2014).

Potter, Sally, *Naked Cinema: Working with Actors* (London: Faber & Faber, 2014).

Rainer, Yvonne, *Feelings are Facts: A Life* (Cambridge MA: MIT Press, 2006).

The Films of Yvonne Rainer (Bloomington: Indiana University Press, 1989).

Rosler, Martha, *Culture Class* (Berlin: Sternberg Press, 2013).

Steyerl, Hito, *The Wretched of the Screen* (Berlin: Sternberg Press, 2012).

Tait, Margaret, *Poems, Stories and Writings*, Sarah Neely (ed) (Manchester: Fyfield/Carcanet Press, 2012).

Taylor, Astra, *The People's Platform: Taking Back Power and Culture in the Digital Age* (London: Fourth Estate, 2014).

Trinh T. Minh-Ha, *Cinema Interval* (London & New York: Routledge, 1999).

The Digital Film Event (London & New York: Routledge, 2005).

Framer Framed (London & New York: 1992).

When the Moon Waxes Red: Representation, Gender and Cultural Politics (Abingdon & New York: 1991).

Woman Native Other (Bloomington: Indiana University Press, 1989).

Varda, Agnès, *Varda par Agnès* (Paris: Cahiers du Cinéma, 1994).

4. Feminist Film Theory and History

Bolton, Lucy, *Film and Female Consciousness: Irigaray, Cinema and Thinking Women* (Basingstoke: Palgrave Macmillan, 2011).

Butler, Alison, *Women's Cinema: The Contested Screen* (London: Wallflower, 2002).

Chaudhuri, Shohini, *Feminist Film Theorists: Laura Mulvey, Kaja Silverman, Teresa de Lauretis, Barbara Creed* (Abingdon & New York: Routledge, 2006).

Clover, Carol, *Men, Women and Chainsaws: Gender in the Modern Horror Film* (Princeton: Princeton University Press, 1993).

Further Reading

Columpar, Corinn, and Sophie Mayer (eds), *There She Goes: Feminist Filmmaking and Beyond* (Detroit: Wayne State University Press, 2010).

Cvetkovich, Ann, *An Archive of Feelings: Trauma, Sexuality, and Lesbian Public Cultures* (Durham, NC: Duke University Press, 2003).

Davis, Therese, Belinda Smaill and Patricia White, *Camera Obscura: Feminism, Culture and Media Studies* 85 29/1 (2014) Special Issue: The Place of the Contemporary Female Director.

Dolan, Jill, *The Feminist Spectator in Action: Feminist Criticism for the Stage and Screen* (New York: Palgrave Macmillan, 2013).

Gledhill, Christine (ed), *Home Is Where the Heart Is: Studies in Melodrama and the Woman's Film* (London: BFI, 1987).

Handyside, Fiona and Kate Taylor (eds), *International Cinema and the Girl: Local Issues, Transnational Contexts* (London: Palgrave Macmillan, 2015).

hooks, bell, *Black Looks: Race and Representation* (Boston: South End Press, 1992).

Reel to Real: Race, Sex and Class at the Movies (London and New York: Routledge, 2008).

Iglesias, Norma, and Rosa Linda Fregoso (eds), *Miradas de Mujer: Encuentro de cineastas y videoastas mexicanas y chicanas* (Tijuana: El Colegio de la Frontera Norte & Davis CA: University of California, 1998).

Keeling, Kara, *The Witch's Flight: The Cinematic, the Black Femme, and the Image of Common Sense* (Durham, NC: Duke University Press, 2007).

Kelly, Gabrielle, and Cheryl Robson (eds), *The Celluloid Ceiling* (Twickenham: Supernova, 2014).

Lant, Antonia, and Ingrid Periz (eds) *Red Velvet Seat: Women's Writing on the First Fifty Years of Cinema* (London: Verso, 2006).

Levitin, Jacqueline, Judith Plessis and Valerie Raoul (eds), *Women Filmmakers: Refocusing* (Vancouver: University of British Columbia Press, 2003).

Mayer, Sophie, and Elena Oroz (eds), *Lo personal es politico: feminismo y documental*, trans. Mar Diestro-D'opido (Pamplona: INAAC, 2011).

Ramanathan, Geetha, *Feminist Auteurs: Reading Women's Films* (London, Wallflower, 2006).

Rich, B. Ruby, *Chick Flicks: Theories and Memories of the Feminist Film Movement* (Durham, NC: Duke University Press, 1998).

New Queer Cinema: The Director's Cut (Durham, NC: Duke University Press, 2013).

Silverman, Kaja, *The Acoustic Mirror: The Female Voice in Psychoanalysis in Cinema* (Bloomington and Indianapolis: University of Indiana Press, 1988).

Taormino, Tristan, Constance Penley, Celine Parreñas Shimizu and Mireille Miller-Young (eds), *The Feminist Porn Book: The Politics of Producing Pleasure* (New York: The Feminist Press, 2013).

Tay, Sharon Lin, *Women on the Edge: Twelve Political Film Practices* (Basingstoke & New York: Palgrave Macmillan, 2009).

Thornham, Sue, *What If I Had Been the Hero? Investigating Women's Cinema* (Basingstoke & New York: Palgrave Macmillan, 2012).

Further Reading

Waldman, Diane, and Janet Walker (eds), *Feminism and Documentary* (Minneapolis: University of Minnesota Press, 1999).

White, Patricia, *Women's Cinema, World Cinema: Projecting Contemporary Feminisms* (Durham, NC and London: Duke University Press, 2015).

Journals

Camera Obscura: Feminism Culture and Media Studies: cameraobscura.dukejournals.org/.
Feminist Media Histories: ucpressjournals.com/journal.php?j=fmh.
Jump Cut: ejumpcut.org/.

5. Feminist Theory and History

Byrd, Rudolph P., Johnnetta Betsch Cole and Beverly Guy-Sheftall (eds), *I Am Your Sister: Collected and Unpublished Writings of Audre Lorde* (Oxford & New York: Oxford University Press, 2009).

Cavarero, Adriana, *Relating Narratives: Storytelling and Selfhood*, 1997, trans. Paul A. Kottman (London: Routledge, 2000).

Cochrane, Kira, *All the Rebel Women: The Rise of Fourth Wave Feminism* (London: Guardianshorts, 2013).

de Beauvoir, Simone, *The Second Sex*, 1949, trans. H.M. Parshley (New York: Avon, 1972).

Faludi, Susan, *Backlash: The Undeclared War against Women* (London: Vintage, 1991).
The Terror Dream: What 9/11 Revealed about America (London: Atlantic, 2008).

Federici, Silvia, *Wages against Housework* (Bristol: Power of Women Collective and Falling Wall Press, 1975).

Friedan, Betty, *The Feminine Mystique* (New York: W.W. Norton & Co., 1963).

Gay, Roxane, *Bad Feminist* (London: Corsair, 2014).

Halberstam, Jack, *Female Masculinity* (Durham, NC: Duke University Press, 1988).

Harris, Anita, *Future Girl: Young Women in the Twenty-First Century* (London: Routledge, 2004).

Irigaray, Luce, *The Way of Love*, trans. Heidi Bostic and Stephen Pluháček (London & New York: Continuum, 2002).

Kaplan, Louise J., *Female Perversions: The Temptations of Emma Bovary* (New York & London: Doubleday, 1991).

Lahiri-Dutt, Kuntala (ed), *Fluid Bonds: Views on Gender and Water* (Kolkata: Stree,2006).

Levy, Ariel, *Female Chauvinist Pigs: Women and the Rise of Raunch Culture* (London: Pocket Books, 2006).

Mies, Maria and Vandana Shiva, *Ecofeminism* (London: Zed Books, 1993).

Riley, Robin L., Minnie Bruce Pratt and Chandra Talpade Mohanty (eds), *Feminism and War: Confronting US Imperialism* (London: Zed, 2008).

Rose, Jacqueline, *Women in Dark Times* (London: Bloomsbury, 2014)

Ross, Karen (ed), *The Blackwell Handbook of Gender, Sexualities and the Media* (Malden, Ox.: Blackwell, & New York: Wiley, 2011).

Scott, Joan, *The Fantasy of Feminist History* (Durham, NC: Duke University Press, 2011).
Warner, Marina, *From the Beast to the Blonde: On Fairy Tales and Their Tellers* (London: Vintage, 1995).
Wolmark, Jenny (ed), *Cybersexualities: A Reader on Feminist Theory, Cyborgs and Cyberspace* (Edinburgh: Edinburgh University Press, 1999).
Yee, Jessica (ed), *Feminism FOR REAL: Deconstructing the Academic Industrial Complex of Feminism* (Ottawa: Canadian Centre for Policy Alternatives, 2011).

Print Journals

Bitch: bitchmagazine.org
Colorlines: colorlines.com
HYSTERIA: hystericalfeminisms.com
make/shift: makeshiftmag.com

6. Feminist Film Online: Sources and Resources

Projects & Organisations

A Nos Amours: anosamours.co.uk/.
Bechdel Test Fest: bechdeltestfest.com
The Bitch Pack: thebitchpack.com.
Birds Eye View: birds-eye-view.co.uk.
Center for the Study of Women in Television and Film (Martha Lauzen): womenintvfilm.sdsu.edu.
Club des Femmes: clubdesfemmes.com.
Directed by Women: directedbywomen.com/en/.
The Director List: thedirectorlist.com.
European Women's Audiovisual Network: ewawomen.com.
Femmes Lab (Ingrid Veninger): punkfilms.ca/.
Films Fatales: filmfatalesnyc.com.
The Geena Davis Institute: thegeenadavisinstitute.org/.
I Am Dora: iamdora.co.uk/.
MDSC Initiative: http://annenberg.usc.edu/pages/DrStacyLSmithMDSCI
Proquote Regie: proquote-regie.de.
Raising Films: raisingfilms.com.
Reel Grrls: reelgrrls.org/.
Sarah Jacobson Film Grant: freehistoryproject.org/sarah-jacobson-film-grant/.
She Must Be Wiki edit-a-thon: en.wikipedia.org/wiki/Wikipedia:SHE_MUST_BE_WIKI:_Feminist_Film_Wiki-a-thon.
VIDA: vidaweb.org.
Women in Film and Television: wftv.org.uk/.

Further Reading

Magazines and Blogs

African Women in Cinema (Beti Ellerson): africanwomenincinema.blogspot.co.uk.
BitchFlicks: btchflcks.com.
Black Girl Dangerous: blackgirldangerous.org.
Centre for the Study of Contemporary Women's Writing: modernlanguages.sas.ac.uk/centre-study-contemporary-womens-writing.
Cléo: A Journal of Film and Feminism: cleojournal.com.
Crunk Feminist Collective: crunkfeministcollective.com.
Dazed Digital Females First: dazeddigital.com/females-first.
The F-Word: Contemporary UK Feminism: thefword.org.uk.
Feminist Killjoys (Sara Ahmed): feministkilljoys.com.
Feral Feminisms: feralfeminisms.com.
Film Studies for Free (Catherine Grant): filmstudiesforfree.blogspot.co.uk.
GUTS Canadian Feminist Magazine: gutsmagazine.ca.
Joan's Digest: joansdigest.com.
On the Issues: A Magazine of Feminist, Progressive Thinking: ontheissuesmagazine.com.
Wellywood Woman (Marian Evans): wellywoodwoman.blogspot.co.uk.
Women and Hollywood (Melissa Silverstein): blogs.indiewire.com/womenandhollywood/.

Index

Bold numbers indicate figures.

1Day (Penny Woolcock) 91
4 Months, 3 Weeks and 2 Days (Cristian Mungiu) 109
8 (various) 49
11'09"01 (various) 23
12 Years a Slave (Steve McQueen) 101
35 Shots of Rum (Claire Denis) 128
52 Tuesdays (Sophie Hyde) 145–146, **145**, 151, 190, 200

Abbott, Michele 17
Abdullah, Reem 143
Abkarian, Simon 77
Academy Awards 12, 14, 15, 161, 199
Acquart, Pauline 126
Adju, Arina 144
Adler, Carine 85
Ado, Adèle 128
Aduviri, Juan Carlos 57
African Women in Cinema 15
'Afronauts' (Frances Bodomo) 132
After Tiller (Martha Shane and Lana Wilson) 21
After the Wedding (Susanne Bier) 180–181
Afternoon Delight (Jill Soloway) 155, 158
Agamben, Giorgio 37
Agbaje, Bola 89
Age of Stupid (Franny Armstrong) 52
Ahmed, Sara 27–28
Ahwesh, Peggy 113
Ai Weiwei: Never Sorry (Alison Klayman) 25
Aïssani, Ghania 60
Akbari, Mania 81–82, 90, 197
Akerman, Chantal 103, 196, 198

Akhavan, Desiree 146–147
Appropriate Behavior 172–173, 182
Slope, The 17
Akhmatova, Anna 49
Akinnagbe, Gbenga 163
Alaverdi (I'm Going to Change My Name) (Maria Saakyan) 144–145, 151
Albelo, Anna Margarita 174, 176
HOOTERS! 174
Who's Afraid of Vagina Wolf? 174–176
Albertine, Viv 156
Alexander, Lexi 8, 13, 116, 188–189
Ali, Monica 91
Alice Walker: Beauty in Truth (Pratibha Parmar) 193, 195–196, 201
All Over Me (Alex Sichel) 4
Alland, Sandra 137
Allen, Joan 77–78
Almada, Natalia 55, 57
al-Mansour, Haifaa
Storm in the Stars, A 119
Wadjda 16, 64, 119, 142–143
Al-Maria, Sophia 22
Almayer's Folly (Chantal Akerman) 103
Alps (Giorgios Lanthimos) 36
Althuizen, Sam 145
Alur, Mithu 170
Alvarez, Mercedes 37
Amagoalik, John 117
Amer (Hélène Cattet and Bruno Forzani) 22
American Horror Story (Brad Falchuk and Ryan Murphy) 119
American Mary (Jen and Sylvia Soska) 22

American Outrage (Beth and George Gage) 130–131
American Revolutionary: The Evolution of Grace Lee Boggs (Grace Lee) 9, 185, 187, 193
Amirpour, Ana Lily 22
Amis, Suzy 112
Amreeka (Cherien Dabis) 138
Anadu, Chika 158
Anatomy of Hell (Catherine Breillat) 178
Anders, Allison 17, 165
Gas Food Lodging 4
Grace of My Heart 166
Mi Vida Loca 4
Sugar Town 166
Andersen, Hans Christian 123, 126
Anderson, Raffaëla 41
Anderson, Sini 2, 9, 142, 193
Andrews, Mallory 138
Ang, Michelle 159
Angel at My Table, An (Jane Campion) 108, 135
Annie Leibovitz: Life Through a Lens (Barbara Leibovitz) 110
Anocha Suwichakornpong 162–163
À nos amours (Maurice Pialat) 134, 137
Anspach, Solveig 103
Antrobus, Corrina 198, 201
Apatow, Judd 7
Apple, The (Samira Makhmalbaf) 23, 142
Appropriate Behavior (Desiree Akhavan) 172–173, 182
Arbor, The (Clio Barnard) 15–16, 86, 87, 95, 98
Aref, Saleha 21
Aristophanes 183

Index

Aristotle 30
Armatage, Kay 33, 147
Armstrong, Franny 52
Armstrong, Gillian
   Little Women 33
   My Brilliant Career 107
Arnatsiaq, Peter Henry 106
Arnold, Andrea 89
   Fish Tank 39–40, 82–83,
      84–85, 92, 96, 140
   Red Road 7
   Wuthering Heights 37–40,
      53, 103, 180
Arraf, Suha 164
Artamonov, Julia 123
Artaud, Antonin 49, 61
Artemisia (Agnès Merlet) 108
Arthur, Imogen 145
Arzner, Dorothy 15, 21,
   111, 198
As If I Am Not There (Juanita
   Wilson) 73–74
Asante, Amma
   Belle 90, 97–98, **99**, 100–103,
      109, 111, 116, 190
   Way of Life, A 83,
      84–85, 89, 98
Aschan, Lisa 39
Asfa, Mahmoud 138
Ashton, Kimberley 68
Ashton, Zawe 87
Asibong, Andrew 75
Assume Nothing (Kirsty
   Macdonald) 186
At Five in the Afternoon
   (Samira Makhmalbaf) 23
Atlas, Maria 144
Attenberg (Athina Rachel
   Tsangari) 36–37, 40
Attenborough, David 36
Atwood, Margaret 113
Audre Lorde: The Berlin Years
   (Dagmar Schultz) 193
Austen, Jane 101
Avatar (James Cameron) 6, 51
Avingaq, Susan 105
Avni, Sheerly 6
Away From Her (Sarah Polley)
   180–181
Ayisi, Florence
   Sisters in Law 9
   Zanzibar Soccer Queens 139
Azmi, Shabana 104

Babadook, The (Jennifer Kent)
   157, 161
Babbit, Jamie
   But I'm a Cheerleader! 174
   *Itty Bitty Titty
      Committee* 174
Bacha, Julia 52
'Bachelor Machines' (Rosalind
   Nashashibi) 90
Backman Rogers, Anna 110
Back to God's Country (Nell
   Shipman) 33–34
Back to Stay (Milagros
   Mumenthaler) 163–165
Bad Girls (Jonathan
   Kaplan) 112
Badawi, Hend 25
Bado, Florencia 67
Bae, Doona 159
BAFTA 12, 80, 83
Baichwal, Jennifer 55
Baise-Moi (Virginie Despentes
   and Coralie Trinh Thi) 41
Baker, Josephine 108
Baker, Natalie 142
Bakri, Saleh 59
Bal, Nilaya 123
Bale, Miriam 116
Ballad of Jack and Rose, The
   (Rebecca Miller) 124
Ballad of Little Jo, The (Maggie
   Greenwald) 112
Bambara, Toni Cade 103
Bani-Etemad, Rakhshan 197
Banks, Elizabeth 13
Barazza, Adriana **26**, 26–27
Barbe, La 188, 199
Barber, Lynn 96
Barkai, Ali 75
Barker, Greg 71
Barlow, Melinda 11
Barnard, Clio
   Arbor, The 15–16, 86,
      87, 95, 98
   Selfish Giant, The 39
Barriga, Cecilia 191–192
Barrymore, Drew 141
Bartana, Yael 21
Barthes, Roland 185
Basile, Giambattista 160
Bassett, Angela 165
*Batman vs. Superman: Dawn of
   Justice* (Zack Snyder) 129

Batmanglij, Zal 51
Baumbach, Noah 127
Bazelon, Emily 71
Beaches of Agnès, The (Agnès
   Varda) 53, 184–187, **186**
Bear, Jeff 58
Beau Travail (Claire Denis)
   60–61, 69, 74
Beautiful Woman Sleeping, The
   (Ulrike Ottinger) 22
Becker, Saga 178
Beer, Shannon 38
Before Tomorrow
   (Marie-Hélène Cousineau
   and Madeline Ivalu)
   104–107, **105**, 117
Begay, Magdalena 20
Beirut (Rahel Zegeye) 162
*Beirut Diaries: Truth, Lies
   and Videos* (Mai Masri)
   196–197
Bellamy, Dodie 152–153
Belle (Amma Asante) 90,
   97–98, **99**, 100–103, 109,
   111, 116, 117, 190
Belle du jour (Luis
   Buñuel) 155
Belle épine (Rebecca
   Zlotowski) 147
Bell, Gertrude 41
Bell, Kristen 1
Bell, Lake 189
Belle (Amma Asante) 90, 97–8,
   99, 100–103, 109, 111,
   116, 117, 190
Belle du Jour (Luis Buñuel) 155
Belle épine (Rebecca
   Zlotowski) 147
Bend it Like Beckham
   (Gurinder Chadha) 90,
   139, 140
Bening, Annette 155
Benioff, David 119
Bennett, Alan 100
Benning, James 142
Benning, Sadie 142
Benzina (Monica Stambrini) 41
Beretta (Sophia Al-Maria) 22
Bergsmark, Ester Martin 20
   'Fruitcake' 178
   Something Must Break 178
Berlant, Lauren 173
Berlinale 63, 97, 161

Index

Berliner, Alain 140
Bertolotto, Sofia 153
Bessie (Dee Rees) 165
Better Man, A (Attiya Khan) 175
Beyoncé 100
Beyond the Lights (Gina Prince-Bythewood) 201
B for Boy (Chika Anadu) 158
Bier, Susanne 6, 67
   After the Wedding 180–181
   Brothers 68–69
   In a Better World 181
   Things We Lost in the Fire 68–69
Bigelow, Kathryn 5, 12, 27, 67, 68, 199
   Hurt Locker, The 6, 69–71
   K-19: The Widowmaker 69
   Point Break 4, 50–51, 69
   Strange Days 120
   Zero Dark Thirty 6, 70–71
Billson, Anne 33
Bilu, Vardit 72
Binder, Maria 193
Binoche, Juliette 108
Bird, Antonia 69, 89
Bispuri, Laura 4
Bitsui, Jeremiah 20
Björk 17
Blackfish (Gabriela Cowperthwaite) 35–36
Blair, Cherie 5
Blame it on Fidel (Julie Gavras) 143–144
Blethyn, Brenda 156
Bling Ring, The (Sofia Coppola) 137
Bloody Beans (Narimane Mari) 60–63, **61**
Bloom, Harold 17
Bluebeard (Catherine Breillat) 122
Blue Black Permanent (Margaret Tait) 198
Blue is the Warmest Colour (Abdellatif Kechiche) 147, 178
Blunt, Emily 173
Bodomo, Frances 132
Bodrov, Sergey 131
Body (Malgorzata Szumowska) 148

Boggs, Grace Lee 9, 184–185
Boggs, James 185
Bolger, Sarah 149
Bollaín, Iciar 58
   Even the Rain 56
   Take My Eyes 7
Bolton, Lucy 17, 83, 200
Bonnaire, Sabine 134–137, **136**
Bonnaire, Sandrine, 147
   Her Name is Sabine 134–137, **136**
Boorman, John 112
Boosheri, Nikohl 114
Borden, Lizzie 27
Borderline (Kenneth Macpherson) 15
Bordwell, David 8
Borg, Maja
   Future My Love 26, 94
   'Ottica Zero' 94
   'We the Others' 131–133
Borges, Graciela 153
Born in Flames (Lizzie Borden) 27, 120
Bornstein, Kate 194, **194**
Bose, Shonali 170
Boström, Tove 131–133
Bouamari, Fettouma 60
Boudica 97
Boudu Saved from Drowning (Jean Renoir) 155, 164
Bouhouche, Sami 60
Bow Wow Wow 110
Bowie, David 3, 127
Boxcar Bertha (Martin Scorsese) 40
Boxing Helena (Jennifer Chambers Lynch) 7
Boy I Am (Sam Feder) 139
Boyhood (Richard Linklater) 166
Boys Don't Cry (Kimberley Peirce) 4
Bradshaw, Asta 1–2, 4, 8, 203
Bradshaw, Peter 157
Brakni, Rachida 60
Bran Nue Dae (Rachel Perkins) 98
Branagh, Kenneth 129
Brant, Martine 103
Brawne, Fanny 111
Break My Fall (Kanchi Wichmann) 94, 176

Breedlove, Lynnee 2
Breillat, Catherine 118, 124
   Anatomy of Hell 178
   Bluebeard 122
   Fat Girl 146–147
   Sleeping Beauty, The 122–123
Brendemühl, Àlex 67
Brick Lane (Sarah Gavron) 89, 91
Bride and Prejudice (Gurinder Chadha) 90
Brides (Tinatin Kajrishvili) 181
Bridesmaids (Paul Feig) 19
Bright, Matthew 125
Bright Star (Jane Campion) 33, 107, 111
Brings Plenty, Moses 58
British Film Institute (BFI) 20, 55, 82, 89, 90, 97, 98, **99**, 114, 192, 197–198
Britton, Connie 166
Brokeback Mountain (Ang Lee) 177
Bronfen, Elisabeth 22
Bronson, Lisa Marie 110
Brontë, Emily 37
Brothers (Susanne Bier) 68–69
Brouillette, Sarah 12
Brown, Renel 139
Brown, Sophie 31
Browning, Emily 123
Bruno, Giuliana 78
Bruzzi, Stella 109
B/Side (Abigail Child) 121
Buchanan, Luke 159
Buck, Chris 1
Buddha Collapsed out of Shame (Hana Makhmalbaf) 23–24, 63–66, **64**, 78
Budrus (Julia Bacha) 52–53
Buffini, Moira 89
Buffy the Vampire Slayer (Joss Whedon) 22, 125
Buñuel, Luis 155
Burley, Nichola 38
Bush, George W. 18, 31, 56, 63, 78, 167
Bush, Laura 5
Bushnell, Candace 17
But I'm a Cheerleader! (Jamie Babbit) 174

243

Index

Butler, Alison 16
Butler, Judith 25, 52–53, 60, 63, 64, 137, 169
Butler, Octavia 117, 120
Butler, The (Lee Daniels) 14
Butter on the Latch (Josephine Decker) 173
Buy, Margherita 164
Byzantium (Neil Jordan) 89

Cadigan, Pat 120
Cahun, Claude 197
Cameron, James 6, 51, 54
Campbell, Deragh 21
Campion, Jane 5, 16, 188
  Angel at My Table, An 108, 135
  Bright Star 33, 107, 111
  In the Cut 22–23, 76–78, 122, 123, 128, 178, 199
  Piano, The 15, 49, 103, 111, 112
  Portrait of a Lady, The 103, 107–108
  Top of the Lake 17, 159–160, 169
  'Water Diary' 49
Canale, María 165
Canby, Vincent 114
Cannes Film Festival 49, 134, 188, 192
Cannon, Kay 13
'Capsule, The' (Athina Rachel Tsangari) 37
Carax, Leos 127
Cardellini, Linda 68
Carradine, David 40
Carrie (Brian De Palma) 157
Carrie (Kimberley Peirce) 157
Carroll, Noël 85
Carter, Angela 124–125
Carter, Lynda 129
Casad, Jen 54
Caton, Rose 150
Cat Power 164
Catching Out: Trainhopping and Living Free (Sarah George) 40
Cathy Come Home (Ken Loach) 83–84
Cattet, Hélène 22
Cavarero, Adriana 196–198

Cavendish, Margaret 120
Cazan, Nadya 94
Chadha, Gurinder
  Bend it Like Beckham 90, 139, 140
  Bride and Prejudice 90
  I'm British But... 90
Chai Jing 191
Chaikin, Ilene 17
Chaiworaporn, Anchalee 19
Chambers, Sara 16
Chapman, Conner 39
Chastain, Jessica 71
Chaudhuri, Shohini 16
Cherkam, Arkaney 162
Cherokee Word for Water, The (Tim Kelly and Charlie Soap) 58
Chib, Malini 170
Chicago, Judy 179
Child, Abigail 196
  B/Side 121
  Is This What You Were Born For? 121
  'Mayhem' 121, 177
  'Perils' 121
  Shape of Error, A 118–119
  'Subtalk' 121–22
  UNBOUND 119–122, **121**, 132
Child of the Revolution (Xoliswa Sithole) 5
Children of the Century (Diane Kurys) 108
Children of Men (Alfonso Cuarón) 82
Chinatown (Roman Polanski) 51
Chocolat (Claire Denis) 75
Cholodenko, Lisa
  Kids Are All Right, The 155
  Laurel Canyon 166
Christie, Julie 180–181, 197
Chuck D 56
Chung, David 112
Chytilová, Věra 197
Ciment, Michel 7
Cinderella (Kenneth Branagh) 129
Cinema of Women 16
Cinenova 16
Cioca, Kori 72–73
Circles 16

Circumstance (Maryam Keshavarz) 114, 141
CITIZENFOUR (Laura Poitras) 7
Citron, Michelle 196
  'Daughter Rite' 168
  Leftovers 169
  Mixed Greens 168–170
  Queer Feast 169
City of Borders (Yun Suh) 177
Clairmont, Claire 118
Clark, Ashley 100
Clarke, Alan 86
Clarke, Shirley 194
  Portrait of Jason 198
Cleghorn, Elinor 197
Clerc, Thérèse 184
Close to Home (Vardit Bilu and Dalia Hager) 72
Clover, Carol 22
Club des Femmes 117, 189–190, 198
Coatman, Anna 8
Cobham-Hervey, Tilda 145–146
Codependent Lesbian Space Alien Seeks Same (Madeline Olnek) 127–128
Cohn, Norman 105
Coixet, Isabel 189
Cole, Joe 150
Colin, Gregoire 60, 128
Collis, Stephen 32
Collyer, Laurie 181
Color Purple, The (Steven Spielberg) 195
Columpar, Corinn 16, 70–71, 105, 190, 196
'Come Together' (Mia Engberg) 178
Comencini, Francesca 164
Company of Wolves, The (Neil Jordan) 124–127
Concussion (Stacie Passon) 155
Condon, Bill 121
Connelly, Jennifer 3
Control Room (Jehane Noujaim) 24–25
Cooper, Catrin 116
Copello, Francisco 162
Coppola, Sofia

Index

Bling Ring, The 137
Little Mermaid, The 126
Marie Antoinette 109–110, 137
Tipping the Velvet 100
Corinealdi, Emayatzy 181
Cornish, Abbie 68, 107
Corpo celeste (Alice Rohrwacher) 147
Costa-Gavras 143–144
Countess, The (Julie Delpy) 109
Cousineau, Marie-Hélène 104, **105**
Cowperthwaite, Gabriela 35–36
Cracks (Jordan Scott) 149
Craft, The (Andrew Fleming) 125
'Creepers on the Bridge' (Colette Ghunim and Tinne van Loon) 175
Crenshaw, Kimberlé 131
Cristo Rey (Leticia Tonos Paniagua) 180
Croc-a-Dyke-Dundee (Fiona Cunningham-Reed) 184–185
Crows (Dorota Kędzierzawska) 82
Crystal 139–140, 202–203, **202**
Cuarón, Alfonso
 Children of Men 82
 Gravity 19
Cullors, Patrisse 24
Cunningham-Reed, Fiona 184–185
Curran, John 41
Curwood, James Oliver 33
Cvetkovich, Ann 110, 169

Dabis, Cherien 164
 Amreeka 138
Daccache, Zeina 183–184, 186
Daguerréotypes (Agnès Varda) 186, 190
'Dahiet Al Bareed, District of the Post Office' (Rosalind Nashashibi) 90
Dalton, Mary 184
Daniels, Lee 14
Dann, Carrie 130
Dann, Mary 130

d'Ansembourg, Muriel 147
d'Antonia, Aurelia 119
Dargis, Manohla 12, 115, 122
Das, Nandita 6
Dash, Julie 196
 Daughters of the Dust 103
 Illusions 103
 Rosa Parks Story, The 103
 Travel Notes of a Geechee Girl 103
'Daughter Rite' (Michelle Citron) 168
Daughters of the Dust (Julie Dash) 103
Daughters of India (Leslee Udwin) 191
Davidson, Robyn 41
Davies, Lottie 87
Davis, Angela Y. 9, **10**, 12, 41
Davis, Essie 157
Davis, Geena 12, 41, 50, 189, 199
Davis, Lennard 120
Davis, Ossie 185
Davis, Therese 17–18
Day I Became a Woman, The (Marzieh Meshkini) 64
Day I Will Never Forget, The (Kim Longinotto) 183
Day, Simon Paisley 150
De Bankolé, Isaach 75
de Beauvoir, Simone 120–121
Deal, Carl 56, 59
Decker, Josephine 173
Dee, Ruby 185
Delaney, Shelagh 86, 89
Deliver (Jennifer Montgomery) 112–113
Deliverance (John Boorman) 112
Delpy, Julie 109
Demerliac, Lou-Léila 148
Dempsey, Anna 6
Demy, Jacques 184–185
Deneuve, Catherine 144
Denis, Claire 6
 35 Shots of Rum 128
 Beau Travail 60–61, 69, 74
 Chocolat 75
 Vendredi soir 128, 178
 White Material 74–76
De Palma, Brian 157
Depardieu, Julie 144

Deren, Maya 15, 194, 197, 198, 200
 'Meshes of the Afternoon' 118, 195
 'Private Life of a Cat, The' 33–34
Derrick, Terreanne 136, 148
Derrida, Jacques 33
Desai, Jemma 198
Descas, Alex 128
Despentes, Virginie 41, 196
Desperate Optimists 93
Desperately Seeking Susan (Susan Seidelman) 192
Devil's Whore, The (Marc Munden) 103
DeWitt, Rosemary 173
Diary of a Teenage Girl, The (Marielle Heller) 133–134
Diaz, Melonie 174
Dick, Kirby 72–73
Dick, Vivienne 49
Dickey, James 113
Dickinson, Emily 111
Dickson Leach, Hope 190
DiFranco, Ani 149
Diop, Mati 128
 'Snow Canon' 123
Dippold, Katie 19
Dirty Diaries (various) 178–179, 186
Dirziute, Aiste 147
Diski, Jenny 33
Disson, Jeanne 140
Dixie Chicks 166–167
Doane, Mary Ann 154
Docter, Pete 154
Dogtooth (Giorgios Lanthimos) 36
Doillon, Lola 22
Dolan, Jill 8
Dolan, Monica 151
Donald, Stephanie Hemelryk, 81
Dones, Elvira 4
Donkeys (Morag McKinnon) 7
Dore, Mary 179
Doron, Anita 138
Double Dare (Amanda Micheli) 129
Double Tide (Sharon Lockhart) 54
Dougherty, Ariel 175

245

Index

Downs, Lila 108
Drakulić, Slavenka 73
Dreamcatcher (Kim Longinotto) 182–183
Dreams of a Life (Carol Morley) 87–89, **88**, 95, 96, 116
Drunktown's Finest (Sydney Freeland) 20
Duchamp, Marcel 76
Duffus, Dylan 91–92
du Fresne, Georges 140
Duggan, Mark 92
Duke of Burgundy, The (Peter Strickland) 178
Dukhtar (Afia Nathaniel) 21
Dulac, Germaine 15
Dunbar, Andrea 16, 86, 89
Dunham, Lena 127
  Girls 7, 124, 172
  Tiny Furniture 156
Dunn, Jan
  Gypo 82
  Sacred Country 99–100
Dunst, Kirsten 109
Dunye, Cheryl 186, 196
  OWLS, The 174, 176
  Stranger Inside 182–183
  Valencia [segment] 176
  Watermelon Woman, The 110–111, 176
Duplass, Mark 173
Dupont, Ewald André 91
Duras, Marguerite 40, 74–75, 144, 196
Duvall, Clea 174
Duvauchelle, Nicholas 75
DuVernay, Ava 132, 133
  Middle of Nowhere 14, 181
  Selma 12, **13**, 14, 20, 103, 115, 203

Earth (Deepa Mehta) 104
East, The (Zal Batmanglij) 51
Eastwood, Clint 112
Eat Pray Love (Ryan Murphy) 41
Education, An (Lone Scherfig) 96, 133
Efron, Ines 126
Eisenberg, Jesse 51
Ekharaga, Destiny 89, 90, 92, 98

Eldaief, Mona 191
El Hoseini, Sally 90, 92
Elie, Lolis Eric 56
El Kashef, Aida **24**, 25
Ellerson, Beti 15, 162
Elsayed, Fady 93
Emak Bakia (Man Ray) 119
Emeke, Cecile 17
Emond, Linda 68
Enchanted (Kevin Lima) 127
Encina, Paz 7
Engberg, Mia
  'Come Together' 178
  Dirty Diaries 178–179, 186
Englert, Alice 49, 95
Enough! (Djamila Sahraoui) 60, 62
Enough Said (Nicole Holofcener) 156
Ephron, Nora 4
Epper, Jeannie 129
Eskridge, Kelley 1
Esma's Secret (Jasmila Žbanić) 73–74
Esmer, Pelin 183
Estate, A Reverie (Andrea Luka Zimmerman) 80
E.T. (Steven Spielberg) 152–153
Euripides 93
Evans, Joel Nathan 138
Evans, Marian 15, 117, 199
Evans, Shaula 116
Even the Rain (Icíar Bollaín) 56
Ewing, Heidi 142
Examined Life (Astra Taylor) 37, 137
Exhibition (Joanna Hogg) 156
Eyo, Alicya 150

Fahrenheit 9/11 (Michael Moore) 56
Falchuk, Brad 119
Falling, The (Carol Morley) 150–152, 157
Faludi, Susan 18, 113, 124–125
Fanning, Dakota 51
Fanning, Elle 95, 119, 197
Fanon, Frantz 100
Faour, Nisreen 164
Farhat, Maymanah 59
Farmiga, Taissa 119

Fassbender, Michael 82
Fast Girls (Regan Hall) 139
Fat Girl (Catherine Breillat) 146–147
Fatal Attraction (Adrian Lyne) 162
Waller, Fats 167
Fawcett, John 125
Featherstone, Lynne 87
Feder, Sam 20
Federici, Silvia 160
  Boy I Am 139
  Kate Bornstein is a Queer and Pleasant Danger 184, 193–95, **194**
Feig, Paul
  Bridesmaids 19
  Heat, The 19
Felperin, Leslie 170
Female Perversions (Susan Streitfeld) 144
Feminist Godzilla 27–28
Fey, Tina 137
Fifty Shades of Grey (Sam Taylor-Johnson) 22, 133, 178
Firaaq (Nandita Das) 6
Fire (Deepa Mehta) 4, 6
Fish Tank (Andrea Arnold) 39–40, 82–83, 84–85, 92, 96, 140
Flag Wars (Laura Poitras) 6–7
Flannery, Peter 103
Fleming, Andrew 125
Fleming, Victor 29
Flores, StormMiguel 20
Flow: For the Love of Water (Irene Salina) 55
Floyd, James 92
'For Cultural Purposes Only' (Sarah Wood) 10
Ford, John 22
Forrest, Diandra 132
Forrest, Katherine V. 120
Forzani, Bruno 22
Fouéré, Olwen 49
Fougere, Myriam 179
Fox, Raphael 20
Foxy Merkins, The (Madeline Olnek) 127
Frame, Janet 108, 135
Frances Ha (Noah Baumbach) 127–128

Index

Frankel, David 32
Frankenstein (James Whale) 121
Franklin, Miles 108
Frears, Stephen
   My Beautiful Laundrette 92
   Tamara Drewe 89
Free Angela and All Political Prisoners (Shola Lynch) 9, **10**, 12, 193
Freeland, Sydney 20
Freeman, Beth 67–68
Freeman, Tamar 68
Freeway (Matthew Bright) 125
Frémaux, Thierry 188
Fresco, Jacque 94
Freud, Sigmund 157
Frida (Julie Taymor) 108, 109
Friedan, Betty 155
Friedrich, Su 113, 198
Friends with Money (Nicole Holofcener) 156
Froggatt, Joanne 68
From the Plantation to the Penitentiary (Tina Gharavi) 92
From the Sea to the Land Beyond (Penny Woolcock) 55–56, 91, 95
From Tehran to London (Mania Akbari) 82
From a Whisper (Wanuri Kahiu) 46–47
Frozen (Chris Buck and Jennifer Lee) 1–4, 8, 10, 12, 13, 123, 201, 203
Frozen River (Courtney Hunt) 57–58
'Fruitcake' (Ester Martin Bergsmark and Sara Kaaman) 178
Fukunaga, Cary 89
'Fuses' (Carolee Schneemann) 33–34
Future, The (Miranda July) 127–128
Future My Love (Maja Borg) 26, 94
Futures Market (Mercedes Alvarez) 37

Gadon, Sarah 101
Gadot, Gal 129
Gage, Beth 130
Gage, George 130
Game of Thrones (David Benioff and D. B. Weiss) 119–120
Gandhi, Mahatma 115
Garbo, Greta 166
Garcia-Pérez, José Luis 59
Garland, Judy 29–30
Garlington, Lee 156
Garner, Eric 115
Garza, Alicia 24
Gas Food Lodging (Allison Anders) 4
Gavras, Julie 143–144
Gavron, Sarah
   Brick Lane 89, 91
   Suffragette 114
   Village at the End of the World 42
Gay, Roxane 1, 19, 25–26
Gazidis, Dorothy 84
Geller, Theresa 194
George, Sarah 40
Gerard, Gilbert 86
Gerwig, Greta 127
Gharavi, Tina 91, 199
   From the Plantation to the Penitentiary 92
   I am Nasrine 39–40, 81, 84–85, 96
Ghazalla, Amira 93
Ghosting (Monika Treut) 178
Ghunim, Colette
   'Creepers on the Bridge' 175
   People's Girls, The 175
Giedroyć, Coky
   Mary Shelley's Monster 119
   Stella Does Tricks 119
Gilbert, Elizabeth 41
Gilbert, Sandra M. 17
Gilder, Sean 39
Gillett, Sue 122
Gilligan, Melanie 132
Gilman, Charlotte Perkins 116
Gilroy, Paul 59
Ginger and Rosa (Sally Potter) 95–96, 98, 113, 119, 197
Ginger Snaps (John Fawcett) 125
Giovanetti, Lola 122
Girl at My Door, A (July Jung) 158–160, 169
'Girl Power' (Sadie Benning) 142
Girl Walks Home Alone at Night, A (Ana Lily Amirpour) 22
Girl with a Pearl Earring, The (Peter Webber) 116
Girlfight (Karyn Kusama) 139–140
Girlhood (Céline Sciamma) 137–138, 151
Girls (Lena Dunham) 7, 124, 172
Glave, Solomon 38
Gleaners and I, The (Agnès Varda) 5, 33, 37
Glick, Maya 130, **130**
Gloeckner, Phoebe 134
Godard, Agnès 60
'God, Construction and Destruction' (Samira Makhmalbaf) 23
Goddess of Mercy (Ann Hui) 159
Gods and Monsters (Bill Condon) 121
Godwin, William 118
Go Fish (Rose Troche) 4, 174, 177
Gold Diggers, The (Sally Potter) 197
Golden Globe awards 14
Gone Too Far (Destiny Ekharaga) 89, 92, 98
Goodbye Gauley Mountain (Beth Stephens) 53
'Good Night' (Muriel d'Ansembourg) 147
Goodwin, Raven 156
Googoosh 165
Gordon, Bette 139
Gordon, Douglas 148
Gordon, Kiowa 138
Gordon-Levitt, Joseph 68
Gore, Al 191
Gould, Judith 134
Goulet, Danis 14, 200
   'Wakening' 8
Govan, Maria 139
Grace Lee Project, The (Grace Lee) 185
Grace of My Heart (Allison Anders) 166

Index

Grady, Rachel 143
'Granada 30 Years On' (Cecilia Barriga) 191–192
Grand Central (Rebecca Zlotowski) 178
Grange Hill (Phil Redmond) 89
Gravity (Alfonso Cuarón) 18
Green Days (Hana Makhmalbaf) 23–24
Green, Eva 149
Green Porno (Isabella Rossellini) 36
Greenberg, Kathy 17
Greenfield, Lauren 144
Greenwald, Maggie 112
Griffith, Nicola 1
Griffiths, Rebecca 82
Grisoni, Tony 87
Grrrl Love and Revolution: Riot Grrrl NYC (Abby Moser) 142
Gubar, Susan 17
Guerrero, Aurora 180
Guerrero, Kimberley 58
Guerrilla Girls 174
Guest, Haden 154
Guevara-Flanagan, Kristy 129
Guggenheim, Davis 191
Gulabi Gang (Nishtha Jain) 130
Gulati, Sonali 196–197
Gulkin, Harry 167, 169
Gupta, Sayani 170
Gutiérrez, Chus 58–59
Guy-Blaché, Alice 15
Guzman, Natasha 72
Gyllenhaal, Jake 156
Gyllenhaal, Maggie 114
Gypo (Jan Dunn) 82

Hadžihalilović, Lucile 148–149
Hager, Dalia 72
Hahn, Kathryn 155
Half Life (Jennifer Phang) 118
Hall, Regan 139
Hall, Stuart 100
Halls, Nicole 39
Hamad, Hannah 23
Hamburg Cell, The (Antonia Bird) 69
Hamed, Farah 59
Hamilton, Tanya 115
Hammad, Suheir 59
Hammer, Barbara 179, 196, 198

'Horse is Not a Metaphor, A' 197
Lover Other: The Story of Claude Cahun and Marcel Moore 197
'Maya Deren's Sink' 195
Hammid, Alexander 33
Hancock, Sheila 77
Handel, Adèle 126
Handmaid's Tale, The (Volker Schlondorff) 113
Handy, Bruce 13
Haneke, Michael 22
Hanna, Kathleen **3**, 4, 11, 12, 25, 133, 134
Hannah Arendt (Margarethe von Trotta) 114
Hannigan, Alyson 125
Hans, Simran 201
Haraway, Donna 31–32, 40
Harb, Shuruq 35
Hard Candy (David Slade) 124–125
Hardie, Kate 198
Hardin, Melora 155
Hardwicke, Catherine
  Red Riding Hood 125
  Thirteen 146
  Twilight 22, 125
Harewood, David 98
Harris, Anita 84
Harron, Mary
  Moth Diaries, The 149–150
  Notorious Bettie Page, The 108–109
Hartley, Hal 141
Harvie, Ian 155
Harwood-Jones, Marcus 20
Haskell, Molly 147
Hattenstone, Simon 83
Hausner, Jessica
  Lourdes 49
  Lovely Rita 147
Haworth, Gwen 20
  She's Just a Boy I Knew 139
Hayek, Salma 108
Haynes, Todd 6
H.D. (Hilda Doolittle) 15
Headless Woman, The (Lucrecia Martel) 126
Heat, The (Paul Feig) 19
Heckerling, Amy 4
Hedges, Chris 69

Helen (Desperate Optimists) 93–94
Heller, Marielle 133–134
Help, The (Tate Taylor) 19
Henderson, Rebecca 172
Henderson, Shirley 100
Hendricks, Christina 197
Henson, Jim 3
Her Name is Sabine (Sandrine Bonnaire) 134–137, 136
Herán, Zoé 139
Herbert-Jane, Del 145–146
Herrera, Viviana 162
Hershey, Barbara 40
Herzog, Werner 41
Heymann, Lindy 139
Hidalgo, Alexandra 197
Hi Ho Mistahey! (Alanis Obomsawin) 7, 8, 12
Hill, Cindy 184
Hill, Natalie 19
History Boys (Nicholas Hytner) 100
Hitchcock, Alfred
  Rebecca 154
  Vertigo 162
Hoffmann, Gaby 155
Hogg, Joanna 198
  Exhibition 156
Hold Me Tight, Let Me Go (Kim Longinotto) 84
Hollis, Kelli 85
Holofcener, Nicole 173
  Enough Said 156
  Friends with Money 156
  Lovely and Amazing 156
  Please Give 156
Holy Girl, The (Lucrecia Martel) 126
Honeytrap (Rebecca Johnson) 93
hooks, bell 3, 103, 125, 173
HOOTERS! (Anna Margarita Albelo) 174
'Horse is Not a Metaphor, A' (Barbara Hammer) 197
Hoseinali, Abdolali 65
Houston, Whitney 165
How to Make an American Quilt (Jocelyn Moorhouse) 112
Howard, Silas 20

248

Index

Howson, James 38
Hui, Ann
  Goddess of Mercy 159
  Simple Life, A 163
Human Rights Watch film festival 65–66
Humpday (Lynn Shelton) 173
Hunger Games, The [quadrilogy] 19
Hunt, Courtney 57
Hunter, Holly 49, 146
Huppert, Isabelle 75
Hurley, Kameron 66–67, 68, 98
'Hurry Up, You Stupid Cripple' (Elle-Máijá Tailfeathers and Terreane Derrick) 136–137, 140, 148
Hurt Locker, The (Kathryn Bigelow) 6, 69–71
Hutcheon, Linda 69
Hyde, Sophie 145–146
Hynes, Jessica 114
Hysteria (Tanya Wexler) 114, 117
Hytner, Nicholas 100

I Am (Sonali Gulati) 196–197
i am a good person/i am a bad person (Ingrid Veninger) 200
I am an Ox, I am a Horse, I am a Man, I am a Woman: Women in Russian Cinema (Sally Potter) 4, 72
I am Curious (Yellow) (Vilgot Sjöman) 178
I am Nasrine (Tina Gharavi) 39–40, 81, 84–85, 96
I'm British But... (Gurinder Chadha) 90
I Can't Think Straight (Shamim Sarif) 94
Ihimaera, Witi 117
Illusions (Julie Dash) 103
imagineNATIVE film festival 14
Imarisha, Walidah 42
In a Better World (Susanne Bier) 181
In a World (Lake Bell) 189
In Our Name (Brian Welsh) 68
InRealLife (Beeban Kidron) 26

In the Cut (Jane Campion) 22–23, 76–78, 122, 123, 128, 178, 199
In the Land of Blood and Honey (Angelina Jolie) 67, 73
In the Mirror of Maya Deren (Martina Kudlacek) 195
In the Turn (Erica Tremblay) 140–141, 202–203, 202
In Your Hands (Lola Doillon) 22
Inconvenient Truth, An (Davis Guggenheim) 191
Innocence (Lucile Hadžihalilović) 148–150
Investigating China's Smog (Chai Jing) 191
Invisible War, The (Kirby Dick) 72–73
Ip, Deanie 163
Irigaray, Luce 17, 122, 173–174
Iron Jawed Angels (Katja von Garnier) 114
Iron Lady, The (Phyllida Lloyd) 89, 113, 114
'Irreducible Difference of the Other, The' (Vivienne Dick) 49
Irreversible (Gaspar Noé) 23
Isabelle, Katharine 125
Ishaq, Sara
  'Karama Has No Walls' 91
  Mulberry House, The 90
Is This What You Were Born For? (Abigail Child) 121
Island President, The (Jon Shenk) 52
Isitt, Debbie 79
Itty Bitty Titty Committee (Jamie Babbit) 174
Ivalu, Madeline, 104–105, 105, 112
Ivalu, Paul-Dylan 105

Jacir, Annemarie
  Salt of this Sea 59
  'Sound of the Street' 34–35
  When I Saw You 138
Jacob, Clarissa 192
Jacob, Nicholas 164
Jacobson, Sarah 142
Jacquot de Nantes (Agnès Varda) 185
Jain, Nishtha 130

James, Diana 48
James, Stephanie 83
Jane Eyre (Cary Fukunaga) 89
Jarnot, Lisa 76
Jarvis, Katie 39
Jelinek, Elfriede 22
Jenkins, Patty
  Monster 36
  Wonder Woman 129, 132
Jenkins, Tamara 163
Jennifer's Body (Karyn Kusama) 22
Jensen, Emma 119
Jesus Camp (Heidi Ewing and Rachel Grady) 143
Jeune et jolie (François Ozon) 147
Joe, Jacqueline 159
Johns, Tara 155
Johnson, Chloé Hope 4
Johnson, E. Pauline (Tekahionwake) 116
Johnson, Liza 68
Johnson, Rebecca 93
Johnston, Claire 15, 120
Jolie, Angelina
  In the Land of Blood and Honey 67, 73
  Unbroken 73
Jones, Marianne 58
Jordan, Neil
  Byzantium 89
  Company of Wolves, The 124–127
Joseph, Samantha 93
Journals of Knud Rasmussen, The (Norman Cohn and Zacharias Kunuk), 105
'Joy of Madness, The' (Hana Makhmalbaf) 23
Judd, Ashley 108
Juhasz, Alex 110, 176, 179
July, Miranda 17
  Future, The 127–128
  Me and You and Everyone We Know 173
Juncadella, Martina 165
Jung, July 158
Jungermann, Ingrid 17

K-19: The Widowmaker (Kathryn Bigelow) 69
Kaaman, Sara 178

249

Index

Kahiu, Wanuri 190
  From a Whisper 46–47
  'Pumzi' 45–48, **48**, 50, 61, 62
Kahlo, Frida 108
Kajrishvili, Tinatin 181
Kamaluddin, Siti 16, 139
Kapaleva, Anna 76
Kaplan, Jonathan 112
Kaplan, Louise J. 144
'Karama Has No Walls' (Sara Ishaq) 91
Karanović, Mirjana 73
Kariyawasam, Sarala 104
Kate Bornstein is a Queer and Pleasant Danger (Sam Feder) 184
Kateb, Reda 71, 193–95, **194**
Kates, Nancy 184, 193
Kavaïté, Alanté 147
Kawase, Naomi 49
Kay, Georgi 17
Kay, Jackie 99
Kaye/Kantrowitz, Melanie 72
Kazemi, Sarah 114
Kechiche, Abdellatif 147
Kędzierzawska, Dorota 82
Keeling, Kara 20, 139
Keener, Catherine 156
Kellaway, Kate 101
Kelly, Tim 58
Kenan, Gil 154
Kennedy, A. L. 87, 119
Kent, Jennifer 157
Kerr, Robyn 176
Kervel-Bey, Nina 144
Keshavarz, Maryam 114
Khan, Attiya 175
Khan, Shahnaz 5
Kher, Kiron 104
Khouri, Callie 15
  Nashville 166
Kiarostami, Abbas 81
Kicks (Lindy Heymann) 139
Kidman, Nicole 41, 108
Kidron, Beeban 26
Kids Are All Right, The (Lisa Cholodenko) 155
Kill Bill Vol. 1 (Quentin Tarantino) 129
Killo Kitty 202
Kim, Sae-ron 159
King Abdullah 143
King, Jamilah 141

King, Martin Luther, Jr. 20, 115
King, Michael Patrick 114
King, Moynan 109
Kipnis, Laura 173
Kirby, Malachi 92
Kitia, Mari 181
Kitch 33–34, 44
Klayman, Alison 25
Klein, Bonnie Sherr 177
Klein, Naomi 84
Klein, Rachel 149
Knudsen, Sidse Babett 180
Koechlin, Kalki 170
Kohan, Jenji 17
Kohler, Sheila 149
Kopple, Barbara 166
Koostachin, Jules 161
Koostachin, Shannen 7, 8, 12
Kristeva, Julia 164
Kudlacek, Martina 195
Kunuk, Zacharias 105
Kureishi, Hanif 92
Kurtz, Hope 66
Kurtz, Steve 66
Kurys, Diane 108
Kusama, Karen 8
  Girlfight 139–140
  Jennifer's Body 22
KUSAMA: Princess of Polka Dots (Heather Lenz) 142

Labaki, Nadine 183
Labed, Ariane 36, 37
LaBerge, Stacey 181
Labyrinth (Jim Henson) 3, 4
Lahiri-Dutt, Kuntala 61
Lajeunesse, Félix 42
Lambert, Christophe 75
Landecker, Amy 155
Landy, Marcia 86
Lane, Penny 113
Lang, Fritz 121
Lansbury, Angela 125
Lant, Antonia 15
Lanthimos, Giorgos 36–37
Last of the Mohicans, The 69
Last Resort (Pawel Pawlikowski) 82
Last Year at Marienbad (Alain Resnais) 119
Lau, Andy 163
Laurel Canyon (Lisa Cholodenko) 166

Lauzen, Martha 12
Lavant, Denis 61
Laverty, Paul 57
Lavie, Talya 72
Lawford, Ningali 98
Lawless, Lucy 129
Lawlor, Joe 93
Lawrence, Francis 19
Lawrence, T. E. 41
Lazón, Bárbara 161
Lea, Frances 147
Lebow, Alisa 69, 75
Leder, Mimi 4
Lee, Ang
  Brokeback Mountain 177
  Sense and Sensibility 101
Lee, Anita 167
Lee, Gerard, 17
Lee, Grace
  American Revolutionary: The Evolution of Grace Lee Boggs 9, 185, 187, 193
  Grace Lee Project, The 185
Lee, Jennifer 1, 14–15
Lee, Spike 56
Leeson, Lynn Hershman
  Strange Culture 66
  !Women Art Revolution 193
Leftovers (Michelle Citron) 169
Le Guin, Ursula K. 120
Leibovitz, Annie 110
Leibovitz, Barbara 110
Leigh, Julia 122–124, 128
Lenkiewicz, Rebecca 100
Lenz, Heather 142
Leo, Melissa 58, 200
Leonard, Joshua 173
Lesage, Julia 18
Lesbiana – A Parallel Revolution (Myriam Fougère) 179, 191
Lesser Blessed, The (Anita Doron) 138
Lessin, Tia 56, 59
Levelling, The (Hope Dickson Leach) 190
Levy, Ariel 146
Lewis, Helen 25
Li Huang 90
Lighthouse, The (Maria Saakyan) 75–76
Lili'uokalani 116
Lima, Kevin 127

250

Index

Limbo (John Sayles) 42
Lindsay, Dido Belle 101, 111
Linklater, Richard 166
Linney, Laura 163
Lioness (Meg McLagan and Daria Sommers) 66, 67, 68
Lions Love (Agnès Varda) 187
Little Mermaid, The (Sofia Coppola) 126
Little Women (Gillian Armstrong) 33
Lives of Performers (Yvonne Rainer) 127
Living in the Overlap (Mary Dalton and Cindy Hill) 184
Llosa, Claudia 161
Lloyd, Phyllida
  Iron Lady, The 89, 113, 114
  Mamma Mia! 89
Loach, Ken 83–84
Lockhart, Sharon 54
Loden, Barbara 40
London Feminist Film Festival 191, 198
London Film Festival 164, 199
London to Brighton (Paul Andrew William) 82
Long, Julia 191
Longinotto, Kim 196
  Day I Will Never Forget, The 183
  Dreamcatcher 182–183
  Hold Me Tight, Let Me Go 84
  Love is All 91, 94–95
  Pink Saris 130–131
  Pride of Place 84
  Runaway 84
  Salma 84, 156–157
  Sisters in Law 8–9
Longoria, Eva 100
Lopes-Benites, Marilou 122
Lopez, Andrea
Lorde, Audre 172, 193
Lords, Traci 146
Lore (Cate Shortland) 67
Lost and Delirous (Léa Poole) 149–150
Louise Michel: La Rebelle (Solveig Anspach) 103
Lourdes (Jessica Hausner) 49
Love is All (Kim Longinotto) 91, 94–95

Love Like Poison (Katell Quillévéré) 147
Lovely and Amazing (Nicole Holofcener) 156
Lovely Rita (Jessica Hausner) 147
Lover Other: The Story of Claude Cahun and Marcel Moore (Barbara Hammer) 197
Lucy 29, 44
Luhrmann, Baz 125
Lumière Brothers 188
L-Word, The (Michele Abbott, Ilene Chaikin and Kathy Greenberg) 17, 174
Lyle (Stewart Thorndike) 157
Lynch, Jennifer Chambers 7
Lynch, Jessica 22
Lynch, Shola 9, 193
Lyne, Adrian 162
Lynskey, Melanie 174

Ma vie en rose (Alain Berliner) 140
Macdonald, Kirsty 186
Mackie, Anthony 69
Macpherson, Kenneth 15
Madame X (Ulrike Ottinger) 22
Madsen, Berit 142
Magic Mirror (Sarah Pucill) 197
Maines, Natalie 167
Maïwenn 159
Makhmalbaf, Hana 25, 65, 81, 142
  Buddha Collapsed out of Shame (Hana Makhmalbaf) 23–24, 63–66, **64**, 78
  Green Days (Hana Makhmalbaf) 23–24
  'Joy of Madness, The' (Hana Makhmalbaf) 23, 63
Makhmalbaf, Mohsen 23, 65, 142
Makhmalbaf, Samira 6, 65, 81
  Apple, The 23, 142
  At Five in the Afternoon 23
  'God, Construction and Destruction' 23
  Two Legged Horse 39

Maleficent (Robert Stromberg) 119, 122, 125, 131
Malik, Aamir 104
Malmborg, Iggy (178)
Mamma Mia! (Phyllida Lloyd) 89
Mammas (Isabella Rossellini) 36
Man Who Envied Women, The (Yvonne Rainer) 127
Mandela, Nelson 87, **88**, 116
Manimekalai, Leena 191
Mankiller, Wilma 58
Man Ray 49
  Emak Bakia 119
Mansfield Park (Patricia Rozema) 103
Mantel, Hilary 151
Maple, Jessie 192
Marazzi, Alina 191–192
Margarita, With a Straw (Shonali Bose) 170–173, **171**, 182, 201
Mari, Narimane 60–61
Marie Antoinette (Sofia Coppola) 109–110, 137
Marinca, Annamaria 109
Marks, Laura U. 54
Marley and Me (David Frankel) 32
Marling, Brit 51
Marroquin, Mariana 177
Marshall, Nadine 158
Marshall, Penny 4
Martel, Lucrecia 49–50, 57, 161, 163
  Headless Woman, The 126
  Holy Girl, The 126
  'Pescados' 44
  Swamp, The 153–154, **154**, 160, 162
Martyn, John 165
Marx, Karl 37
Mary Shelley's Monster (Coky Giedroyć) 119
Maskharashvili, Giorgi 181
Masri, Mai 196–197
Mastroianni, Chiara 143
Matten, Jessica 70
Maurice, Gail 8
'Maya Deren's Sink' (Barbara Hammer) 195

251

Index

Mayer, Ursula 79
'Mayhem' (Abigail Child) 121, 177
Mbatha-Raw, Gugu 98
McDermott, Kathleen 85
McDonough, Jill 15
McDormand, Frances 166
McDowell, Malcolm 50
McFadden, Davenia 182
McKellen, Ian 112
McKenzie, Mia 27
McKenzie, Rocky 98
McKinnon, Morag 7
McLagan, Meg 66
McLaren, Michelle 129
McLaughlin, Sheila 177
McLynn, Pauline 82
McMahon, Laura 128
McMullan, Chlesea 140
McQueen, Steve
   12 Years a Slave 101
   Shame 89
McTeer, Janet 114
MDSC Initiative 12, 19, 199
Me and You and Everyone We Know (Miranda July) 173
Mean Girls (Mark Waters) 137, 151
Meek's Cutoff (Kelly Reichardt) 41, 53, 111–113, 116
Meek, Stephen 111
Mehta, Deepa 16
   Earth 104
   Fire 4, 6
   Water 104, 115
Melville, Herman 60
Mengele, Josef 67
Menzel, Idina 1
Merlet, Agnès 108
'Meshes of the Afternoon' (Maya Deren) 118, 195
Meshkini, Marzieh 64, 81
Metropolis (Fritz Lang) 121
Meyer, Stephenie 37
Mi Vida Loca (Allison Anders) 4
Michael, Frann 182
Micheli, Amanda 129
Middle of Nowhere (Ava DuVernay) 14, 181
Midnight's Children (Mira Nair) 104

Mihai, Teodora Ana 79
Mikkelsen, Mads 180–181
Milk (Gus van Sant) 114
Milk of Sorrow (Claudia Llosa) 161–164, 169
Miller, Liz 48
Miller, Rebecca
   Ballad of Jack and Rose, The 124
   Private Lives of Pippa Lee, The 155
Miller, T'Nia 176
Milović, Luna 73
Mir-Hosseini, Ziba 84
Misadventures of an Awkward Black Girl, The (Issa Rae) 17
Mischief Night (Penny Woolcock) 85
Miss Representation (Jennifer Siebel Newsom) 19
Mitchell, Joni 46
Mitchell, Mani Bruce 186
Mixed Greens (Michelle Citron) 168–170
Mlambo-Ngcuka, Phumzile 18–19
Mobarak, Nour 123
Modra (Ingrid Veninger) 200
Moffatt, Tracey 16
Mohammed, Waad 143
Mohammed, Yanar 73
Mohanty, Chandra Talpade 66
Mol, Gretchen 108
Molina, Alfred 108
Molina, Juana 44
Molloy, Christine 93
Mongol (Sergey Bodrov) 131
Monroe, Marilyn 21
Monster (Patty Jenkins) 36
Monster House (Gil Kenan) 154
Montgomery, Jennifer 112–113
Moodysson, Lukas 139
Moore, Carmen 20
Moore, Jason 13
Moore, Julianne 155
Moore, Michael 56
Moorhouse, Jocelyn 112
Morán, Mercedes 153
Morgan, Abi 89, 114
Morgan, Frances 190
Morley, Carol 134

Dreams of a Life 87–89, **88**, 95, 96, 116
Falling, The 150–152, 157
'Stalin My Neighbour' 150
Morrar, Ayed 52
Morrar, Iltezam 52
Morris, Courtney Desiree 51
Morrison, Toni 55
Mort, Cynthia 165
Morton, Samantha 80, 83, 85–86
   Unloved, The 80–87, **81**, 89, 93, 95, 96, 134
Morvern Callar (Lynne Ramsay) 85, 87, 90
Moseley, William 171
Moser, Abby 142
Mosquita y Mari (Aurora Guerrero) 180, 182
Moss, Elisabeth 159
Moswela, Kudzani 46
Moth Diaries, The (Mary Harron) 149–150
Moulin Rouge! (Baz Luhrmann) 125
Mourikis, Vangelis 36
Mulberry House, The (Sara Ishaq) 90
Mullan, Peter 159
Mulligan, Carey 96
Mulvey, Laura 5, 15, 18, 120, 185
   Penthesilea, Queen of the Amazons 129
   Riddles of the Sphinx 192
Mumenthaler, Milagros 163–164
Mumolo, Annie 19
Mumtaz, Samiya 21
Mundane History (Anocha Suwichakornpong) 162–163
Munden, Mark 103
Mungiu, Cristian 109
Murakami, Nijiro 49
Murch, Walter 30
MURDER and Murder (Yvonne Rainer) 197
Murphy, Ryan 41, 119
Murray, Alison 40
Mutu, Wangechi 118
Muybridge, Eadweard 38
My Beautiful Laundrette (Stephen Frears) 92

Index

My Brilliant Career (Gillian Armstrong) 107
My Brother the Devil (Sally El Hoseini) 90, 92–93
Myers-Powell, Brenda 182–183
My Name is Hmmmm… (Agnès Troublé) 147–148
My Prairie Home (Chelsea McMullan) 140
Myers-Powell, Brenda 182–183

Nacro, Fante Régina 65
Nair, Mira 4
  Midnight's Children 104
  Vanity Fair 103
Nas 83
Nash, Sydney Mary 82
Nashashibi, Rosalind
  'Bachelor Machines' 90
  'Dahiet Al Bareed, District of the Post Office' 90
  'This Quality' 89
  'University Library' 89
Nasheed, Mohammed 52
Nashville (Callie Khouri) 166
Nathaniel, Afia 21
National Film Board of Canada (NFB) 167, 177
Native Dancer (Gulshat Omarova) 131
Nayman, Adam 128
NDiaye, Marie 75
Neely, Sarah 198
Negrón-Muntaner, Frances 175–176, 179
Neill, Sam 77
Nelson, Marion 41
Neshat, Shirin 116
Netanel, Sa'ar 177
Nevin, Robin 160
Newsom, Jennifer Siebel 19
Newsome, Bree 132
Ng, Iris **168**
Ngassa, Vera 9
'Nguva' 118
Night Catches Us (Tanya Hamilton) 115
Night is Young, The (Leos Carax) 127
Night of Truth, The (Fante Régina Nacro) 65
Night Moves (Kelly Reichardt) 23, 51

Nina (Cynthia Mort) 165
Nivola, Alessandro 96
No. 73 (J. Nigel Pickard) 89
Noé, Gaspar 23
Noruz, Nikbakht 63
Not a Love Story (Bonnie Sherr Klein) 177
Notorious Bettie Page, The (Mary Harron) 108–109
Noujaim, Jehane 52
  Control Room 24–25
  Rafea: Solar Mama 191
  Square, The 24–25
Novak, Matt 42
Ntuba, Beatrice 9
Nungak, Zebedee 117
Nwadili, Uche 158

Obomsawin, Alanis 8
Obvious Child (Gillian Robespierre) 21
O'Connell, Jack 67
Oduye, Adepero 141
Offside (Jafar Panahi) 81
Of Girls and Horses (Monika Treut) 39
O'Keeffe, Georgia 152
Okeke, Frances 158
O'Leary, Barbara Ann 199
Oler, Tammy 157
Olnek, Madeline
  Codependent Lesbian Space Alien Seeks Same 127–128
  Foxy Merkins, The 127
Omarbekova, Nespkul 131
Omarova, Gulshat (Guka) 131
Omran, Radia 25
One Mile Away (Penny Woolcock) 91–93, 138
Ono, Yoko 197
Onwurah, Ngozi 90, 98
Open Bethlehem (Leila Sansour) 90
Orange is the New Black (Jenji Kohan) 17, 181–182
Orlando (Sally Potter) 15, 103, 104, 112, 116, 117, 124
Oroz, Elena 190–191
Ostrowska, Ania 114, 190
'Ottica Zero' (Maja Borg) 94
Ottinger, Ulrike 177, 198

Beautiful Woman Sleeping, The 22
Madame X 22
Ouedraogo, Rasmane 65
Owczarek, Marta 191
OWLS, The (Cheryl Dunye) 174, 176
Oyelowo, David 14, 115
Ozon, François 147

Page, Ellen 125, 141
Palafox, Teofilia 107
Pal, Sampat 130–131
Panahi, Jafar 6, 81
Panetierre, Hayden 166
Panh, Rithy 75
Paniagua, Leticia Tonos 180
Paquin, Anna 103
Parade's End (Susanna White) 114
Paraguayan Hammock (Paz Encina) 7
Paré, Jessica 149
Parekowhai, Cushla 117
Pariah (Dee Rees) 141–142
Parkerson, Michelle 192
Parmar, Pratibha 90
  Alice Walker: Beauty in Truth 193, 195–196, 201
Paronnaud, Vincent 65
Parrella, Valeria 165
Parsipur, Sharnush 116
Passon, Stacie 155
Patterson, Sarah 124
Pawlikowski, Pawel 82
Peck, Cecilia 166
Peirce, Kimberley
  Boys Don't Cry 4
  Carrie 157
  Stop-Loss 68–69
Pejíc, Andreja 126
Pekün, Didem 165
Pelo Malo (Mariana Rondon) 139
People's Girls, The (Colette Ghunim and Tinne van Loon) 175
Penny, Laurie 119–120
Penthesilea, Queen of the Amazons (Laura Mulvey and Peter Wollen) 129
Perabo, Piper 149
Perestroika (Sarah Turner) 55, 94

Index

Perhacs, Linda 165
'Perils' (Abigail Child) 121
Periz, Ingrid 15
Perkins, Claire 156
Perkins, Emily 125
Perkins, Rachel 98
Perrault, Charles 123, 160
Perry, Grayson 14
Persepolis (Marjane Satrapi and Vincent Paronnaud) 65–66, 142–143
'Pescados' (Lucrecia Martel) 44
Petersen, Anne Helen 159–160
Peterson, Bob 152
Petrovic, Natasha 73–74
Petty, Lori 50
Phang, Jennifer 118
Phillippe, Ryan 68
Phoenix, Woodrow 10
Pialat, Maurice 134
Piano, The (Jane Campion) 15, 49, 103, 111, 112
Piano Teacher, The (Michael Haneke) 22
Piccadilly (Ewald André Dupont) 91
Pick, Anat 35
Pickard, J. Nigel 89
Pidduck, Julianne 101
Pink Saris (Kim Longinotto) 130–131
Pink Saris 130–131
Pinsent, Gordon 180
Pitch Perfect (Jason Moore) 13
Pitch Perfect 2 (Elizabeth Banks) 13
'PLACEnta' (Jules Koostachin) 161
Play (Alicia Scherson) 162–163
Play, The (Pelin Esmer) 183
Please Give (Nicole Holofcener) 156
Podemski, Sarah 8
Point Break (Kathryn Bigelow) 4, 50–51, 69
Poitras, Laura 6–7, 193
Polanski, Roman
  Chinatown 51
  Rosemary's Baby 157
Polisse (Maïwenn) 159
Polley, Diane 167–169
Polley, Michael 167, 169

Polley, Sarah 175
  Away From Her 180–181
  Stories We Tell 167–169, **168**
  Take this Waltz 178
Poole, Léa 149
Popular Unrest (Melanie Gilligan) 132
Porter, Dawn 17
Portrait of Jason (Shirley Clarke) 198
Portrait of a Lady, The (Jane Campion) 103, 107–108
Potter, Sally 10, 16, 89, 91, 99, 192, 197
  Ginger and Rosa 95–96, 98, 113, 119, 197
  Gold Diggers, The 197
  I am an Ox, I am a Horse, I am a Man, I am a Woman: Women in Russian Cinema 4, 72
  Orlando 15, 103, 104, 112, 116, 117, 124
  Rage **26**, 26–27
  Tango Lesson, The 196
  Thriller 106
  Yes 77–79
Pounder, CCH 139
Powley, Bel 133
Pratt, Minnie Bruce 66
Price, Elizabeth 79
Price, Erika 124
Pride (Matthew Warchus) 95
Pride of Place (Kim Longinotto and Dorothy Gazidis) 84
Prince-Bythewood, Gina 201
Principles of Lust (Penny Woolcock) 178
'Private Life of a Cat, The' (Maya Deren and Alexander Hammid) 33–34
Private Lives of Pippa Lee, The (Rebecca Miller) 155
Profession: Documentarist (various) 165
Program, The (Laura Poitras) 7
Puccini, Giacomo 106
Pucill, Sarah 197, 198
Puenzo, Lucia
  Wakolda 67
  XXY 126
Pugh, Florence 150

'Pumzi' (Wanuri Kahiu) 45–48, **48**, 50, 61, 62
Punk Singer, The (Sini Anderson) 2, **3**, 4, 9, 12, 133, 142, 175, 193
Pussy Riot 25

Qallunaat! Why White People are Funny (Zebedee Nungak and Mark Sandiford) 117
Queen of the Desert (Werner Herzog) 41
Queer Feast (Michelle Citron) 169
Quezada, Juan Pablo 162
Quillévéré, Katell 147

Rabin, Nathan 134
Rae, Issa 17
Rafea: Solar Mama (Mona Eldaief and Jehane Noujaim) 191
Rage (Sally Potter) **26**, 26–27
Rain (Maria Govan) 139
'Rain' (Maya Glick) 130, **130**
Rainer, Yvonne 18, 21, 85, 128, 196
  Lives of Performers 127
  Man Who Envied Women, The 127
  MURDER and Murder 197
Raising Films 189–190
Ramanathan, Geetha 16
Ramsay, Lynne
  Morvern Callar 85, 87, 90
  We Need to Talk about Kevin 157–158
Randou, Evangelia 36
Rape Nation (Leena Manimekalai) 191
Raphaël, Paul 42
Ravenhill, Mark 100
Rebecca (Alfred Hitchcock) 154
'Rebel Menopause' (Adèle Tulli) 184, 187
'Red Girl's Reasoning, A' (Elle-Máijá Tailfeathers) 70–71, 74, 131, 136
Redmond, Phil 89
Red Riding Hood (Catherine Hardwicke) 125
Red Road (Andrea Arnold) 7

Index

Reed, Nikki 146
Rees, Dee
  Bessie 165
  Pariah 141–142
Reeves, Jennifer
  Time We Killed, The 76–78
  When It Was Blue 54
Reeves, Keanu 51
Regarding Susan Sontag (Nancy Kates) 184, 193
Reichardt, Kelly 42
  Meek's Cutoff 41, 53, 111–113, 116
  Night Moves 23, 51
  River of Grass 41
  Wendy and Lucy 29–32, **30**, 34, 36, 40–44, 47, 201
Reid, Sam 102
Reiniger, Lotte 15
Renner, Jeremy 69
Renoir, Jean 155
Resnais, Alain 119
Return (Liza Johnson) 68
Return to Hansala (Chus Gutiérrez) 58–59
Return to Oz (Walter Murch) 30
Revathi 170
Reynaud, Bérénice 40
Rhodes, Liz 197
Richardson, Tony 86, 87
Rich, B. Ruby 4, 11, 49–50, 176, 195
Riddles of the Sphinx (Laura Mulvey and Peter Wollen) 192
Riel, Jørn 105
Riley, Robin L. 66
Rimes, Shonda 17
Riot Club, The (Lone Scherfig) 89
Riseborough, Andrea 103
Rita, Sue and Bob Too (Alan Clarke) 86
River of Grass (Kelly Reichardt) 41
Roberts, Adam 198
Roberts, Kimberley
  Rivers 56–57
Roberts, Scott 56
Robertson, Selina 190, 200
Robespierre, Gillian 21
Robinson, Tasha 19
Rodriguez, Michelle 139

Roger, Elena 67
Rohrwacher, Alice
  Corpo celeste 147
  Wonders, The 36
Roman, Shari 5
Romney, Mitt 120
Rondeaux, Ron 111
Rondon, Mariana 139
Rosa Luxemburg (Margarethe von Trotta) 114
Rosa Parks Story, The (Julie Dash) 103
Rose, Gillian 173
Rose, Jacqueline 21, 121, 123
Rosemary's Baby (Roman Polanski) 157
Rosendahl, Saskia 67
Rosler, Martha 196
Rossellini, Isabella 36
Ross, Gary 19
Ross, Stanley Ralph 129
Ross, Yolonda 182
Rotberg, Dana 117
Rozema, Patricia 103
Rudychenko, Diana 123
Ruffalo, Mark 122
Runaway (Kim Longinotto and Ziba Mir-Hosseini) 84
Russ, Joanna 120
Ryan, Eileen 119
Ryan, Meg 76
Ryan, Robbie 38
Ryan, Thomas Jay 66
Ryberg, Ingrid 179

Saakyan, Maria
  Alaverdi (I'm Going to Change My Name) 144–145, 151
  Lighthouse, The 75–76
Sacred Country (Jan Dunn) 99–100
Sadeghi, Mischa 39
Sadowska, Maria 191
Sahraoui, Djamila 60
Salas, Ailín 165
Salina, Irene 55
Salma (Kim Longinotto) 84, 156–157
Salma, Rajathi 156–157
Saltfish & Ackee (Cecile Emeke) 17

Salt of this Sea (Annemarie Jacir) 59, 62
Samaqan: Water Stories (Jeff Bear) 58
Samson and Delilah (Warwick Thornton) 180
Sanchéz, Suis 161
Sandberg, Sheryl 157
Sandiford, Mark 117
Sandoval, Chela 172
Sansour, Leila 90, 91
Sarandon, Susan 41
Sarif, Shamim 174
  I Can't Think Straight 94, 173
  World Unseen, The 94, 173
Sarkeesian, Anita 25
Sarris, Andrew 16
Satrapi, Marjane 65–66, 142–143
Savages, The (Tamara Jenkins) 163
Sayad, Cecilia 197
Sayar, Smadar 72
Sayles, John 42
Scacchi, Greta 151
Scandal (Shonda Rimes) 17
Scheherezade's Diary (Zeina Daccache) 183–184
Schendar, Naama 72
Scherfig, Lone
  Education, An 96, 133
  Riot Club, The 89
Scherson, Alicia 162
Schlondorff, Volker 113
Schneemann, Carolee 10, 179
  'Fuses' 33–34
Schulian, John 129
Schulman, Sarah 176
Schultz, Dagmar 193
Sciamma, Céline 9, 49
  Girlhood 137–138, 151
  Tomboy 50, 126, 139–140
  Water Lilies 50, 126
Scodelario, Kaya 38
Scorsese, Martin 40
Scott, Joan 116
Scott, Jordan 149
Scott, Ridley 15
Sea, Daniela 174
Sea Wall, The (Rithy Panh) 74–75
Searchers, The (John Ford) 22, 69

Index

Second Coming (debbie tucker green) 89, 98, 158
Seduce Me (Isabella Rossellini) 36
Seidelman, Susan 192
Seif, Sanaa 24
Selfish Giant, The (Clio Barnard) 39
Selma (Ava DuVernay) 12, **13**, 14, 20, 103, 115, 203
Senior, Antonia 1
Sense and Sensibility (Ang Lee) 101
Sepideh (Berit Madsen) 142
Serner, Anna 200
Severson, Anne 179
Sex and the City (Candace Bushnell) 17
Sex and the City (Michael Patrick King) 114
Seyfried, Amanda 125
Seyrig, Delphine 144
Shabba 91–92
Shah, Tejal 198
Shaka Zulu 66
Shakespeare, Willian 180
Shame (Steve McQueen) 89
Shane, Martha 21
Shape of Error, A (Abigail Child) 118–119
Shapiro, Isabel 86
Sharifi, Farahnaz 165
Sharp, Anastasia 177
Shaw, Lee 38
She, A Chinese (Xiaolu Guo) 90
She's Beautiful When She's Angry (Mary Dore) 179
She's Just a Boy I Knew (Gwen Haworth) 139
Shelley, Mary 118–120, 132
Shelley, Percy Bysshe 118
Shelly, Adrienne 141
Shelton, Lynn
 Humpday 173
 Your Sister's Sister 173
She Monkeys (Lisa Aschan) 39, 139
She Must Be Seeing Things (Sheila McLaughlin) 177
Shenk, Jon 52
Shepitko, Larisa 67
Sherrybaby (Laurie Collyer) 181

Shimizu, Jenny 174
Shipman, Nell 33–34
Shiva, Vandana 45
Shohat, Ella 92
Shortland, Cate 67
Shriver, Lionel 157
Shukla, Shilpa 104
Shut Up and Sing (Barbara Kopple and Cecilia Peck) 166–167
Sichel, Alex 4
Sicinski, Michael 40
Sight & Sound 18, 198, 201
Silent Waters (Sabiha Sumar) 104, 117
Silverman, Kaja 164
Silverstein, Melissa 14, 129, 189
Simone, Nina 165
Simple Life, A (Ann Hui) 163
'Sinalela' (Dan Taulapapa McMullin) 126
Sirene, Chloe 82
Sisters in Arms (Beth Freeman) 67–68
Sisters in Law (Kim Longinotto and Florence Ayisi) 8–9
Sithole, Xoliswa 5
Sjöman, Vilgot 178
Slade, David 124
Sleeping Beauty (Julia Leigh) 122–124, 128
Sleeping Beauty, The (Catherine Breillat) 122–123
Slope, The (Desiree Akhavan and Ingrid Jungermann) 17
Smaill, Belinda 17–18, 181
Smart-Grosvenor, Vertamae 103
Smith, A. C. H. 3
Smith, Ali 99, 198, 201
Smith, Bessie 165
Smith, Jacqui Ashton 134
Smith, Stacy L. 1, 12, 14, 199
'Snow Canon' (Mati Diop) 123
Snyder, Zack 129
Soap, Charlie 58
Sobchack, Vivian 148
Socha, Lauren 82, 87
Solid Women (Tracey Moffatt) 16

Solier, Magaly 161
Solnit, Rebecca 28, 57, 152
Solomon, David 125
Soloway, Jill
 Afternoon Delight 155, 158
 Transparent 17, 155
Somerville, Jimmy 103
Something Must Break (Ester Martin Bergsmark) 178
Sommers, Daria 66
Sontag, Susan 179, 193
Soska, Jen 22
Soska, Sylvia 22
'Sound of the Street' (Annemarie Jacir) 34–35
'Space Dog Assassin' (Bev Zalcock and Sara Chambers) 16
Spheeris, Penelope 4
Spielberg, Steven
 Color Purple, The 195
 E.T. 152–153
Spivak, Gayatri Chakravorty 20
Spoon, Rae 140
Sprinkle, Annie 53
Square, The (Jehane Noujaim) **24**, 24–25
'Stalin My Neighbour' (Carol Morley) 150
Stam, Robert 92
Stambrini, Monica 41
Steinem, Gloria 44
Stein, Gertrude 121–122
Stella Does Tricks (Coky Giedroyć) 119
Stephens, Beth 53
Stephenson, Janey 183
Steponaityte, Julija 147
Stewart, Clare 199
Steyerl, Hito 196
Still the Water (Naomi Kawase) 49
St. John, Bridget 165
Stop-Loss (Kimberley Peirce) 68–69
Stories We Tell (Sarah Polley) 167–169, **168**
Storm in the Stars, A (Haifaa al-Mansour) 119
Strange Culture (Lynn Hershman Leeson) 66
Strange Days (Kathryn Bigelow) 120

256

Index

Stranger Inside (Cheryl Dunye) 182–183
Strawberry Fields (Frances Lea) 147
Strayed, Cheryl 41
Streitfeld, Susan 144
Strickland, Peter 178
Stromberg, Robert 119
Stud Life (Campbell X) 176
Stukan, Fedja 74
Sturges, Fiona 159
Subcomandante Marcos 22
'Subtalk' (Abigail Child) 121–22
Suffragette (Sarah Gavron) 114, 199
Sugar Town (Allison Anders and Kurt Voss) 166
Suh, Yun 177
Sukkhapisit, Tanwarin 19
Sukowa, Barbara 114
Sumar, Sabiha 104
Summer of Sangaile, The (Alanté Kavaïté) 147
Sumner, Mickey 127
Sundance 103, 141
Surapongsanuruk, Phakpoom 163
Susskind, Yifat 73
Suwala, Justyna 148
Sverisson, Skuli 54
Swamp, The (Lucrecia Martel) 153–154, **154**, 160, 162
Swan, Rebecca 186
Swan, Susan 149
Swayze, Patrick 50
Swinton, Tilda 66, 104, 158
Sworn Virgin (Laura Bispuri) 4
Sylla, Assa 138
Szumowska, Malgorzata 148

Tabari, Ula 164
Tagaq (Gillis), Tanya 42–43, **43**
Taghmaoui, Saïd 92
Tailfeathers, Elle-Máijá
  'Hurry Up, You Stupid Cripple' 136–137, 140, 148
  'Red Girl's Reasoning, A' 70–71, 74, 131, 136
Tait, Margaret 198
Take My Eyes (Iciar Bollaín) 7

Take this Waltz (Sarah Polley) 178
bin Talal, Alwaleed, Prince 143
Talalay, Rachel 4, 8, 50
Tale of Love, A (Trinh T. Minh-Ha) 179–180
Tamara Drewe (Stephen Frears) 89
Tambor, Jeffrey 155
Tango Lesson, The (Sally Potter) 196
Tank Girl (Rachel Talalay) 50
Tapert, Robert G. 129
Tarantino, Quentin 129
Tarquini, Holly 198
Taskafa: Stories of the Street (Andrea Luka Zimmerman) 32, 44
Taste of Honey, A (Tony Richardson) 86, 96
Taubin, Amy 158
Taulapapa McMullin, Dan 126
Taylor, Astra 26, 37, 193
Taylor, Sunaura 137
Taylor, Tate 19
Taylor-Johnson, Sam 22, 89
Taymar 93
Taymor, Julie 108
Tay, Sharon Lin 8, 48–49
Tea, Michelle 176
Temple, Juno 155
Ten (Abbas Kiarostami) 81
Testud, Sylvie 49
Thatcher, Margaret 114
Thelma and Louise (Ridley Scott) 15, 41, 60
Thiele, Alex 190
Thin (Lauren Greenfield) 144
Things We Lost in the Fire (Susanne Bier) 68–69
Thirteen (Catherine Hardwicke) 146
'This Quality' (Rosalind Nashashibi) 89
Thomas, Shaun 39
Thompson, Bertha 40
Thompson, Emma 101
Thorndike, Stewart 157
Thornham, Sue 85
Thornton, Warwick 6, 180
Thriller (Sally Potter) 106
Tilikum 35
Tiller, Isidore 49

Time We Killed, The (Jennifer Reeves) 76–78
Tina Goes Shopping (Penny Woolcock) 85
Tiny Furniture (Lena Dunham) 156
Tipping the Velvet (Sofia Coppola) 100
Tirado, Linda 31
Tlatli, Moufida 6
'Tombeau de Zgougou, Le' (Agnès Varda) 33
Tomboy (Céline Sciamma) 50, 126, 139–140
Tometi, Opal 24
Tong, Allan 200
Top of the Lake (Jane Campion and Gerard Lee) 17, 159–160, 169
Toronto International Film Festival (TIFF) 8, 24, 104, **105**, 106, 164, 199
Tosar, Luis 57
Touré, Karidja 137
Townend, Thomas 81
Townsend, Annie 93
Townsend, Shakilus 93
Tracks (John Curran) 41
Train on the Brain (Alison Murray) 40
Transparent (Jill Soloway) 17, 155
Trans X Istanbul (Maria Binder) 193
Travel Notes of a Geechee Girl (Julie Dash) 103
Tremain, Rose 99
Tremblay, Erica 140–141, 202
Treslove, Kyle 176
Treut, Monika 177, 198
  Ghosting 178
  Of Girls and Horses 39
Trinh Thi, Coralie 41
Trinh T. Minh-Ha 179–180, 182, 196
Troche, Rose 4
Troublé, Agnès 147–148
Trouble the Water (Tia Lessin and Carl Deal) 56–57, 59
Tsai Ming-Liang 177
Tsangari, Athina Rachel
  Attenberg 36–37, 40
  'Capsule, The' 37

257

Index

Tsang, Wu 20, 176
Tsyganov, Evgeniy 144
tucker green, debbie 89, 91, 98, 158
Tulay German: Years of Fire and Cinders (Didem Pekün) 165
Tulli, Adèle 184
'Tungijuq' (Félix Lajeunesse and Paul Raphaël) 42–43, **43**
Turner, Guinevere 174
Turner, Sarah 55, 57, 94
Turner, Sophie 119
Tushingham, Rita 86
Twilight (Catherine Hardwicke) 22, 125
Two Legged Horse (Samira Makhmalbaf) 39

Udwin, Leslee 191
Ukeje, O. C. 92
Ulloa, Andrez 162
UNBOUND (Abigail Child) 119–122, **121**, 132
Unbroken (Angelia Jolie) 67
Under the Skin (Carine Adler) 85–87
Unforgiven (Clint Eastwood) 112
United Nations (UN) 18–19, 21, 45–46, 48, 74
'University Library' (Rosalind Nashashibi) 89
Unloved, The (Samantha Morton) 80–87, **81**, 89, 93, 95, 96, 134
Up (Pete Docter and Bob Peterson) 154
Upham, Misty 57–58
Up the Women (Jessica Hynes) 114

Vagabond (Agnès Varda) 134, 147
Valencia (various) 176
Vallée, Jean-Marc 41
Vand, Sheila 22
Vanity Fair (Mira Nair) 103
van Loon, Tinne
  'Creepers on the Bridge' 175

People's Girls, The 175
van Sant, Gus 114
Varda, Agnès 16, 144, 188, 196, 198
  Beaches of Agnès, The 53, 184–187, **186**
  'Black Panthers' 184
  Daguerréotypes 186, 190
  Gleaners and I, The 5, 33, 37, 185
  Jacquot de Nantes 185
  Lions Love 187
  'Tombeau de Zgougou, Le' 33
  Vagabond 134, 147
  'Widows of Noirmoutier, The' 184
  'Women Reply' 184, 189–190
Vaughn, Matthew 95
Vendredi soir (Claire Denis) 128, 178
Veninger, Ingrid
  i am a good person/i am a bad person 200
  Modra 200
Verhoeven, Deb 179
Vertigo (Alfred Hitchcock) 162
Vessel (Diana Whitten) 21
Vicius, Nicole 174
Vidal, Belén 100, 103, 116
Vigo, Jean 60
Viktoria (Maya Vitkova) 79
Villa Touma (Suha Arraf) 164–166
Village at the End of the World (Sarah Gavron) 42
Vincent, Joyce 87–88, **88**, 95, 96, 116
Virgin With a Memory (Sophia Al-Maria) 22
Vitkova, Maya 79
Viva 187
Vizenor, Gerald 106
von Garnier, Katja 114
von Harbou, Thea 121
von Kleist, Heinrich 129
von Trotta, Margarethe 113, 123
  Hannah Arendt 114
  Rosa Luxemburg 114
Voss, Kurt 166

Wachowski, Lana 20
Wade, Laura 89
Wadjda (Haifaa al-Mansour) 16, 64, 119, 142–143
Waiting for August (Teodora Ana Mihai) 79
Waitress (Adrienne Shelly) 141
'Wakening' (Danis Goulet) 8
Wakolda (Lucia Puenzo) 67
Walker, Alice 195–196, 201
Waller, Fats 167
Wanda (Barbara Loden) 40–41
Warchus, Matthew 95
Wareing, Kierston 83
Warner, Alan 85
Warner, Marina 128, 160
Washuta, Elissa 70, 139
Wasikowska, Mia 41
Water (Deepa Mehta) 104, 115
'Water Diary' (Jane Campion) 49
Water Front, The (Liz Miller) 48–49
'Water Has a Perfect Memory' (Natalia Almada) 55
Water Lilies (Céline Sciamma) 50, 126
Watermarks (Jennifer Baichwal) 55
Watermelon Woman, The (Cheryl Dunye) 110–111, 176
Waters, Mark 137
Waters, Sarah 100
Watkins, Elizabeth 107
Way of Life, A (Amma Asante) 83, 84–85, 89, 98
Wayne, John 111
We Are the Best (Lukas Moodysson) 139
We Need to Talk about Kevin (Lynne Ramsay) 157–158
We Want Roses Too (Alina Marazzi) 191–192
Wearing, Gillian 89
Webber, Peter 116
Wedekind, Frank 148
Weerasethakul, Apichatpong 6, 163, 177

Index

Weil, Simone 35
Weiss, D. B. 119
Welcome II the Terrordome (Ngozi Onwurah) 98
Welles, Orson 6
Wellywood Woman 15
Welsh, Brian 68
Wendy and Lucy (Kelly Reichardt) 29–32, **30**, 34, 36, 40–44, 47, 201
Wenham, David 160
West, Cornell 170
Westwell, Guy 5
'We the Others' (Maja Borg) 131–133
Wexler, Tanya 114
Whale, James 121
Whedon, Joss 6, 22
When I Saw You (Annemarie Jacir) 138
When It Was Blue (Jennifer Reeves) 54
When the Levees Broke: A Requiem in Four Acts (Spike Lee) 56
Where Do We Go Now? (Nadine Labaki) 183
Whip It (Drew Barrymore) 141
Whishaw, Ben 107
White, Carol 83
White Lies/Tuakiri Huna (Dana Rotberg) 117
White Material (Claire Denis) 74–76
White, Patricia 5, 16, 65, 67, 153, 162
White Space, The (Francesca Comencini) 164
White, Susanna 114
Whitman, Richard Ray 20
Whitney (Angela Bassett) 165
Whitsitt, Sam 69
Whitten, Diana 21
Who's Afraid of Vagina Wolf? (Anna Margarita Albelo) 174–176
Wichmann, Kanchi 94, 176
'Widows of Noirmoutier, The' (Agnès Varda) 184
Wieland, Joyce 197, 198
Wiig, Kristen 19
Wild (Jean-Marc Vallée) 41

Wilde, Oscar 39
Wilding, Nick 119
Wildness (Wu Tsang) 176–177
Wilkinson, Tom 101, 115
Will (Jessie Maple) 192
Willard, Trina 173
William, Paul Andrew 82
Williams, Maisie 150
Williams, Michelle 29, 111
Willmore, Alison 17
Wilson, Emma 9, 50, 81, 126
Wilson, Jacqueline 84
Wilson, Juanita 73–74
Wilson, Lana 21
Wilson, Morning Star 20
Windsor, Molly 80, 87
Winfrey, Oprah 14, 115
Wings (Larisa Shepitko) 67
Wiseman, Noah 157
Witherspoon, Reese 41, 125
Wizard of Oz, The (Victor Fleming) 29–30, 43
Wollen, Peter
  Penthesilea, Queen of the Amazons 129
  Riddles of the Sphinx 192
Wollstonecraft, Mary 118
Women and Hollywood 12, 15, 188–189
!Women Art Revolution (Lynn Hershman Leeson) 193
Women Make Movies 5, 193–194
'Women Reply' (Agnès Varda) 184, 189–190
Women without Men (Shirin Neshat) 116
Women's Day (Maria Sadowska) 191, 36
Wonders, The (Alice Rohrwacher) 36
Wonder Woman (Patty Jenkins) 129, 132
Wonder Woman (Stanley Ralph Ross) 129
Wonder Women! The Untold Story of American Superheroines 130, 142
Wong, Anna May 91
Wongsompetch, Sarasawadee 19
Wood, Evan Rachel 146

Wood, Sarah 10, 190, 200
Woolcock, Penny 57, 89, 134
  1Day 91
  From the Sea to the Land Beyond 55–56, 91, 95
  Mischief Night 85
  One Mile Away 91–93, 138
  Principles of Lust 178
  Tina Goes Shopping 85
Woolf, Virginia 80, 154, 189, 194
Woolverton, Linda 119
World Unseen, The (Shamim Sarif) 94
Wright, Robin 155
Wuthering Heights (Andrea Arnold) 37–40, 53, 103, 180
Wyornos Allen, 36
Wright, Thomas M. 160
Wuornos, Aileen, 36

X, Campbell 91, 117, 176, 192
Xena Warrior Princess (John Schulian and Robert G. Tapert) 129
Xiaolu Guo 89–91
X-Men: First Class (Matthew Vaughn) 95
XXY (Lucia Puenzo) 126

Yaa Asantewaa 97
Yasmine (Siti Kamaluddin) 16, 139
Year Dolly Parton Was My Mom, The (Tara Johns) 155
Yee, Jessica 26
Yes (Sally Potter) 77–79
Yoshinaga, Jun 49
Young, Stella 137
Younge, Gary 14
Your Sister's Sister (Lynn Shelton) 173

Zak, Dan 143
Zalcock, Bev 16
Zanzibar Soccer Queens (Florence Ayisi) 139
Zbanić, Jasmila 73–74
Zegeye, Rahel 162

Index

Zeig, Sande 139
Zeitoun, Mark 52
Zero Dark Thirty (Kathryn Bigelow) 6, 70–71
Zero for Conduct (Jean Vigo) 60
Zero Motivation (Talya Lavie) 72

Zhao Wei 159
Ziegler, Kortney Ryan 20
Zimmerman, Andrea Luka
Estate, A Reverie 80
Taskafa: Stories of the Street 32, 44

Žižek, Slavoj 37
Zlotowski, Rebecca
Belle épine 147
Grand Central 178
Zoffany, John 101
Zreik, Maria 164